T0350137

The Rise of the Dutch New Right

In the past 20 years, a wave of right-wing populist movements has swept over Europe, changing the face of European politics. The Netherlands has been one of the more iconic countries to partake in this shift. Known internationally as an emblem of progressivism and tolerance, the country soon became a frontrunner in the revival of nationalist and anti-immigrant sentiment. This is the first study to offer an extensive engagement with the ideas behind the Dutch swing to the right.

The emergence of Dutch populism, this book shows, formed an integral part of a broader conservative tendency, identified as the Dutch New Right. In the US and the UK, the term New Right has been used to describe conservative backlash movements that arose in opposition to the progressive movements of the 1960s. The Dutch swing to the right, this book argues, formed a belated iteration of the New Right backlash that occurred overseas.

This text will be essential reading for students and scholars in the fields of European Studies and Political Science, and Dutch politics and society more specifically.

Merijn Oudenampsen is a sociologist and political scientist. He works as a post-doc researcher at the University of Amsterdam (UvA), The Netherlands.

Routledge Studies in Fascism and the Far Right
Series editors
Nigel Copsey
Teesside University, UK
and
Graham Macklin
Center for Research on Extremism (C-REX),
University of Oslo, Norway

This new book series focuses upon fascist, far right and right-wing politics primarily within a historical context but also drawing on insights from other disciplinary perspectives. Its scope also includes radical-right populism, cultural manifestations of the far right and points of convergence and exchange with the mainstream and traditional right.

Titles include:

American Antifa
The Tactics, Culture, and Practice of Militant Antifascism
Stanislav Vysotsky

Lost Imperium
Far Right Visions of the British Empire, c.1920–1980
Paul Stocker

Hitler Redux
The Incredible History of Hitler's So-Called Table Talks
Mikael Nilsson

Researching the Far Right
Theory, Method and Practice
Edited by Stephen D. Ashe, Joel Busher, Graham Macklin and Aaron Winter

The Rise of the Dutch New Right
An Intellectual History of the Rightward Shift in Dutch Politics
Merijn Oudenampsen

Anti-fascism in a Global Perspective
Transnational Networks, Exile Communities and Radical Internationalism
Edited by Kasper Braskén, Nigel Copsey and David Featherstone

For more information about this series, please visit: www.routledge.com/Routledge-Studies-in-Fascism-and-the-Far-Right/book-series/FFR

The Rise of the Dutch New Right

An Intellectual History of the Rightward Shift in Dutch Politics

Merijn Oudenampsen

Routledge
Taylor & Francis Group

LONDON AND NEW YORK

First published 2021
by Routledge
2 Park Square, Milton Park, Abingdon, Oxon OX14 4RN

and by Routledge
52 Vanderbilt Avenue, New York, NY 10017

Routledge is an imprint of the Taylor & Francis Group, an informa business

© 2021 Merijn Oudenampsen

The right of Merijn Oudenampsen to be identified as author of this work has been asserted by him in accordance with sections 77 and 78 of the Copyright, Designs and Patents Act 1988.

All rights reserved. No part of this book may be reprinted or reproduced or utilised in any form or by any electronic, mechanical, or other means, now known or hereafter invented, including photocopying and recording, or in any information storage or retrieval system, without permission in writing from the publishers.

Trademark notice: Product or corporate names may be trademarks or registered trademarks, and are used only for identification and explanation without intent to infringe.

British Library Cataloguing-in-Publication Data
A catalogue record for this book is available from the British Library

Library of Congress Cataloging-in-Publication Data
A catalog record has been requested for this book

ISBN: 978-1-138-62415-3 (hbk)
ISBN: 978-0-429-45260-4 (ebk)

Typeset in Times New Roman
by Wearset Ltd, Boldon, Tyne and Wear

Contents

Acknowledgements

In the 1950 essay *The Dutch Author and the World Crisis*, the writer W.F. Hermans noted that the world didn't really care what the Dutch had to say, since the Dutch never dealt with crises that 'exceeded a fire in an ashtray'. Hermans admonished Dutch authors to stop trying to copy foreign examples and to become fully provincial. Writing this book often felt like following Hermans along that path, since this study departs from an insistence on the particularity of the Dutch political tradition, even if it does so through international comparisons. At conferences abroad, I sometimes felt I had become fully provincial, and somehow blamed Hermans for it. I have dug myself deep into the Dutch context, in the hope that I can escape the dilemma, and that the Dutch case is indeed more compelling than a fire in an ashtray.

At the same time, this thesis has been the work of a relative outsider. Someone with no obvious belonging to a single academic discipline in the Netherlands. A relative outsider, too, when it comes to the Dutch political culture of consensus and moderation. Prominent inspirations such as Stuart Hall and Edward Said have written on the scholarly merits of being a relative outsider. Arguably, it allows one to develop a critical vision of the things that insiders generally take for granted. Stuart Hall's saying that 'fish have no concept of water', is something that stuck with me with respect to Dutch consensus culture. You need to be located outside of that political culture, banging your head against it so to say, to be able to trace its contours.

Let me thank those who have helped me along on my path to completing this manuscript. First my PhD supervisors, Odile Heynders and Piia Varis, who have pushed me to make the most of it, at a moment when I was ready to submit 'the damned thing' in suboptimal condition. Paul Mepschen and Sinan Cankaya have been an important source of feedback and moral support. Bram Mellink has been a great co-conspirator on the neoliberalism project that I'm currently working on. Bram has read almost everything there is to read and he serves as an endless source of the finest quality academic gossip. Ido de Haan and Ewald Engelen have been a much-needed source of encouragement and emotional blackmail to get me to finish this book. Thanks also to Naomi Woltring and again Bram, for all the bizarre jokes on our pilgrimage to Mont Pèlerin and the many more that are to come. Finally, my parents, Cilia and Dick, have been a crucial source of support. They have had the much-appreciated tactfulness to stop asking at a given moment, when I realistically planned to finish. Last but not least, I should thank Iris and Max, for allowing this young father to sleep, and have some brain functions left. Let me also extend my gratitude in advance to all the readers, critics, adversaries and kindred spirits to come. Writing can be a lonely activity. It need not be so.

Abbreviations

CDA   Christen-Democratisch Appèl (Christian Democratic Appeal)
LPF   Lijst Pim Fortuyn (List Pim Fortuyn)
PvdA Partij van de Arbeid (Labour Party)
PVV   Partij voor de Vrijheid (Party for Freedom)
VVD   Volkspartij voor Vrijheid en Democratie (People's Party for Freedom and Democracy)

Newspapers and magazines mentioned

De Volkskrant	Former Catholic newspaper, centrist orientation with social democrat affinity
NRC Handelsblad	Former liberal newspaper, centrist orientation with progressive-liberal affinity
Trouw	Former Protestant newspaper, centrist orientation with Christian affinity
Elsevier Weekblad	Secular right-wing weekly

Introduction
The Dutch swing to the right

A wave of right-wing anti-establishment movements has swept over Europe in the past 20 years, changing the face of European politics. The Netherlands has been one of the more iconic countries to partake in this right-wing upsurge. Known internationally as an emblem of progressivism and tolerance, the country soon became a frontrunner in the European revival of nationalist and anti-immigrant sentiment.

The turning point occurred around the turn of the century, with the meteoric rise and dramatic assassination of the right-wing populist Pim Fortuyn in May 2002. In the elections that followed, his party List Pim Fortuyn (LPF) went on to score a stunning victory. With 17 per cent of the vote, it became the second largest party out of the blue, in what is commonly called 'the Fortuyn revolt'. It set the stage for a Dutch culture war that made national identity, immigration and law and order into the dominant themes of Dutch public debate. In the ensuing decade, the entire political landscape shifted to the right, while the Party for Freedom, led by Geert Wilders continued Fortuyn's legacy.[1]

The central question of this book is how to make sense of this shift in ideological terms. So far, the European right-wing surge of the past decades has generally been analysed through the lens of (radical right-wing) populism.[2] It is a focus that foregrounds style and rhetoric, but undervalues ideas. Populist leaders have been portrayed above all, as savvy political entrepreneurs expressing the repressed sentiments of a marginalized electorate, but have less frequently been analysed in terms of their political ideas, as part of a larger ideological constellation. Not the head but the underbelly, not ideas but the attitudes of 'the man on the street' were presumed to be the decisive factors, reinforced by the new-found power of the media and the personal charisma of the populist leader.

The prevailing focus on populism has produced a large and rich literature.[3] But to analyse the profound political changes in the Netherlands, populism can only be part of the story. How to explain that a political current that never managed to capture more than a fraction of the vote, has been able to exercise such an outsized influence on the Dutch political climate? After the rapid demise of Fortuyn's LPF party in 2003, Dutch populism remained an electorally marginal phenomenon for the rest of the decade. The right-wing populist Geert Wilders, who successfully positioned his Party for Freedom (PVV) as the heir of

Fortuyn's legacy, could count on only nine out of 150 seats until 2010. Yet there was no let-up in the Dutch culture war on national identity, immigration and integration.

As this book will show, the rise of radical right-wing populism in the Netherlands formed part of a broader conservative backlash against the 'permissiveness' of the 1960s and the 'relativism' of progressive baby boomers. A new conservative ' sentiment emerged in the 1990s, voiced by a loose and eclectic coalition of journalists, politicians and intellectuals. It blamed the anti-authoritarian ethos of the 1960s for the rising crime rates, the stalling integration of immigrants, the erosion of national identity and wide-ranging moral decline. This new cultural controversy cut straight across party lines, and resonated in the conservative wings of the three major Dutch political parties (the right-wing liberal VVD, the Christian democratic CDA, and the social democratic PvdA). After failing to win over the mainstream parties, Dutch conservatives established an influential conservative think tank in December 2000, the Edmund Burke Foundation. It formed part of a long-lasting intellectual offensive. Through a series of polemical interventions, conservatives helped prepare the ideological ground for the Fortuyn revolt. In the years after 9/11, they remained at the centre of Dutch public debate, pleading for the defence of Dutch culture against the threat of radical Islam.[4] This eclectic conservative current was highly influential in shaping the Dutch debate and formed a crucial inspiration for the right-wing populist leaders Pim Fortuyn and Geert Wilders.

Vice versa, the breakthrough of right-wing populism was seen as a windfall for Dutch conservatism. For the motley alliance that made up the conservative current, 'the Fortuyn revolt' was first and foremost a conservative uprising. The conservatives grouped around the Edmund Burke Foundation described Pim Fortuyn as the 'originator of the conservative moment' and awarded him the prize 'conservative of the year' in 2002.[5] H.J. Schoo, the conservative editor of the largest Dutch weekly *Elsevier*, approvingly observed that the Fortuyn revolt 'could be compared with American neoconservatism'.[6] Both in the United States and in the Netherlands, Schoo observed a modernized conservatism that promoted a moral restoration, opposed the ideals of the 1960s and stressed the capacity of ordinary citizens to shape their own destiny without the welfare state. Jos de Beus, a leading professor of political theory and a conservative social democrat, proclaimed an 'implosion of the progressive consensus from the 1960s' after the breakthrough of Fortuyn and prophesized a conservative 'paradigm-shift', a change towards a 'neoconservative consensus'.[7]

As a result of the dominant focus on populism, this broader conservative current has generally been ignored. The ideology behind the Dutch revolt has never been taken very seriously. Prominent politicians and opinion makers qualified the ideas of Fortuyn as 'twaddle written out', 'political postmodernism', or 'political kitsch, a potpourri of blather and folk wisdoms'.[8] In the process of writing this book, I received similar responses. When I explained my ambition to explore the political ideas behind the Fortuyn revolt at the proverbial birthday parties, the prevailing reaction was one of amused scepticism: 'Are there any?'

As a result, in the public imagination the Dutch revolt has been reduced to the triumph of style over content. Due to this common underappreciation of the role of ideas, the change in the Dutch opinion climate has often elicited a sense of bafflement from observers. As the late law professor and social democrat senator Willem Witteveen remarked in 2005: 'The Netherlands has become more conservative. Sometimes it seems like the entire political discourse after the murder of Fortuyn has been picked up by an invisible hand, and brusquely put down again several meters to the right'.[9]

A series of studies have sought to question this view by pointing to the debates on immigration and national identity that formed the long run-up to the voter rebellion.[10] Yet, there is still a common conception that Fortuyn appeared like a *deus ex machina* on the stage of Dutch politics, boldly picking up political discourse and bluntly hurling it to the right. This book aims to further dispel that *idée recue*, by exploring the ideological origins of the Dutch revolt, drawing on intellectual history and ideology studies.[11] Rather than looking at individual actors or parties, the aim is to trace the contours of a conservative 'movement of ideas' that transcends parties, by examining the writings of leading Dutch politicians, journalists and academics in the 1990s and 2000s. The focus in this book, then, is on the intellectual dimension of the political turnabout; the revolt of the mind rather than that of the underbelly.

From New Left to New Right

An important stepping-stone in my analysis of the swing to the right is that other seismic shift in Dutch political culture, the 'cultural revolution' of the 1960s. The analysis developed in this book draws on the influential interpretation of that period developed by the American-Dutch historian James Kennedy and builds on his suggestion that there are important parallels between the two instances of political metamorphosis.[12]

In the US and the UK, the 1960s and 1970s were a period of polarization that gave rise to both the progressive movements of the New Left and their conservative counterparts, the New Right. To echo one of the book titles on this period, the baby-boomer generation was in a very real sense 'a generation divided'.[13] Especially in the US, the conservative response to the 1960s took hold at an early stage, when Nixon assumed power in 1969 and administered a devastating defeat in 1972 to McGovern, the candidate of the New Politics and the New Left. In that same year, the writer and 'gonzo' journalist Hunter S. Thompson famously chronicled the turning point:

> San Francisco in the middle sixties was a very special time and place to be a part of. [...] There was a fantastic universal sense that whatever we were doing was right, that we were winning. And that, I think, was the handle. That sense of inevitable victory over the forces of Old and Evil. [...] We had all the momentum, we were riding the crest of a high and beautiful wave. So, now, less than five years later, you can go on a steep hill in Las Vegas and look

west. And with the right kind of eyes you can almost see the High-Water Mark. That place where the wave finally broke and rolled back.[14]

In the Netherlands, the image of this historical period is strikingly different. The 1960s and 1970s had an almost singularly progressive character. The country changed in a short period of time from a conservative, conventional and overwhelmingly Christian society, to a progressive, critical and secular one. The breadth, speed and depth of this transformation were exceptional from an international point of view. In a matter of years, the country became susceptible to progressive politics; it embraced a hedonistic attitude to life and criticism of the constraints of Christian morality developed into a new, established tradition. Meanwhile, a convincing conservative countertendency failed to emerge. Not for nothing, a classic work on the period describes it as 'the endless 1960s', with a life span lasting till at least 1977.[15] The wave met no resistance and kept on rolling until its momentum dissipated of its own accord, until its mercurial fluids were fully absorbed in the Dutch mud.

The predominant narrative of the Dutch 1960s identifies the baby-boomer generation as the primary engine of that transformation. The innovative contribution of the American-Dutch historian James Kennedy was to point to the crucial role of traditional Dutch elites. Kennedy attributed the profundity of the changes to a peculiar dialectic between the romantic radicalism of the youth and the old-fashioned views of Dutch elites. It was not the boisterous political activism of the baby-boomer generation that set the Netherlands apart. What stood out internationally were the ideas and behaviour of Dutch elites who chose to embrace the changes, rather than digging in their heels. Kennedy attributed this to Dutch elites' 'dread of conflict and violence – coupled with a belief that the inevitable tide of modernity was better channelled than blocked'.[16]

Instead of resisting, mobilizing a Gaullist majority or Nixon's silent minority in defence of the moral order, Dutch elites focused on restoring equilibrium by organizing a new consensus, accommodating and depoliticizing protests from below by means of a passive revolution from above. As Kennedy observed, 'an effective "reactionary" rhetoric, that either advocated maintenance of the status quo or a return to a previous glorious age', was absent among Dutch elites.[17] The belief of Dutch elites in the inevitability of historical change and modernization led them to facilitate and stimulate behaviour that was met with elite hostility in other countries. This response to the progressive wave functioned as a double-edged sword. The traditional Dutch elites let their hair down (sometimes literally) and rapidly became more progressive.

The baby boomers, in their long march through the institutions, soon repudiated their youthful belief in social engineering and adopted the moderate, consensual and historicist views of their previous adversaries. In proper Hegelian fashion, the dialectic of the 1960s evolved into a 'prudently progressive' synthesis. It was a term used in 1989 by the Christian Democrat Prime Minister Ruud Lubbers to qualify the sentiments of the Dutch population: 'Before, people wanted to be progressive, even if they were conservative. Nowadays there is a trend to be *prudently* progressive'.[18] Intellectually, the dominant sentiment was expressed in a 'Burkean progressivism' articulated by baby-boomer intellectuals such as Dick Pels, Bas van Stokkom and Hans Achterhuis.[19]

In the 1990s and 2000s, however, a New Right countertendency emerged that took aim against the legacy of the 1960s and 1970s and strove to undo the 'prudent progressive' consensus. In an essay from 2010 on the Fortuyn revolt, Kennedy pondered on the remarkable similarities between the transformation of the 1960s and that of the 2000s. In this latter period, Kennedy observed another sweeping change, this time in the opposite direction: a swing to the right. It reached its full momentum after the brutal political assassinations of Pim Fortuyn (by an animal rights activist) in 2002 and the filmmaker and columnist Theo van Gogh (by a Dutch-Moroccan Muslim Extremist) in 2004. Where conservatism was repudiated in the 1960s, now it was at least partially embraced: law and order, Dutch national identity, immigration and moral restoration were at the centre of the debate. In a short period of time, criticism of the 1960s and the baby-boomer generation, associated with permissiveness, moral relativism, political correctness and multiculturalism, became the omnipresent tune that all contenders on the public stage had to tailor their steps to.[20]

When Fortuyn launched an election campaign centred on immigration and Islam in the autumn of 2001, initially the attempt was to marginalize him in the same way as the Dutch far-right had historically been contained. Leading up to the 2002 municipal elections that preceded the national elections by only two months, politicians and journalists tried to disqualify Pim Fortuyn by comparing him with far-right leaders, such as Jean-Marie Le Pen (FN), Filip de Winter (VB), Jörg Haider (FPÖ) or even Benito Mussolini. Fortuyn, whose main ideological inspirations derived from Anglo-American (neo)conservatism rather than the European far-right, managed to effectively distance himself from the far-right. The marginalization strategy backfired when Fortuyn won the local elections in March 2002, leading to a rapid shift in strategy from marginalization to accommodation, here described by Dutch political scientists in one of the most convincing analyses of the Fortuyn revolt to date:

> After the electoral success of Fortuyn in the local elections of March 2002 – especially his triumph in Rotterdam, the second largest city in the Netherlands – the main parties used a different strategy in their attempt to block him: they followed his lead. The PvdA, CDA and VVD changed their draft versions of the election programmes of 2002 and copied Fortuyn's proposals. This bandwagon behaviour of the main parties further legitimized Fortuyn's programme. The change of strategy also implied that the established parties could no longer present their own campaign with their own items and issues. They now had to explain what their position was on the immigration question in comparison to the views of Fortuyn.[21]

The assassination of Pim Fortuyn on 6 May 2002 proved to be the final straw for the marginalization strategy. The politicians and journalists that had associated

Fortuyn with the far-right were publicly blamed for creating the polarized climate that led to his assassination. They were accused of 'demonization', a watchword frequently employed by right-wing populist politicians and opinion makers in the following years to invoke the haunting memory of the death of Fortuyn. The LPF was politically accommodated and included in the new first Balkenende cabinet (2002–2003) led by the Christian Democrats, described by many as the only realistic option after the dramatic elections.[22] The accommodating approach of Dutch elites in the 2000s came to resemble the attitude described by James Kennedy in the 1960s and 1970s.

Not the content of these two political shifts, but their consensual nature fascinated Kennedy the most. To him the remarkable aspect was that the whole of Dutch society seemed to shift in unison to the right, as it had collectively swerved to the left in the 1960s and 1970s. In both periods, he observed a 'decisive collective break with the past, in which confident defenders of the *ancien régime* are difficult to find and new dogmas are proclaimed with missionary zeal'.[23] Perhaps, Kennedy suggested, 'sudden, radical and massive conversions and huge paradigm shifts are the more or less predictable result of a political culture in which the desire for consensus hinders the continuous debate'.[24] In such a context, opposing visions do not clash but succeed one another in time. In contrast to the US and the UK, where the progressive New Left and the conservative New Right confronted each other head-on, in the Netherlands the two movements seemed to follow each other in time. The Netherlands experienced a New Left tendency in the 1960s and 1970s and a New Right countertendency in the 1990s and 2000s.

Kennedy attributed the collective nature of both shifts to the importance attached to consensus in the Netherlands. In ordinary times, the aversion to political disagreement and ideological conflict restricts Dutch public debate to a limited spectrum of opinion. Eventually, the dominant consensus erodes, due to societal changes and contestation. At first, the gatekeepers of the existing consensus resist outside critique. But soon, the dominant narrative collapses, and work starts on negotiating a new consensus. As the sociologist and senior public official Paul Schnabel observed in relation to the Dutch swing to the right, change in the Netherlands generally occurs in shockwaves across the entire political spectrum: 'For long periods, there is consensus and understanding, until things don't work any longer, and then there is a radical impulse. The undercurrent becomes the mainstream'.[25]

The conservative undercurrent

The conservative undercurrent, referred to by Schnabel, started to emerge in the beginning of the 1990s. In his first book published in 1990, Frits Bolkestein, who had just been appointed as leader of the centre-right liberal party (VVD), proclaimed the beginning of a sustained battle of ideas to contest the legacy of 1968 and what he described as a progressive *pensée unique*. Bolkestein expressed his astonishment about the ease with which the 'hare-brained schemes' of the *soixante huitards* had found their way into Dutch government policy. He blamed Dutch elites, who 'had surrendered without firing a shot'. In his view, the Dutch political culture of consensus and the lack of civil courage among Dutch elites to confront the protest generation had deepened the hubris of the 1960s. 'The tidal wave of the New Left has swept the country and flowed away again', Bolkestein wrote. 'Here and there it has left residues: corroded cans, stained pieces of wood'. Now was the time for a conservative countercurrent to clear away the mess.[26]

The 1990s saw a build-up of critiques of the anti-authoritarian ethos of the 1960s and the baby boomers, and a pervasive nostalgia for Dutch national identity, depicted as lost or in a state of prolonged (progressive) neglect. A series of publications gave testimony to this rising undercurrent. In an essay titled *The Conservative Offensive*, the journalist Marcel ten Hooven observed that 'the unrestrained tolerance of the permissive society had awakened a conservative temperament'. He cited pleas from Christian Democrats (CDA) and right-wing Liberals (VVD) for a 'conservative alliance', focused on moral restoration and a concerted campaign against 'the legacy of the 1960s'.[27] In his book *The Conservative Wave*, the conservative social democrat journalist Hans Wansink announced with much fanfare the rise of a new conservatism in the Netherlands, inspired by Margaret Thatcher, Ronald Reagan, John Gray and Francis Fukuyama. 'Conservative thinkers and politicians reveal themselves as the social critics of the 1990s', he observed. 'Leftist illusions are challenged; old-fashioned virtues and traditional forms of community are infused with new life'.[28]

Pim Fortuyn joined the conservative wave in 1995, when he published *The Orphaned Society*. In this book, Fortuyn argued that the anti-authoritarian revolt of the 1960s had 'orphaned' the Dutch and deprived them of paternal and maternal authority figures. What was needed was a new moral order that would resolve the crisis of authority. *The Orphaned Society* received high praise in Dutch conservative circles, 'as the most conservative Dutch book' since 'the beginning of the twentieth century'.[29]

Similar observations about the shifting ideological tides were made from the other end of the political spectrum. Left-wing commentators Jos van der Lans and Antoine Verbij noted in surprise how a new conservative cultural critique emerged in the 1990s, 'borne by what increasingly looks like a right-wing conservative consensus': 'The excessive tolerance, social indifference, moral decline, coarsening of society, disdain for authority and erosion of norms and values – all moral shortcomings of contemporary society are supposedly rooted in the 1970s'.[30]

Dutch conservatives ascribed the relative late occurrence of the conservative response in the Netherlands to the penchant for consensus among Dutch elites, which became a central target of critique. The figureheads of the New Right undercurrent, in particular Frits Bolkestein and Pim Fortuyn, wrote searing condemnations of consensus politics, now depicted as the reason for elite negligence of societal problems. We live in a 'consensus society', Bolkestein noted in 1990, where 'the ideal is not to cut the Gordian knot, but to strive for political accommodation'. It frustrated the ability of politics to deal with controversial issues such as immigration and integration. In order to solve a societal problem, Bolkestein argued, 'it has to be addressed in a frank and incisive manner, but that evokes so much irritation and opposition that it delays a possible solution'.[31] Not much later came the opening salvo of Pim Fortuyn's career as a right-wing opinion maker, a polemical plea to 'remove the gloriously warm blanket of consensus from our Dutch little bed'.[32] Similar discontent resounded in the conservative wing of the social democrat party. The most powerful intellectual attack on Dutch consensus politics was provided by the award-winning book *Correct*, written by the conservative social democrat journalist Herman Vuijsje.[33] His indictment of the political correctness of the baby-boomer generation soon developed into a central reference point for the coming conservative assault on the institutions. The argument of the book echoed existing critiques of the 'permissive society' of the 1960s and the 'crisis of authority' that had been voiced in the decades before by the New Right in the US and the UK.

According to Vuijsje, the baby-boomer generation had never really challenged the prevailing culture of consensus in the Netherlands. The baby boomers claimed to be self-asserted individualists who had broken with the taboos and conformism of their parents. But the protest generation had simply erected a new series of totems and taboos on terrains such as race relations, migration, government compulsion and privacy. Because the Dutch were not allowed to talk frankly about the problems created by the anti-authoritarian and progressive ideals of the 1960s, problems had festered and struck the most vulnerable: exactly those that the baby boomers had vowed to protect. Consensual conformism had delayed a much-needed conservative correction to the 1960s from arising. Vuijsje employed an arsenal of metaphors to explain this Dutch particularity. In his introduction, he described the situation in the 1970s and 1980s in the Netherlands in terms of a *surplace* (tactical standstill) in a cycling race:

> The moment the cyclists stand motionless on the track, balancing and closely keeping check on one another. No one dares to move first, but as soon as one departs, everyone has to sally forth. Only in the 1990s did it finally happen: a sudden and wild sprint erupted, in which the unassailable dogmas were finally breached.[34]

Naturally, by writing this book, Vuijsje positioned himself at the head of the race, guiding the Dutch to a new, more conservative consensus. True to the transgressive ethos of the 1960s, he proclaimed this new consensus to be free from conformism and taboos. The Dutch were finally liberated. In paradoxical fashion, the transgressive, taboo-breaking imaginary of the 1960s was now mobilized against the baby boomers themselves. Vuijsje presented the first copy of his book to Frits Bolkestein, for having done the most to negate progressive totems and taboos.

At the turn of the century, the conservative undercurrent came to the surface. In December 2000, the aforementioned Edmund Burke Foundation (EBF) was established, an influential conservative think tank with close links to the centre-right parties. The members of the foundation came out of the closet as conservatives and forcefully presented themselves on the public stage. In a series of controversial opinion pieces, they declared that 'the conservative moment' had come, and proclaimed a 'conservative revolution' against the baby boomers and the spirit of 1968.[35] The foundation was modelled on the American Heritage Foundation and funded by large grants from American corporations such as Pfizer and Microsoft. Its immediate aim was to strengthen the conservative wings of the centre-right parties (VVD, CDA) and the small Christian parties (CU, SGP). In the long term, the aspiration was to restructure the Dutch landscape and assemble the fragmented conservative forces in a new fusionist party, inspired by the New Right in the US.[36]

After 9/11, the EBF became a central node in a broader intellectual network that proposed to bring a 'neoconservative revolution' to the Netherlands. The ideas of American neoconservatives inspired a reinvention of Dutch right-wing politics on two fronts. On the one hand, neoconservative ideas were important in articulating opposition to Islam. Especially the clash of civilizations theory, as developed by Bernard Lewis and Samuel Huntington, became a leitmotif of the Dutch revolt. Frits Bolkestein framed the integration of Muslim immigrants as a civilizational confrontation between the West and Islam, Pim Fortuyn branded himself 'the Samuel Huntington of Dutch politics' and publicly called for a cold war against Islam in the week before 9/11, while Geert Wilders' core issue was countering Islam, which was seen as a civilizational threat.[37] Similarly, the EBF member Paul Cliteur and Islam critic Ayaan Hirsi used neoconservative inspirations to develop an early Dutch version of New Atheism, the famed international intellectual movement led by Richard Dawkins, Christopher Hitchens and Sam Harris.[38] On the other hand, neoconservative ideas were important in framing opposition to the legacy of 1968 and progressive baby boomers. Dutch progressives were described as a 'new class', a concept used by US neoconservatives to refer to an entrenched progressive intellectual elite dominating the institutions that shape public opinion.[39]

As mentioned, there is a close relationship between this (neo)conservative intellectual current and the future populist leaders. During his time as a columnist for the Dutch conservative weekly *Elsevier* in the mid-1990s, Pim Fortuyn came under the influence of its editor H.J. Schoo, a self-declared neoconservative, who later became part of the circle around the EBF. In these years, Fortuyn's politics made a marked shift in conservative direction. Geert Wilders, before becoming the founder of the right-wing populist Party for Freedom in 2006, referred to the publications of the EBF as a guideline for a shift to the right in Dutch politics.[40] Wilders had contacted Bart Jan Spruyt in 2003 to discuss future cooperation. One year later, Spruyt became the ideologue and second in command of Wilders' fledgling party. Together they made a weeklong visit to a series of American (neo)conservative think tanks in 2005, before finally falling out with each other in 2006.[41] Wilders' ideologue and speech writer after 2006, Martin Bosma, claimed inspiration from US neoconservatism.

In a 2011 book, he described Geert Wilders' Party for Freedom as a Dutch equivalent to the US neoconservative movement, since both were comprised of people who had moved to the right in response to 1968, the New Left and multiculturalism.[42]

The rise of right-wing populism in the Netherlands was thus preceded and accompanied by a broader conservative backlash that resonated in the conservative wings of the major Dutch parties. Paraphrasing Hunter S. Thompson, Fortuyn and Wilders were riding the crest of a larger conservative wave. The political success of right-wing populism in the Netherlands cannot be understood in separation from the broader accomplishments of this loose and heterogeneous current of conservative politicians, journalists and intellectuals in gaining acceptability for a series of once marginal and now pervasive ideas.

Between Anglo-American conservatism and European populism

What analytical framework can we use to make sense of this broader ideological constellation? The argument in this book straddles two different lines of scholarship that have become oddly disconnected over the decades. On one side there is the literature on the Anglo-American conservative movement, also known as the New Right. In both the UK and the US, this latter term came into use to describe conservative movements that emerged in parallel with – and in response to – the rise of the New Left in the 1960s and 1970s. Most prominently, the politics of Thatcher and Reagan are associated with the term. The newness of the New Right, on the one hand, lies in the combination of a free market strand and a culturally conservative strand. The ideology of the New Right has been described as a complex and often contradictory fusion of neoliberal and (neo) conservative ideas.[43] On the other hand, the New Right is seen as a departure from the more moderate, gradualist politics of the post-war consensus, when liberal and conservative forces participated in the construction of the welfare state. The politics of the New Right was more radical in nature; it sought to contest and replace the existing social contract. The 'backlash politics' of the New Right challenged existing elites and institutions, seen as tarnished by the legacy of the 1960s, with the aim of reinstituting the free market and traditional forms of moral authority. In so doing, it accorded an important role to the 'battle of ideas' in achieving political change, with a prominent role for conservative and free market think tanks.[44] Not surprisingly, the study of ideas has been central to the scholarship on the New Right, represented by a series of well-known intellectual histories of (neo)conservatism and neoliberalism.[45]

On the European continent, a similar conservative tendency expressed itself in a more diffuse and fragmented manner. On the one hand, it was taken up in a more moderate manner by the established centre-right parties, who shifted to the right in the 1980s and achieved political power in West Germany, the Netherlands, Denmark, Belgium and Portugal.[46] On the other hand, the counter-tendency manifested itself in a more radical fashion with the rise of populist radical right and extreme right parties.[47] It is these latter currents, especially radical right-wing populism, that have become the major focus of scholarly study. Typically, these parties are defined in terms of their nativist, populist and authoritarian positions and their radical stance on immigration and ethnic diversity.[48] The predominant object of research is not so much ideas or ideology, but rather the development of populist parties and the empirical analysis of voting behaviour.

Originally, these two strands of scholarship overlapped. The first authoritative studies of the populist radical right in Europe portrayed these parties as a more radical embodiment of the neoliberal and (neo)conservative ideas that had been popularized by the New Right overseas. Herbert Kitschelt, in his comparative overview of the European radical right, famously identified a 'winning formula', which consisted of a combination of neoliberal and culturally conservative (or authoritarian) positions.[49] He saw it as part of a larger restructuring of the political landscape, in which an opposition between left-libertarian and right-authoritarian came to increasingly prevail. Similarly, Hans-Georg Betz identified the 'neoliberal creed' of Thatcher and Reagan and 'the neo-conservative turn of the 1980s' as important reference points for the radical right.[50] With 'regard to their economic policies most radical right-wing populist parties have been close to the positions advanced by Margaret Thatcher', he observed.[51]

In an essay entitled *The Silent Counterrevolution*, Piero Ignazi highlighted the role of neoconservatism in setting the scene for a backlash against the post-material agenda of the New Left. He observed that 'the new cultural movement of neoconservatism' had 'legitimized a series of "right-wing" themes which were previously almost banned from political debate'. Ignazi concluded that this 'neoconservative cultural mood' became 'highly influential all over Western societies in the 1980s'.[52] It occasioned a rightward shift of the established right-wing parties, enlarging the political space, and thus allowing the populist radical right and extreme right parties to get a foot in the door. In Germany, authors such as Claus Offe, Michael Minkenberg and Jürgen Habermas described the popularity of neoconservative ideas in Europe as a countertendency to the post-material agenda of the new social movements.[53] In an influential essay, Jürgen Habermas identified such an intellectual movement on both sides of the Atlantic, represented by the work of Samuel Huntington, Irving Kristol and Daniel Bell in the US, and that of Arnold Gehlen, Helmut Schlesky and Ernst Forsthoff in West Germany.[54]

In short, scholars analysed the emergence of radical right-wing populism on the European continent, in conjunction with a broader ideological transformation of right-wing politics, in which the New Right synthesis of neoliberal and (neo) conservative ideas played an important role.[55] This appreciation of the inherent ideological hybridity of populist politics also resounds in the influential definition by Cas Mudde, which identifies populism as a 'thin ideology' that occurs in conjunction with a 'thick ideology'. In the Dutch press, Mudde pointed to the connection between populism and neoconservatism, suggesting that 'the ideology and priorities of Wilders are very similar to those of American neoconservatives'.[56] Similar connections between 'thin' and 'thick' ideology have been made in the case of Fortuyn's party (LPF), as populism scholar Sarah de Lange argued that 'the position of the LPF is neoliberal'.[57] These scattered observations, however, haven't prompted more extensive studies of neoconservatism and neoliberalism. And as the field of populism studies has consolidated itself, this appreciation of populist hybridity has receded. Scholars increasingly treat radical right-wing populism as an independent phenomenon, considered separate from the established right-wing parties and the wider ideological transformation of the right. This is curious, since the defining phenomena of our 'populist Zeitgeist' – Brexit and Trump – can hardly be understood in isolation from the Anglo-American conservative parties.

In fact, the disproportionate focus on populism has at times led to a wholesale depoliticization of mainstream politics. In prominent studies on the rise of radical right-wing populism in Europe, populist parties are considered to be the only ideological actors in the game, the only actors with 'transformative aspirations' and 'anti-establishment attitudes'. The mainstream parties, in contrast, are depicted as non-ideological, and 'committed to the status quo'.[58] As we will see, this framework does not fit the Dutch case very well, where it has been the political and intellectual mainstream that pioneered a conservative anti-establishment discourse. This study seeks to correct this narrowing of scholarly vision, by charting the broader ideological constellation – or 'thick ideology' – that informed the Dutch revolt.

A 'complex' conservative backlash

This book identifies this broader constellation as the Dutch New Right. My proposition is that the New Right synthesis of free market ideas and cultural conservatism, combined with opposition to the 1960s and a critique of political moderation, provides a useful analytical framework for understanding the politics of figures such as former VVD leader Frits Bolkestein, the right-wing populist Pim Fortuyn, the early Geert Wilders ideologue Bart Jan Spruyt, the conservative New Atheist Paul Cliteur, the conservative social democrat journalist H.J. Schoo, Islam critic Ayaan Hirsi Ali and Geert Wilders himself, the leader of the Freedom Party (PVV). The central thesis of this book is that the swing to the right in the Netherlands can be understood as a belated iteration of the New Right backlash that occurred overseas.

At the same time, the Dutch New Right is not a simple copy of its Anglo-American counterparts. Due to the late birth of the Dutch New Right and the exceptional impact of the progressive wave of the 1960s and 1970s, the Dutch current had to contend with an overwhelming progressive common sense on the so-called 'social issues' that were the subject of the culture wars in the US: sexual morality, abortion, euthanasia, drugs. The rise of the Dutch New Right is the result of a messy process of translation of political ideas between very dissimilar contexts.

Crucial is the contradictory character of the conservatism of the New Right. It emerged as a backlash movement, an anti-establishment current challenging existing elites and institutions. Of course, conservatism is often understood as an ideology that emerged in defence of existing institutions and elites, in opposition to radical challenges to the status quo. When progressives are seen to have taken over the institutions, however, conservatives have little choice but to adopt an anti-establishment position and to vie for popular appeal. The American political scientist Seymour Martin Lipset used the term 'backlash politics' to express the contradictory nature of such a conservative anti-establishment politics. With that term, Lipset referred to the paradoxical reality of 'right-wing groups [that] have to appeal to the populace in a framework of values which are themselves a source of right-wing discontent in the first place: anti-elitism, individualism and egalitarianism'. The reason was simple: these were the 'supreme American political values' that no movement could ignore. 'Commitment to these values is the American ideology', Lipset proposed.[59]

Such a contradictory logic seems to apply to an even greater extent in the Dutch case. A Dutch conservative backlash needed to frame its appeal within the context of supreme Dutch values. And the depth of the wave of the 1960s meant that commitment to progressive sexual and secular morality had become 'the Dutch ideology'. Due to its belated occurrence, the conservative countercurrent came to incorporate to a much larger degree the progressive sexual, anti-authoritarian and secular ethos that had become engrained in the Netherlands after the 1960s and 1970s. While right-wing leaders such as Bolkestein still opposed gay marriage and defended Christian morality in the late 1990s, that soon changed.[60] In the wake of Pim Fortuyn, Dutch New Right intellectuals embraced the Enlightenment and progressive values such as individualism, secularism, women's equality and gay rights, presenting themselves as the true defenders of the progressive accomplishments of Dutch culture against the 'backward culture' of Muslim immigrants.

The sociologist Paul Schnabel called this 'modern conservatism':

> Wilders wants to hold on to the country's achievements. He does not want to go back to the time where gays and women were rated inferior. He does not want to restore old values, he wants to maintain new ones.[61]

In his acclaimed book on the murder of Theo van Gogh, the essayist Ian Buruma commented extensively on this contradictory conservative politics:

> Because secularism has gone too far to bring back the authority of the churches, conservatives and neo-conservatives have latched onto the Enlightenment as a badge of national or cultural identity. The Enlightenment, in other words, has become the name for a new conservative order, and its enemies are the aliens, whose values we can't share.[62]

On the one hand, this conservative co-optation of progressive values has an instrumental quality to it. The conservative interest in feminism and gay rights is largely a function of their opposition to Islam and does not seem to have much salience on its own. Many have pointed out that women's rights and gay rights have been instrumentalized for a nationalist and anti-Muslim politics, a development that has been debated by scholars under terms such as sexual nationalism, homonationalism and femonationalism.[63] On the other hand, this paradoxical position expresses a reality on the ground: the aforementioned depth and uncontroversial nature of the sexual revolution of the 1960s has led to a widely shared progressive sexual morality in the Netherlands that could no longer be challenged by a conservative countercurrent. Pim Fortuyn, himself an openly gay baby boomer and a product of the 1960s, described this legacy as an unassailable cultural sediment and advised Dutch conservatives against attempts to overturn it.

The conservatism of the Dutch New Right is therefore a far more ambiguous and contradictory affair than that of its British and American counterparts. Drawing on Angela McRobbie's notion of a 'complex' conservative backlash, I describe the Dutch New Right as a conservative countercurrent that selectively incorporates some of the accomplishments of the 1960s, while successfully challenging the progressive agenda on a broader set of terrains, such as law and order, immigration, social policy, environmental policy, internationalism, cultural policy and development aid.[64] In this way, the Netherlands has served as the laboratory for a new form of right-wing politics, and functions as an ideal type for a broader transformation on the right that is becoming increasingly prominent on the European continent as a whole.[65]

Structure of the book

In line with Karl Mannheim's thesis that political thought is inherently context-bound, the first chapter is dedicated to a critical exploration of the Dutch political tradition. While this book seeks to explore the ideological dimension of the Dutch revolt, the Netherlands has often been portrayed as a country that has moved beyond ideology altogether. The belief in 'the end of ideology' and the feasibility of an 'objective' politics has long been a powerful sentiment in Dutch politics. Hans Daalder and Arend Lijphart, the founding fathers of Dutch political science, attributed this to a peculiar political culture of depoliticization among Dutch elites. In a country of political minorities, framing one's ideas as non-ideological allows one to build coalitions with other parties. Based on the work of Daalder and Lijphart, this chapter shows how this traditional consensus culture became the target of critique of the new social movements in the 1960s. And it explains how in the 1990s, conservative critics such as Bolkestein, Vuijsje and Fortuyn took up the old consensus critique, this time to challenge the protest generation itself.

Chapters 2, 3 and 4 lay out the main thesis of the book: the interpretation of the Dutch swing to the right as a belated and complex pendant of the New Right backlash in the US and the UK. The New Right is introduced as a fusionist project combining free market ideas and cultural conservatism. The transfer of political ideas from the Anglo-American context facilitated political innovation and inspired the Dutch conservative backlash in the 1990s against existing elites and institutions. The Dutch New Right is the product of a rather messy process of translation of neoliberal and neoconservative ideas. It consists of an eclectic coalition of Christian conservatives, conservative liberals, conservative social democrats and provocative nihilists. In so doing, the analysis takes issue with a still prevalent image of the 1990s as the supposed era of the end of ideology. While this is true to a degree for the leftist spectrum, on the other side of the aisle, the 1990s have been a period of politicization and ideological renewal.

Chapter 5 qualifies the argument of the previous chapter. It deals with the complexity of the Dutch New Right. The crucial difference between the Dutch New Right and its Anglo-American counterparts is that Dutch conservatives have come to incorporate progressive values such as women's rights and gay rights. The belated occurrence of the New Right backlash in the Netherlands meant that progressive sexual morality was seen as ingrained to such a degree that a conservative countercurrent could no longer hope to overturn it. The 'social issues' that became the subject of the culture wars in the US – women's emancipation, gay rights, abortion, drugs, euthanasia – were not up for discussion in the Netherlands. Instead, Dutch conservatives reinvented themselves as defenders of the progressive accomplishments of Dutch culture against the perceived threat of Muslim immigrants. The Dutch New Right can be seen as a 'complex backlash' against the legacy of the 1960s. Put differently, it is a countercurrent that selectively incorporates elements of the tendency that it opposes, while contesting that tendency on a broader set of terrains. The chapter introduces a situational perspective on conservatism that allows us to make sense of these contradictory aspects of the Dutch conservative backlash.

Chapter 6 is dedicated to Islam critic Ayaan Hirsi Ali, and develops a relational analysis of her autobiographical writing. Due to the fact that Hirsi Ali's views on Islam are often seen as her personal opinions, comparatively little attention has been given to her intellectual development. Hirsi Ali became part of the Islamic fundamentalist movement in her teenage years, and joined an influential circle of neoconservative intellectuals after her arrival in the Netherlands and her study in Leiden. This chapter situates her writing in relation to these two formative intellectual influences. It traces the development of Hirsi Ali's perspective on Islam, which consists of a paradoxical combination of ideas drawn from Islamic fundamentalism and Western Orientalism and neoconservatism. And it shows how these adopted views are – in important respects – in open contradiction with her personal life story, as told in her biography, *Infidel*. The work of Olivier Roy on Islamic fundamentalism is used as an interpretive lens to create an alternative interpretation of her life story.

Chapters 7 and 8 delve into Dutch nihilism and the internet. The Fortuyn revolt coincided with the ascendency of the internet as a major factor in shaping public opinion. After the assassination of Fortuyn and Van Gogh, the nihilist weblog *GeenStijl* developed into one of the most popular and influential websites in the Netherlands. It became the central node in an online right-wing social movement. In terms of its style and rhetoric, *GeenStijl* can be seen as an early pendant of what is known internationally as the alt-right, even though *GeenStijl* has kept more distance to the extreme right than its famous American counterpart. Using the work of Raymond Williams, the chapter considers the relation between technology and ideological form, and proceeds to trace the intellectual origins of the discourse of *GeenStijl*. The website has a nihilist orientation that is Nietzschean in inspiration. *GeenStijl* presents the nihilist breaking of norms and the disregard for etiquette as a progressive movement towards greater transparency. *GeenStijl's* ironic and nihilist discourse has its roots in the Dutch literary field, in particular the work of the leading Dutch post-war writers W.F. Hermans and Gerard Reve.

The conclusion sums up the argument and expands on the central themes of this book. It elaborates on the contradictory nature of the conservative backlash against the legacy of the 1960s and 1970s as both a revolt and an echo. And it addresses the common intellectual underestimation of the right, even though the widely shared belief in the power of ideas is arguably the most striking feature of the Dutch New Right.

Notes

1 Jos de Beus, 'Een Derde Eeuw van Nederlands Conservatisme', in *Ruimte Op Rechts? Conservatieve Onderstroom in de Lage Landen*, ed. Huib Pellikaan and Sebastiaan van der Lubben (Utrecht: Spectrum, 2006), 221–37; Huib Pellikaan, Sarah de Lange and Tom van der Meer, 'The Centre Does Not Hold: Coalition Politics and Party System Change in the Netherlands, 2002–12', *Government and Opposition* 53, no. 2 (2018): 231–55; Willem Schinkel, *Denken in Een Tijd van Sociale Hypochondrie: Aanzet tot wen Theorie Voorbij de Maatschappij* (Kampen: Klement, 2007); Justus Uitermark, *Dynamics of Power in Dutch Integration Politics: From Accommodation to Confrontation* (Amsterdam: Amsterdam University Press, 2013).

2 Cas Mudde, *Populist Radical Right Parties in Europe* (Cambridge: Cambridge University Press, 2007); Jasper Muis and Tim Immerzeel, 'Causes and Consequences of the Rise of Populist Radical Right Parties and Movements in Europe', *Current Sociology* 65, no. 6 (2017): 909–30; Tjitske Akkerman, Sarah L. de Lange and Matthijs Rooduijn, *Radical Right-Wing Populist Parties in Western Europe: Into the Mainstream?* (London: Routledge, 2016).

3 Paul Lucardie, 'The Netherlands: Populism versus Pillarization', in *Twenty-First Century Populism* (Springer, 2008), 151–65; Cas Mudde, 'The Populist Zeitgeist', *Government and Opposition* 39, no. 4 (2004): 541–63; Pellikaan, de Lange and van der Meer, 'The Centre Does Not Hold: Coalition Politics and Party System Change in the Netherlands, 2002–12'; Joost van Spanje, 'Contagious Parties', *Party Politics* 16, no. 5 (2010): 563–86.

4 For a collection of prominent Dutch neoconservative essays, see Jaffe Vink and Chris Rutenfrans, *De Terugkeer van de Geschiedenis: Letter & Geest* (Amsterdam: Trouw/ Augustus, 2005).

5 Bart Jan Spruyt, *Lof van het Conservatisme* (Amsterdam: Balans, 2003), 10; Tom Jan Meeus and Guus Valk, 'De Buitenlandse Vrienden van Geert Wilders', *NRC Handelsblad*, 15 May 2010.

6 Hendrik Jan Schoo, *Republiek van Vrije Burgers: Het Onbehagen in de Democratie*, 2e dr. (Amsterdam: Bert Bakker, 2008), 264.

7 Beus, 'Een Derde Eeuw van Nederlands Conservatisme', 237.

8 Ton de Graaf, 'Entree Fortuyn in de Politiek Is Bedenkelijk Voor Leefbaarheid', *De Volkskrant*, 13 November 2001; Jet Bussemaker, 'Pim Fortuyn: De Eerste Politieke Postmodernist', *Socialisme & Democratie* 59, no. 4 (2002): 8–9; Jos van der Lans, 'De Kreet des Volks', *Vrij Nederland*, 22 June 2002.

9 Willem Witteveen, 'Edmund Burke, Profeet van de Vooruitstrevendheid', *Socialisme En Democratie* 62, no. 1 (2005): 48.

10 Jan Willem Duyvendak, *The Politics of Home: Belonging and Nostalgia in Western Europe and the United States* (Basingstoke: Palgrave Macmillan, 2011); Leo Lucassen and Jan Lucassen, *Winnaars en Verliezers: Een Nuchtere Balans van Vijfhonderd Jaar Immigratie* (Amsterdam: Bakker, 2011); Baukje Prins, 'The Nerve to Break Taboos: New Realism in the Dutch Discourse on Multiculturalism', *JIMI/RIMI* 3, no. 3–4 (2002): 363–79; Willem Schinkel, *Denken in een Tijd van Sociale Hypochondrie: Aanzet tot een Theorie Voorbij de Maatschappij* (Kampen: Klement, 2007); Rogier van Reekum, 'Out of Character: Debating Dutchness, Narrating Citizenship' (PhD thesis, Amsterdam, University of Amsterdam, 2014).

11 Terry Eagleton, *Ideology*, Longman Critical Readers (London: Longman, 1994); Andrew Heywood, *Political Ideologies: An Introduction* (London: Macmillan, 1992); Michael Freeden, *Ideology: A Very Short Introduction* (Oxford: Oxford University Press, 2003), Michael Freeden, Lyman Tower Sargent and Marc Stears, *The Oxford Handbook of Political Ideologies* (Oxford: Oxford University Press, 2013).

12 James Kennedy, 'Building New Babylon: Cultural Change in the Netherlands during the 1960s' (PhD thesis, Iowa, Iowa University, 1995).

13 Rebecca E. Klatch, *A Generation Divided: The New Left, the New Right, and the 1960s* (Berkeley, CA: University of California Press, 1999); Geoff Andrews, *New Left, New Right and Beyond: Taking the Sixties Seriously* (Basingstoke: Palgrave Macmillan, 1999); Paul Lyons, *New Left, New Right, and the Legacy of the Sixties* (Philadelphia, PA: Temple University Press, 1996).

14 Hunter S. Thompson, *Fear and Loathing in Las Vegas: A Savage Journey to the Heart of the American Dream* (London: Paladin, 1972), 72.

15 Hans Righart, *De Eindeloze Jaren Zestig: Geschiedenis van een Generatieconflict* (Amsterdam: Amsterdam University Press, 2006).

16 Kennedy, 'Building New Babylon', 20.

17 Kennedy, 21.

18 Syp Wynia and Sytze van der Zee, 'Lubbers: "Geen Zin in nog een Sanering"', *Het Parool*, 10 June 1989.

19 Lubbers derived the term from a leading empirical study that characterized the value patterns of the Dutch population since the 1970s in terms of a 'prudently progressive' consensus: a self-evident progressive morality regarding sexual morality and hierarchical authority, connected with a widespread belief in the necessity of redistribution of wealth. This progressive 'common sense' also contains a more prudent – or conservative – stress on the need to restrict government bureaucracy and an endorsement of disciplinary intervention on crime and other socially deviant behaviour. See SCP, *Sociaal en Cultureel Rapport 1998: 25 Jaar Sociale Verandering* (Rijswijk: Sociaal en Cultureel Planbureau, 1998).

20 James Kennedy, *Bezielende Verbanden: Gedachten over Religie, Politiek en Maatschappij in het Moderne Nederland* (Amsterdam: Bert Bakker, 2009).

21 Huib Pellikaan, Sarah L. de Lange and Tom van der Meer, 'Fortuyn's Legacy: Party System Change in the Netherlands', *Comparative European Politics* 5, no. 3 (2007): 294.

22 Paul Lucardie, 'The Netherlands', *European Journal of Political Research* 42, no. 7–8 (2003): 1029–36.

23 Kennedy, *Bezielende Verbanden*, 148–49.

24 Kennedy, 150.

25 Cited in Martin Sommer, 'Steeds Harder Lopen', *De Volkskrant*, 4 September 2008.

26 Frits Bolkestein, *De Engel en Het Beest* (Amsterdam: Prometheus, 1990), 238.

27 Marcel ten Hooven, 'Het Conservatieve Offensief', 9 September 1995.
28 Hans Wansink, *De Conservatieve Golf* (Amsterdam: Prometheus, 1996).
29 Spruyt, *Lof van het Conservatisme*, 10.
30 Jos van der Lans and Antoine Verbij, 'Manifest voor de Jaren Zeventig', *Vrij Nederland*, 23 March 2005.
31 Bolkestein, *De Engel En Het Beest*, 70.
32 Pim Fortuyn, *Een Toekomst Zonder Ambtenaren* (Den Haag: SDU Juridische & Fiscale Uitgeverij, 1991), 8.
33 Herman Vuijsje, *Correct: Weldenkend Nederland sinds de Jaren Zestig* (Amsterdam: Contact, 1997); Published in English as: Herman Vuijsje, *The Politically Correct Netherlands since the 1960s*, trans. Mark T. Hooker (Westport, CT: Greenwood Press, 2000).
34 Vuijsje, *Correct*, 10. My translation. All Dutch-language sources have been translated to English by the author. While the original Dutch text of large quotes has been left out in this book, it is included in the original PhD manuscript, see Merijn Oudenampsen, 'The Conservative Embrace of Progressive Values: On the Intellectual Origins of the Swing to the Right in Dutch Politics' (PhD thesis, Tilburg, Tilburg University, 2018).
35 Paul Cliteur, 'Conservatieven Hebben een Revolutie Nodig', *NRC Handelsblad*, 5 May 2001.
36 Guus Valk, 'Het Conservatieve Moment is Voorbij', *NRC Handelsblad*, 26 August 2006.
37 Matthew Kaminski, 'Pim's Misfortune', *Wall Street Journal*, 7 May 2002.
38 For an overview of New Atheism, see Thomas Zenk, 'New Atheism', in *The Oxford Handbook of Atheism*, 2013, 245–62.
39 Hendrik Jan Schoo, *De Verwarde Natie: Dwarse Notities over Immigratie in Nederland* (Amsterdam: Prometheus, 2000); Peter Steinfels, *The Neoconservatives: The Origins of a Movement*, 1st Touchstone ed. (New York: Simon and Schuster, 2013).
40 Elaine de Boer and Theo Koelé, 'Een Rechtse Directe', *De Volkskrant*, 20 November 2003.
41 Koen Vossen, *The Power of Populism: Geert Wilders and the Party for Freedom in the Netherlands* (London: Routledge, 2017).
42 Martin Bosma, *De Schijn-Élite van de Valsemunters: Drees, Extreem Rechts, de Sixties, Nuttige Idioten, Groep Wilders en ik* (Amsterdam: Bert Bakker, 2011).
43 Andrew Gamble, *The Free Economy and the Strong State: The Politics of Thatcherism* (Basingstoke: Macmillan, 1994); Desmond S. King, *The New Right: Politics, Markets and Citizenship* (Basingstoke: Macmillan Education, 1987); John Gray, *Beyond the New Right: Markets, Government and the Common Environment* (London: Routledge, 1993).
44 Richard Cockett, *Thinking the Unthinkable: Think-Tanks and the Economic Counter-Revolution 1931–1983*, Rev. ed. (London: HarperCollins, 1995); Sidney Blumenthal, *The Rise of the Counter-Establishment: The Conservative Ascent to Political Power* (New York: Union Square Press, 2008); Stuart Hall and Martin Jacques, *The Politics of Thatcherism* (London: Lawrence and Wishart, 1983); Petrus Willem Zuidhof, 'Imagining Markets: The Discursive Politics of Neoliberalism' (PhD thesis, Rotterdam, Erasmus Universiteit, 2012).
45 George H. Nash, *The Conservative Intellectual Movement in America since 1945* (Wilmington, DE: ISI Books, 2014); Justin Vaïsse, *Neoconservatism: The Biography of a Movement* (Cambridge, MA: Belknap Press of Harvard University Press, 2010); Peter Steinfels, *The Neoconservatives: The Origins of a Movement* (New York: Simon and Schuster, 2013); Francis Fukuyama, *America at the Crossroads: Democracy, Power, and the Neoconservative Legacy* (New Haven, CT: Yale University Press, 2006); Irving Kristol, *Neoconservatism: The Autobiography of an Idea* (New York: Free Press, 1995); Kim Phillips-Fein, *Invisible Hands: The Making of the Conservative Movement from the New Deal to Reagan* (New York: W. W. Norton & Company, 2009); Angus Burgin, *The Great Persuasion: Reinventing Free Markets*

since the Depression (Harvard University Press, 2012); Colin Crouch, *The Strange Non-Death of Neo-Liberalism* (Cambridge: Polity, 2011); Daniel Stedman Jones, *Masters of the Universe: Hayek, Friedman, and the Birth of Neoliberal Politics* (Princeton, NJ: Princeton University Press, 2014); Jamie Peck, *Constructions of Neoliberal Reason* (Oxford: Oxford University Press, 2010); Philip Mirowski and Dieter Plehwe, *The Road from Mont Pèlerin: The Making of the Neoliberal Thought Collective* (Cambridge, MA: Harvard University Press, 2009).

46 Piero Ignazi, 'The Silent Counter-Revolution. Hypotheses on the Emergence of Extreme Right-Wing Parties in Europe', *European Journal of Political Research* 22, no. 1 (1992): 3–34; Brian Girvin, *The Transformation of Contemporary Conservatism* (London: SAGE, 1988).

47 Piero Ignazi, *Extreme Right Parties in Western Europe* (Oxford: Oxford University Press, 2003); Hans-Georg Betz, *Radical Right-Wing Populism in Western Europe* (Basingstoke: MacMillan, 1994); Herbert Kitschelt and Anthony J. MacGann, *The Radical Right in Western Europe: A Comparative Analysis* (Ann Arbor, MI: The University of Michigan Press, 1995); Michael Minkenberg, 'The New Right in Germany. The Transformation of Conservatism and the Extreme Right', *European Journal of Political Research* 22, no. 1 (1992): 55–81.

48 Mudde, *Populist Radical Right Parties in Europe*; Muis and Immerzeel, 'Causes and Consequences of the Rise of Populist Radical Right Parties and Movements in Europe'; Akkerman, Lange and Rooduijn, *Radical Right-Wing Populist Parties in Western Europe: Into the Mainstream?*

49 Kitschelt and MacGann, *The Radical Right*, viii.

50 Betz, *Radical Right-Wing Populism*, 89, 109.

51 Betz, 171.

52 Ignazi, 'The Silent Counter-Revolution', 16, 19.

53 Claus Offe, 'New Social Movements: Challenging the Boundaries of Institutional Politics', *Social Research* 52, no. 4 (1985): 817–68; Piero Ignazi, 'The Silent Counter-Revolution'; Michael Minkenberg, *Neokonservatismus Und Neue Rechte in Den USA: Neuere Konservative Gruppierungen Und Strömungen Im Kontext Sozialen Und Kulturellen Wandels* (Baden-Baden: Nomos, 1990).

54 Jürgen Habermas, 'Neoconservative Culture Criticism in the United States and West Germany: An Intellectual Movement in Two Political Cultures', *Telos* 1983, no. 56 (1983): 75–89.

55 Mudde, *Populist Radical Right Parties in Europe*.

56 Cas Mudde, 'Wilders is de Meest Succesvolle Neocon', *Trouw*, 6 November 2009.

57 Sarah de Lange, 'A New Winning Formula? The Programmatic Appeal of the Radical Right', *Party Politics* 13, no. 4 (2007): 426.

58 Akkerman, Lange and Rooduijn, *Radical Right-Wing Populist Parties*, 7–8.

59 Seymour Martin Lipset and Earl Raab, *The Politics of Unreason: Right Wing Extremism in America, 1790–1970* (New York: Harper & Row, 1970), 29–30.

60 Jan Willem Duyvendak, 'Zijn We Dan Niet Altijd Modern Geweest? Over Collectief Geheugenverlies in Nederland en de Overwinning van de Jaren Zestig', *Socialisme & Democratie* 73, no. 1 (2016): 13–19.

61 Cited in Sommer, 'Steeds Harder Lopen'.

62 Ian Buruma, *Murder in Amsterdam: Liberal Europe, Islam and the Limits of Tolerance* (New York: Penguin, 2007).

63 Sara R. Farris, *In the Name of Women's Rights: The Rise of Femonationalism* (Durham, NC: Duke University Press, 2017); Paul Mepschen and Jan Willem Duyvendak, 'European Sexual Nationalisms: The Culturalization of Citizenship and the Sexual Politics of Belonging and Exclusion', *Perspectives on Europe* 42, no. 1 (2012): 70–6; Paul Mepschen, Jan Willem Duyvendak and Evelien H. Tonkens, 'Sexual Politics, Orientalism and Multicultural Citizenship in the Netherlands', *Sociology* 44,

no. 5 (2010): 962–79; Jasbir K. Puar, *Terrorist Assemblages: Homonationalism in Queer Times*, Next Wave (Durham, NC: Duke University Press, 2007).

64 Angela McRobbie, 'Post-feminism and Popular Culture', *Feminist Media Studies* 4, no. 3 (2004): 255–64.

65 See Rogers Brubaker, 'Between Nationalism and Civilizationism: The European Populist Moment in Comparative Perspective', *Ethnic and Racial Studies* 40, no. 8 (2017): 1191–1226.

1 Struggling with depoliticization

This book takes issue with a common perception of the Netherlands, as a country that has moved beyond ideology. The most renowned exponent of that view was Francis Fukuyama, who had published his famous essay *The End of History?* in the summer of 1989. On a visit to the Netherlands in 1992, Fukuyama debated VVD leader Frits Bolkestein, and argued that the Dutch were among the first to have reached the end of history, by which he meant the final resolution of ideological conflict:

> It is part of human nature to take risks and struggle, to pursue big ideas and historic deeds. In a country like the Netherlands, where the end of history has been reached some time ago, it is questionable whether the desires inspired by this aspect of human nature can be satisfied. If people want to live with struggle and ordeals, and society is decent and just, it seems to me they will resist that society. It could be the impetus for the entire historical process to begin anew.[1]

After the collapse of the Soviet Bloc, the idea of an end of ideology was enthusiastically embraced by Dutch political, intellectual and journalistic circles. The leading Dutch historian Piet de Rooy noted that the 1990s seemed to be the time 'of overcoming all ideological differences that had come into being since the second half of the nineteenth century'. According to De Rooy, this was not an entirely new development. The Netherlands has been suffering from an acute case of 'ideological hypothermia' ever since the late 1970s. In his eyes, the Dutch peace movement of the 1980s formed 'the final possibility to divide the country in a progressive and a conservative part'.[2] When social democrat leader Wim Kok made a landmark speech in 1995, in which he proclaimed a 'definitive farewell to socialist ideology' and spoke of 'the liberating feeling of shedding one's ideological feathers', many felt confirmed in their vision of a future without ideology.[3] While this common perception was not altogether unfounded when it concerned developments on the left, the right experienced an ideological renewal that many had overlooked. A conservative undercurrent emerged, articulated around a new and enduring cultural cleavage on immigration, law and order and national identity. This book casts the Dutch 1990s and 2000s not as the era of the end of ideologies, but rather as a time of renewed ideological controversy.

Fukuyama had not been altogether wrong to single out the Netherlands as a frontrunner in the abolition of history. The belief in 'the end of ideology' and the feasibility of an 'objective' politics has long been a powerful sentiment in Dutch politics. In the 1950s and 1960s, there had been an earlier 'end of ideology' debate, initiated by authors such as Daniel Bell, Edward Shils, Seymour Martin Lipset, Ralf Dahrendorf and Raymond Aron. Also back then, the Netherlands was seen as exceptional for its 'highly apolitical atmosphere'.[4] Hans Daalder and Arend Lijphart, considered by many as the founding fathers of Dutch political science, attributed this to a peculiar culture of depoliticization among Dutch elites.

In the post-war rise of Dutch political science, a strong tendency towards depoliticization and an antipathy towards ideology were identified as pivotal elements of Dutch political culture, and a particularity of the Dutch political – and intellectual – tradition. Daalder argued that the proportional political system in the Netherlands offers obvious incentives for Dutch political, academic and journalistic elites to frame their ideas as non-ideological, as 'pragmatism', 'objectivity' or 'realism'. In a country of political minorities, it makes it possible to build consensus and win majorities for political ideas. Daalder called this 'depoliticization-out-of-political-interest'.[5]

Drawing on Daalder's and Lijphart's groundbreaking work, this first chapter serves as an introduction to the Dutch political tradition. It argues that ideology is ever-present yet often disavowed in the Netherlands, due to the dominant culture of depoliticization. Subsequently, it shows how Daalder's and Lijphart's theory of Dutch political culture became a powerful instrument in the hands of protest movements. The first wave of consensus critique appeared in the 1960s and 1970s, when progressive protest movements appealed to the work of Daalder and Lijphart to critique the restricted nature of Dutch democracy. A second wave emerged in the 1990s, when conservatives such as Bolkestein, Vuijsje and Fortuyn repurposed the old consensus critique, this time to challenge the 'baby boomer' elites seen as representatives of the legacy of the 1960s.

Power and passivity

In 1964, Hans Daalder gave his inaugural lecture as chair in the science of politics at Leiden University, titled *Power and Passivity in Dutch Politics* (*Leiding en Lijdelijkheid in de Nederlandse Politiek*). The lecture grew out to become a foundational text and Daalder a founding father of Dutch political science. In his lecture, Daalder explored the major obstacles for the study of politics in the Netherlands. He wondered what could explain the 'Dutch tepidity towards political life' and the country's peculiar 'highly apolitical atmosphere'.[6] Of course, Daalder was writing in a time when a prominent international debate was taking place on the slackening of political passions and the waning of ideology more generally. The American sociologist Daniel Bell had famously

published *The End of Ideology* in 1960, in which he identified modernization
and the increasing complexity of state intervention as the underlying trends.
Daalder similarly noted that in large parts of the western world 'the complex
negotiation and the concrete goal dominate, where once revolutionary, eschatological hope and counter-revolutionary fear and repression prevailed'.[7] On the
other hand, Daalder contended that the apolitical atmosphere he observed in the
Netherlands had specific Dutch roots.

There was certainly no lack of subject matter that lent itself for political conflict in the Netherlands. For Daalder, the crucial factor needing explanation was
the fact that 'many essentially political matters aren't presented as such in Dutch
society'.[8] He located the key to this phenomenon in the behaviour of Dutch
elites that had long pursued 'a more or less conscious policy of depoliticizing
key political issues'. As a result, politics in the Netherlands was perceived by
the larger population to be a largely technocratic and tedious affair, the private
domain of the various political and administrative elites. It contributed to a
'large distance between those that make policy and those that are subject to it'.[9]
The lack of clear political contrasts and meaningful choice for the electorate led
to widespread political disenchantment and passivity, which could, in times of
crisis, foster the appeal of extremism. In his inaugural lecture, Daalder
developed a wide-ranging historical-sociological explanation of the Dutch predi-
lection for depoliticization. Since the text is not available in English, I will
briefly reproduce his argument here.[10]

History had endowed the Netherlands with a particular elite political culture,
which Daalder called 'regent mentality' after the regent class of the Dutch
Republic. Dutch public office had grown from a peculiar marriage of the plural-
istic regent traditions dating back to the Dutch Republic of the sixteenth and
seventeenth century, and the incomplete adoption of Napoleonic centralization
under French rule (1795–1813). The fruit of this strange marriage was the
so-called 'regent mentality'. With this term, Daalder referred to the belief of
Dutch elites that political authority was not based on popular sovereignty, it was
self-evident and self-legitimizing. Dutch elites did not necessarily see themselves
as representatives of the people, nor did they engage in political controversies and
conflicts on the people's behalf. This 'regent mentality' was reinforced in the
twentieth century by the fact that the first mass political party was the Protestant
Anti-Revolutionary Party (ARP). In line with Christian anti-revolutionary ideology, justification of political power was sought in conservative notions of natural
inequality, the rule of the wise or the natural order. The result, Daalder observed
while pointing to the contrast with the more self-asserted and adversarial British
political elite, is an establishment that 'doesn't see or show itself as such'. The
Dutch elite does not 'engage with conviction in the public political struggle, but
isolates itself in private, while consciously conforming itself'. In so doing, Daalder
contended, 'it robs us of public politics', presenting not only the electorate, but
also the Dutch political scientist with a rather nebulous image.[11]

The 'regent mentality' had been able to maintain its hold on Dutch society
due to the fact that the impact of the differing Dutch emancipation movements

(liberals, Protestants, Catholics and socialists) had been partial and fragmented. Each political movement brought a democratizing impulse, as synthesized in a famous line by the liberal professor Van Vollenhoven, mentioning respectively the founding fathers of the liberal, Catholic, Protestant and socialist Dutch currents:

> First Thorbecke learned the merchant to look up from his account book and pipe rack, and understand his political rights and duties, then Schaepman and Kuyper learned the petty bourgeois and farmer to look up from counter, chisel, cows; finally Domela Nieuwenhuis and Troelstra have liberated the spirit of the worker from his machine.[12]

However, due to the fact that none of these movements were able to confront the political establishment on their own, they fused with the existing elite rather than opposing it as a whole. The result, Daalder argued, was a particular form of political ambiguity. Outwardly, the emancipatory parties were focused on testimonial politics, professing the ethical principles of their current and socializing their base. Inwardly, the elites of the oppositional currents refrained from effective political organization and mobilization to realize these principles. They accepted the overarching framework in which they were accommodated, resulting in a conciliatory attitude towards government and the eager acceptance of positions and resources granted to them. This, Daalder concluded, was largely to the benefit of the colourless 'quasi-neutralistic currents' in either movement.

The diffused character of the political and policy-making process reinforced political obscurity. In any coalition of a sufficiently broad basis, there was ample space for each party to claim certain political measures and to distance itself from other, unpopular decisions, attributing them to coalition partners. Parties could switch between their testimonial role in parliament and their administrative role in government. The results of elections left ample room for interpretation, and could even be ignored to some extent, allowing the coalition game to continue unhampered. A similar situation occurred at the policy level, due to the complex interaction with a range of different bureaucratic advisory councils, civil society organizations and corporatist bodies, in which anonymous bureaucrats and specialists were often more at home than politicians themselves. In such a context of complex multi-party negotiations, the leaders of organizations necessarily have a large degree of autonomy with respect to their base. The elaborate play with responsibilities that developed in this space, Daalder argued, obscured the outsider's vision. In his view, it clashed with the norm stipulated by John Stuart Mill: 'It should be apparent to all the world, who did everything, and through whose default anything was left undone'.[13] The relative stability of the Dutch political system was thus bought at the expense of a passive or frustrated electorate, who were denied insight into the political choices that were made and had few possibilities to enforce meaningful change. Daalder concluded by citing Montesquieu's *De l'Esprit des Lois* to the effect that if the electorate is deprived of possibilities to oust an unpopular government, 'the people upon seeing it once corrupted would no longer expect any good from its laws; and of course they would either become desperate or fall into a state of indolence'.[14]

In this context there are clear political benefits in depoliticizing key issues, which Daalder called 'depoliticization-out-of-political-interest'. While the Dutch political field was structured along two major axes of competition, the religious-secular cleavage and the socio-economic left-right cleavage, political action along these axes soon revolved around distribution rather than competition. In this process of depoliticization, the state was neutralized, an organ deciding over a 'correct' balance of interests, according to commonly agreed norms, in which every subgroup is 'done justice', and each is tolerated and guaranteed their own space.[15] Daalder elaborates mainly on the socio-economic issue. The politically dominant Christian parties had made the appeasement of social conflict the key point of their programme. Due to the fact that the electoral base of the Christian parties was heterogeneous in its class makeup, socio-economic polarization represented a political threat. To counteract such a development, opposing socio-economic interests – trade unions and employers associations – were brought together politically in the same Christian organizations. Complicated compromises were made behind closed doors, often expressed in technocratic language, to gloss over conflicting class interests. In this process, Daalder highlights the role of a 'centrist mythology' that serves to deny conflict, and that allows decrees and accords to be clothed in the appearance of scientific neutrality.[16]

As a paradoxical result of the dominance of Christian parties, scientific technocracy became the lingua franca of Dutch politics. For citizens and political scientists alike, this made Dutch politics a difficult process to understand. 'Centrism, centralization, and depoliticized expertise create a complex and obscure political space in which even experts are often lost', and where constituents feel ill represented.[17] When the political effort of mobilization and struggle is eclipsed, passivity of the public is the natural result. As long as the economy does well, this leads to a situation Daalder describes with reference to the Dutch writer Simon Carmiggelt: 'being satisfied in a dissatisfied manner'.[18] In less fortunate times, Daalder warned, passivity can lead to extremism: 'recalcitrant extremism can paradoxically be the unexpected flipside of a centrist satisfaction'.[19] Daalder's analysis seems to have lost little relevance when considering political developments at the turn of the millennium.

Finally, Daalder argued that the press and the universities had an important role in reproducing the regent mentality. There was seldom an attempt to break through the depoliticized façade of Dutch politics, since both institutions considered themselves to be a functional part of that system.[20] In a response to the lecture, the leading sociologist Joop Goudsblom observed that Dutch universities functioned as the site where Dutch political elites were trained and the attitudes conducive to the politics of accommodation were reproduced. Even 'the modern university graduates', Goudsblom wrote in the 1960s, 'have generally tended without questioning to adopt this paternalistic attitude, known in Dutch as *regentenmentaliteit*, or "regent mentality"'.[21]

The study of politics as the unmasking of political power

There are interesting parallels between Daalder's lecture and Daniel Bell's end of ideology thesis. Both observed the substitution of ideological competition with technocratic deliberation surrounding the 'correct' distribution of resources. Both noted the marginalization of revolutionary and counter-revolutionary tendencies that had made their mark on the political landscape of the 1930s. But Daalder saw the end of ideology in Dutch politics as a form of mystification rather than political reality. It was an unnatural – and undesirable – effect of the depoliticizing tendency of both the Dutch political system and the political philosophy of Dutch elites: the 'regent mentality'. The task of the scholar, Daalder argued, was to reach beyond the depoliticized façade of Dutch politics. Daalder ended his lecture by outlining a research agenda and defining a spirited mission statement for the study of Dutch politics. In the eyes of Daalder, the task of the political scholar is one of unmasking:

> The science of politics can only contribute to a real insight into Dutch political realities, if it does not hesitate in desecrating many sacred cows. The masking of political power and political ambitions is in all political systems a means of governing. All scientific research into such phenomena runs the risk of thwarting established interests. If the need arises, political science will need to enter into conflict with these interests, or else it risks becoming an accessory. As the result of research and reflection it offers, not so much normative guidelines as more openness and a better understanding of relationships.[22]

While there is much to admire in this critical motto that Daalder would continue to invoke over his long and fruitful career, the concluding Weberian appeal to a non-normative science of politics is perhaps somewhat misleading. After all, the power and thrust of the argument in Daalder's lecture derives from a thoroughly normative appeal to an open and competitive conception of democracy expressed in the liberal philosophy of Stuart Mill and Montesquieu. Daalder's argument is founded on an implicit comparison of the consensual Dutch political system to the adversarial Westminster model. A comparison that is normative in character. In fact, Daalder's perspective closely resembles that of the American political scientist Schattschneider, who defended the essential role of conflict in modern democracy, as a precondition for popular participation in his 1960 classic *The Semi-Sovereign People*.[23] In an early critical essay that formed the basis for his inaugural lecture, Daalder is even more explicit:

> Pressure politics and political struggle aren't just the essence but even the justification for the existence of political parties. This seems a truism, but it is necessary to repeat it, seeing that an entire mythology has developed that obscures this. A mythology that speaks of the perversion of Politics by

politics, that posits an objective 'common interest' against 'narrow' party interests and speaks of the 'proportional' distribution of burdens, according to an 'objective criterion'. Oftentimes such a myth serves as a cover for actions of self-confident political and economic interest groups. But it is even more the result of an anti-political tradition, whose roots can be traced back to constitutional law, in as much as it abstracts from parties; to the aforementioned bureaucratic and sometimes clearly technocratic regent mentality, in which one rules for 'the' people; and to the entire Dutch party system, which constantly necessitates compromises that give off a pretence of objectivity, on the one hand because all those who are 'compromised' will defend the decision as such, on the other hand, because some parties also have internal interests in not sketching essential oppositions too clearly.[24]

At the time of writing this essay, Daalder worked at the University of Amsterdam as an assistant for Professor Barents, who prevented him from publishing the text. 'Icebags on the head!' and 'do not presuppose popular sovereignty!' were Barents' injunctions to his hot-headed assistant.[25] More important for our purposes here, however, is that the lecture that Daalder had written as a trenchant critique of the Dutch political system was soon turned into its very opposite by his close colleague and collaborator Arend Lijphart. In a curious twist of fate, the lecture became the key inspiration for a political theory that would serve as a legitimization for the political mentality Daalder originally set out to censure: Lijphart's famous model of consociational democracy. While always retaining a critical distance to Lijphart's work, Daalder proved surprisingly supportive of this effort. He personally brought over Lijphart from the US and introduced him in the Netherlands, and effectively worked with him in establishing Lijphart's theory on the international academic scene, dominated by the American pluralist tradition. In so doing, political science seemed to take on the accessory role Daalder had warned about in his credo.

Arend Lijphart and the legitimating formula

After finishing his PhD in political science on Dutch decolonization in 1963 at Yale University, the American-Dutch scholar Arend Lijphart went on to write the single most famous text on Dutch politics. In 1968, Arend Lijphart published *The Politics of Accommodation*.[26] It became the textbook description of the Dutch political system, identified as a 'consociational democracy'. The notion of consociationalism, a seminal topic of discussion in comparative politics, denotes a particular brand of politics that developed in societies that were deeply divided in ethnic or religious terms. More specifically, the term refers to an elite political culture of overarching compromise and non-competitive acceptance of ideological differences to ensure political stability. Lijphart proposed it as an alternative model to the more competitive and majoritarian Westminster model of parliamentary democracy in the US and the UK. Lijphart depicted the Netherlands as the primary example of this alternative political model, next to countries such as Belgium, Austria and Switzerland.

Lijphart's study draws heavily on the analysis by Daalder, only with opposite appreciation. Daalder saw the dominance of depoliticization and the wilful practice of obscuring political contrasts and responsibilities as shortcomings of Dutch democracy; Lijphart defended these practices as necessary for containing societal cleavages and praised them as key to the strength of Dutch democracy. Daalder deplored the large distance between rules and subjects; Lijphart saw the freedom of Dutch elites to act independently from their base as vital to the success of overarching elite cooperation. Daalder lamented the political apathy of the Dutch electorate as a breeding ground for extremism; Lijphart lauded political passivity, or deference, as a cornerstone of democratic stability. And finally, while Daalder aimed to unmask the centrist mythology governing Dutch politics, Lijphart's work can itself be read on an ideological level as an expression of that mythology, its codification in pluralist theory and its extension to the terrain of political science.

Lijphart's basic argument is that Dutch elites developed a particular political culture in the early twentieth century, a specific set of 'rules of the game', to deal with the fragmented nature of the country's political landscape. Central to this culture was the stress on harmony and the pragmatic toleration of differing political and religious beliefs rather than political struggle and ideological contestation. For Lijphart, 'the pragmatic acceptance of ideological differences which cannot and should not be changed', was central to Dutch political culture. 'The fundamental convictions of other blocs must be tolerated, if not respected. Disagreements must not be allowed to turn into either mutual contempt or proselytizing zeal'.[27]

The major innovation is that Lijphart introduced an eschatological element: without the political culture of depoliticization, Dutch society would erupt into a semi-Hobbesian civil war. Due to the fact that the country was divided from 1917 to 1967 into four minority socio-religious groups – Protestants, Catholics, socialists and liberals – the elites of these groups gave rise to an overarching politics of accommodation to keep the country stable and governable. This political reality was neatly captured by Lijphart in the eloquent and powerful metaphor of pillarization: the four separate pillars were united in a stable structure by a common roof: the culture of elite accommodation. Under the consociationalist system, the subcultures each developed their own public infrastructure, facilitated by the state: schools, universities, newspapers, radio and later television channels, political parties, trade unions and employer federations, housing corporations, culture and sports facilities, even neighbourhood life could be segregated in terms of denomination. Lijphart's study describes the emergence of this system in the beginning of the twentieth century, and its decline in the 1960s, with secularization and the rise of the 'neo-democrat' protest movements.

On a more theoretical level, Lijphart's study was intended as an amendment to American pluralist theory, which held that the homogeneity of the electorate and cross-cutting cleavages (groups and individuals having multiple and overlapping affiliations with differing class, ethnic and religious identities) were a precondition for democratic moderation and political stability. These cross-cutting cleavages were deemed absent from the Netherlands, leading the intellectual godfather of pluralism, Robert Dahl, to drily remark to Daalder: 'You know, your country theoretically cannot exist'.[28] Lijphart even cited Robert Dahl, to the effect that civil war was deemed a real possibility in such instances. In contrast, Lijphart argued that the Dutch case showed that deeply divided societies could still be governed in a democratically stable fashion, if elites were aware of the grave dangers of political disintegration and prudently took action to dampen and pacify conflict while maintaining a 'healthy element of authoritarianism'.[29] Lijphart famously called this the self-denying prophecy.

Depoliticization was one of the most important 'rules of the game'. Echoing the ambiguity Daalder wrote of, Lijphart observed that ideological discourse served to socialize the base of the different pillars and obtain voter adherence, while at the intra-elite level, politics was decreed to be technical, pragmatic and collegial. The compromises arrived at by different coalition governments had to be described in a depoliticizing language that appeased all parties. Potentially destabilizing ideological conflict had to be curtailed to keep the system manageable. One way of doing that was the rule of proportionality: making decisions in a proportional manner, dividing resources equally. Another way of depoliticizing matters was to deliberately clothe decisions in a technocratic language, so that ordinary voters could not understand them. As Lijphart approvingly observed, Dutch elites engaged in 'complicated economic arguments and the juggling of economic facts and figures incomprehensible to most people'.[30]

> The art is to present political matters which tend to evoke emotions and can lead to discord in society, as if they are not political matters at all, but issues that can be dealt with according to objective, established principles of economic doctrine, of accounting (distribution), or law.[31]

In other words, the depoliticizing technocratic rationality criticized by Daalder as 'centrist mythology' became a centrepiece of Lijphart's theory. The most dangerous political controversies for the stability of the Dutch political system are those that cannot be resolved through rules of proportionality. In that case, Dutch elites resort to a conscious policy of putting things on ice, not addressing them. Lijphart called this the 'icebox policy', 'allowing a vexatious issue to be temporarily frozen'.[32]

Over the years, critics have argued that Lijphart's model paints an overly schematic picture at best, and a rather deceptive one at worst.[33] One of the most significant criticisms is that Lijphart's argument is inherently tautological: the political system that divided Dutch society in pillars was supposedly created to further political stability. While at the same time, the extent of pillarization was used by Lijphart as an indication of how intensely divided Dutch society was, and why pillarization was needed for stability in the first place. There is little doubt that Dutch elites actively fomented socio-religious fragmentation, by creating the very educational institutions that divided people. The attitudes of elites were, more often than not, a driver of fragmentation rather than a response to it.[34] Moreover, cross-cutting cleavages were prominent features of the Dutch political context. After all, the Christian subcultures brought together voters of different class affiliations, and functioned as a bulwark against class polarization. Lijphart's premise of the ever-present threat of social disintegration – or even civil war – has since been refuted as unfounded and far-fetched.[35] A final objection is that Lijphart sketches a harmonized model of four political currents proportionally dividing resources, while it is more reasonable to describe Dutch pillarization in terms of the dominance of the Christian bloc that managed to exclude the social democrats from power until the onset of the Second World War. Alternative and more plausible explanations have described the genesis of the Dutch political system as a control mechanism.[36] It was the product, on the one hand, of a successful attempt by Catholic and Protestant forces to contain the forces of modernization and stave off an emerging labour movement. And on the other, the product of a contest between Christian and liberal currents over control of the Dutch state apparatus, leading to the political compromise of pillarization and proportionality.[37]

Despite the model's shortcomings, Lijphart's theory of accommodation has continued to exert a pronounced influence over Dutch political science, sociology and public administration, as a foundational text.[38] Its description of Dutch political culture at the elite level has become, rather ironically, a self-fulfilling prophecy, as Lijphart's work became a central reference point in the political socialization of Dutch elites at universities. *The Politics of Accommodation* became a manual on how to do Dutch politics. The basic black-or-white argument – accommodate or disintegrate – still resonates powerfully in Dutch political life. Influential academics referred to Lijphart to advocate the accommodation and depoliticization of right-wing populism.[39] This lasting authority can perhaps partly be explained by the important ideological function that Lijphart's theory served in underpinning the Dutch political system. In his 1964 inaugural lecture, Daalder referred to Gaetano Mosca's elite theory and the need for a 'political formula' legitimizing the exercise of power. In more egalitarian-democratic times, authority needs 'an ideological justification', Daalder argued.[40] He went on to trace a short history of Dutch conservative-liberal theories legitimizing authority. I would suggest that Lijphart's theory of the politics of accommodation can be read on such an ideological level, as a post-war extension of that conservative-liberal tradition. The fear of instability, social disintegration and civil war was much overstated, but the theory can be analysed in terms of an origin myth or a Hobbesian social contract theory that served to legitimize the relatively closed and hierarchical Dutch political system, while giving a positive twist to the passivity of the electorate.

The 1960s and the breakdown of the politics of accommodation

The political turmoil of the 1960s threw Dutch political culture into disarray. Lijphart's landmark study appeared just at a time when the Dutch system of pillarization started to fall apart. In the 1960s and 1970s, the pillars rapidly disintegrated due to a process of secularization and modernization, going hand in hand with open contestation by new social movements. In an afterword to his book, Lijphart wrote of a breakdown of the politics of accommodation. He saw it as part of a transformation from consociational democracy (fragmented electorate, cooperative/closed elites) to a cartel democracy (homogeneous electorate, cooperative/closed elites). The dissatisfaction caused by cartel democracy gave rise to a 'neo-democratic ideology' that challenged the closed character of Dutch politics. Lijphart saw this democratizing impulse as a worrying source of instability, 'undermining the homogeneous political culture of cartel democracy'.[41] The historical irony is that Lijphart's theory formed a major inspiration for the 'neo-democrats' criticizing the system. One of the most significant 'neo-democrat' voices was the leading journalist and essayist Henk Hofland who wrote a powerful and unsparing takedown of the Dutch political elite in 1972, titled *Tegels Liften* (Lifting Tiles). He based himself on the work of Lijphart and used it to frontally attack the Dutch authorities that he famously accused of having 'colonized' the Dutch citizen. In so doing, Hofland gave the wheel of Dutch political theorizing yet another twist, reverting back to Daalder's original critical intent. What was written as an instruction manual for Dutch elites on how to maintain political order now became an instrument for the decolonization efforts to come:

> Reading Lijphart's book made me extremely content, since it confirmed the sentiment many of us walked around with, lacking scientific understanding. How do the elites manage to persuade the common people to move in the direction they desire, wilfully complying with peace and order?[42]

Hofland gave voice to a strong sentiment in the 1970s that the Dutch political system was in fact, not very democratic. The problem was not so much malevolent despotism, but 'the sentiment held by many an administrator, authority, politician, director and magistrate, that they had the monopoly to "scheme and concoct"'. The problem was that Dutch elites, once in private, had a different set of political values and priorities than they let on towards their base. It was not a typical kind of authoritarianism, but rather 'the continuous taking of "calm, considerate decisions" hidden under the magic of secrecy and a suitable ideology for the occasion'.[43]

In the years before, Daalder's analysis had been smuggled out of the Leiden University lecture hall and had been warmly received by the protest movements of the 1960s. The Dutch countercultural movement Provo took up Daalder's terminology and the Dutch novelist Harry Mulisch wrote his controversial book *Message to the Rat King* (*Bericht aan de Rattenkoning*, 1966) as an indictment of the regent mentality. Building on Daalder's definition of the regent mentality as a form of political authority that sees no need to publicly legitimize itself, Mulisch argued that Provo was not against authority as such, but against a specific form of authority, called AUTHORITY. This form of authority was typically Dutch, a legacy of the colonial paternalism of the old patrician regent elite, who had colonized the Dutch people. 'Like the Russians that suffer from the tsar mentality, we suffer from the regent mentality. I freely admit, that we are still relatively lucky, but only in a relative sense'.[44] The main problem was the 'paternalist desire of the regents, to work undisturbed on other issues' than the pressing matters brought forward by Dutch society itself. 'It is this regent mentality, this paternalist obduracy that is being demolished presently. A job that has been taken on in July 1965 and that will be completed marvelously, that much has been made clear, I think'.[45]

In 1974, ten years after his inaugural lecture on 'the regent mentality', Daalder returned to the topic, this time with opposite conclusions. The politics of accommodation, he observed, had given way to a period of politicization with a different set of rules of the game. The strategy of depoliticization, identified by Lijphart as central to Dutch politics, had been substituted for a progressive insistence on 'unmasking the ideology of the establishment'. Meanwhile, in Dutch parliamentary politics, the traditional toleration of opponents, and the reduction of politics to that of finding a 'correct' technocratic balance of interests, had given way to open contestation. It formed part of the 'polarization strategy' of the social democrats and the smaller, newly formed progressive parties, in order to break the traditional dominance of the Christian centre. In the words of Daalder: 'polarization to form an exclusive majority'. A series of attempts were made by the progressive parties at forming a progressive bloc that could attain an electoral majority.

Over the years, Daalder's personal enthusiasm for democratization and politicization had subsided, not in the least due to his negative personal experiences with the Dutch student movement and the push for democratization at Dutch universities. Yet it was his 1964 lecture and the writings of Lijphart and Hofland that became important reference points in the attempt to transform and democratize Dutch politics. Also the progressive majoritarian strategy was partly inspired by Daalder's critique of Dutch political culture. In particular the Dutch progressive Shadow Cabinet of 1971–1972, copied from the UK, formed a clear attempt at introducing elements of the more open and competitive Westminster model in Dutch politics. While a clear progressive majority was never reached, the polarization strategy resulted in the leftist Den Uyl cabinet (1972–1977), generally seen as the high tide of the progressive wave in the Netherlands.

This period of politicization proved to be an interlude. As we have seen in the introduction, the progressive wave was accommodated into a new 'prudent-progressive' paradigm. From 1977 onwards, scholars identified a return to the political patterns of old, leading Lijphart to conclude that while the pillars had gone, the roof of elite accommodation remained.[46] 'It is as if some of the old rules of the game that Lijphart once identified for Dutch politics, have returned, if only in another guise', Daalder observed in 1984.[47] With one big difference: the political ambiguity of the pillarized parties (ideological towards the base, pragmatic at the top) changed into a more monistic technocratic political culture. Daalder described the appetite for politicizing issues in the 1970s – 'for some, politicization has become a goal in itself' – with reference to Kwame Nkrumah, the first president of Ghana, and his dream of the 'Political Kingdom': 'a means to save humanity by entering into one hundred percent political activity'.[48] In contrast, the no-nonsense technocratic atmosphere that enveloped Dutch politics in the 1980s and 1990s can best be described as the dream of the 'Post-political Kingdom', a society where politics had ostensibly been reduced to administration.

An interesting illustration is *The Ideological Triangle (De Ideologische Driehoek)*, a classic on Dutch political thought published by three leading Dutch academics and intellectuals in 1989. The book describes the ideological development of the three main political traditions in modern Dutch politics: Christian democracy, social democracy and liberalism. From the 1980s onwards, the authors observed the erasure of ideology from the Dutch political sphere, a process described as destiny:

> In a complex society such as ours, in which at a thousand different points, government, bureaucracy and society have become interwoven with one another in what can be called an intervention state, politics can no longer be a grand and compelling adventure. The term policy is in this process key. It has nothing of what characterised politics before: utopia's, ideals, visions, societal images, doctrines, traditions; neither does policy give much space to that other aspect of democratic politics: political imagination, independent judgement, personal conviction, government by discussion. Policy is cool, rationalist, as far as possible grounded in quantitative analysis, specialist, scientific, or pretending to be scientific. Policy means technocracy. This does not imply disapproval. [...] This is reality. Politics will have to accord with reality to not render itself powerless.[49]

As in the 1960s, when a similar end of ideology had been proclaimed, the dream proved short-lived. In the 1990s, a new wave of politicization emerged. This time, the signs had been reversed: the challenge to the prevailing consensus came from a conservative undercurrent while the political establishment was now portrayed as a 'leftist elite'. The 1960s critiques of Dutch political culture were now taken up by authors on the right.

The return of consensus critique

When the future right-wing populist Pim Fortuyn started his career as a right-wing commentator in the early 1990s, he began by highlighting the problems of Dutch consensus democracy. 'A long tradition of building consensus, has made us into true specialists in subduing conflict and conceiving of pragmatic solutions', Fortuyn argued in his pamphlet *Without Bureaucrats (Zonder Ambtenaren)*. 'Handling conflict by exploring our differences in perspectives and experiences is not one of our strengths. A major tradition of debate concerning societal, philosophical and religious questions is lacking'. For Fortuyn, adopting his characteristic tone of motivational speaker, the clash of ideas was a prerequisite for modernization, and even a way to 'release emotional energy necessary to realize our creative potential'.[50]

Drawing on the work of Daalder, Lijphart and Hofland, Fortuyn argued that the pillars had disappeared, but the overarching roof of elite consensus culture had remained. Over the years, the composition of the governing elite had become more diverse, but Dutch elites still behaved in accordance with Daalder's regent mentality. They kept on running the country in a rather closed fashion, without much democratic participation. Only now they had become an insulated political caste, lacking a pillar or social base legitimating their decisions:

> Most of our institutions, together with the organs of formal democracy, are faced with a problem of legitimacy. The traditional rank and file have long since disappeared or have been significantly reduced, but the bureaucracies administered by professional elites keep on governing, without the legitimacy provided by the pillars of old.[51]

Paraphrasing Hofland, Fortuyn pleaded for the 'political decolonization of the Dutch citizen'. The accomplishments of the progressive movements of the 1960s and 1970s had led to an emancipated, independent and self-assertive citizenry, who no longer needed the welfare state nor the attentions of paternalistic Dutch elites. Fortuyn now equated emancipation with the curtailment of the state and the embrace of the free market. The inevitable rise of the market, the processes of European unification and economic globalization meant that Dutch bureaucratic institutions needed to be radically curtailed and reformed. The political culture of consensus formed an obstacle to free market reform that needed to be cleared:

> Too often it [consensus society] rewards conformism and discourages dissidence; too often it promotes convention and hinders renewal; too often it takes care of the insiders and hinders the outsiders. Too frequently it contributes to the atrophy of the community while undermining its vitality; too frequently it standardizes where diversity is needed; too frequently it sticks to procedures where flexibility could offer a solution.[52]

Fortuyn initially focused his consensus critique on the economy, but would soon develop a similar position when it came to immigration and multiculturalism. Open and sharp debate on immigration and Islam was needed to deal with the problems of integration and to defend Dutch culture.

We find a similar, paradoxical mobilization of the critiques of the 1960s in the work of the conservative social democrat Herman Vuijsje. His bestselling critique of Dutch political correctness, the book *Correct*, was inspired by the work of Hans Daalder. For Vuijsje, the main problem with Dutch political culture was its passive and accommodating character, its *lijdelijkheid* (passivity), a reference to the title of Daalder's 1964 lecture. Vuijsje proposed that the major failure of the baby-boomer generation consisted of having drawn the wrong conclusions from the Second World War. The real lesson of the war was not to guard against the revival of racism and fascism, since these phenomena never amounted to much in the Netherlands, in the eyes of Vuijsje.[53] The problem was political passivity and accommodation.

By being passive in the face of immigration, segregation and criminality, the baby boomers had repeated the mistakes of their parents. Rather than contesting the politics of accommodation wholesale, the baby boomers had become 'new regents' themselves. They had simply substituted the religious and sexual taboos of their parents for a series of new totems and taboos springing forth from the anti-authoritarian and antiracist ethos of the 1960s.[54] Vuijsje employed the intellectual version of the jujitsu move, in which the momentum of opponents is used against them. The taboo-breaking ethos of the baby boomers was now mobilized against the progressive ideals of the baby-boom generation themselves.[55] Vuijsje's rhetorical strategy of presenting an impressive array of social problems as the singular result of progressive taboos dating back to the cultural revolution of the sixties and seventies, became a leitmotif in the swing to the right in Dutch politics.[56]

A similar criticism of Dutch consensus culture as the cause for Dutch difficulties with immigration resounded in a landmark essay on the failure of multiculturalism, published in January 2000 by the social democrat intellectual Paul Scheffer. In *The Multicultural Drama*, a major turning point in the immigration debate, Scheffer criticized Dutch elites for thinking that the traditional Dutch 'politics of accommodation could be used to deal with the new divisions'.[57] Elite consensus culture, Scheffer contended, had led to a tendency to evade and deny the problems of immigration and integration. In his 2007 bestseller *Country of Arrival* (*Land van Aankomst*), he maintained that consensus culture had fostered a relativist conception of Dutch national identity.

> Dutch society has a great ability to blunt sharp edges. The desire to avoid conflict is undeniable, but the downside to this attitude generally escapes attention: the avoidance of conflict can all too easily lead to avoidance of a more general kind. The Netherlands lacks a culture of debate, whether in parliament, academic life or literature, since the life of the mind is permeated by that same sense of give and take. This has turned out to be a weakness in dealing with immigration.[58]

According to Scheffer, the dominant accommodating tendency was to accord the Muslim minority their own religious and political subculture, as in the pillarization of old, and tolerate their presence in the same way that other religious minorities had been tolerated. But this would not work with Islam because of the lack of a shared language and the rise of Muslim fundamentalism. What was needed, instead, was an assertive and self-conscious Dutch majority culture that could forcefully integrate Muslim immigrants, by highlighting Dutch core values and openly debating and critiquing Islam. 'Criticism of religion, however narrow-minded it may sometimes be, should never be confused with ethnic or racial prejudice', Scheffer argued.[59]

These critiques of Dutch political culture were built on a kernel of truth. But looking at immigration and integration in the 1990s through the lens of the 1960s analyses of Dutch pillarization also distorted matters. Scheffer's contention that Dutch elites intended to organize the Dutch Muslim community as an independent pillar, with its own schools and political subculture, ignored the reality of Dutch integration policy. Since the very beginning of integration policy in the 1980s, the idea of a pillar for Muslim immigrants was considered undesirable. Integration into the dominant majority culture had always been the norm. The overwhelming majority of Muslim children went to Dutch public and Christian schools; politicians with a Muslim background became active in existing parties, rather than forming a party of their own.[60]

In this way, the 1960s critique formed the inspiration for the conservative 1990s indictment against progressive baby boomers and their excessive tolerance towards immigrants. More ironic, even, is that this critique of baby boomers was voiced most prominently by baby boomers themselves: Fortuyn, Vuijsje and Scheffer had all been active in the leftist student movement of the 1960s and 1970s. By presenting their critique as courageous realism and the old 'prudent progressive' consensus as stifling conformism, the undercurrent of the 1990s could present itself as a new wave of emancipation from the yoke of the 'regent mentality'.

The return of the conflict model

By way of conclusion, let's return to James Kennedy's framework of Dutch consensual change as outlined in the introduction. The tendency of Dutch elites to pacify conflict can serve as an explanation for the observation by Kennedy that, in the Dutch context, differing political perspectives tend to succeed one another diachronically, rather than synchronically confronting each other head-on. In the US and the UK, the baby boomers were seen as a divided generation, spawning both the New Left and the New Right. In the Netherlands, in contrast, the image is that of a generalized progressive movement in the 1960s and 1970s and a generalized conservative counter-reaction that materializes at a much later point, surfacing in the 1990s and finally hitting it off politically in the 2000s.

This perhaps also explains the attraction of a generational narrative of political change in the Netherlands: generations serve as a depoliticized indication of the path of the future. It could explain why the baby-boomer generation became such a central signifier for the conservative countermovement of the 2000s, to the point that the Fortuyn revolt was seen as a rebellion against that generation as such. This generational perspective is alluring, but it omits the fact that some of the most incisive critics of the legacy of the 1960s and 1970s were baby boomers themselves, with Fortuyn, Vuijsje and Spruyt as the most obvious examples. It also further obscures the fact that the movements in the 1960s and

1970s were led politically and intellectually by the so-called silent generation (*oorlogsgeneratie*) born before the Second World War. Some of the most famous figureheads of the progressive wave of the 1960s and 1970s were people like Joop den Uyl, Harry Mulisch and Henk Hofland, who had the required age to play a leading role.

The political breakthrough of the conservative undercurrent in the 2000s can be interpreted as another period of politicization, like the 1960s and 1970s. A time in which the dominant paradigm enters into crisis, resulting in a breakdown of consensus politics. In the 2000s, the rules of the conflict model as identified by Daalder entered back into operation, this time centred on the 'unmasking of the multicultural ideology of the establishment'. The climax of this new period of polarization is formed by the two governments that accommodated the right-wing populist surge: the first Balkenende cabinet that was brokered after the 2002 election victory of Fortuyn's party LPF (2002–2003), and the first Rutte cabinet (2010–2012), formed with the support of Geert Wilders' Party for Freedom.

Both can be seen as the conservative counterparts to the progressive government of Den Uyl in the 1970s. The formation of these right-wing cabinets can fittingly be described as 'polarization as a means to form an exclusive majority'. In fact, the official promise of the first Rutte cabinet was a policy that those on the right 'could lick their fingers to'. This in flagrant contradiction with Lijphart's rules of proportionality and depoliticization. In terms of establishment critique, the revolt of the 2000s contains obvious parallels to the 1960s and 1970s. In both periods, we see a radical critique of consensus politics, a celebration of the breaking of taboos, a challenge to the entire political system, an appeal to referenda and political reforms, and a reliance on new communication technologies (first the television, then the internet) to break open what is perceived as a closed regime.

Notes

1 Frits Bolkestein, *Woorden Hebben hun Betekenis* (Amsterdam: Prometheus, 1992), 69.
2 Piet de Rooy, *A Tiny Spot on the Earth: The Political Culture of the Netherlands in the Nineteenth and Twentieth Century* (Amsterdam: Amsterdam University Press, 2015), 275.
3 Wim Kok, 'We Laten Niemand Los' (Den Uyl-lezing, Amsterdam, 11 December 1995).
4 Hans Daalder, *Politisering En Lijdelijkheid in de Nederlandse Politiek* (Assen: Van Gorcum, 1974), 10.
5 Hans Daalder, *Van Oude en Nieuwe Regenten: Politiek in Nederland* (Amsterdam: Bakker, 1995), 36.
6 Daalder, 10.
7 Daalder, 10.
8 Daalder, 12.
9 Daalder, 13.
10 Parts of the argument are present in his chapter in a volume edited by Robert Dahl, see Hans Daalder, 'The Netherlands: Opposition in a Segmented Society', in *Political Oppositions in Western Democracies*, ed. Robert Dahl (New Haven, CT: Yale University Press, 1966), 188–236. Daalder has been criticized for his stress on historical

continuity and his lack of attention for material factors, such as industrialization. See Siep Stuurman, *Verzuiling, Kapitalisme En Patriarchaat: Aspecten van de Ontwikkeling van de Moderne Staat in Nederland* (Nijmegen: Sun, 1983), 307–36.

11 Daalder, *Politisering en Lijdelijkheid*, 18.

12 This harmonious vision of a shared movement towards emancipation has been justifiably criticized by Stuurman. The liberal and Christian currents weren't merely movements of emancipation, they also acted as conservative bulwarks in opposition to emancipation. Here Von der Dunk's remark mentioned earlier, concerning the mixed character of Dutch liberalism and Christian conservatism, needs to be considered. Daalder, *Politisering en Lijdelijkheid*, 22.

13 Daalder, 24.

14 Daalder, 25.

15 Daalder, 27.

16 Daalder, 28.

17 Daalder, 28.

18 Daalder, 28.

19 Daalder, 28.

20 Daalder, 36.

21 Johan Goudsblom, *Dutch Society*, Studies in Modern Societies, 31 (New York: Random House, 1967), 70. Arend Lijphart, *The Politics of Accommodation: Pluralism and Democracy in the Netherlands* (Berkeley, CA: University of California Press, 1968), 133.

22 Daalder, *Politisering en Lijdelijkheid*, 36.

23 E.E. Schattschneider, *The Semisovereign People: A Realist's View of Democracy in America* (New York: Holt, Rinehart and Winston, 1960).

24 Hans Daalder, *Politiek en Historie: Opstellen over Nederlandse Politiek en Vergelijkende Politieke Wetenschap*, ed. J.T.J. van den Berg (Amsterdam: Bakker, 1990), 91–2.

25 Daalder, *Politiek en Historie*, 81.

26 Lijphart, *The Politics of Accommodation: Pluralism and Democracy in the Netherlands*.

27 Lijphart, 124.

28 Hans Daalder, 'The Consociational Democracy Theme', *World Politics* 26, no. 4 (1974): 606.

29 Lijphart, 179.

30 Lijphart, 129.

31 The Dutch translation of *The Politics of Accommodation* is a little bit more extensive on 'the rules of the game', at times I have used that version. See Arend Lijphart, *Verzuiling, Pacificatie en Kentering in de Nederlandse Politiek* (Amsterdam: De Bussy, 1976), 135.

32 Lijphart, *The Politics of Accommodation*, 125.

33 Cees Middendorp, *Ideology in Dutch Politics: The Democratic System Reconsidered, 1970–1985* (Assen: Van Gorçum, 1991); Ilja Scholten, *Political Stability and Neo-Corporatism: Corporatist Integration and Societal Cleavages in Western Europe* (London: SAGE); Rinus Van Schendelen, 'Consociational Democracy: The Views of Arend Lijphart and Collected Criticisms', *The Political Science Reviewer* 15 (1985): 143; Stuurman, *Verzuiling, Kapitalisme En Patriarchaat: Aspecten van de Ontwikkeling van de Moderne Staat in Nederland*.

34 Hans Daalder, 'On the Origins of the Consociational Democracy Model', *Acta Politica* 19, no. 1 (1984): 97–116.

35 Ilja Scholten, 'Does Consociationalism Exist? A Critique of the Dutch Experience', in *Electoral Participation: A Comparative Analysis*, ed. Richard Rose, SAGE Studies in Contemporary Political Sociology (London: SAGE, 1980), 329–55.

36 Rudy Andeweg and Galen A. Irwin, *Governance and Politics of the Netherlands*, Comparative Government and Politics (Basingstoke: Palgrave Macmillan, 2009), 34.

37 See Scholten, *Political Stability and Neo-Corporatism*; Stuurman, *Verzuiling, Kapitalisme En Patriarchaat.*
38 Andeweg and Irwin, *Governance and Politics of the Netherlands.*
39 Frank Hendriks and Mark Bovens, 'Pacificatie En Polarisatie: Kentering En Continuïteit in Politiek En Bestuur in Nederland Post 2002', *Bestuurskunde* 17, no. 3 (2008): 56–63.
40 Daalder, *Politisering en Lijdelijkheid*, 15.
41 Lijphart, *The Politics of Accommodation*, 234.
42 Henk Hofland, *Tegels Lichten of Ware Verhalen over Autoriteiten in het Land van de Voldongen Feiten* (Amsterdam: Contact, 1973), 93–4.
43 Hofland, *Tegels Lichten*, 79.
44 Harry Mulisch, *Bericht aan de Rattenkoning* (Amsterdam: De Bezige Bij, 1966), 97.
45 Mulisch, *Bericht aan de Rattenkoning*, 90.
46 Arend Lijphart, 'From the Politics of Accommodation to Adversarial Politics in the Netherlands: A Reassessment', *West European Politics* 12, no. 1 (1989): 139–54. There is no dominant image or theory of Dutch political reality that has emerged after depillarization. It is difficult to come up with a metaphor as alluring as that of pillarization. Perhaps one can argue that instead of the multiple pillars and the roof, the Dutch political system now consists of a single pillar, following the description of the depoliticized Dutch political system of the nineties as a cartel or a one-party state. See: Piet de historicus Rooy, *Republiek van Rivaliteiten: Nederland sinds 1813* (Amsterdam: Mets & Schilt, 2002), 278.
47 Daalder, 'On the Origins of the Consociational Democracy Model', 100.
48 Daalder, *Politisering en Lijdelijkheid*, 39.
49 Jos de Beus, Jacques van Doorn and Piet de Rooy, 'De Ideologische Driehoek', *Nederlandse Politiek in Historisch Perspectief* (1989), 60.
50 Pim Fortuyn, *Zonder Ambtenaren. De Ondernemende Overheid* (Amsterdam: Van Veen, 1991), 8.
51 Fortuyn, 9.
52 Fortuyn, 9.
53 In that sense, Vuijsje is a principal intellectual exponent of what Gloria Wekker has called 'white innocence', the Dutch way of dealing with the postcolonial legacy, in which Dutch culture is described as innocent and inherently non-racist. See Gloria Wekker, *White Innocence: Paradoxes of Colonialism and Race* (Durham, NC: Duke University Press, 2016).
54 Herman Vuijsje, *Correct*, 80.
55 Vuijsje's analysis is fast-paced, well-written and polemical, but his argument often lacks coherence. There is an open contradiction in his core thesis. On the one hand, he indicts the baby boomers for failing to break with the passivity and conformism of the old 'regent mentality'. On the other hand, he blames baby boomers for 'having annihilated the old elite' and for refusing to adhere to the old regent mentality and 'flexibly adapt themselves to the renewals experienced as historically inevitable'. In sum, the baby boomers are simultaneously too radical and not radical enough; too much and not enough in thrall to Dutch regent mentality. See: Herman Vuijsje, *Correct*, xix.
56 Taken as a whole, the political character of Vuijsje's argument differs markedly from that of Fortuyn. As a conservative social democrat, Vuijsje is no fan of the free market. In fact, in his book *Correct*, he (erroneously) portrays the neoliberal reforms of the 1980s as yet another unwanted outcome of the anti-authoritarian ideals of the 1960s. Despite these differences, Fortuyn and Vuijsje shared a common position due to their critique of the 'leftist elite' and their desire to contest the progressive consensus on cultural issues.
57 Paul Scheffer, 'Het Multiculturele Drama', *NRC Handelsblad*, 29 January 2000.
58 The English translation is titled *Immigrant Nations*. Paul Scheffer, *Immigrant Nations*, trans. Liz Waters (Cambridge: Polity Press, 2011), 110.

59 Scheffer, *Immigrant Nations*, 127.
60 See Leo Lucassen and Jan Lucassen, *Winnaars en Verliezers: Een Nuchtere Balans van Vijfhonderd Jaar Immigratie* (Amsterdam: Bakker, 2011); Leo Lucassen and Jan Lucassen, 'The Strange Death of Dutch Tolerance: The Timing and Nature of the Pessimist Turn in the Dutch Migration Debate', *Journal of Modern History* 87, no. 1 (2015): 72–101. On Dutch education, the historian Bram Mellink has shown in his PhD that there was an intensive involvement with the integration of minorities, rather than the 'culture of avoidance' Scheffer criticized. As Mellink concluded, Scheffer's 'image of indifference isn't based on historical research, but on a political stance'. Bram Mellink, *Worden Zoals Wij: Onderwijs en de Opkomst van de Geïndividualiseerde Samenleving sinds 1945* (Wereldbibliotheek Amsterdam, 2014), 183.

2   The rise of the Dutch New Right

The swing to the right in the Netherlands has often been cast as a return of the repressed, as a politics of the gut. Long-ignored feelings concerning immigration, integration and Islam are seen to have given rise to the 'voter revolt' of 2002. The focus in this book is on the intellectual dimension of the political turnabout: not a politics of the gut, but a revolt of the mind. The Dutch swing to the right was preceded and accompanied by a conservative intellectual revolt against the 1960s, against the welfare state, against permissiveness, against cultural relativism. First coming to the fore in the intense debates on immigration, multiculturalism and national identity in the 1990s, this conservative tendency remains an underestimated factor in the rightward shift in Dutch politics. Right-wing politicians such as Bolkestein, Fortuyn, Hirsi Ali and Wilders, I argue, are merely the most eye-catching members of a broader conservative political and intellectual movement that I call the Dutch New Right. This loose and heterogeneous current of conservative politicians, journalists and intellectuals has been able to set the terms of the debate. In so doing, this broader tendency has preceded, accompanied and preconditioned the rise of radical right-wing populism.

The use of the term New Right can be seen as a somewhat surprising analytical move, since the label never really caught on in the Netherlands.[1] What further complicates the situation is that there exist different uses of the term. On the European continent, the label New Right has long been used as a moniker for far-right movements, in particular the French *Nouvelle Droite* and the German *Neue Rechte*. The Netherlands also featured a Dutch far-right splinter party in the early 2000s that named itself *Nieuw Rechts* (New Right), in an appeal to this continental tradition.[2] The last decade has seen a remarkable resurgence of the European far-right, also due to the rise of the online alt-right movement, which has again popularized older European far-right ideas.[3]

The label New Right as it is employed here, however, stems from the US and the UK, and refers to a more mainstream part of the right-wing spectrum. It came into common use to denote conservative movements that emerged in the 1950s, 1960s and 1970s, both in opposition and in parallel to the New Left. The high-water mark of the New Right is generally associated with the politics of Thatcher and Reagan. What is considered to be 'new' about the New Right is, on the one hand, its combination of free market ideas with cultural conservatism, and, on the other, the radical break with the moderate conservatism and liberalism of the post-war period. The New Right sharply challenged existing elites and institutions, seen as compromised by the progressive legacy of the 1960s. My argument is that a similar conservative movement has made its mark on Dutch politics, but in a delayed and peculiar fashion. It took the form of a conservative undercurrent that emerged only fully in the 1990s, and that experienced its political breakthrough around the Fortuyn revolt in 2002. While the coming two chapters are dedicated to a historical overview of the neoliberal and neoconservative strands of this movement, this introductory chapter deals with the issue of conceptualization and motivates the use of the (Anglo-American) New Right as a framework for analysis.

Anglo-American inspirations

The motivation to apply an Anglo-American frame to Dutch politics is straightforward: the principal political and intellectual inspiration for Dutch conservatives was provided by Anglo-American example. Of course, the Netherlands has long been known for its Atlanticist outlook. Ever since the Second World War, the US and Great Britain have been the main source for new intellectual and policy ideas in the Netherlands. Of all European countries, the Netherlands is arguably most oriented towards the Anglo-American context, in both a political and intellectual sense. The social democrat intellectual Bart Tromp once sarcastically proposed to make things official and have the Netherlands join the United States as its 51st state.[4]

At the same time, the lack of an established conservative tradition in the Netherlands added to the importance of Anglo-American inspirations. For the larger part of the twentieth century, Christian parties advocating centrism and social harmony dominated Dutch politics and prevented a right-wing conservative party from emerging. Ongoing secularization and the decline of Christian Democracy in the 1990s provided the space for a renewal of Dutch conservatism. At this point in time, the ideological renascence of conservatism under Reagan and Thatcher made the US and the UK into a crucial reference point to re-establish Dutch conservatism on a new footing. When we look at some of the leading Dutch right-wing figures in the 1990s and 2000s, we find that they have all been profoundly shaped by Anglo-American influences.

The most prominent figurehead of the Dutch New Right, the VVD leader and future European Commissioner Frits Bolkestein, distinguished himself from other Dutch politicians through his international career for the Anglo-Dutch oil corporation Shell. Bolkestein was stationed in London in the 1970s, and experienced the fallout of 1968 largely through an Anglo-American lens. He often referred to American neoconservative journals such as *Commentary* and *Encounter*, and described himself as an avid reader of the free market publications of the British Institute of Economic Affairs. In the early 1990s, he proposed to reform Dutch socio-economic policy in the direction of his

Anglo-American inspirations, recommending a 'mid-Atlantic model' with flexible labour markets, lower minimum wages and modest social security.[5] Referencing the writings of the American neoconservative Daniel Bell, Bolkestein advised his party in the mid-1990s to combine a free market agenda with cultural conservatism.[6]

H.J. Schoo, the influential editor of the largest Dutch (right-wing) weekly *Elsevier*, had studied and taught in Chicago in the polarized years from 1968 till 1973. He later confided that 'since his long-gone American years', he had felt a kinship with US (neo)conservatives such as Daniel Moynihan, Nathan Glazer, John Podhoretz, Irving Kristol, James Buckley and Gertrude Himmelfarb.[7] Schoo was an important conservative influence on Pim Fortuyn in the 1990s and argued that his politics could well be compared with American neoconservatism.[8] For Pim Fortuyn himself, the liberalized economies of the United States and Great Britain served as indications of the future, whereas the Dutch corporatist welfare state with its consensual mores was a mouldy artefact of the past.[9] Reagan and Thatcher were for him examples of decisive and visionary politics, qualities that Dutch politicians lacked.

Anglo-American inspirations were also front and centre for the founders and members of the Edmund Burke Foundation, the Dutch conservative think tank that powerfully shaped the Dutch debate in the early 2000s. The controversial opinion piece that announced the establishment of the think tank referred to the ideological renewal of conservatism under Reagan and Thatcher as an inspiration. It argued that 'in the past twenty-five years a true revolution had taken place in conservative thought in the Western world'. It called on Dutch conservative forces, still divided between the different Dutch parties, to join together and 'reap the harvest'.[10] As the think tank's president Bart Jan Spruyt later conceded, the foundation was explicitly modelled on the American Heritage Foundation and formed part of a long-term fusionist strategy inspired by the US Republican Party.

When Geert Wilders clashed with the VVD leadership in 2004 and began work on the establishment of his right-wing populist Party for Freedom, Bart Jan Spruyt became his first ideologue. Not surprisingly, Wilders' party was heavily influenced by the US conservative movement. In the process of establishing his Party for Freedom in 2005, Wilders made a weeklong visit to a series of (neo)conservative think tanks in the US.[11] American neoconservative networks, in particular the Middle East Forum, Jihad Watch and the David Horowitz Center, would provide Wilders with a crucial form of ideological and financial support.[12] Martin Bosma, from 2006 onwards, the ideologue and speechwriter of Geert Wilders, pointed to the US conservative movement as a formative influence on his politics. Bosma had studied and worked in New York, where he became inspired by neoconservatives such as Norman Podhoretz, Leo Strauss and Irving Kristol. In a book from 2011, Bosma described the US conservative backlash against the New Left in the 1960s and argued that the Party for Freedom formed part of a similar backlash against Dutch progressive baby boomers.[13]

As this short revision serves to show, the Anglo-American framework used in this study is not a foreign artefact that I seek to artificially impose on the Dutch source material; rather, it emerges quite naturally from that source material itself.

Introducing the Anglo-American New Right

What does the Anglo-American New Right concretely entail? In the US, the origins of the New Right lie in the Cold War politics of the 1950s, when a new conservative current emerged that repudiated the isolationist and elitist conservatism of the Old Right. The first generation of the New Right coalesced around William F. Buckley's *National Review*. It embraced 'fusionism', a conservative strategy to build a broad coalition based on the cohabitation between a free market strand (called libertarianism in the US), a traditionalist Burkean and Christian conservative strand, and an anti-communist strand with foreign policy hawks and – from the 1970s on – neoconservatives.[14]

The New Right sought to challenge the centrist establishment in the Republican Party and supported candidates on the right flank of the party, beginning with the presidential candidacy of Barry Goldwater in 1964. While Goldwater's campaign became a failure, the election victory of Ronald Reagan in 1980 signalled the breakthrough of the movement conservatism of the New Right. 'It's very simple. The Left is old and tired. The New Right is young and vigorous', the marketeer Richard Viguerie wrote in his 1981 book *The New Right: We're Ready to Lead*.[15] Fusionism continued to be an important characteristic. Ronald Reagan famously referred to the US conservative movement as a 'three-legged stool', comprised of free markets, conservative family values and military hawks. The metaphor expresses the fusionist conviction: lacking one of the legs, the stool will fall.[16]

In the UK, the term New Right had a different trajectory and came into use with the rise of Thatcher to describe a new insistence on economics and ideas on individualism and markets.[17] The Old Right, conversely, was defined as a more philosophical current, with ideas stressing tradition and hierarchy. However, others soon pointed to the fact that with the rise of the New Right, the ideas of the Old Right also enjoyed a new ascendency, most notably the Bloomsbury group and conservative thinkers such as Roger Scruton.[18] Thatcher and Reagan were seen as combining (neo)liberal economics with authoritarian culturally conservative ideas. Many soon argued that the newness of the New Right resided not so much in the ideas as such, but in the fact that various strands of right-wing ideas were welded together in a new synthesis, with neoliberalism and (neo)conservatism being the most notable of these strands.[19] In the UK, Thatcherism became the political expression of that fusion, as Andrew Gamble argued in *The Politics of Thatcherism*:

> The New Right is the seedbed from which Thatcherism has grown and is composed of two rather different strands. There is the revival of liberal

political economy, which seeks the abandonment of Keynesianism and any kinds of government intervention; and there is a new populism – the focusing on issues like immigration, crime and punishment, strikes, social security abuse, taxation and bureaucracy.[20]

Gamble went on to conclude that the newness of Thatcherism resided in the linkage between these two currents:

> The real innovation of Thatcherism is the way it has linked traditional Conservative concern with the basis of authority in social institutions and the importance of internal order and external security, with a new emphasis upon re-establishing free markets and extending market criteria into new fields.[21]

What is further seen as particular to the British and the American New Right is the break with the moderate, gradualist politics of the conservatism and liberalism of the post-war consensus, currents that participated in the construction of the welfare state. The neoliberal and neoconservative strands that made up the New Right were more radical in nature, and aimed to unsettle and undermine the previous social contract, reconstructing the free market and restoring – or rather reinventing – moral authority. Faced with the magnitude of this task, the New Right ditched the traditional scepticism and relativism of the Old Right, and embraced a belief in social engineering that is more commonly associated with the left. There is Ronald Reagan's Hollywoodian idea of a government that encourages us in reaching for the stars: 'We must always ask: is government working to liberate and empower the individual? [...] Is it encouraging all of us to reach for the stars?'[22] And there is Thatcher's famous statement at the start of her first term: 'Economics are the method, the object is to change the heart and soul' of the nation.[23] In working towards those ambitious goals, the New Right has pursued a politics of ideas. Following the philosophy of Friedrich Hayek, a foundational figure for both the British and American New Right, shaping the intellectual climate is seen as a precondition for taking power.

New Right versus populist radical right

It is not my intention to argue that the New Right should supplant radical right-wing populism as the analytical framework of choice. Both have strengths and weaknesses and can contribute to a fuller understanding of the recent wave of right-wing anti-establishment movements. Since it refers to an eclectic ideological coalition rather than a political party, the label of the New Right is definitely more diffuse than that of the populist radical right, which refers to a concrete party family. It does, however, shed light on a series of aspects that have thus far been underappreciated by scholars. First of all, it foregrounds the crucial role of the 1960s, and the conservative discomfort with the legacy of this period. As we've seen in the introduction, for many on the right, the Dutch revolt formed a challenge to the anti-authoritarian ethos of the 1960s and the pervasive influence of progressive baby boomers. Pim Fortuyn framed his politics as a correction to the 1960s, a period in which 'the moral foundation of society had been swept away', 'leading to egoism, boredom and banal materialism'.[24] According to Martin Bosma, the ideologue of Geert Wilders, the Party for Freedom was founded to oppose the legacy of 1968.[25] Analytical frames that restrict themselves to anti-immigrant, nativist or anti-Islam sentiment elide this broader dimension of the Dutch revolt.

Furthermore, the term New Right includes the mainstream parties and allows us to capture the heterogeneous cross-party alliances that make up the Dutch conservative countercurrent. Studies of populism take the established parties out of the picture, and tend to ignore the role of prominent figures therein. In the Netherlands, it was the political mainstream that developed an anti-immigration politics long before the official emergence of political populism in the Netherlands. In fact, the presence of populist parties in Dutch politics has been fragmented and marginal in the period till 2010. Yet in the literature on radical right-wing populism, it is the populist parties who are commonly attributed with most of the agency, while the politics of mainstream parties on hot-button topics such as immigration, Islam and law and order are reduced to a more passive role of accommodating populism or being contaminated by it.[26]

Finally, the New Right framework stresses the importance of political ideas. The prevailing image of the populist leader as someone who attempts to embody the *vox populi* leaves little room for political ideas. Rather, the populism scholarship tends to ignore the role of intellectuals and opinion makers in providing the ideological foundation for right-wing populists. Populism is often characterized as a style, a technique, a form of rhetoric in which the populist leader purports to embody a monolithic, pure people while opposing an estranged establishment.[27] Populism can take shape on the left or on the right and has in itself only limited predetermined content. At most, it is a 'thin ideology' that attaches itself in almost parasitic fashion to another 'thick' ideology of stronger solidity.[28] It is that 'thick' ideology we are interested in here.

Interestingly, the picture of the New Right we have outlined above bears a surprising resemblance to the character profile of the radical right, the 'thick' ideology that right-wing populism is generally associated with. In his classic overview of the European radical right in the 1990s, Kitschelt identified a 'winning formula' of economic neoliberalism and cultural authoritarian and protectionist views.[29] Similarly, in his influential comparative analysis of radical right-wing populism, Hans-Georg Betz wrote how these parties tend to blend a 'radical neoliberal program', with 'opposition to immigration'. Betz argued that the radical right takes much after Thatcher and the British New Right. Both currents promote neoliberal economic policies and appeal to a popular pragmatism that 'put[s] the family, respectability, hard work, "practicality", and order first'.[30] Similar to Thatcherism, Betz states, the radical right has offered 'an exclusionary ideology as a compensation for the anxieties inevitably created by the new insecurities generated by the globalization of the market place'. And he went on to cite Simon During's analysis of 'the rationale behind the political strategy employed by Thatcherism'. Betz saw it as central to the radical right:

> The more the market is freed from state intervention and trade and finance cross national boundaries, the more the nation will be exposed to foreign influences and the greater the gap between the rich and the poor. Thatcherism's appeal to popular values can be seen as an attempt to overcome this tension. In particular, the New Right gives the family extraordinary value and aura just because a society organized by market forces is one in which economic life expectations are particularly insecure (as well as one in which, for some, the rewards are large and life exciting). In the same way, a homogenous image of national culture is celebrated and enforced to counter the danger posed by the increasingly global nature of economic exchanges and widening national economic divisions. The New Right image of a mono-culture and hard-working family life, organized through traditional gender roles, requires a devaluation not just of other nations and their cultural identities, but of 'enemies within': those who are 'other' racially, sexually, intellectually.[31]

Perhaps this notion of the conservative component of the New Right assemblage functioning merely as a compensation mechanism is too reductionist. But the example shows the clear lines of continuity between the New Right and the radical right. The major point of distinction lies in their respective radicalisms. The American and British New Right were radical with regards to the legacy of the 1960s and the prevailing socio-economic order, Johnson's Great Society and the British welfare state. In contrast, the radical right is deemed radical because it exists in a state of tension with aspects of liberal democracy. While radical right parties (unlike the extreme right) accept the basic parameters of the democratic

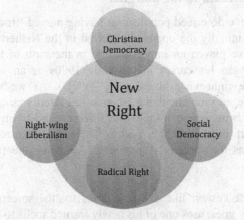

Figure 2.1 A Venn diagram roughly indicating the political space of the Dutch New Right.

system, there is a commonly perceived tension when it comes to issues such as pluralism, the protection of minorities from the will of the majority, and checks on executive authority.[32] Furthermore, in the course of the 1990s the neoliberal aspect of the radical right agenda became less salient, as radical right-wing populists tried to broaden their appeal to disheartened social democrat voters. Their focus increasingly centred on cultural themes, especially immigration.[33]

The radical right can therefore be seen as a subset of the New Right. In other words, the New Right refers to a larger political space that includes the radical right. This is due to the term's provenance from the Anglo-American context, where the first-past-the-post electoral system does not easily allow radical right-wing parties to emerge. In the Anglo-American context, radical currents tend to operate in a more fluid manner within the mainstream parties. When we transfer the label to the Dutch political context, it demarcates a space that includes both the conservative currents within the mainstream parties and the populist radical right. Because this study is oriented at political ideas and our focus therefore does not restrict itself to party ideologies, adopting the broader framework of the New Right allows us to trace the development of ideas in a more precise manner. After all, the origins of the ideas of the radical right, both when it comes to neoliberalism and when it comes to authoritarianism, law and order and anti-immigration politics, derive for an important part from the New Right of the 1970s and 1980s. The relationship between the conservative currents in the mainstream parties and the radical right is often fraught with difficulties. At times they contest one another, at times they collaborate. Their political development from the 1990s onwards can be described in terms of what historians call a *histoire croisée*: 'an interwoven or interconnected history where it is no longer very clear who is innovating, who is transmitter and who is receiver'.[34]

From the mainstream to the margins

While scholars have described populism as having moved 'from the margins to the mainstream', initially the opposite occurred in the Netherlands. The mainstream parties have played an important role in the birth of the radical right. Geert Wilders began his career in the early 1990s as an assistant of Frits Bolkestein in the right-wing liberal party (VVD). As we will see, it was Bolkestein who began problematizing Islam as 'an inferior culture', long before Wilders acquired fame as one of the world's fiercest anti-Islam campaigners. In a profile on Geert Wilders in the *New York Times*, Bolkestein described his former assistant as the sorcerer's apprentice, following the famous poem by Goethe:

Today Mr. Bolkestein likens Mr. Wilders to 'the sorcerer's apprentice', who, the story goes, uses one of his newly learned spells to enchant a broom into washing the floor for him. Soon the water is all over, and he realizes that he does not know how to stop the broom. He tries splitting it in two with an axe, but then there are two brooms, then four. 'The apprentice can't stop', Mr. Bolkestein said.[35]

In the poem, the old sorcerer admonishes his student that only a master should invoke powerful spirits. In similar fashion, Bolkestein accused Wilders of having adopted his political ideas, without understanding how to apply the brakes and exercise political restraint.

Pim Fortuyn, in turn, had a close relationship with the Christian Democrat Party (CDA). The first copy of Fortuyn's 1995 book *The Orphaned Society* (*De verweesde samenleving*) was warmly received by Enneüs Heerma, then party leader of the CDA, who gave a speech at the book launch. According to senior Christian Democrats, there were important overlaps between the 'ideology critique' developed by Fortuyn and that of the Christian Democrat Party. Fortuyn, who was indeed an intellectual sponge of sorts, had taken much of his conservative ideas from the CDA.[36] Fortuyn criticized the anonymity of large-scale government bureaucracy and pleaded for a return to the 'human scale'. It was one of the ideas from *The Orphaned Society* that would become a well-known political slogan. But it actually derived from the conservative wing of the CDA. In the year before Fortuyn's book was published, the head of the Christian Democrat think tank had proposed a 'return to the human scale' in reaction to trends such as globalization, social insecurity, anonymity and feelings of unsafety.[37] The relationship between Fortuyn and the CDA went further than that of an ideological overlap. In the campaign for the 2002 elections, Fortuyn's party and the Christian Democrat Party agreed not to attack each other. In the autumn of 2001, Fortuyn is said to have privately professed his faith in the Christian Democrat leader Balkenende, who was 'okay' and 'a real conservative'.[38]

In this way, the conservative currents within the mainstream right played an important role in assisting in the birth of the populist radical right. The relationship also worked the other way around. Conservatives in the mainstream parties have been able to realize some of their political agenda thanks to the electoral successes of the populist radical right. Illustrative here is a discussion within the Christian Democrat Party (CDA) after the extraordinary election victory of Pim Fortuyn's party in 2002. It resulted in the formation of the first Balkenende cabinet, based on a coalition of the CDA, the VVD and the List Pim Fortuyn (LPF). As Thijs Jansen, the editor-in-chief of the journal of the Christian Democrat Party, went on to write:

> Important elements of Fortuyn's political agenda matched with the reform plans of the CDA, or had even been derived from there, I sometimes had the impression. In this way, Fortuyn functioned as a battering ram for the CDA to realize that agenda. In the existing literature up to now, there has absolutely been a lack of attention to the fact that the alliance between Balkenende/Fortuyn was for *both* parties a tactical and a strategic, content-focused alliance. Balkenende has used the momentum to realize his reform agenda that had been developed by the CDA in the years before.[39]

The New Right coalition was built on this intricate form of two-way traffic: the right-wing populists derived much of their politics from the mainstream parties, while the conservatives within the mainstream parties used the populist radical right as a battering ram. Or to put it less dramatically, as an instrument to realize their own agenda, often while confronting the centrist or progressive forces within their own party. As the conservative Christian Democrat Hans Hillen argued: 'Pim ploughs the field from which we can reap the harvest'.[40]

The electoral success of Wilders' Party for Freedom (PVV) in 2010 – the party won 16 per cent of the vote, which was in that sense an eerie repetition of 2002 – led again to a tactical and strategic content-focused alliance with the VVD and the CDA in the first Rutte cabinet (2010–2012). The Party for Freedom became the official support party for this right-wing minority cabinet. The leading parliamentary journalist Max van Weezel interviewed the conservative Christian Democrat Hans Hillen, who told him that the one-and-a-half million people that had voted for Wilders could not be ignored:

> In the turbulent 1960s, Catholic politicians such as Piet de Jong and Gerhard Veringa succeeded in accommodating the leftist student protests. The motto of the time was to listen to the idealists, make concessions and give them jobs if need be. 'Elastic absorption', De Jong called that strategy. The Dutch administrative apparatus was kept intact, and that example is worth imitating, according to Hillen. In 2010, it was the right-wing populists that had to be 'accommodated' by the CDA. By creating an alliance with them.[41]

In a similar dynamic, conservative social democrats have pushed for a stricter immigration agenda within the social democrat party, by pointing to the right-wing populist challenge.[42] The social democrat party eventually changed its tune and adopted a tougher position on immigration and integration in 2008. Party leader Wouter Bos defended the polarizing debate on the problems posed by immigrants in colourful fashion, while attempting to equate it with Marxist theory:

> In the debate on integration I hear repeated calls for less polarization. Unbelievable. My position is: stop complaining about the tone of the debate! No emancipation without polarization. The emancipation of the worker, the woman and the homosexual has only succeeded through struggle, by confrontation. It is classically Marxist: thesis-antithesis-synthesis.[43]

Of course, not all proponents of the accommodation of right-wing populism necessarily share the New Right agenda. Here it is pertinent to recall James Kennedy's remarks concerning the undervalued role of traditional elites in realizing the changes in the 1960s. Many of the traditional elites did not necessarily share the agenda of the protest generation back then. Their actions were motivated by the perceived need to adapt in order to channel historical trends and maintain equilibrium. A similar motivation accounts for the accommodating role of centrist elites. The conundrum of Dutch politics is that it is often difficult to distinguish the active drivers of a trend from those politically accommodating that trend.

As a consequence of the eye-catching role of the populist radical right, the important role of the mainstream parties in achieving the shift to the right has been far less conspicuous. And as a result of a lingering adherence to a pluralist 'end of ideology' framework, many studies of populism conceive of populists as the only ideological player in the game. In this way the impression has been able to take hold that the populist radical right is the only historical actor in the arena, while the mainstream parties are merely accommodating and reacting to historical trends.

Using the analytical framework of the New Right allows us to better address the complex political dynamic described above. In the next two chapters, I will address the neoliberal strand within the Dutch New Right, followed by the (neo) conservative strand.

Notes

1 The term has been used in a similar manner by prominent Dutch politicians and intellectuals such as Joop den Uyl, Jos de Beus and Dick Pels, but it is not commonly used in the Netherlands. See Joop den Uyl, 'Tegen de Stroom In' (Paradiso, Amsterdam, 3 May 1981); Jos de Beus, 'Een Derde Eeuw van Nederlands Conservatisme', in *Ruimte Op Rechts? Conservatieve Onderstroom in de Lage Landen*, ed. Huib Pellikaan and Sebastiaan van der Lubben (Utrecht: Spectrum, 2006), 221–37; Dick Pels, *Een Zwak voor Nederland: Ideeën voor een Nieuwe Politiek* (Amsterdam: Anthos, 2005).
2 Trouw, 'Nieuw Rechts Opgeheven', *Trouw*, 22 December 2007.
3 See Pierre-André Taguieff, *Sur la Nouvelle Droite: Jalons d'une Analyse Critique* (Paris: Descartes & Cie, 1994); Roger Woods, *Germany's New Right as Culture and Politics* (Basingstoke: Palgrave Macmillan, 2007). But still another usage of the term exists. For some sociologists and political scientists, the label 'New Right' is a means to distinguish the primarily cultural concerns of radical right-wing populist parties from what they see as the principally economic concerns of the 'Old Right': the free market politics of Reagan and Thatcher. See Willem De Koster et al., 'Progressiveness and the New Right: The Electoral Relevance of Culturally Progressive Values in the Netherlands', *West European Politics* 37, no. 3 (2014): 584–604.
4 Bart Tromp, *Geschriften van een Intellectuele Glazenwasser: De Draagbare Tromp* (Amsterdam: Bert Bakker, 2010), 152–72.
5 Frits Bolkestein, *Het Heft in Handen* (Amsterdam: Prometheus, 1995), 15–41.
6 Bolkestein, 132.
7 Bart Jan Spruyt, 'In memoriam H.J. Schoo', in *Dwars en bewogen: Afscheid van H.J. Schoo (1945–2007)*, ed. Arendo Joustra et al. (Amsterdam: Elsevier/de Volkskrant, 2007), 84.
8 Hendrik Jan Schoo, *Republiek van Vrije Burgers: Het Onbehagen in de Democratie* (Amsterdam: Bert Bakker, 2008), 264.
9 Pim Fortuyn, *Uw Baan Staat op de Tocht! De Overlegeconomie Voorbij* (Utrecht: Bruna, 1995).
10 Joshua Livestro, 'Het Conservatieve Moment is Gekomen', *NRC Handelsblad*, 3 February 2001.
11 Koen Vossen, 'Classifying Wilders: The Ideological Development of Geert Wilders and His Party for Freedom', *Politics* 31, no. 3 (2011): 179–89.

12 Tom Jan Meeus and Guus Valk, 'De Buitenlandse Vrienden van Geert Wilders', *NRC Handelsblad*, 15 May 2010.
13 Martin Bosma, *De Schijn-Élite van de Valsemunters* (Prometheus, 2011).
14 See George H. Nash, *The Conservative Intellectual Movement in America since 1945* (Wilmington, DE: ISI Books, 2014), 17.
15 Richard A. Viguerie, *The New Right: We're Ready to Lead* (Falls Church, VA: Viguerie Co., 1981), 1.
16 For studies of the US New Right see Geoff Andrews, *New Left, New Right and Beyond: Taking the Sixties Seriously* (Basingstoke: Palgrave Macmillan, 1999); Rebecca E. Klatch, *A Generation Divided: The New Left, the New Right, and the 1960s* (Berkeley, CA: University of California Press, 1999); Desmond S. King, *The New Right: Politics, Markets and Citizenship* (Basingstoke: Macmillan Education, 1987); Joseph E. Lowndes, *From the New Deal to the New Right: Race and the Southern Origins of Modern Conservatism* (New Haven, CT: Yale University Press, 2008); Paul Lyons, *New Left, New Right, and the Legacy of the Sixties* (Philadelphia, PA: Temple University Press, 1996).
17 Nicholas Bosanquet, *Economics: After the New Right* (Leiden: Kluwer Academic Pub, 1983).
18 Stuart Hall and Martin Jacques, *The Politics of Thatcherism* (London: Lawrence and Wishart, 1983); Ruth Levitas, ed., *The Ideology of the New Right* (Cambridge: Polity Press, 1986).
19 Levitas, *The Ideology of the New Right*.
20 Andrew Gamble, 'Thatcherism and Conservative Politics', in *The Politics of Thatcherism*, ed. Stuart Hall and Martin Jacques (London: Lawrence & Wishart, 1983), 115.
21 Gamble, 121.
22 Ronald Reagan, *Public Papers of the Presidents of the United States: Ronald Reagan, 1982* (New York: Best Books, 1984), 938.
23 Ronald Butt, 'Interview with Margaret Thatcher', *Sunday Times*, 3 May 1981.
24 Bart Jan Spruyt, 'Heer van Stand in de Politiek', *Reformatorisch Dagblad*, 8 September 2001. On the connection between Christian conservatives and Fortuyn, see Christophe van der Belt, ' "Fortuyn Is Aanwinst, Maar Geen Behoudende Bondgenoot": Het Reformatorisch Dagblad over de Opkomst van Een Populistisch Fenomeen', in *Theocratie En Populisme: Staatkundig Gereformeerden En de Stem van Het Volk* (Houten: Den Hertog, Forthcoming).
25 Bosma, *De Schijn-Élite van de Valsemunters*.
26 For a good example of that perspective, see Tjitske Akkerman, Sarah L. de Lange and Matthijs Rooduijn, *Radical Right-Wing Populist Parties in Western Europe: Into the Mainstream?* (London: Routledge, 2016).
27 Margaret Canovan, 'Trust the People! Populism and the Two Faces of Democracy', *Political Studies* 47, no. 1 (1999): 2–16; Paul A. Taggart, *Populism* (Buckingham: Open University Press, 2000).
28 Cas Mudde, *Populist Radical Right Parties in Europe* (Cambridge: Cambridge University Press, 2007).
29 Herbert Kitschelt and Anthony J. MacGann, *The Radical Right in Western Europe: A Comparative Analysis* (Ann Arbor, MI: The University of Michigan Press, 1995).
30 Hans-Georg Betz, *Radical Right-Wing Populism in Western Europe* (Basingstoke: Macmillan, 1994).
31 Betz, 171–2. A similar compensatory strategy has been observed in the US concerning the 'paradox of blue-collar conservatives' in the 1980s. See John Fiske, *Media Matters: Everyday Culture and Political Change* (London: Routledge, 1994), 32.
32 David Art, *Inside the Radical Right: The Development of Anti-Immigrant Parties in Western Europe* (New York: Cambridge University Press, 2011), 11; Mudde, *Populist Radical Right Parties in Europe*.

33 See Betz, *Radical Right-Wing Populism*; Herbert Kitschelt, *Diversification and Reconfiguration of Party Systems in Postindustrial Democracies* (Bonn: Friedrich Ebert Stiftung, 2004).
34 Henk te Velde, 'Political Transfer: An Introduction', *European Review of History: Revue Europeenne d'histoire* 12, no. 2 (2005): 211.
35 Alissa Rubin, 'Geert Wilders, Reclusive Provocateur, Rises Before Dutch Vote', *New York Times*, 27 February 2017.
36 This point is made by the former leader of the Christian Democrat Party, Sybrand van Haersma Buma (CDA leader from 2012 till 2019) in his book *Against Cynicism* (*Tegen het Cynisme*). A political assistant at the time, Buma wrote Heerma's lecture at Fortuyn's book presentation in 1995. Buma stresses the similarities of the 'ideological critique' of Fortuyn and the CDA. See Sybrand van Haersma Buma, *Tegen het Cynisme: Voor een Nieuwe Moraal in de Politiek* (Prometheus, 2016), 25, 56.
37 Marcel ten Hooven, 'Een Machtspartij met Idealen: Een Geschiedenis van het CDA, 1980–2010', in *De Conjunctuur van de Macht: Het Christen Democratisch Appèl 1980–2010*, ed. Gerrit Voerman (Amsterdam: Boom, 2011), 93.
38 Hendrik Jan Schoo, *Een Bitter Mensbeeld: De Transformatie van een Ontregeld Land* (Amsterdam: Bakker, 2004), 12.
39 Thijs Jansen, 'CDA Moet Conservatieve Verleiding Weerstaan', *Christen Democratische Verkenningen*, Winter (2004): 10.
40 Cited in Servatius W. Couwenberg, *Opstand Der Burgers: De Fortuyn-Revolte en het Demasqué van de Oude Politiek* (Damon, 2004), 151.
41 Max van Weezel, 'De Inkapselingsstrategie van het CDA', *Vrij Nederland*, 25 April 2012.
42 A recent example of that type of discourse is Paul Scheffer's 2016 essay on the politics of the border. He argues that the progressive '*bien-pensants*' foment populism with their calls for hospitality for refugees. When the established parties fail to establish borders, then 'sooner or later – probably sooner – the moment will come that people with an authoritarian mindset will draw those borders'. Scheffer, cited in: Femke Halsema, *Nergensland: Nieuw Licht op Migratie* (Amsterdam: Ambo Anthos, 2017), 46.
43 Cited in Marc Peeperkorn and Martin Sommer, 'Hoofdpijn van de Partij', *De Volkskrant*, 3 March 2008.

3   The neoliberal strand

The intellectual and political movement known as neoliberalism is a central reference point for the New Right. Though there has been a lot of scholarly and public controversy surrounding the concept of neoliberalism, a recent series of intellectual histories built on extensive archival research has provided the analysis of this movement with a more solid footing.[1]

Neoliberalism's earliest intellectual origins can be traced back to discussions on economic planning in the 1920s. Broadly conceived, it is fair to say that neo-liberalism emerged as a reaction to the economic crisis of the 1930s, as a response to the perceived shortcomings of laissez-faire liberalism on the one hand, and the emergence of Keynesianism on the other. In the post-war years, neoliberalism developed into a broad intellectual current that resisted economic planning and the Keynesian welfare state.

A pivotal figure in the neoliberal movement is the Austrian philosopher and economist Friedrich Hayek, later hailed as an intellectual inspiration by both Reagan and Thatcher. When Hayek published *The Road to Serfdom* in 1944, it soon became a foundational text of the neoliberal movement. In the book, Hayek portrayed central planning and government intervention in the economy as a slippery slope towards the bondage of man: totalitarian society. The intended target of his critique was above all democratic socialism and the dominant influ-ence of the ideas of John Maynard Keynes. To contest Keynesianism, socialism and communism, seen as different stages in a continuum of state intervention, Hayek proposed a renewal of liberalism.

This renewal departed, on the one hand, from a critique of the old, fossilized classic-liberal doctrines, which had led to liberal passivity. 'Probably nothing has done so much harm to the liberal cause as the wooden insistence of some liberals on certain rough rules of thumb, above all the principle of laissez-faire', Hayek stated.[2] The core of the renewal proposed by Hayek in relation to classic-liberal doctrine – why neoliberalism is 'neo' – is the idea that the state needs to actively foster the market mechanism, beginning with a proper juridical frame-work. Hayek called this 'planning for competition'. In so doing, attaining the free market becomes a form of social engineering.

On the other hand, the liberal tradition needed to be warded off from its problematic progressive-liberal offshoot, originating in John Stuart Mill and subsequently leading to Keynes, the welfare state and finally – even inevitably in the eyes of Hayek – to socialism and totalitarianism. While the neoliberal movement contained a lot of internal diversity and disagreement, they shared a similar vision on what Michel Foucault called the 'field of adversity': the manner in which they framed their relation to opponents and competitors.[3] The shared position of the neoliberal movement was defined by a negative view of Keynesian economic planning as a slippery slope towards totalitarianism, a critical attitude towards laissez-faire, and the idea that a long-term battle of ideas was needed to turn the tide.

In April 1947, under the leadership of Friedrich Hayek and the Swiss businessman Albert Hunold, a group of economists and intellectuals converged on the Swiss mountain village Mont Pèlerin. In the days that followed they conferred and founded the Mont Pèlerin Society (MPS), an intellectual network that soon became the incubator and nerve centre of the global neoliberal movement. This network presented itself explicitly in the 1950s, in a series of texts, as 'the neoliberal movement'. 'Gone are the days when the few outmoded liberals walked their paths lonely, ridiculed and without response from the young', Hayek would write after the first MPS gatherings, 'at least personal contact among the proponents of neoliberalism has been established'.[4] Milton Friedman wrote a text with a comparable sentiment in 1952, titled *Neo-Liberalism and its Prospects*, in which he presented 'the doctrine sometimes called neoliberalism' as 'a new faith' that is 'in many ways ideally suited to fill the vacuum that seems to me to be developing in the beliefs of intellectual classes the world over'.[5] In the decades that followed, thousands of researchers, politicians, businessmen and journalists would attend the yearly meetings, continuing up to the present moment. Directors of neoliberal think tanks such as the Heritage Foundation and the Institute of Economic Affairs took part, and later helped shape the Reaganite and Thatcherite policies of liberalization, privatization and deregulation. The leading intellectual histories of neoliberalism have used the networks of the MPS as a pragmatic indication of the bandwidth of neoliberal ideology.

From the very beginning, there was a focus on a 'politics of ideas', a conviction that ideas play a central role in achieving political change. Hayek spoke at the foundational meeting of the MPS while referencing the renowned conclusion from Keynes' classic *The General Theory of Employment, Interest and Money*:

> [T]he ideas of economists and political philosophers, both when they are right and when they are wrong, are more powerful than is commonly understood. Indeed the world is ruled by little else. Practical men, who believe themselves to be quite exempt from any intellectual influences, are usually the slaves of some defunct economist. Madmen in authority, who hear voices in the air, are distilling their frenzy from some academic scribbler of a few years back. I am sure that the power of vested interests is vastly exaggerated compared with the gradual encroachment of ideas.[6]

According to Hayek, the rise of socialism was a result of the effort of socialist intellectuals in the preceding decades. Over a similarly long period of several decades, Hayek told his MPS associates in 1947, they would need to set their aims. Hayek called on the MPS to focus on a long-term battle of ideas. A great intellectual task had to be performed before political action could be undertaken: the renewal of liberalism that had petrified into a rigid and unpractical ideology. On the second gathering of the MPS, Hayek circulated a now famous essay – *The Intellectuals and Socialism* – in which he argued that a long-term radical vision was needed to win that battle:

> A program which seems neither a mere defence of things as they are nor a diluted kind of socialism, but a truly liberal radicalism which does not spare the susceptibilities of the mighty (including the trade unions), which is not too severely practical, and which does not confine itself to what appears today as politically possible.[7]

What was politically feasible in the current moment should not be the first concern, Hayek noted. Of primary importance was the spreading of ideas that he considered necessary for the attainment of a free society in the long term. For that purpose, the neoliberals needed a utopian ideal, like the socialists:

> The main lesson which the true liberal must learn from the success of the socialists is that it was their courage to be Utopian which gained them the support of the intellectuals and therefore an influence on public opinion which is daily making possible what only recently seemed utterly remote.[8]

Friedman shared this belief in the necessity of a long-term battle of ideas.[9] Due to their role in developing this idea-driven political strategy, Friedrich Hayek and Milton Friedman are seen as pivotal figures for both the American and the British New Right. George Nash opens his classic *The Conservative Intellectual Movement in America* with a discussion of the formidable impact of Hayek's *Road to Serfdom*.[10] A condensed version was spread by Reader's Digest in an edition of 600,000 copies. It was hailed by conservatives as a foundational text for the libertarian, free market wing of US conservatism. In the British case, Friedrich Hayek is known both as the most important personal inspiration of Margaret Thatcher and, together with Friedman, the principal reference point for Thatcherite economic policy. The Institute of Economic Affairs, the powerful think tank seen as the originator of Thatcherism, was founded on Hayek's explicit instruction by a wealthy reader of *The Road to Serfdom*. A famous scene at a Conservative Party meeting in the late 1970s perhaps best illustrates Hayek's significance. Margaret Thatcher, confronted with a plea for centrist pragmatism by one of her colleagues, reached into her briefcase and took out a book. 'It was Friedrich von Hayek's *The Constitution of Liberty*. Interrupting, she held the book up for all of us to see. "This", she said sternly, "is what we believe", and banged Hayek down on the table'.[11]

A depoliticized neoliberal turn

Neoliberalism first emerged in the Netherlands in the late 1940s and 1950s. There was an explicit neoliberalism debate in the Dutch media at the time, with reference to Hayek and the MPS. Liberal and Christian politicians were receptive to neoliberal ideas, but this early wave of free market advocacy ultimately failed to break through.[12] A second neoliberal wave in the 1980s proved more successful but had a more depoliticized and rhetorically subdued character. The curious story of Dutch neoliberalism in the 1980s is perhaps best started by reference to a landmark political speech.

On 3 May 1981, a large crowd gathered in Paradiso, the illustrious Amsterdam church-turned-music-hall. They came to hear Joop Den Uyl speak, then leader of the Dutch social democrat party (PvdA) and arguably the most formidable intellectual figure of the Dutch post-war left. The speech lasted for a solid two-and-a-half hours. Over time, it developed into a historical reference point for a younger generation of centre-left intellectuals and politicians coming of age in the 1980s. The Paradiso lecture came to represent the swan song of Keynesian social democracy. Den Uyl impressed upon his public that this was a pivotal moment. With the elections around the corner, Dutch society stood at a crossroads. The choice was either to walk the democratic road, or the road pointed out by the New Right, understood by Den Uyl as 'in essence a fusion of conservative and certain liberal beliefs'. The New Right was represented by the threatening rise of Reagan and Thatcher and the growth in popularity of the 'free market ideology' of Hayek and Friedman, also in the Netherlands:

> One shouldn't underestimate the influence of the New Right. As much as the movement towards societal change in the middle of the 1960s was an international phenomenon with similar features in countries with differing degrees of development, one can find traces everywhere of New Right thinking.[13]

What is striking about the lecture is that Den Uyl identified the anti-democratic threat of the New Right in the Netherlands primarily as one of depoliticization and popular acquiescence. After evaluating the democratization movement of the 1960s and 1970s that took aim against the closed political culture of pillarization, Den Uyl argued that there was now an attempt to turn back the clock; an effort to pacify the electorate and undermine their belief in participatory politics. The New Right, Den Uyl explained to his audience in Paradiso, 'intended to return the steering wheel of society to a small group of strong but mostly powerful people. The state turned back in on itself. The motto is peace and order. Or: acquiescence without ordering'.[14]

The intriguing paradox here is that the breakthrough of a new free market ideology, which purportedly served as a 'legitimation to attack the welfare state', appeared in the form of depoliticization. In fact, Den Uyl was not alone in this perception. The Dutch political science literature identifies the previous national elections of 1977 as a turning point from a more open, polarized and politicized decade, towards the 'no-nonsense politics' of the 1980s: a more closed period of pacification and depoliticization, in which Lijphart's 'rules of the game' of the politics of accommodation entered back into operation.[15]

This contradiction did not go unnoticed at the time. Hans Daalder argued that the aim of the Lubbers cabinets to 'roll back the state' had an obvious ideological character. In his eyes, it was inspired by a 'neoliberal or if you will, neoconservative ideal that has also made great strides elsewhere in the Western world'.[16] At the same time, Daalder noted, Lubbers ushered in a revival of the old Dutch tradition of 'depoliticizing political choices'. The neoliberal turn was sold to the Dutch public as an apolitical and technocratic fix, with slogans as 'no-nonsense' and 'finishing the job'. Similar observations are made in recent historical studies that aim to correct the prevailing non-ideological image of the 1980s. Rather than doing away with ideology altogether, the 1980s saw a shift from a more public and open engagement with politics and ideology to a more private and closed way of dealing with these matters.[17] That could explain the observation that neoliberal ideas were actively circulated and promulgated among policy elites, while the reforms of the 1980s were not presented as such in public discourse. Instead, they were depoliticized as largely technocratic, pragmatic measures.

The Dutch counterpart to Thatcher and Reagan was formed by the coalitions led by Ruud Lubbers (1982–1994) and his Minister of Finance Onno Ruding (1982–1989). Shortly before, Ruding had been executive director at the IMF, at that time an institution at the very heart of the neoliberal 'revolution' in economic policy. The rapidly deteriorating condition of Dutch public finance and the declining rate of corporate profitability in the late 1970s led to a concerted attempt by political and business elites to sideline the corporatist institutions. These deliberative bodies, where Dutch trade unions and employers traditionally presided over socio-economic policy, had been in a state of deadlock for years. After increasingly anxious attempts to reach a compromise with trade unions and employers at the end of the 1970s, it was finally decided to unilaterally implement harsh austerity measures and cut public sector wages under the first Lubbers cabinet of 1982, comprised of Christian Democrats (CDA) and right-wing liberals (VVD).

Instead of Thatcherite all-out confrontation, however, Lubbers chose to pacify the opposition – the leadership of the trade unions and later the social democrats – resulting in the Wassenaar Agreement of 1982 and the Dutch wage moderation strategy. This was clearly an agreement that was imposed by the state and Dutch business, signifying a historical retreat by the Dutch trade unions. Not for nothing, in their classic *A Dutch Miracle*, Visser and Hemerijck described the reforms of the 1980s as an expression of 'a shift in the balance of power between the separate interests of organized capital and labour', where 'those who lose power must learn'.[18] Yet it was successfully sold to the public, as a voluntary, consensual agreement, soon to assume mythical proportions in the Dutch public imagination as the birth of the 'polder model'. Here we should remember Lijphart's argument concerning the politics of accommodation. Dutch politics is a game where all parties are supposed to win, where painful (read: polarizing) political defeats, or at least the impression thereof, have to be prevented as much as possible.[19]

The reinvigorated politics of accommodation resulted in a markedly different historical development than the path taken in the US and the UK. The neoliberal turn in the Dutch context did not lead to an open confrontation with the previous political order and was ultimately more moderate than its Anglo-American counterparts. There was no settling of accounts with the progressive legacy of the 1960s and 1970s, no public battle of ideas with the adherents of Keynesianism, or epic confrontations with the trade unions. Yes, there were large demonstrations and strikes against the austerity measures of the Lubbers cabinets and there was obvious political polarization. But the ideological nature of the political turn was carefully downplayed and the policies of the subsequent Lubbers cabinets were depoliticized and framed using the technocratic label of 'no-nonsense' politics.[20] Dutch Christian Democrats were partly confronting their own Christian trade union, the progressive or corporatist wing of their own party, and a considerable part of their voter base – Christian workers – so they had little incentive to aim for open confrontation.

In 1984, *Time Magazine* portrayed Lubbers as Ruud 'Shock', supposedly tougher than the Iron Lady. The article featured a reverential quote by Margaret Thatcher on a state visit to the Netherlands:

> 'Mr. Lubbers, are you really intending to cut the salaries of your public employees by more than 3%?' she demanded. 'That's a disaster. I am supposed to be the toughest in Europe. You are going to ruin my reputation as the Iron Lady'.[21]

But Lubbers never attained the tough image of 'iron lad' in the Netherlands. In fact, it would have been more appropriate for *Time Magazine* to call him Ruud 'Smog', due to his reputation as a living smoke machine. Among others, Pim Fortuyn later pointed to Lubbers' 'sphinx-like character' and remarked on his consensual 'magic formulas', so 'Jesuitically unclear' that 'all participants left with the impression that they had been proven right'.[22] Bolkestein called Lubbers 'compromise incarnate'.[23] The implicit ideological profile of the reforms of the 1980s made it rather difficult for all parties involved to distinguish it from mere pragmatism.

The Rutten Boys and the political nature of technocracy

In the UK and the US, the switch from a Keynesian demand-side model to a neoliberal supply-side model has been studied as a policy paradigm shift in which political and media elites ideologically confronted the established economic policy elites, who held Keynesian views.[24] Surprisingly, in the Netherlands, the more radical and ideological role was taken up by established economic policy elites. The man that is often mentioned as the ideological linchpin of the economic reforms of the 1980s is Frans Rutten, an economist from a Catholic background who served as the head of the department of Economic Affairs from 1973 till 1990. A senior figure at the Dutch Employers Federation hailed him as 'the man that has made the case for Reaganomics in the Netherlands'.[25] Rutten headed the taskforce General Economic Policy (*Algemene Economische Politiek*, AEP), an elite ministerial policy unit overseeing macro-economic policy. Echoing the famous name of the Chilean 'Chicago Boys' trained by Milton Friedman, the group serving under Rutten were dubbed the 'Rutten Boys'. In a retrospective interview, Jarig van Sinderen, one of the Rutten Boys, highlighted the trailblazing role of the AEP in its turn from the demand-side economics of Keynesianism to the supply-side model inspired by Reaganomics:

'There was a huge crisis, incomparable to what we experience now, a budget deficit of eight, nine percent. Something had to happen, and at AEP we reflected on it with a lot of creativity. Traditionally, the commission had a strong connection with economics departments at the universities. But if we were to depart from the views that were held there, the budget deficit was allowed to be even higher. Cutbacks are bad for expenditures and as such for the economy, that was the dominant theory'. The AEP directorate was thinking of a change in policy. AEP-members had looked around in the United States, where Reagan aimed for economic recovery with his Reaganomics recipes: cut taxes and let the market do its work. The committee adopted ideas that had not reached the Netherlands yet. 'We were vilified for it', says Van Sinderen.[26]

Politically, the shift from Keynesianism to Reaganomics had been prepared and proposed by the Wagner commission, a powerful extra-parliamentary committee of technocrats and business leaders installed by the previous government in 1980. The committee was named after its chairman, the former chairman of Shell, Gerrit Wagner, also a prominent Christian Democrat. Again, it was Frans Rutten who had selected and screened the members of the Wagner commission, who headed the secretariat and who can be considered the intellectual godfather of its policy ideas. The first Lubbers cabinet adopted almost all of the reform measures proposed by the Wagner commission without much alteration. Understandably, Rutten took full credit for the economic policies of the Lubbers cabinets in an interview in *Trouw* at his resignation:

In the beginning of the 1980s, the Dutch economy was in a deep recession. The Social Economic Council (SER) stopped functioning, the labour movement was obstructing and politicians would not come to their senses. On the initiative of two senior officials of the Finance Ministry and Economic Affairs, an informal club was created with business leaders and civil servants. That group set out a new economic course. When at the end of

1982, the first Lubbers cabinet entered power, the case had already been thought out. It is one of the most impressive feats in the sphere of economics in the Netherlands of the past century.[27]

Rutten had formulated his economic views in a series of articles in the leading Dutch economics journal, *ESB*. Taken together, it amounted to a surprisingly radical reform agenda inspired by Reaganomics. In his article of 1987, he retrospectively called this programme The New Objectivity (*De Nieuwe Zakelijkheid*). The core idea is that the 'government needs to concentrate on its primary tasks (such as justice, education, roads, defence) and should limit its less essential tasks (all sorts of subsidies and other interventions in the market economy)'. In the long run, the government should stop taking care of 'quasi-public goods (social security, healthcare, education)' altogether, and transform these terrains into markets through vouchers.[28] An approach famously advocated by Milton Friedman. Not surprisingly, Rutten wrote that Dutch economic policy was in need of a long-term radical vision, and that he based his vision on the writings of Adam Smith and Milton Friedman.[29] This vision, however, remained in the sphere of technocracy and was not publicly advocated by the Lubbers cabinets. It highlights the political nature of ostensibly depoliticized technocratic knowledge in the Netherlands. Frans Rutten later remarked that the political controversy surrounding the reforms had led the government to reduce its political ambitions to a mere technocratic exercise:

> Critical remarks by the Minister of Finance Ruding [...] and the President of the Dutch Central Bank, Duisenberg about the tenability of the welfare state, provoked storms of critique during the period of the first Lubbers cabinet. The question was raised whether the bank director could be ejected from the social democrat party. The officials in question soon had no other choice but to keep their mouths shut about socially sensitive issues. On instructions from the government, deregulation was reduced to a technocratic exercise.[30]

Ideological critiques of the new course were rare and largely restricted to the technocratic sphere. A good example is Wim Kok, the former trade union leader who succeeded Den Uyl as leader of the Dutch social democrats in 1986. He criticized the technocratic appearance of the New Objectivity in a dense, technocratic contribution to an anniversary publication of the Dutch Association of Economists. Kok indicted it as a clear-cut ideological programme dressed in a 'seemingly objective garment': 'The ideological dimension of the new objectivity is clearly expressed in the plea of Rutten for a concentration of the government on its primary tasks (such as justice, education, roads, defence); so a concentration on "core business"'.[31] According to Kok, the New Objectivity was part of a historical development, in which 'the free play of [market] forces triumphs over the striving towards social consensus'. According to the free market perspective, Kok argued, 'a government that goes beyond its night-watch tasks is seen as ruining the game. This overreach could consist of an "artificial" aim of full employment, or a less skewed income distribution'.[32]

As a result of the closed, technocratic and depoliticized nature of the Dutch neoliberal turn, the word neoliberalism was not frequently invoked in Dutch public debate. Prominent observers, however, have pointed to the neoliberal character of the reforms. A case in point is Wil Albeda, a leading economist who had been Minister of Social Affairs under the previous Van Agt-Wiegel cabinet (1977–1981). Albeda was the face of the progressive, pro-union wing of the Christian Democrats. In a retrospective on Dutch economic policy written after his retirement in 1999, he referred to Rutten's abovementioned interview in *Trouw*, in which Rutten applauded himself for the reforms. Albeda argued that Rutten should have been a bit more modest: 'That seems too much honour. A small group like this could draw on the neo-liberal arsenal, as it had been thought out in the US'.[33] Referring to Hayek and Friedman, Albeda argued that the Dutch economic reforms inspired by their views implied something more than mere pragmatism. Rather, it was a 'sea-change in the ideological thinking of economists'. Referring to neoclassical and monetarist economists, Albeda concluded that 'presently a new ideology comes to the fore, that chooses for the minimal state, not out of necessity but out of conviction'.[34]

Right-wing discontent with the reforms of the 1980s

Returning to Den Uyl's cautionary lecture on the ascendency of the New Right in 1981, the question is whether the three Lubbers cabinets can be fully equated with the New Right. At most, it was a half-hearted variant; Lubbers lacked the radical impulse of Thatcher and Reagan. As the conservative journalist Hans Wansink noted with disappointment: 'Ruud Lubbers is no Margaret Thatcher. Her 1980s had truly been a revolution, she did engage in a politics of confrontation, but Lubbers let things slide after his first government, lacking the conviction'.[35] All in all, the Dutch rightward turn of the 1980s was a more muted and moderate affair compared to the UK and the US. In the Dutch case, conflict has been more subdued, the dialogue with trade unions has ultimately been maintained and most of the political transformations have been discussed and enacted behind the scenes, in technocratic language.

A second important contrast is the relative weakness of the cultural conservative strand in the Netherlands. The conservative law professor Couwenberg had welcomed the economic crisis in 1981 as a 'blessing in disguise' that would put short order to the hedonistic 1960s rebellion against duty and decency.[36] Similarly, Jos de Beus concluded that the conditions for a 'conservative backlash' against 'the explosion of progressiveness from the 1960s' were present. But all in all, conservative efforts had been 'rather limited and moderate'. Consensus needed to be maintained, the trade unions needed to be accommodated and there was a peak of progressive and Christian mobilization around nuclear proliferation.[37] We might add that the legacy of pillarization and the lingering presence of the religious cleavage in Dutch politics prevented a broad conservative mobilization. The VVD was economically on the right but culturally progressive, due to its historical opposition to religious morality. The right-wing liberals won big in the 1982 elections with the free and easy slogan 'simply allowed to be yourself'. The subdued breakthrough of neoliberalism under Lubbers did, however, lead to a new radicalism on the right, as free market thought increasingly became the prevailing policy consensus. It seems fair to argue that the Dutch New Right only fully emerged as a response to the Lubbers cabinets, as an attempt to fulfil a job seen as half-done, tainted by too much compromise.

In a bid to placate the progressive wing of his party and to keep the Christian Democrats in the centre, Ruud Lubbers discarded the right-wing liberals (VVD) in 1989 as a coalition partner and invited the social democrats (PvdA) to partake in the third Lubbers cabinet (1989–1994). This development was made possible by the (cautious) embrace of free market ideas in the PvdA in the late 1980s, culminating in the Dutch Third Way in the 1990s.[38] Still, the new government was seen as an explicit choice for a more centrist course by Lubbers. Many on the right were deeply disappointed. The chance of making a radical break with the progressive legacy of the Dutch welfare state and its corporatist socio-economic arrangements seemed to have subsided. Frustration with Lubbers and the reforms of the 1980s became a central theme of the New Right undercurrent of the 1990s, who increasingly came to see the Dutch political culture of consensus and corporatist compromise as a bulwark against neoliberal reform that needed to be challenged. Among the disappointed was Frans Rutten, who was asked to leave his powerful position as head of Economic Affairs in 1989. The disenchantment was also felt in the conservative wing of the CDA, personified by Elco Brinkman, the doomed successor of Lubbers. Brinkman would lead the Christian Democrat Party in the elections of 1994 by insisting on the need for a more radical right-wing turn, 'a watershed'. Amid great controversy, Lubbers advised against his successor, resulting in historic Christian Democrat losses in the elections.[39]

But the most significant expression of right-wing discontent was – poignantly enough – Frits Bolkestein's contribution to Lubbers' *liber amicorum (festschrift)*. In a text that is traditionally supposed to be a celebratory salute, Bolkestein launched a litany of complaints against Lubbers. The problem was that Lubbers had been politically formed under Den Uyl and 'never developed into a convinced supply-side economist'. Lubbers 'never squarely positioned himself behind his Minister of Finance Onno Ruding'. He was too soft on social security and did not have 'a clear vision on the future of the welfare state'. Lubbers was too corporatist and insisted too much on cooperation with the trade unions; and he had started moderating the government's stance from 1986 onwards, in a conscious effort to move back to the centre and the social democrats. Lubbers would not go down in history as 'the Prime Minister who has buried the legacy of the 1970s', Bolkestein's illuminating measure of achievement. In short: Lubbers was not radical and neoliberal enough.

In his typical measured, dry and evocative prose, Bolkestein described Lubbers as 'a politician with a perfect radar but with a defective gyroscope'.

In other words, Lubbers received signals from all directions flawlessly, but he lacked a long-term vision, an internal conviction that kept him on course. Not that everything was the fault of Lubbers, who had to contend with the progressive current within the CDA. Bolkestein also blamed the centrists and progressives in his own party: due to its lack of 'internal cohesion', the VVD had 'offered too little resistance against the watering down of the austerity policies at the end of the 1980s'.[40] But what had been half-done could still be fully achieved. In the years that followed, Bolkestein became the principal standard-bearer of the Dutch New Right, inspiring a generation of conservative politicians and intellectuals while exercising a dominant influence on the Dutch opinion climate.

Bolkestein and the battle of ideas

Because of his well-known aversion to the Dutch political culture of consensus and ideological toleration, Bolkestein is often described as an un-Dutch politician, a rather polarizing and even unsociable figure. In the Dutch political tradition, it is common for politicians and intellectuals alike to praise the golden mean, to practice self-doubt, to build bridges and to compromise. Bolkestein's approach was radically different: 'A bridge is not a stance. A bridge is to sleep under or to walk over'.[41] Bolkestein had joined the VVD parliamentary party in the run-up to the elections of 1977. He had worked for Shell from 1960 to 1976 in East Africa, Honduras, El Salvador, London, Indonesia and Paris. During this period, he developed his political views, in the crucible of Cold War and decolonization.[42] Returning to the Netherlands, he described himself after the John Le Carré novel as 'the man who came in from the cold'.[43] Unpleasantly surprised by the progressive opinion climate in the Netherlands, he took up a position on the conservative flank of the VVD.

Besides their common distaste for compromise and the centrists in their parties, Bolkestein shared with Thatcher a fascination for the work of Friedrich Hayek. He described the Austrian thinker as 'perhaps the most important liberal political philosopher of the twentieth century' and Hayek is a recurring presence in his books.[44] It is not surprising, then, that Bolkestein subscribed to Hayek's belief in the power of ideas. 'The primary resource of politics is formed by public opinion, that is to say the outlook that can be considered dominant at a certain point in time', Bolkestein often argued.[45] The notion of a long-term battle of ideas, as the authors of Bolkestein's biography rightly state, is fundamental to his political career. 'To bring about a new consensus', Bolkestein argued, 'you first need a collision of perspectives, a *choc des opinions*. Politics is about achieving dominance for one body of ideas above another'.[46] In the Dutch context, however, Friedrich Hayek is hardly known, and many observers have expressed their bewilderment concerning the political views of what journalists have called 'the enigma-Bolkestein'. The leading political journalists who wrote Bolkestein's otherwise carefully researched biography, fail to mention Hayek's name even once in the entire book. Nevertheless, they capture some of the essence when they portray Bolkestein in the introduction as 'the first Gramscian thinker in Dutch political history', more interested in fighting the intellectual hegemony of the left, than to jostle for positions in The Hague.[47]

His first book *The Angel and the Beast* (*De Engel en het Beest*), a collection of his many lectures and opinion pieces from the 1980s, reads as a fierce and sustained attack on Dutch progressive intellectuals. He describes them as a 'passionate minority' blinded by their ideology, which had 'dominated the opinion climate', influencing an 'entire generation of policy makers'.[48] This belief that the ideas of a passionate minority had moved the country to the left had as its corollary the conviction that another passionate minority could perform the opposite feat and move the country back to the right. Bolkestein's sentiment here can be compared with that other disciple of Hayek, the American libertarian Frank Chodorov:

> We are not born with ideas. We learn them. If socialism has come to America because it was implanted in the minds of past generations, there is no reason for assuming that the contrary idea cannot be taught to a new generation. What the socialists have done can be undone.[49]

At the same time, Bolkestein was very much aware of the logic of the Overton window, the famous theory stipulating the bandwidth of acceptable opinions in a given opinion climate. In the short term, he needed to tactically curtail his radicalism to curry influence with his views, so as to move the Overton window in his direction in the long term:

> The reigning intellectual fashion naturally leaves space for dissenting views, but that space is limited. The Dutch political debate takes place between the far ends of a range of opinions. Politicians who move outside of that bandwidth of acceptable opinion, lose credibility. What you say is heard, but not understood. You lose your effectiveness and will not be considered for an electable position [on the list of candidates] in the next nomination procedure.[50]

At the same time, it is also true that 'the enigma-Bolkestein' employs a confusing amount of differing registers in his thinking. Citing Hayek, he accused Dutch progressive intellectuals of being 'second-hand dealers in ideas', who lacked the ability to develop a progressive philosophy of their own. They were a *lumpenintelligentsia* whose bric-a-brac mindset was a product of the trauma of secularization. They had filled the void of Christian redemption for a secular messianism, expressed in a vulgarized Marxism.[51]

It is all too fitting that Bolkestein's counteroffensive consisted of a similar ideological bric-a-brac, an unstable *bricolage* of second-hand ideas borrowed from international neoliberal, conservative and neoconservative thinkers. The resulting contradictions in his views make it difficult at times to lend these a coherent description.[52]

The best approach is perhaps to differentiate these registers. There is a conservative Bolkestein who entertains a pessimistic perspective on man, who is sceptical about the capacity of politics to change the world. The conservative Bolkestein poses as a sober realist and distances himself from ideology and abstract ideas.[53] There is a neoliberal Bolkestein, who embraces the power of ideas and the capacity of politics to radically change the world in the direction óf a Hayekian ideal image. The neoliberal Bolkestein warns us for the use of morality in politics and public life and sees Christian ethics as the problematic source of Dutch leftist politics. He cites Mandeville's 'private vices, public benefits' and has made Mandeville's anti-moralistic philosophy into his personal motto, the so-called 'thesis of Frits'.[54] And there is a neoconservative Bolkestein, as we will soon see, who laments the erosion of moral values in the Dutch public sphere and pleads for a moralizing politics. The neoconservative Bolkestein appeals to Christian identity as a foundation for the Dutch moral order.

These three voices continuously intermingle in his speeches and writings. In short, Bolkestein embodies all the contradictions of the fusionist project of the New Right. He is the personification of the three-legged stool. To be fair, as a prominent politician, Bolkestein simply did not have the time to develop a consistent philosophy. He admitted as much in interviews, he was not a real intellectual, but rather a 'pamphleteer and a politician'. Dutch political journalists were simply too intellectually underdeveloped to notice the difference.[55] Many of Bolkestein's articles, essays and lectures were (co-)written by his staff, which naturally leads to some eclecticism. Considering these limiting conditions, Bolkestein was surprisingly productive, well read and eloquent, fulfilling a crucial role as 'broker' of foreign intellectual currents that were largely unknown in the Netherlands.

Bolkestein was most explicit about these international inspirations when he went abroad. He gave an insightful lecture at the Institute of Economic Affairs (IEA) during his time as European Commissioner. As noted before, the IEA played a fundamental role in providing the ideological foundation for Thatcherism, by popularizing the work of leading members of the Mont Pèlerin Society. But it also had a significant part in Thatcher's famous internal struggles with the centrists in the Conservative Party, the so-called 'wets'. Bolkestein opened his speech at the IEA with the claim that 'ideas have consequences', a slogan used by New Right conservatives to express their belief in the political importance of ideas:

> Ideas have consequences. I have always been persuaded of the truth of this statement and so it was only logical that, as a budding young MP (well, young, I was a sprightly 45 year-old), I decided to take a subscription to the publications of a free market research institute which at that time was very much at the forefront of the battle of ideas. That research institute was the IEA and I owe it a profound debt of gratitude. The Institute and its authors, many of them Nobel laureates, have equipped people such as myself with the intellectual tools to fight, and win, the great political debates of the 1980s and 1990s.[56]

Moving Dutch liberalism to the right

It is tempting to see Bolkestein's battles with the centrists in his party as a less dramatic reiteration of the efforts of Thatcher and the IEA in the 1970s, even though the contexts and periods are somewhat different. Together with a group of intellectuals at the VVD think tank, the Telders Foundation, Bolkestein sought to provide a new ideological foundation for Dutch liberalism. That new foundation departed from the views of Hayek. This took shape through a series of publications. The historical development of neoliberalism was chronicled in *Liberalism and Political Economy* (*Liberalisme en Politieke Economie*) a remarkably thorough study by Telders Stichting members Andreas Kinneging and Klaas Groenveld.[57] Kinneging had only just finished his studies in political philosophy, and rapidly became a rising star within the VVD. Kinneging also worked on a subsequent publication, the study *Liberalism, a Search for Philosophical Foundations* (*Liberalisme, een Speurtocht naar de Filosofische Grondslagen*) published in 1988.[58] Kinneging was assisted this time by a commission of political heavyweights, amongst whom the later Minister Uri Rosenthal, coming party leader Frits Bolkestein and the leading sociologist Jacques van Doorn. As Gerry van der List, a colleague at the Telders Foundation confirmed, 'the theories of Hayek were adopted as a guideline' for the report.[59] In classic Hayekian fashion, the report made a black-and-white distinction between two forms of liberalism, a conservative 'utilitarian liberalism' (or neoliberalism) and a progressive liberalism epitomized by John Stuart Mill, the ideology that allegedly formed the basis for the welfare state.

Hayek's negative appreciation of the progressive-liberal tradition had been elaborated by Isaiah Berlin, in his famous distinction between negative and positive freedom. In short, the freedom from (the absence of compulsion and external government intervention as a condition for freedom) and the freedom to (the availability of resources as a condition for freedom), the principle that forms the basis of the welfare state. Like Hayek, Berlin saw positive freedom – and in extension progressive liberalism – as a pathway to totalitarianism.[60] The Telders study adopted this position. 'The pursuit of positive freedom to the detriment of negative freedom', it stated, 'does not lead to greater freedom, but entails a destruction of both aspects of freedom and that what one seeks to achieve with positive freedom, will naturally arise out of negative freedom'.[61] Also present in the study is Hayek's liberal utopian ideal, a long-term radical vision that does not confine itself to what is politically feasible at the moment. This was the 'gyroscope' that Lubbers lacked. The study identified this ideal as the minimal state, or guarantor state (*waarborgstaat*), based philosophically on Hayek's conception of the Rule of Law. This minimal state does not engage in socio-economic redistribution. The only exception identified by the report is a remittance for those that fall below an absolute minimum. This framework echoes Milton Friedman's plea for a basic income, a measure he promoted as a way to minimize more extensive welfare state programmes and forego any other form of redistribution or welfare state arrangements.

Bolkestein later expanded on the report in an essay titled *Modern Liberalism* (*Modern Liberalisme*).[62] He wrote that the radical restructuring of the Dutch welfare state in the direction of a guarantor state would mean going 'back to the future', to a point in Dutch history before the expansion of the welfare state. Bolkestein referred to the Dutch social democrat Prime Minister of the 1950s, Willem Drees, who coined the term *waarborgende staat* (guaranteeing state), a state that only guarantees minimal social security.[63] Using Drees as a reference allowed Bolkestein to present his neoliberal programme as a return to the roots of social democracy, rather than an attack on its legacy:

> Drees remained as relevant as ever for Bolkestein, if not in all respects. 'The Old Left is neo-liberal' the VVD-leader states, 'and with that I have said everything there is to say. We propagate the guarantor state of Drees in which an existence at subsistence level is guaranteed for everyone. In that respect, my party is the heir of social democracy. What Drees called the guarantor state, we call a basic system (*basisstelsel*). We also advocate the same sober realism'.[64]

In the US, it would be the equivalent of a return to the time before the civil rights movement and the Great Society programmes under Lyndon Johnson. As Bolkestein outlined in *Modern Liberalism* (*Modern Liberalisme*), regulation needed to be diminished, government services privatized and decentralized, and taxes lowered. At the same time, Bolkestein (and the Telders study) noted that the expansion of the caring functions of the state had marginalized its traditional law and order tasks: security, police, justice and infrastructure. In addition, Bolkestein proposed a radical assault on 'the decayed structures of corporatism': social security should be reduced to 60 per cent of the minimum wage, collective labour agreements should no longer be declared universally valid by the state, the labour market needed to be flexibilized and the Socio-Economic Council (where trade unions and employers deliberate over policy-making) could be abolished. Bolkestein presented these measures as a change from a Rhineland model to a 'mid-Atlantic model'. All in all, it amounts to a surprisingly radical neoliberal programme, legitimized with an extensive philosophical underpinning.[65]

What sparked controversy is that the commission of heavyweights that signed off on the report explicitly recommended the neoliberal vision of the guarantor state 'as a basis for political action'.[66] It was meant as a challenge to the still powerful centrist and progressive currents within the VVD. The study of the Telders Foundation served as the basis for the discussion paper *Liberal Compass '90* (*Liberaal Bestek '90*). The discussion paper was headed by an epigraph taken from Friedrich Hayek's *The Constitution of Liberty*: 'The main point of liberalism is that it wants to go elsewhere, not to stand still'.[67] The document proposed to sharply move the party to the right, both in terms of the proposed restructuring of the welfare state towards a guarantor state, and in terms of the restriction of immigration and the intensification of law and order policies. Sharp reactions followed. According to the party leader of the Christian Democrats, the report brought VVD and CDA 'further apart'. Wim Kok characterized the report as a 'swing to the right' and warned the VVD to not marginalize itself. *De Volkskrant* described it as 'a return to Dickens', or 'unfiltered bourgeois conservatism'.[68] The threat was clear: the VVD was isolating itself from possible future coalitions. The centrist leadership in the VVD resisted the proposed changes. A record amount of two thousand amendments were filed by party members at the annual party conference in May 1988, effectively burying the report.[69] While Bolkestein was made party leader in 1990 and stayed on till 1998, the conservative Bolkestein wing of the party remained in a minority position. Uri Rosenthal later looked back at the controversy of 1988 by commenting that it formed part of Bolkestein's grand strategy of a long-term *choc des opinions*. Rosenthal concluded that the strategy clearly paid off in the 1990s.[70]

Neoliberalism as a formative influence on Fortuyn and Wilders

Against the background of this neoliberal discontent, the figures that would become part of the populist movements of the 2000s enter the scene. Before immigration and integration became the all-important topics, their radicalism was defined much more in terms of their opposition to corporatism and the Dutch welfare state.

Pim Fortuyn, the former Marxist professor and future right-wing populist leader, joined the wave of free market enthusiasm sweeping the country at the end of the 1980s. In 1991, Fortuyn kicked off his new career as a right-wing opinion maker with his inaugural lecture at the Erasmus University Rotterdam, titled *A Future Without Civil Servants* (*Een Toekomst Zonder Ambtenaren*). The lecture was soon published as the first in a series of popularizing books in which Fortuyn developed a radical neoliberal critique of Dutch bureaucracy and Dutch political elites.[71] Fortuyn's vision of Dutch consensus culture, as we have seen in the first chapter, was inspired by Hans Daalder's 1964 analysis of pillarization and the 'regent mentality'. The 1960s critique of Dutch political culture was given a new twist by Fortuyn, who now portrayed the free market as a force of emancipation and corporatism and state bureaucracy as the principal source of oppression. A state-led modernization programme aimed at privatization, flexibilization and decentralization was needed to set Dutch citizens free.

Like Bolkestein, Fortuyn blamed the first Lubbers cabinet for having squandered a wonderful opportunity. Lubbers had assembled his government of 'vital men of action' and confronted the Dutch public sector workers, achieving a great victory in 1983, thanks to broad popular support.

> The great blunder of the first Lubbers cabinet is that he did not use that political capital to tackle the problem of high expenditures on public sector wages once and for all. [...] We would have been much further ahead if Lubbers had chosen the method of amputation instead of servicing a medicine that offered only temporary relief.[72]

Fortuyn elaborated enthusiastically on the meaning of this proposed amputation: he proposed to dismiss half of all Dutch public sector workers. The third Lubbers cabinet was in his eyes so incredibly boring and decent that it failed to inspire anyone, not even negatively. Perhaps Lubbers' discursive agility had masked the fact that he did not have any political views at all. Fortuyn called for a 'Dutch Margaret Thatcher' to deal with the trade unions, by which he most likely meant himself.[73] In a series of booklets, he proposed a 'rigorous alteration' of the Dutch welfare state, substituting it with a negative income tax, an idea popularized by Milton Friedman. All other benefits would make way for private insurance schemes. Fortuyn also envisaged radical change on the Dutch labour market. He proposed to strip Dutch corporatist institutions of their official public role, and to abolish the universal status of collective labour agreements. Pointing to the low unemployment figures in the United States, Fortuyn argued that indefinite-term labour contracts needed to be abolished altogether and exchanged for short-term contracts with a maximum of five years. This would lead the worker to make sure that 'his labour would remain valuable, no longer as the result of the care of others, but as a result of self-care'.[74] The Dutch citizen, Fortuyn argued, had to become an entrepreneur of the self, a central theme in neoliberal philosophy as chronicled by Michel Foucault.[75]

Seeing that Fortuyn was a fascinating and eccentric figure, it is not strange that his political views have often been explained in psychological terms. The single most accomplished analysis of Fortuyn's ideas, the intellectual biography by the Dutch sociologist Dick Pels is – despite its merits – a good example of the limitations of that approach. In the enticing psychological analysis of Pels, Fortuyn's evolving political views are depicted as a mirror of his personal trajectory. His rejection of the Dutch political establishment is understood in terms of his 'eccentricity' and 'outsider-status'. His switch to neoliberalism is connected with a career change to the private sector: 'Fortuyn privatizes himself in this period, and switches to a neoliberal ideology in which free market thought, calculating citizenship and contractual society are the central themes'.[76]

The problem with this psychological explanation is that it is possible to make the very opposite claim: Fortuyn's views can just as well be portrayed as an expression of his normalcy and insider-status. His political trajectory from leftist sociologist in the 1970s to neoliberal firebrand in the 1990s was not unusual. In fact, it conformed to dominant trends in the Dutch opinion climate. In the year 1986, presented by Pels as Fortuyn's moment of conversion to the free market, Fortuyn had been posted by his university at the Scientific Council for Government Policy (WRR). At this influential state think tank, the neoliberal turn was actively discussed at the time. The Wagner commission had been formed in reaction to a report published by the WRR in 1980 and the think tank had close links to the 'Rutten Boys' at Economic Affairs. Frans Rutten actually served as chairman of the WRR not long after, from 1990 till 1993. Fortuyn's political views in the 1990s are clearly derived from the ideas circulating among the highest levels of Dutch economic policy elites, and they have much in common with Frans Rutten's 'New Objectivity' agenda.

Fortuyn's inaugural lecture consisted in large parts of a popularization of reports from the AEP think tank, explicitly mentioned in the references, as well as Bolkestein's abovementioned book, *The Angel and the Beast*.[77] Of course, Fortuyn added some unique touches of his own, in particular the democracy critique from the 1960s. But overall, his proposals were eerily similar to those of Economic Affairs and Bolkestein. Fortuyn also pleaded for an end to corporatist institutions such as the Social Economic Council and the universal status of collective labour agreements. He copied Bolkestein's Friedmanian plea for reducing social security provision to a basic income at subsistence level. Although Fortuyn shifted his emphasis to cultural conservatism and immigration in the mid-1990s, free market themes remained an important element in his politics, a fact often ignored by scholars and commentators. In interviews Fortuyn stated that 'the poor should learn to care for themselves', that the welfare state took people's soul, and that he considered it his 'calling to proclaim that not only Dutch politics is worthless, but also that many citizens are'.[78] The critique of the large-scale bureaucracy of the corporatist welfare state, contrasted with the diversity of consumer choice in the free market, provided the core of his analysis in *The Disasters of Eight Years Purple* (*De Puinhopen van Acht Jaar Paars*), his bestselling critique of the liberal/social democrat (purple) coalitions. The book famously accompanied Fortuyn's spectacular electoral breakthrough in 2002.[79]

The election platform of Fortuyn's party in 2002 pleaded for the marketization of health care, 8.6 billion in tax cuts, wage moderation, deregulation of education, radical cuts in disability benefits, and the wholesale elimination of rent subsidies and family allowances.[80]

Similarly, for Geert Wilders, the later leader of the Party for Freedom, neoliberal views formed the original inspiration of his anti-establishment stance. Wilders began his political career as a staff member of Frits Bolkestein in 1990. He was hired as an expert on social security, and his first notable contribution was the background research for a 1991 opinion piece by Bolkestein on the neoliberal policy plank of a radical reform of corporatist structures in social security.[81] It would be his foremost topic of expertise for some time. During his time as an MP for the VVD, Wilders called the Netherlands 'the village idiot' of Europe, the system of disability benefits was 'a directionless super tanker unavoidably heading towards a sandbank', and on issues of social security, Dutch parliament was a 'socialist feast'.[82] In February 2001, Wilders published the opinion piece 'Stop Trade Union Power' in which he argued that 'the exaggerated pursuit of societal consensus takes the dynamism out of socio-economic activities, which the Netherlands can hardly afford'.[83] Wilders pleaded for a smaller welfare state and the curtailment of Dutch trade unions, in order to restore the entrepreneurial freedom of the Dutch citizen.

Wilders referred to these neoliberal inspirations when he started his rebellion against the centrist party leadership of the VVD in 2003, culminating eventually in his break with the party in the following year. In an interview from 2003 in *de Volkskrant*, Wilders suggested that

> it would be worthwhile to excavate an old VVD-document from the archives. The document *Liberalism, a Search for Philosophical Foundations* written in 1988 by the think tank of the VVD, was professionally swept under the carpet by then VVD-leader Voorhoeve, Wilders remembers. The report was crafted under the leadership of his great example, the current European Commissioner Frits Bolkestein. In [the Dutch weekly] *HP/De Tijd* Wilders told what he had learned from him: 'That you need to with-stand great resistance, that you need to set the agenda, have a thick skin, and that being proven wrong today does not mean that you are wrong tomorrow'.[84]

When Wilders left the VVD to create his own party in 2005, he published the pamphlet *Choose for Freedom* (*Kies voor vrijheid*). It refers again to the publication of the Telders Foundation on utilitarian liberalism. In the pamphlet, Wilders laments the lack of ideological substance of VVD parliamentarians, who had not read the Telders publications and did not even know what utilitarian liberalism was.[85] Neoliberal ideas remained an important element in Wilders' first official party documents, in his Declaration of Independence (*Onafhankelijkheidsverklaring*) from 2005, in *Straight-Talk* (*Klare Wijn*) from 2006 and the accompanying economic proposal, the *Plan for a New Golden Age* (*Plan voor een nieuwe Gouden Eeuw*).[86] The latter proposed a €16 billion reduction in government expenditure, a staggering 13 per cent of the total budget. It would be given back to citizens as tax cuts, to make room for 'freedom, responsibility, creativity, innovation and entrepreneurialism'. 'Lowering taxes, reducing the role of government, and minimal regulation' had proven to be the 'only engine of economic growth'.[87] In the years after, Wilders has tactically chosen to adopt a more centrist rhetoric on socio-economic issues. His programme and voting record have remained fiscally conservative, however, with some notable exceptions, such as health care.[88]

In conclusion, rather than foregrounding personal psychology as an explanation for the political views of Bolkestein, Fortuyn and Wilders, it arguably makes more sense to take a step back and consider these figures in the larger ideological context of the time. Seen from a Kuhnian perspective, it is a moment in Dutch political history when the old Keynesian corporatist paradigm had been discredited and the new paradigm was still taking shape. Like the entrepreneurial scientists in Kuhnian paradigm shifts, the radical views of the 1980s and 1990s reflect a period of 'exceptional science' that allows for more far-reaching changes to the existing socio-economic paradigm. Unlike the UK or the US, where neoliberalism entailed an all-out confrontation with the trade unions, the Dutch reforms were eventually channelled through neo-corporatist structures. After a period of unilateral government intervention, the trade unions were brought back into the fold in the 1990s, in what is known as 'responsive corporatism' or more commonly, the Dutch polder model.[89] Some scholars have described Dutch neoliberalism as a – restructured – continuation of the corporatist model, rather than a departure from it.[90] Such a hybrid reality is not exceptional when we consider the recent literature on neoliberalism. 'To the extent that neoliberalism has been, since the 1970s, "victorious" in the war of ideas', Jamie Peck argued in his well-crafted study, 'its victories have always been Pyrrhic and partial ones'. 'As a result, it is doomed to coexist with its unloved others, be these the residues of state socialism, developmental statism, authoritarianism, or social democracy'.[91] In the Dutch case, those 'unloved others' have been corporatism and consensus politics. The Dutch New Right arose out of dissatisfaction with the emerging synthesis, and tried to take the newly forming paradigm several steps further in the direction of their Anglo-American inspirations.

Neoliberal ideas, however, were not the sole or even main driver of the political breakthrough of the Dutch New Right. Free market thought was accompanied by a new body of conservative ideas, which forms the subject of the following chapter.

Notes

1 See Angus Burgin, *The Great Persuasion: Reinventing Free Markets since the Depression* (New Haven, CT: Harvard University Press, 2012); Colin Crouch, *The Strange Non-Death of Neo-Liberalism* (Cambridge: Polity, 2011); Philip Mirowski and Dieter Plehwe, *The Road from Mont Pèlerin: The Making of the Neoliberal Thought Collective* (Cambridge, MA: Harvard University Press, 2009); Jamie Peck, *Constructions of Neoliberal Reason* (Oxford: Oxford University Press, 2010), Daniel Stedman Jones, *Masters of the Universe: Hayek, Friedman, and the Birth of Neoliberal Politics* (Princeton, NJ: Princeton University Press, 2014); Bernhard Josef Antonio Walpen, '"Der Plan, das Planen zu Beenden": Eine Hegemonietheoretische Studie zur Mont Pèlerin Society' (PhD thesis, Amsterdam, University of Amsterdam, 2004). For a good Dutch study written by an adherent and MPS member, see Gerrit Meijer, 'Het Neoliberalisme: Neoliberalen over Economische Orde en Economische Theorie' (PhD thesis, Assen, Koninklijke Van Gorcum, 1988).
2 Friedrich A. Hayek, *The Road to Serfdom: With the Intellectuals and Socialism* (London: Institute of Economic Affairs, 2005), 18.
3 Michel Foucault, *The Birth of Biopolitics: Lectures at the Collège de France, 1978–1979*, trans. Arnold I. Davidson and Graham Burchell (Basingstoke: Palgrave Macmillan, 2004), 107.
4 Cited in George H. Nash, *The Conservative Intellectual Movement in America since 1945* (Wilmington, DE: ISI Books, 2014), 69. The concept was used in a comparably neutral or positive way by MPS members such as Milton Friedman, Ludwig von Mises, Walter Eucken, Jacques Rueff, Ludwig Erhard, Albert Hunold, Alfred Müller-Armack, Wilhelm Röpke and Alexander Rüstow. See: Walpen, 'Der Plan, Das Planen Zu Beenden' (2004), 48.
5 Milton Friedman, 'Neo-Liberalism and its Prospects', *Farmand* 17 (1951): 89–93.
6 Cited in Walpen, 'Der Plan, Das Planen Zu Beenden', 73.
7 Hayek, *The Road to Serfdom*, 128–9.
8 Hayek, 128–9.
9 Burgin, *The Great Persuasion*.
10 Nash, *The Conservative Intellectual Movement in America*, 1–50.

11 John Ranelagh, *Thatcher's People: An Insider's Account of the Politics, the Power and the Personalities* (London: Fontana, 1992), ix.

12 Bram Mellink, 'Politici Zonder Partij: Sociale Zekerheid En de Geboorte van Het Neoliberalisme in Nederland (1945–1958)', *BMGN – Low Countries Historical Review* 132, no. 4 (2017): 25–52; Merijn Oudenampsen, 'A Dialectic of Freedom: The Dutch Post-War Clash Between Socialism and Neoliberalism', *Socialism and Democracy* 30, no. 1 (2016): 128–48.

13 Joop den Uyl, 'Tegen de Stroom In' (Paradiso, Amsterdam, 3 May 1981). The ideas of Hayek and Friedman enjoyed a new ascendency at the time, in books such as Hans Daudt and Ernst van der Wolk, eds., *Bedreigde Democratie? Parlementaire Democratie en Overheidsbemoeienis in De Economie* (Assen: Van Gorcum, 1978); Theo Stevers, *Na Prinsjesdag in De Volkskrant: Kritische Beschouwingen Over de Economische en Politieke Zijden van het Begrotingsbeleid Der Rijksoverheid* (Leiden: Stenfert Kroese, 1979). Den Uyl had framed his own political views in opposition to Hayek's neoliberalism ever since the 1950s. The stark opposition Den Uyl sketched between a democratic road and a road to authoritarianism can be read as a response to Hayek's own use of that motif in *The Road to Serfdom*. See Oudenampsen, 'A Dialectic of Freedom'.

14 Den Uyl, 'Tegen de Stroom In'.

15 Rudy Andeweg and Galen A. Irwin, *Governance and Politics of the Netherlands* (Basingstoke: Palgrave Macmillan, 2009), 41.

16 Daalder, *Politiek en Historie*, 98–9.

17 Jouke Turpijn, *80's Dilemma: Nederland in de Jaren Tachtig* (Amsterdam: Bakker, 2011); Kees-Jan van Klaveren, 'Het Onafhankelijkheidssyndroom: Een Cultuurgeschiedenis van het Naoorlogse Nederlandse Zorgstelsel' (PhD thesis, Amsterdam, University of Amsterdam, 2015).

18 Jelle Visser and Anton Hemerijck, *'A Dutch Miracle': Job Growth, Welfare Reform and Corporatism in the Netherlands*, Changing Welfare States (Amsterdam: Amsterdam University Press, 1997), 78. See also Anton Hemerijck, 'The Historical Contingencies of Dutch Corporatism' (PhD thesis, Oxford, Oxford University, 1992), 330.

19 Arend Lijphart, *The Politics of Accommodation: Pluralism and Democracy in the Netherlands* (Berkeley, CA: University of California Press, 1968), 125.

20 Daalder, *Politiek en Historie*, 98–9.

21 Time Magazine, 'The Netherlands: Ruud Shock', *Time Magazine*, 23 January 1984.

22 Pim Fortuyn, *Aan het Volk van Nederland: De Contractmaatschappij, Een Politiek-Economische Zedenschets* (Amsterdam: Contact, 1992), 111.

23 Frits Bolkestein, *Het Heft in Handen* (Amsterdam, Prometheus, 1995), 217.

24 Mark Blyth, *Great Transformations: Economic Ideas and Institutional Change in the Twentieth Century* (Cambridge University Press, 2002); Peter A. Hall, 'Policy Paradigms, Social Learning, and the State: The Case of Economic Policymaking in Britain', *Comparative Politics* 25, no. 3 (1993): 275–96. Dutch scholars have used Peter Hall's work on Kuhnian paradigm shifts in economic policy to describe Dutch developments, but they have left out the role of ideological confrontation, which is deemed crucial in Peter Hall's model and the analysis of the transformation in the Anglo-American context more generally. See Jeroen Touwen, 'How Does a Coordinated Market Economy Evolve? Effects of Policy Learning in the Netherlands in the 1980s', *Labor History* 49, no. 4 (2008): 439–64; Visser and Hemerijck, *'A Dutch Miracle'*.

25 Elsje Jorritsma and Michèle de Waard, 'De SG Is Weer Staatsdienaar, Geen Mooie Zangvogel', *NRC Handelsblad*, 5 January 2009.

26 Jarig van Sinderen, 'Beleidseconomen zijn het tegenwoordig veel te veel eens', interview by Hans Obbink, *SER Magazine*, 2003. For a more extensive analysis of the role of the AEP, see Louis Raes et al., 'Het Maken van Economisch Beleid: De Rol van AEP in de Afgelopen Vijftig Jaar', *Tijdschrift Voor Politieke Economie* 24, no. 1 (2002): 7–50.

27 Chris Rutenfrans, 'Simonis is Net zo Oppervlakkig als ik Vroeger Was', *Trouw*, 3 July 1999.

28 Frans Rutten, *Zeven Kabinetten Wijzer: De Nieuwe Zakelijkheid bij het Economische Beleid* (Groningen: Wolters-Noordhoff, 1993), 55.

29 Frans Rutten, *Verval, Herstel en Groei: Lessen voor het Economisch Beleid Gelet op het Leergeld van Twintig Jaar* (Utrecht: LEMMA, 1995), 37.

30 Rutten, 58.

31 Wim Kok, 'Het Bestuurlijke in de Economie: Een Kritiek op de Nieuwe Zakelijkheid', in *Lessen Uit Het Verleden: 125 Jaar Vereniging Voor Staathuishoudkunde*, ed. Antonie Knoester (Leiden: Stenfert Kroese, 1987), 368.

32 Kok, 373.

33 Wil Albeda, 'De Droom van een Humaan Kapitalisme', *Maandschrift Economie* 63, no. 6 (1999): 420.

34 Albeda, 424.

35 Hans Wansink, *De Conservatieve Golf* (Amsterdam: Prometheus, 1996), 167.

36 Servatius W. Couwenberg, *Op de Grens van Twee Eeuwen: Positie en Perspectief van Nederland in Het Zicht van het Jaar 2000* (Kok Agora, in samenwerking met Stichting Civis Mundi, 1989), 196.

37 Jos de Beus, 'Een Derde Eeuw van Nederlands Conservatisme', in *Ruimte Op Rechts? Conservatieve Onderstroom in de Lage Landen*, ed. Huib Pellikaan and Sebastiaan van der Lubben (Utrecht: Spectrum, 2006), 223.

38 See Merijn Oudenampsen, 'Opkomst En Voortbestaan van de Derde Weg: Het Raadsel van de Missende Veren', *B En M: Tijdschrift Voor Beleid, Politiek En Maatschappij* 43, no. 3 (2016): 23–45.

39 Bert De Vries, *Overmoed En Onbehagen: Het Hervormingskabinet-Balkende II* (Amsterdam: Bert Bakker, 2005), 40.

40 Bolkestein, *Het Heft in Handen*, 217–20.

41 Bolkestein, 159.

42 In his biography, Bolkestein states that he first became interested in politics during his work for Shell in El Salvador. "El Salvador was a polarized society, with big contrasts between rich and poor. You were automatically sucked into politics. I developed more of an eye for the relations between Shell and the trade unions. At Shell, the norm is to not get involved in politics, but that was impossible there." Significantly, at the time of Bolkestein's stay, El Salvador was run by the US-backed colonel Rivera Carballo, who organized paramilitary death squads to deal with leftists and trade unionists. In that context, Bolkestein's comments are intriguing to say the least. Max van Weezel and Leonard Ornstein, *Frits Bolkestein: Portret van een Liberale Vrijbuiter* (Amsterdam: Prometheus, 1999), 52.

43 Van Weezel and Ornstein, 64.

44 Bolkestein, *Het Heft in Handen*, 15. See also the opinion piece by Edwin van de Haar, who described Bolkestein as the Dutch exponent of Hayek's battle of ideas, Edwin van de Haar, 'De Ideeënoorlog van Friedrich Hayek', *Trouw*, 12 June 2004. Van de Haar, at that time, was a member of the Edmund Burke Foundation.

45 Bolkestein, *Het Heft in Handen*, 58.

46 Van Weezel and Ornstein, *Frits Bolkestein:* (1999), 159.

47 Van Weezel and Ornstein, 14.

48 Frits Bolkestein, *De Engel en het Beest* (Amsterdam: Prometheus, 1990), 17.

49 Cited in Nash, *The Conservative Intellectual Movement in America*, 39.

50 Bolkestein, *De Engel en het Beest*, 69.

51 One of the oft-returning themes of Bolkestein is that he criticized baby boomers for being more interested in intentions than results. He relied on the Weberian distinction between *Gesinnungsethik* and *Verantwordungsethik*, proclaiming the superiority of the latter. Daniel Bell had used this Weberian distinction to criticize the American left in his book *The End of Ideology*. While *Gesinnungsethik* departs from

the intention of an ethical deed, *Verantwordungsethik* focuses on the estimated results. Originally, Weber argued that politics needed to contain both ethics, but Daniel Bell presented it as a dilemma, a choice between one or the other. Bolkestein here echoed Bell. It allowed Bolkestein to take up the position of the realist, while skilfully masking a more prosaic reality, namely that Bolkestein had markedly different intentions and aspirations than his progressive opponents. Bolkestein, *De Engel en het Beest*, 75.

52 One brief example: central to Bolkestein's intellectual project, in socio-economic terms, was to locate the ideas on which the Dutch welfare state was based. On the one hand, he argued that the Dutch welfare state departed from an ideology of personal development (*ontplooiingsideologie*) premised on a pessimistic image of man, in need of constant improvement. Bolkestein argued that his own views, in contrast, were founded on a positive image of man as strong and independent. In the very same book, Bolkestein argues that the welfare state arose out of a positive image of man as inherently good and strong, a view that completely dominated Dutch politics. In contrast, his own politics were based on a pessimist vision of man. See: Bolkestein, *Het Heft in Handen* (1995), 20, 59.

53 This voice prevails in Bolkestein's most accomplished book: Frits Bolkestein, *De Intellectuele Verleiding* (Amsterdam: Prometheus, 2012).

54 Bolkestein, *De Engel en het Beest*, 43.

55 In an interview with the magazine of the youth department of the VVD, Bolkestein suggested that the founder of his party, P.J. Oud, was a 'real intellectual'. He himself was not. 'I am a pamphleteer and a politician', Bolkestein said. See JOVD, 'Frits Bolkestein over Duitsland, P.J. Oud En de Liberale Doorbraak', *Driemaster*, 1995.

56 Frits Bolkestein, 'The EU's Economic Test: Meeting the Challenges of the Lisbon Strategy' (17th Annual State of the International Economy Conference, IEA, London, 19 November 2001). The opening words 'ideas have consequences' refer to the eponymous title of a 1948 book by the US conservative thinker Richard Weaver, which has since become a famous conservative slogan. See Nash, *The Conservative Intellectual Movement in America*, 82.

57 Karel Groenveld and Andreas Kinneging, *Liberalisme en Politieke Economie*, Geschrift; 54 ('s-Gravenhage: Prof. Mr. B.M. Teldersstichting, 1985). While the study used the word neoliberalism for the earlier period of the neoliberal movement, it reverted to 'classical economic liberalism' to describe its later offshoots such as the Chicago School, the neo-Austrian school and supply-side economics.

58 Andreas Kinneging, *Liberalisme: Een Speurtocht naar de Filosofische Grondslagen*, Geschrift Prof. Mr. B.M. Teldersstichting; 65 (Den Haag: Teldersstichting, 1988).

59 Gerry van der List, 'Hayek En de Nederlandse Politiek', *De Vrijbrief*, 1993, 30.

60 See Zeev Sternhell's discussion of Isaiah Berlin in Zeev Sternhell, *The Anti-Enlightenment Tradition* (New Haven, CT: Yale University Press, 2010).

61 Kinneging, *Liberalisme*, 55.

62 Bolkestein, *Het Heft in Handen*, 15–41.

63 The Dutch New Right has an intriguing fondness for Willem Drees. Drees was the Dutch social democrat leader and Prime Minister during the sober period of post-war reconstruction, from 1948 to 1958. New Right politicians admire Drees for his opposition to the expansion of the Dutch welfare state in the 1960s and for his sharp critiques of immigration and the New Left. In a prominent speech in 2013, the Prime Minister Mark Rutte presented Drees as an important inspiration for his ambition to further curtail the Dutch welfare state. Rutte hailed Drees as a 'realist' and argued that the realism of Drees 'resounded in his preference for the guarantor state rather than the welfare state'. See Mark Rutte, 'Sterke Mensen, Sterk Land: Over het Bezielend Verband in de Samenleving' (Dreeslezing, Den Haag, 14 October 2013). Martin Bosma, the ideologue of Geert Wilders, presented Drees as a political forefather of

the PVV. Bosma saw Drees as the Dutch equivalent of the first generation of US neoconservatives, such as Kristol and Bell. Not wholly without reason, as we shall soon see. Martin Bosma, *De Schijn-Élite van de Valsemunters: Drees, Extreem Rechts, de Sixties, Nuttige Idioten, Groep Wilders en ik* (Amsterdam: Bert Bakker, 2011), 205.

64 Kees Versteegh, 'Het Sociaal-Democratische Verleden van de VVD-Top; De Linkse Wortels van het Liberale Succes', *NRC Handelsblad*, 13 May 1995.
65 Bolkestein, *Het Heft in Handen*, 15–41.
66 Kinneging, *Liberalisme*, v.
67 VVD, *Discussienota Liberaal Bestek '90: Een Kansrijke Toekomst – Verantwoorde Vrijheid* (Den Haag: VVD).
68 Lidie Koeneman et al., *Kroniek 1988: Overzicht van Partijpolitieke Gebeurtenissen van het Jaar 1988* (Groningen: Documentatiecentrum Nederlandse Politieke Partijen, 1989).
69 Piet van de Breevaart, 'Liberalen: Bestek op de Schroothoop', *Reformatorisch Dagblad*, 28 May 1988.
70 Van Weezel and Ornstein, *Frits Bolkestein*, 93.
71 Fortuyn, *Het Zakenkabinet Fortuyn*, 113.
72 Fortuyn, *Aan het Volk van Nederland*, 111.
73 Fortuyn, *Het Zakenkabinet Fortuyn*, 113.
74 Fortuyn, *Uw Baan Staat op de Tocht!*, 68–72.
75 Fortuyn, 31.
76 Dick Pels, *De Geest van Pim: Het Gedachtegoed van een Politieke Dandy* (Amsterdam: Anthos, 2003).
77 Fortuyn, *Een Toekomst zonder Ambtenaren*, 36.
78 Bart Jan Spruyt, 'Heer van Stand in de Politiek', *Reformatorisch Dagblad*, 8 September 2001.
79 Pim Fortuyn, *De Verweesde Samenleving: Een Religieus-Sociologisch Traktaat* (Uithoorn Rotterdam: Karakter, 1995).
80 LPF, *Politiek is Passie: Verkiezingsprogramma Lijst Pim Fortuyn 2003–2007* (Rotterdam: Lijst Pim Fortuyn, 2002).
81 Meindert Fennema, *Geert Wilders: Tovenaarsleerling* (Amsterdam: Bakker, 2010), 14.
82 Cited in Bert Snel, 'Zijn Wilders en Fortuyn Vergelijkbaar?', *Civis Mundi Digitaal* 5 (2011).
83 Geert Wilders, 'Stop de Vakbondsmacht', *NRC*, 15 February 2001.
84 Elaine de Boer and Theo Koelé, 'Een Rechtse Directe', *De Volkskrant*, 20 November 2003.
85 Geert Wilders and Wilders Groep, *Kies voor Vrijheid: Een Eerlijk Antwoord* (Den Haag: Groep Wilders, 2005), 26–7.
86 PVV, 'Klare Wijn', 2006, www.pvv.nl/index.php/component/content/article/30-publicaties/706-klare-wijn.html; PVV, 'Een Nieuw-Realistische Visie', 2006, www.pvv.nl/30-visie/publicaties/707-een-nieuw-realistische-visie.html; PVV, 'Plan Voor Een Nieuwe Gouden Eeuw', 2006, www.pvv.nl/30-visie/publicaties/703-een-nieuwe-gouden-eeuw.html. For a more extensive discussion of these reports, see Koen Vossen, *The Power of Populism: Geert Wilders and the Party for Freedom in the Netherlands* (London: Routledge, 2017).
87 PVV, 'Plan Voor Een Nieuwe Gouden Eeuw'.
88 Tom van der Meer, 'Ook het Verkiezingsprogramma van de PVV is niet Links', 5 March 2017, http://stukroodvlees.nl/ook-het-verkiezingsprogramma-van-de-pvv-niet-links/.
89 Visser and Hemerijck, *'A Dutch Miracle'*.
90 Ilja Scholten, *Political Stability and Neo-Corporatism: Corporatist Integration and Societal Cleavages in Western Europe* (London: SAGE, 1987), 120–52.
91 Peck, *Constructions of Neoliberal Reason*, 7.

4   The neoconservative strand

The neoliberal elements of the Dutch New Right form a complex assemblage with ideas drawn from another powerful intellectual movement, that of US neo-conservatism. Similar to neoliberalism, neoconservatism refers to a movement with a lot of internal diversity and historical dynamism, a movement that has chosen to influence existing parties rather than forming a political organization of its own. Like neoliberalism, it is therefore a rather vague and often contested label. In one of the more widely acclaimed studies of neoconservatism, the French scholar Justin Vaïsse has resolved the problem of the current's historical and political heterogeneity by subdividing the movement into 'three different formative impulses': the three ages of neoconservatism.[1]

Neoconservatism gradually developed out of the anti-Stalinism of the 1930s and the Cold War liberalism of the 1950s and 1960s. Anti-communism was a prominent theme from the beginning, with many neoconservatives participating in the Congress for Cultural Freedom, an anti-communist advocacy group staffed by intellectuals and funded by the CIA. But the focus in the first age lies more in the realm of domestic rather than foreign policy. The immediate cause for the rise of neoconservatism was the leftward turn of US liberalism exempli-fied by Johnson's Great Society programmes and the rise of the New Left in the 1960s. A group of liberal intellectuals moved to the right in response to these developments (some of them had been founders of pluralism as we have seen in the previous chapter). These 'neoconservatives' criticized the perverse effects of Johnson's welfare programmes. They introduced the 'culture of poverty' thesis that linked the poverty of the black population to cultural deficiencies, in par-ticular the lack of family values. They opposed the New Left, criticizing 'the adversary culture' of the baby-boomer generation: its individualism, hedonism and moral relativism. And they rallied against attempts to diversify the academic curriculum, criticizing these developments under the labels of 'multiculturalism' and 'political correctness'. In so doing, neoconservatives played a crucial part in igniting the *culture wars* that determine American politics up to the present day.[2] Two intellectual journals had a formative function for this first generation: *The Public Interest*, founded by Irving Kristol and Daniel Bell, and *Commentary*, edited by Norman Podhoretz. Around these journals, a larger group of intellectuals gathered, some of the leading lights included Nathan Glazer, Seymour Martin

Lipset, Gertrude Himmelfarb and Daniel Patrick Moynihan. This first generation can be considered centrist on socio-economic issues and conservative on cultural issues.

The second age begins in the early 1970s when the New Left, represented by George McGovern's *New Politics* in the 1972 elections, is powerfully defeated by Richard Nixon. Neoconservatives saw the electoral defeat of the Democrat Party as a result of the abandonment of the 'silent majority', in particular culturally conservative blue-collar workers, who felt sidelined in favour of a 'rainbow coalition' of students, blacks, Hispanics, women and homosexuals. Neoconservatives opposed the counterculture and pleaded for a return to the defence of law and order and family values. Some neoconservatives, such as Kristol and Moynihan, now jumped ship to Nixon and the Republican Party. Others formed the conservative wing of the Democrat party, where foreign policy became the major focus, promoted by figures such as Richard Perle, Frank Gaffney, Paul Wolfowitz, Elliot Abrams and Douglas Feith. The most prominent object of discontent was the 'détente' with the Soviet Union, advocated by Republicans such as Richard Nixon and Henry Kissinger. As part of this political stance, ardent support for Israel became a major policy plank, portrayed as the defence of a democracy threatened by (secular) Arab regimes in league with the Soviet Union. In 1980, neoconservatives entered the halls of power under Ronald Reagan, where they successfully pushed for an intensification of the Cold War. At this point, many neoconservatives switched from the Democratic to the Republican Party. The neoconservative movement had become a fixture of the right, even though many still referred to their liberal origins, most notably Irving Kristol, who defined neoconservatives as 'liberals mugged by reality'.

A third phase in neoconservatism started in the 1990s, when the Cold War is finished and neoconservatism has become a fully fledged element of the Republican Party. Newcomers such as William Kristol, Robert Kagan (both editors of the *Weekly Standard*), Francis Fukuyama, David Brooks, Max Boot and David Frum no longer had leftist or even Democrat origins. The emergence of a unipolar world furthered global ambitions of neoconservatives. The only remaining progressive legacy of neoconservatism at this point is the rhetoric of Wilsonian liberalism ('Wilsonianism with boots') that resounded in foreign policy. Military intervention was defended in terms of the universal values embodied by American democracy. Progressive thinking about domestic policy had by now fully disappeared. After the 9/11 attacks, the neoconservatives infamously become the initiators of the *War on Terror* and the invasion of Afghanistan and Iraq. In the public view, the epic scale of these events has had the effect of reducing the meaning of neoconservatism to this last episode in its variegated history.

Leo Strauss and the philosophical inspirations of neoconservatism

Turning to the more philosophical aspect of neoconservatism, a core element connecting the different periods is the conviction that the struggle against an external threat has politically beneficial effects in sustaining a community.[3] Neoconservatives have championed an image of the world as divided by a dramatic conflict of starkly contrasted forces of good and evil. They have stressed the benevolent nature of America's dominant global role, as a harbinger of democracy and human rights. Particularly the philosophy of Leo Strauss would become one of the foremost sources of inspiration.[4] Strauss, a Jewish refugee from the Nazi regime, rose to prominence at the University of Chicago in the 1950s. He founded a Straussian school of philosophy. Among the Straussians were many neoconservatives who would later acquire positions of power in government, in military and foreign policy circles, and in neoconservative think tanks.[5] Elaborating on the thesis of the German jurist Carl Schmitt that friend-enemy distinctions form the essence of politics, Strauss saw the struggle against an enemy – portrayed as an absolute moral evil – as a necessary condition for the construction and safeguarding of a healthy moral community.[6]

For Strauss, the problem of Burkean conservatism was that it had developed a relativist philosophy in opposition to radical Enlightenment thought. Philosophically, the French Revolution had been grounded in the universalist appeal to natural law, to the inalienable and universal rights of man. Burke had responded in relativistic terms, by positing the unique nature of national traditions, and by appealing to historical contingency. In his seminal response to the French Revolution, Burke framed human rights as the historic accomplishments of specific national traditions. Instead of abstract principles as 'the rights of men', he argued that 'the rights of Englishmen' were based on their 'entailed inheritance derived to us from our forefathers, and to be transmitted to our posterity'.[7] In the Burkean perspective, national traditions were spontaneously grown, naturally evolved, complex organisms that defied human reason and could not be reduced to abstract formulas.

In *Natural Right and History*, Strauss took aim against the cultural relativism of Burkean conservatism and the rejection of universal standards and natural law. Without such a higher standard, Strauss contended, conservatism would revert to accepting whatever history imparted and what a particular society's way of life and institutions had come to accept. From such a point of view 'the principles of cannibalism are as defensible or sound as those of civilized life', Strauss argued.

> It is only a short step from this thought of Burke to the supersession of the distinction between good and bad by the distinction between the progressive and the retrograde, or between what is and what is not in harmony with the historical process.[8]

Strauss went back further in history to classical thought, in particular Plato, to articulate a new conservatism grounded in a metaphysics that could do away with relativism and properly distinguish good and evil. As Francis Fukuyama noted, of particular importance for Strauss and the neoconservatives was Plato's plea for the necessity of a civil religion in *Laws*. Reason does not suffice to obtain obedience to the law; a higher truth supplied by myth and religion is required. 'Non-rational claims of revelation' can never be expelled from politics.[9] Hence, neoconservatives, although secular in conviction, saw religion as a necessary foundation for a non-relativist notion of identity and moral order. Leo Strauss thus supplied the philosophical basis for neoconservatives to criticize cultural relativism, to defend the Christian identity of the US, to define cultures in terms of their core values and to pinpoint enemies of the West as an axis of evil. Under Reagan, this led to anti-western regimes being labelled as morally evil. After 1989, Islamic fundamentalism took over the role of communism as the dominant enemy image, as articulated in the clash of civilizations thesis developed by Bernard Lewis and Samuel Huntington.

The Dutch reception of neoconservatism

In the Netherlands, US neoconservatism has remained relatively unknown to the larger public and there are few studies of its Dutch reception.[10] The period that has rightly received attention from journalists and academics is that of the controversial 'coming out' of self-proclaimed Dutch neoconservatives in the years from 2000 till 2006.[11] After 9/11, neoconservative ideas were at the centre of the public conversation, while the Dutch left had fallen silent. In 2003, the conservative social democrat Jos de Beus famously proclaimed the 'vacuity of the left', which he contrasted to the audacity of Dutch neoconservatives:

> It's the neoconservatives that take the initiative in foreign and domestic policy. They put on the agenda the democratization of Arabia, the defence of freedom against Islamism, the norms and values in public space, the social duties in a welfare state and the corporate social responsibility of multinationals. The left follows, divided, confused and aggrieved.[12]

But neoconservative ideas had been circulating among Dutch intellectuals long before 9/11. They played an essential role in the debates on national identity, Islam, integration and immigration of the 1990s, which has generally been ignored by scholars and journalists. Again, there is a leading part for Frits Bolkestein as a 'broker' and translator of ideas. As the Dutch Minister of Foreign Affairs in the 1980s, Bolkestein was well aware of US foreign policy debates, spearheaded by neoconservatives. He frequently referred to neoconservative authors such as Nathan Glazer, Daniel Patrick Moynihan, Francis Fukuyama, Daniel Bell, Irving Kristol, Gertrude Himmelfarb and Samuel Huntington in his lectures and books and engaged some of them in debate on their visits to the Netherlands.[13]

In that same period, the journalist Hendrik Jan Schoo became another important bridgehead for neoconservative ideas. In the 1990s, Schoo served as editor-in-chief of the largest Dutch (right-wing) weekly *Elsevier*. He appointed Pim Fortuyn as a columnist in 1993 and is said to have been an important influence on Fortuyn's conservative turn in the mid-1990s.[14] From 1999 onwards,

Schoo became sub-editor and then columnist for the social democrat leaning newspaper *de Volkskrant*, which made a shift in conservative direction in that period. An influential circle of conservative (former) social democratic journalists and intellectuals such as Martin Sommer, Herman Vuijsje, Hans Wansink, Jos de Beus, René Cuperus, Paul Scheffer and Chris Rutenfrans would take up Schoo as their inspiration. This group remained somewhat critical of neoliberalism and can be equated politically with the first age of neoconservatism.

A third significant figure is Paul Cliteur, law professor in Leiden, former custodian of the VVD think tank and occasional text writer for Bolkestein. He published an ambitious 600-page dissertation on legal philosophy, European conservatism and US neoconservatism in 1989 and described himself as an early fan of Irving Kristol. Cliteur became the principal exponent of the Dutch New Atheist current, and an influential critic of Dutch multiculturalism. (He would soon be outdone by a brighter star, his former pupil Ayaan Hirsi, to whom Chapter 6 is dedicated.) In what follows, the chapter explores the reception of four core neoconservative ideas: the clash of civilizations thesis, the notion of civil religion, the cultural contradictions of capitalism and the theory of the new class.

The clash of civilizations thesis

While there had been some loose references to neoconservatives before, Dutch engagement with this current really picked up during the neoconservative discussion surrounding the fall of the Berlin Wall. In the summer of 1989, Francis Fukuyama's famous essay *The End of History?* was published in *The National Interest*, a neoconservative foreign policy journal founded by Irving Kristol in the 1980s.[15] The publication of the essay marked a phase of crisis and transformation for the neoconservative movement. The implosion of communism, the archenemy that neoconservatives had directed their daunting intellectual energies against since the very beginning of the movement, led to the search for a new grand narrative. What story could give meaning and coherence to the newly emerging world order, with the US as sole superpower? Fukuyama's thesis of the end of ideological rivalry was an attempt at creating such a narrative.

The essay immediately provoked a flurry of responses. Many argued that communism was far from dead and buried, others pointed at Islam as a new rival for liberal democracy.[16] The neoconservative political scientist Samuel Huntington, the former PhD supervisor of Fukuyama, qualified his thesis in the autumn edition of *The National Interest* as 'an intellectual fad'.[17] Huntington referred back to the end of ideology debate in the 1960s, when the idea took hold that the power of religion, ethnicity and nationalism would diminish due to modernization. That turned out to be premature, since these identities had developed in the 1980s into 'the dominant bases of political action in most societies'. 'The revival of religion is now a global phenomenon', Huntington concluded. With that response, Huntington already gave a first sketch of what would become his own attempt to formulate a new grand narrative. In 1993, Huntington published the essay *The Clash of Civilizations?* where he identified Islamic civilization as a new source of hostility for the West, allowing history to proceed its course.[18]

The debate was closely followed in the Netherlands. The newspaper *NRC Handelsblad* devoted a spread to Fukuyama's thesis in August 1989.[19] Frits Bolkestein became actively involved in the discussion. He wrote a public response (in Dutch) to Fukuyama in December 1989 and debated him at two occasions in the Netherlands in 1992 and 1995. In his public reaction to Fukuyama in 1989, Bolkestein took Huntington's side. He identified Islam as a new ideological rival for the West: 'The fact remains that the world contains a billion Muslims, of which many consider their ideology superior to the "godless, materialist, and egoistic liberalism of the West"'. Bolkestein pointed to demographic factors, to a frustrated Islamic intelligentsia 'confronted with television images of our post-modern societies', to the Rushdie affair and the French controversy surrounding the veil.[20] The clash of civilizations thesis became a central touchstone for the development of the Dutch New Right in the 1990s and 2000s, as the cultural conservative strand of the New Right became more and more prominent. Pim Fortuyn would introduce himself to American journalists as 'the Samuel Huntington of Dutch politics'.[21] The first manifesto of Geert Wilders' PVV couched immigration in terms of a civilizational clash, arguing that 'Islam orients itself against Western civilization as such'.[22] And Hirsi Ali depicted her life story as an illustration of Huntington's theory, as a 'personal journey through the clash of civilizations', the subtitle of her book *Nomad*.[23]

The thesis of the clash of civilizations, however, did not originate with Huntington. Bernard Lewis, the Princeton-based Orientalist, had been promoting the idea of such a clash on and off ever since the 1960s.[24] In 1990, a month after the beginning of the First Gulf War, Lewis published the essay *The Roots of Muslim Rage* in *The Atlantic*. In this text, Lewis described the rise of Islamic fundamentalism and argued that Islamic civilization was inherently hostile to the West: 'This is no less than a clash of civilizations – the perhaps irrational but surely historic reaction of an ancient rival against our Judeo-Christian heritage, our secular present, and the worldwide expansion of both'.[25] The rhetoric of the clash of civilizations performed several political functions simultaneously. To begin with, the thesis effectively transposed the image of a centrally organized political adversary, Soviet Russia, unto a world religion that was in reality deeply divided. As the leading French Islamic fundamentalism scholar Gilles Kepel pointed out, the Islamic world is a civilization more at war with itself than with the West.

> The clash of civilizations theory facilitated the transfer to the Muslim world of a strategic hostility the West had inherited from decades of Cold War. And the neoconservative movement played a crucial role in bringing about this rhetorical and theoretical permutation.[26]

At the same time, the clash of civilizations thesis also served to redefine the image of the West. Crucial is that the neoconservatives portrayed the secular modernity of the West as the product of Christianity, as 'Judeo-Christian heritage'. Modern liberal values were culturalized and historicized, they were portrayed as a specific product of the religious legacy of the West. In so doing, liberal modernity was presented as wholly absent in Islam. Thirdly, the clash assumes an incompatible, antagonistic relation between the West and Islam, both framed as neatly contained cultural monoliths without internal contradictions or overlaps. This opposition between the West and Islam is presented as the terrain for a new ideological conflict, a new Cold War. The field of struggle revolves around two options: wholesale rejection of the West by Muslims or their assimilation to Western values.

These very same themes come to the fore in a contentious lecture by Frits Bolkestein during the congress of the Liberal International in 1991 in Luzern. Bolkestein mainly spoke on the collapse of the Soviet Union, but it was his remarks on the integration of Muslim minorities that courted controversy. He expanded on his lecture in an opinion piece in *De Volkskrant*. The text sparked an avalanche of responses in the Netherlands and kicked off the Dutch integration debates that came to dominate Dutch politics in the next decades:

> European civilization, even if it has a lot to answer for, is saturated with the values of Christianity. A liberal politician acknowledges that too. Rationalism, humanism and Christianity have, after a long history that includes many black pages, brought forth a number of fundamentally important political principles, like the separation of Church and State, freedom of speech, tolerance and non-discrimination. Liberalism claims universal validity and significance for these principles. That is its political vision. This means that according to liberalism, a civilization that affirms these values, is superior to a civilization that does not. Liberalism cannot accept the relativity of these political values without renouncing itself.[27]

Bolkestein depicted 'the Islamic world' as both inferior and 'antithetical' to liberalism. He saw the presence of a large number of Muslim immigrants as a threat to European values, and he called for the uncompromising defence of these values. This threat was compounded by the spectre of 'cultural relativism', a common tendency of Dutch progressive intellectuals to deny the superiority of their culture. Bolkestein's minorities lecture closely follows the logic of Lewis' clash of civilizations theory. The integration of Muslim immigrants in the Netherlands was framed by Bolkestein as an ideological conflict between Western liberalism and Islamic backwardness.

The central contradiction in Bolkestein's discourse is the notion of universal values, which are at the same time presented as belonging to a specific cultural tradition. Access to these universal values can only be gained through acculturation, through the assimilation to (superior) Western culture. Universal values are thus enlisted in the service of a particularistic discourse of Western superiority and cultural confrontation. Moreover, if one takes the 'culturalist' view that human behaviour is primarily determined and contained by culture, to assert the superiority of Western culture is to claim the superiority of its people. Culture, if conceived in sufficiently static, self-contained and monolithic terms, can thus serve to redraw the boundaries between insider and outsider groups, between the white Dutch population and the Muslim minorities.[28] In this way, in the early 1990s, the Dutch New Right found a way to talk about immigration without conjuring the memory of the Second World War and the image of right-wing extremism.

This paradoxical idea of universal values, enclosed in a particular cultural tradition, is a prominent theme of US neoconservatism. It undergirded American military intervention abroad, depicted as a way to spread the universal values that the American tradition embodied. Meanwhile, the anti-war movement and the counterculture of the 1960s and 1970s were derided as cultural and moral relativists.[29] In the Netherlands, that same formula has been used as a tool on the domestic front to plead for tougher immigration and integration policies and to reinvent Dutch identity in opposition to both progressive 'cultural relativists' and a 'backward' Islam. This discourse soon came to dominate the Dutch integration debate. Whereas before, the socio-economic aspect (work, education) was seen as central to the integration of immigrants, in the 1990s that view was increasingly marginalized in favour of a socio-cultural insistence on the need to assimilate Western values.

Civil religion as a foundation for Dutch identity

A consequence of the adoption of the clash of civilizations thesis is the affirmation of the religious identity of Europe and the Netherlands. Progressive values that have historically been claimed in confrontation with Christianity were now depicted as the accomplishments of (Judeo-)Christian culture. Bolkestein, Fortuyn, Wilders and consequent political leaders of the CDA and VVD employed a variety of these formulas in Dutch integration politics. They defined Dutch identity in terms of rationalist-humanist-Christian values, Judeo-Christian values or Judeo-Christian-humanist values. Pim Fortuyn posited 'unbridgeable differences' between the 'Judaeo-Christian humanist culture' of the Netherlands and the culture of Islam, even in its 'liberal variants'.[30] Geert Wilders proposed to replace the first article of the Dutch constitution – which contains the principle of equality and the proscription of discrimination – with a reference to a *Leitkultur* of Judeo-Christian-humanist values.[31] In this way, right-wing politicians sought to distinguish the identity of the dominant white majority in the Netherlands from first- and second-generation Muslim immigrants. As the religion scholar Ernst van den Hemel points out in a sharp analysis of this new discourse, we are not dealing with historically accurate, neutrally descriptive terms for existing religious-cultural affinities. There is no such thing as a unitary Judeo-Christian tradition. Rather it should be seen as an invented tradition:

> [T]he appeal to Judeo-Christian roots should be seen as a performative linguistic act, an invocation rather than a description, that has as its goal the simultaneous defence and construction of a community that is perceived to

be under threat, by appealing to a tradition that cannot be grasped in rational, objective terms.[32]

Van den Hemel traces this appeal to the Christian roots of Dutch culture back to Leo Strauss and the neoconservative idea that some conception of natural right, bolstered by religion and myth, is needed to sustain a moral order and inspire obedience to the law. In March 1994, Bolkestein gave a controversial interview, again igniting a flurry of debate, in which he adopted this approach and pleaded for a *bezielend verband* (spiritual bond):

> A society needs a bond. That is why I have attacked cultural relativism in the framework of the minorities debate. The laws are the walls of the state, the Old Greeks said. Except that the government is powerless faced with a massive breach of the law. When the sense is lacking that it is morally bad to break the law, the walls of the state have no foundation. In the past, the manifesto of the VVD stated that the party based itself on a series of fundamental values, among which Christianity. In the 1970s, when everything was possible and allowed, it was dropped. This makes sense, seen purely from the liberal tradition. But we now live in a society that is adrift, with a million of allochtons [minorities] in the year 2000. Perhaps the reference to Christianity needs to be included once more in our program.[33]

For some, the neoconservative origin of this argument concerning religious morality as the foundation of the 'walls of the state' was obvious. According to Paul Cliteur, Bolkestein's 'reference to Christianity as a foundation for our moral values, is found in Kristol'.[34] (Kristol, in turn, attested to inspiration by Leo Strauss.) Cliteur saw Bolkestein's intervention as part of a wider embrace of neoconservative ideas among the intellectuals of the VVD:

> When I wrote an article in 1987 on Irving Kristol, I did not think there was anyone in the Netherlands that seriously studied his work. But who compares the book of Kristol with the ideas of the aforementioned thinkers [VVD-intellectuals such as Bolkestein, Kinneging and Van der List] will find significant similarities. [...] The ideologues of the VVD have gone through a trajectory from Rawls to Hayek, and from Hayek to Kristol, or so it seems.[35]

These neoconservative inspirations remained controversial in the Netherlands. Elsewhere, Cliteur noted that the label neoconservatism was so contentious that the conservative wing of the VVD was wary of identifying itself as such:

> In the time that he was director of the Wiardi Beckman Stichting, the [social democrat] senator Joop van den Berg characterized the VVD as a 'neo-conservative party'. In the US, such a characterization wouldn't have provoked any resistance. It couldn't be more different in the Netherlands!

Here Bolkestein for example, would never dare to characterize his essays as neoconservative. [...] Klaas Groenveld, director of the Teldersstichting, the think tank of the VVD, would introduce himself in the US as 'head of a neoconservative think tank'.[36]

In the debate that followed Bolkestein's opinion piece, Dutch Christian Democrats expressed their doubts concerning the instrumental nature of his appeal to Christian values. Why did Bolkestein take recourse to something he himself did not believe in? Here the conservative idea that Christianity can bolster conservative values provides the answer. Bolkestein's relation to Christianity, however, is far more troubled than that of the American neoconservatives. His view of the Dutch Christian tradition is marked by a deep ambivalence. Looking back at Bolkestein's writings, a largely negative picture of the legacy of Dutch Christianity appears. He criticized Dutch Protestants for having abandoned the Heidelberg Catechism on the inherent sinfulness of man.[37] As a result, Protestantism had stopped being a conservative force in Dutch society, and instead fostered the progressive movements of the 1960s and 1970s. Both the Dutch welfare state and the progressive ideals of the protest generation were in Bolkestein's opinion a product of Christian feelings of guilt and sympathy with the suffering of one's fellow man. He reserved specific scorn for the influential Christian pacifist organizations protesting the Cold War arms race in the 1980s. That negative attitude never fully subsided. In a prominent intervention at a later date, Bolkestein attributed the Western penchant for cultural relativism to Christian values. The Christian ethic of 'turning the other cheek', Bolkestein argued, spelled doom for European civilization in the struggle with Islam.[38]

Within the Dutch New Right, not everyone was content with Bolkestein's appeal to Christianity. Paul Cliteur, who had been one of the earliest to introduce neoconservative ideas to the VVD, rejected the use of religion to reframe Dutch identity. Cliteur published a philosophically worded response to Bolkestein at the end of 1994, in which he outlined his objections and proposed an alternate approach. He agreed with Bolkestein on the need for a metaphysical foundation of moral values, in which some conception of natural law was used. Drawing on the work of American conservatives, Cliteur alternately called this a 'cosmic police agent', a 'metaphysical dream' or a 'civil religion'.[39] But in contrast to Bolkestein, Cliteur proposed to use appeals to the Enlightenment and universal human rights as a foundation for Dutch identity, as a way of declaring Western culture superior to Islam.

In his PhD thesis, Cliteur had taken up a position in between Burke and Strauss, and in between positive law and natural law. Taking from Burke the notion of evolutionary development of national traditions, and from Strauss the idea of the need for natural law and universal standards, Cliteur formulated a synthesis that he called *cultuurrecht* (cultural law). The core idea is that evolutionary development of a culture can give rise to moral standards that are superior to those of other cultures. He elaborated on that vision in books such as *Filosofie van Mensenrechten* (*Philosophy of Human Rights*) published in 1999 and *Moderne Papoea's* (*Modern Papuans*) in 2002, an influential critique of multiculturalism and cultural relativism. In these books, Cliteur did with universalism and Enlightenment values what Bolkestein had tried to do with Christian religion: he used them in an instrumental and paradoxical fashion to construct a particularistic discourse of cultural superiority:

> For a cultural relativist there can be no such thing as the superiority of one culture. But from the perspective of the universalist it is self-evident that the question can be resolved. If we can outline one corpus of universal values, it is possible to identify one culture where those values are, by and large, best protected. The culture in which that is the case, is the best culture. And 'the best', is 'superior'.[40]

Cliteur and his former student Hirsi Ali became the Dutch representatives of a hugely influential anti-religious tendency within the New Right. They were the Dutch representatives of New Atheism, the current that achieved prominence internationally after 9/11 through the work of intellectuals such as Christopher Hitchens, Richard Dawkins and Sam Harris. Eventually Cliteur (and Hirsi Ali) were dubbed 'Enlightenment fundamentalists' by the sociologist Dick Pels.[41] Curiously, this has been the charge that seems to have stuck over time. The caveat here is that Cliteur's embrace of Enlightenment values is as ambivalent as Bolkestein's embrace of Christianity. We should not forget that Cliteur is a self-declared conservative thinker and member of the Edmund Burke Foundation. He is one of the most prolific authors on conservatism in the Netherlands, a tradition he himself describes as 'resistance to the Enlightenment'.[42] Cliteur's most important inspirations, Hayek and Burke, whose writing has supplied the building blocks for his own philosophy, were both avowed critics of universal human rights. And when push comes to shove, Cliteur has a rather spotty record as a defender of human rights. When discussing the torture of suspected terrorists in his 2002 book on multiculturalism, Cliteur writes that universal human rights are, as a rule, not absolute: exceptions should be allowed.[43] A similar contradiction is found in the politics of Ayaan Hirsi Ali, who defends universal human rights fervently and at the same time pleads for a liberal jihad, meaning the suspension of human rights for Islamic radicals.[44] If Cliteur and Hirsi Ali are truly fundamentalists, they are strikingly flexible in their fundamentalism. And if Cliteur and Hirsi Ali are truly universalists, they are strikingly tribal in their universalism.

A true proponent of universalism would argue that universal values transcend cultures, and can therefore also be found within the Islamic world. Cliteur and Hirsi Ali enlist universalism and the Enlightenment in the service of a patriotic discourse of cultural superiority and conflict. As Ian Buruma observed sharply: 'the Enlightenment has a particular appeal to some conservatives because its values are not just universal, but more importantly, "ours", that is, European, Western values'.[45] Neoconservatives have historically used the universalist discourse of Wilsonian liberalism to bolster American patriotism. Similarly, in the Dutch context, universalism came to denote a new Dutch patriotism.

The cultural contradictions of capitalism

Neoconservative theory also helped to underpin the Dutch New Right strategy of combining neoliberal and (neo)conservative convictions. A central reference point, introduced by Bolkestein at a Telders Foundation conference on liberalism, conservatism and communitarianism in 1994, was the book *The Cultural Contradictions of Capitalism* by Daniel Bell. The basic thesis of this classic from 1976 is that capitalism is inherently prone to create its own gravediggers.[46] It undermines the cultural preconditions of its very existence. Bell's analysis was inspired by Max Weber's sociological classic *The Protestant Ethic and the Spirit of Capitalism*. On the one hand, capitalism functions thanks to an underlying conservative (Protestant) morality based on frugality, a strong work ethic, patience, self-discipline, perseverance and so on. On the other hand, capitalism is a system of ongoing rationalization. Its technology and dynamism are revolutionary and derive from the spirit of modernity. It is the dynamic of capitalism itself that threatens to destroy existing traditions and communities. Irving Kristol's slogan *Two Cheers for Capitalism* aptly expressed the neoconservative reservation.

The image of capitalism evoked by neoconservatives is perhaps best explained by reference to a passage from *The Communist Manifesto*. Here, Marx depicted capitalism as 'the sorcerer who is no longer able to control the powers of the nether world that he has called up by his spells':

> Constant revolutionising of production, uninterrupted disturbance of all social conditions, everlasting uncertainty and agitation distinguish the bourgeois epoch from all earlier ones. All fixed, fast-frozen relations, with their train of ancient and venerable prejudices and opinions, are swept away, all new-formed ones become antiquated before they can ossify. All that is solid melts into air, all that is holy is profaned, and man is at last compelled to face with sober senses his real conditions of life, and his relations with his kind.[47]

Marx welcomed this cultural dynamic as a historically necessary liberation from feudalist bondage, while critiquing capitalism largely on socio-economic grounds. The neoconservatives chose the opposite approach, and wanted to defend capitalism by counteracting its corrosive influence in the cultural field. Ever since Edmund Burke, conservatives have cherished the 'ancient and venerable prejudices' as essential to the maintenance of the social order. The neoconservatives were no exception to that rule. Daniel Bell saw the emergence of the libertine and hedonistic culture of the 1960s and 1970s as an outgrowth of the revolutionary nature of capitalism, in particular its consumer culture. Above all, the progressive elites in the culture industry – where all sorts of profanity was on offer – undermined the conservative morality necessary for the continued existence of capitalism.

At the time of the appearance of *The Cultural Contradictions of Capitalism*, the neoconservatives were drifting further to the right. They joined Reagan's

New Right coalition. As part of that new reality, they were proponents of unleashing capitalism through free trade and globalization, through liberalization, deregulation and flexibilization. At the same time, at the cultural level, they refused the norms and values that capitalist modernity entailed, while pointing to progressive cultural elites as the cause of the problem. Bell's analysis became the intellectual expression of a broader strategy of the American conservative movement: the discontent and anxiety generated by an unbridled capitalism was addressed on the terrain of culture. In *What's the Matter with Kansas*, Thomas Frank called this political strategy 'the Great Backlash'. It allowed the Republican Party to garner support for free market policies by foregrounding conservative cultural discontent.[48]

In his presentation at the Telders Foundation conference in 1994, Bolkestein made the case for a similar two-pronged strategy. On the economic terrain he was a strong proponent of globalization, privatization, flexibilization and deregulation. On the cultural sphere he advocated conservatism:

> We need to take into account the different domains that Daniel Bell has distinguished within society. The Dutch economy is not very flexible and progress can be made by getting rid of unnecessary rules and decayed corporatist structures. But on the cultural level, partly due to the arrival of lots of people with other norms and values, instability and fragmentation pose a greater danger than rigidity. Hence the importance of the Christian and humanist tradition for our society as a binding element. This combination of economic progressivity and cultural conservatism is not opportunistic, but a consequence of the analysis of the present social condition of the Netherlands.[49]

The sociologist Dick Pels described Fortuyn as the 'eclectic forerunner' of 'the intriguing convergence between market-liberalism and neoconservatism'.[50] In reality, Bolkestein preceded Fortuyn in articulating this convergence. Again the historical irony is stark: at the very moment of liberal triumphalism concerning the fall of the Berlin Wall, the VVD of all parties was reintroducing a critique of capitalism. The right-wing liberals turned to (cultural) conservatism at a time when all other parties turned to embrace liberalism. Like the above-mentioned rationale of Thatcherism spelled out by During, the insecurity created by economic developments was addressed in the sphere of culture. The most devastating political strategy, Schattschneider argued, is to change the conflict that is central to the political field. The Dutch New Right did just that, by moving the major left-right opposition from the socio-economic to the cultural terrain.

The leading sociological analyses of the emergence of the radical right, such as those of Kitschelt and Betz, point to deindustrialization and the rapid socio-cultural and socio-economic changes of the 1980s and 1990s as the driver of the success of this radical right politics.[51] Similarly, the Netherlands in the 1990s was subject to sweeping changes due to processes such as deindustrialization, globalization, individualization and neoliberalization. The consequences of deindustrialization were specifically harsh for the former guest workers who had decided to stay and bring their families over in the 1980s. For them, the difficulty of accommodating themselves to the new context was compounded by the spectre of mass unemployment. Meanwhile, the Netherlands signed the Maastricht Treaty formalizing the European Monetary Union in 1992 and was swept up in the wave of globalization and free market reform. The civil society institutions that had become part of the Dutch welfare state were drastically scaled back under the cutbacks and privatizations of the 1980s and 1990s. Concurrently, the massive introduction of part-time employment for Dutch women meant a momentous break with the old Fordist breadwinner model. In this turbulent context of rapid socio-cultural and socio-economic change, a conservative discourse emerged that self-assuredly pointed to immigration, Islam, the 1960s and the cultural relativism of baby boomers as the source of the erosion of community, the loss of tradition and the attrition of national identity.

After the 1994 conference *Liberalism, Conservatism and Communitarianism*, the Telders Foundation came with the publication *Between Permissiveness and Paternalism (Tussen Vrijblijvendheid en Paternalisme).*[52] Cliteur, Kinneging and Van der List were among its authors. In the publication, the Dutch debate on communitarianism, excessive individualization and moral decline was subtly channelled in the direction of the ideas of Hayek and the neoliberal reform programme outlined in the 1988 Telders publication *Liberalism, a Search for Philosophical Foundations*. The 1995 report expressed the fusionist ambition of uniting conservative and neoliberal convictions. Gerry van der List, the secretary of the working group that produced the report was quite explicit about this motivation: 'We want in some way or other, to incorporate conservative morality in the liberal creed of freedom'.[53] The report referred to Bolkestein's plea for a 'spiritual bond', and proposed to include a reference to Christian foundations in the party programme. Gerry van der List argued for a 'conservative alliance' with the CDA to fight together against the 'culture of permissiveness' and 'the legacy of the 1960s'. The core of this agenda would be a restoration of 'common decency', next to cutbacks in government spending, the encouragement of business initiative, the promotion of law and order policies and a 'civilized nationalism'.[54] It is this combination that forms the hallmark of the New Right.

New class theory and the assault on the 1960s

The neoconservatives had formulated a theory about the progressive elites who were the target of the backlash strategy in the US. This was the notion of the 'new class', described by Steinfels in his influential study of neoconservatism as 'half-analytical concept, half-polemical device'.[55] The protest movements of the New Left, neoconservatives had argued in the 1960s, threatened to undermine the stability of American democracy. It wasn't Vietnam or the situation in the inner cities. The crisis was above all moral and cultural. The problem was the decay of values, the decline of moral standards and the corruption of manners. Individualism and hedonism had replaced traditional conventions of family, community and work. The breeding ground for this erosion was the new class: a new cultural elite comprised of erstwhile students who had climbed the ladder to become society's intellectuals, academics, bureaucrats, social workers, managers, consultants, lawyers and so forth. Leftist politics, the neoconservatives argued in the 1970s, is a rationalization of the interests of this class: a way to increase their power by expanding the (welfare) institutions they dominated. This new class was described as culturally progressive, hostile to traditional morality and the working-class politics of the Old Left.[56]

Almost a quarter century later, new class theory turned into an important inspiration for the Dutch backlash. In April 1995, a landmark essay appeared in the Dutch weekly *Elsevier*, titled *Commemorating with Humility* (*Herdenken in Deemoed*). In this text, H.J. Schoo argued that the progressive counterculture of the 1960s still presided over Dutch politics, due to the rise of a new social class. This 'new class', Schoo argued, dominated the sphere of knowledge production: the fields of policy formulation, academia, culture and the media. The 'new class' in the Netherlands had monopolized the memory of the Second World War and used it to push through its egalitarian agenda while stifling the debate.

> [T]he baby boomers, presently in their fifties, have been in command of the country for the past twenty-five years. Not economically (business has other masters) or even in a strictly political sense. No, their ideology sets the tone in the 'consciousness industry': in administration, policy, education, culture, science and the media. They have the power over the written and the spoken word, formulate ideas, set the agenda and define reality.[57]

Here we find *in nuce* an idea that would become extremely popular during the Fortuyn revolt: the idea of the 'leftist elite', portrayed as a dominant force in Dutch society even if the Dutch left had been excluded from political power in the 1980s and remained in electoral retreat ever since. That Schoo used neoconservative ideas to theorize Dutch developments was not a coincidence. Schoo had studied in the US in the polarized period of the late 1960s. When Bart Jan Spruyt described Schoo in an essay as one of the leading Dutch neoconservatives, Schoo responded privately as follows:

> It is strange to see myself named among the 'hall of fame' of Dutch neocons. The reason of course, is that I prefer to remain unlabelled and indefinable, but on balance I think it is correct. I have since my distant American years felt a kinship with people such as Moynihan, Glazer, Podhoretz, the old Kristol, Buckley. Later came Himmelfarb, first as 'psychohistorian', then as the author of *The Demoralization of Society*. And Lasch has of course been an important influence; he is never seen as a neocon, but in many respects he really is.[58]

In public, though, Schoo remained in the closet and was careful to not out himself as a neoconservative, for fear of being sidelined in the debate. It underlines the earlier observation of the incentives in Dutch society to not make the ideological character of one's ideas explicit.[59] One of the outstanding qualities of US neoconservatism as an intellectual movement was its use of sociological journalism, combining an accessible style with an admirable grasp of social theory and a passionately pursued political agenda. While translating US neoconservative ideas to the Netherlands, Schoo developed an incisive form of sociological journalistic commentary that stood out in the Dutch media landscape and ultimately became very influential.

The major difference with the US, Schoo contended in his essay, was that the new class in the Netherlands had been more powerful than anywhere else, due to the weakness of traditional Dutch institutions, as a result of depillarization and secularization. From the ruins of the old pillars, the 'new class' in the Netherlands had crafted a more or less cohesive new moral order, embodied by the welfare state. This progressive ideology had been constructed in opposition to National Socialism and the German occupation during the Second World War. Consequentially, the new class saw hierarchy and authority as overwhelmingly negative. Any appeal to repressive measures by the state had been made suspicious by using references to the war. In their generational rebellion, the new class had taken its revenge on the moral failings of their parents under German occupation by embracing an anti-authoritarian welfare state and by welcoming mass immigration.

While Schoo observed in 1995 that the belief in the welfare state had subsided somewhat, he argued that the first article of the Dutch constitution had become a new object of national veneration, enshrining anti-racism as a public religion. The official activities surrounding the public remembrance of the war and the celebration of liberation on the fifth of May connected Dutch identity to a 'harnessed anti-fascism': 'The memory of the war is made to serve the utopian creed of the coming multicultural society'.[60] In this way, Schoo reconstructed the messy, improvised and in reality rather negligent record of Dutch immigration and integration policy – that began with the pragmatic and economically motivated decision of a right-wing government to invite guest workers – as a consistent, intentional and deeply idealistic multicultural agenda of the Dutch left.[61]

His treatment of the ideas of the 'new class' and the baby-boomer generation had a similar sharpening effect. The protest generation of the 1960s was critiqued from both left and right for its lack of a clear political vision, its arrested intellectual development and its ideological vacuity. In the hands of Schoo, what was in reality a rather spontaneous and practical movement without an exceedingly coherent agenda, suddenly became a streamlined ideological operation of unreconstructed radicals, controlling the minds of the Dutch population well into the 1990s. Ironically, this notion of an all-pervasive 'leftist elite' was brought in circulation by Schoo at the same time that leftist intellectuals such as Bart Tromp and Ruud Koole were busy debating the terminal decline of the Dutch left.[62]

That sentiment was broadly shared. None other than Frits Bolkestein observed with glee in 1994 that the left had entered its 'terminal phase'. If anything, it was the pragmatists who were the dominant force on the left in the 1990s, not the ideological hardliners. In 1995, social democrat leader Wim Kok famously spoke on how liberating it was for the social democrat party to shed its 'ideological feathers'. Schoo had transposed an image of the baby-boomer generation dating from the politicized period in the 1960s, straight into the technocratic reality of the 1990s.

Schoo's new class theory formed the early echo of the revisionist immigration narrative put forward by Fortuyn and Wilders, stipulating that the Dutch left had orchestrated mass immigration. The problem with that accusation, of course, was that the left was not in power when the most important decisions were made.[63] The new class theory neatly worked around that problem, by arguing that mainstream Dutch right-wing parties were also dominated by a leftist elite in 'the consciousness industry'. As Jos de Beus correctly observed, 'a conservative critique of progressive hegemony has to devolve in our case into a critique of the softening of Christian Democrats and right-wing liberals'.[64] The new class theory was eminently suitable for this purpose. It actually served to attack the pragmatist centre in Dutch politics, policy and media by linking it to an ephemeral, omnipresent spirit of 1968. The added advantage was that the spirit of 1968 would not fight or talk back, since it had long since departed.[65] Schoo connected this critique of the new class with a forceful attack on political correctness:

> The liberators, the generation of the 1960s, quickly became the gatekeepers of political correctness. [...] The Dutch public domain is littered with pitfalls, with emergency triangles; with zones we cannot enter unpunished. Almost anyone that writes or speaks on the market place of public opinion, does so with the aid of an ever-vigilant internal censor.[66]

Next to his personal influence on Fortuyn whose views on immigration and globalization were still very (neo)liberal in the early 1990s, perhaps the biggest impact of Schoo was in conservative social democrat circles. Schoo described himself as a 'right-wing social democrat' and formed part of a larger group of social democrat opinion makers that moved to the right in the 1980s and 1990s. As noted before, in 1997 the sociologist and journalist Herman Vuijsje published his influential book *Correct*, in which he reiterated and elaborated on Schoo's baby-boomer theory of an entrenched leftist elite.[67] Vuijsje represented a growing conservative sentiment among Dutch social democrat circles in the 1990s, famously dubbed *Nieuw Flinks* (a contraction of 'New Left' and 'toughness') by Dutch comedians Van Kooten en De Bie. These conservative social democrats aligned themselves with the New Right in the Dutch culture wars of the 1990s and 2000s. The basic thesis of Schoo and Vuijsje would later be taken up in the landmark essay titled *The Multicultural Drama* (*Het Multiculturele Drama*), by social democrat intellectual Paul Scheffer.[68] His bestselling book

Immigrant Nations (*Land van Aankomst*) can be read as a dialogue with US neoconservatism.[69]

A failed palace revolution

Figures such as Pim Fortuyn and Geert Wilders have often been cast as the original innovators who for the first time represented the sentiments of long-ignored segments of the population, who made debatable what had been considered taboo. What this chapter has shown is that both Fortuyn and Wilders were part of a larger and longer conservative wave. They drew on ideas that had been introduced by politicians and intellectuals of the Dutch New Right. Almost all of the major themes that were central to the breakthrough of right-wing populism in 2002 had been formulated and passionately discussed by the mid-1990s. Already in 1995, Hendrik Jan Schoo argued that the debate on national identity implicitly revolved around the lack of political conservatism in the Netherlands. He predicted that 'the large political parties, with the exception of D66, will in this sense become conservative'.[70]

This conservative undercurrent has gone strangely unnoticed by many prominent authors. The aforementioned Dutch historian Piet de Rooy depicted the Dutch 1990s as post-ideological. He observed a 'worrying degree of unanimity', and noted that 'lively debate or political oppositions were sadly missed'.[71] Another illuminating example is the newspaper *NRC Handelsblad*, which wrote in 1990, during a veritable peak of intellectual activity within the VVD: 'Is it that they are not allowed, or is [it] that they're not willing to discuss matters in the VVD? [...] Intellectual laziness and poverty are catchwords that seem to cling to the party'.[72] Perhaps the intellectual debates covered in this chapter were not taken very seriously at the time, or unfamiliarity with conservative ideas has hindered analysis, perhaps some have been looking in the wrong places. Perhaps some Dutch scholars really *wanted* to believe in the end of ideology.

This chapter has shown how neoconservative ideology inspired the conservative wave in the 1990s and provided much of its political idiom. The contention is not that these ideas were ideological in the sense of being completely false. As Terry Eagleton has argued, an ideology can only be effective if it is convincing, if it corresponds in some degree to an existing reality. But the transposition of neoconservative ideas from the far more politicized and polarized American context helped Dutch conservatives in painting a much more dramatic, radical and ideological portrait of the Dutch left and the baby-boomer generation than the existing 'prudent progressive' consensus allowed for. Especially on immigration policy, Dutch conservatives succeeded in popularizing a revisionist history, in which mass immigration was framed as an idealistic agenda of the left.

Neoconservative theory assisted Dutch conservatives in this dramatization and helped them in tying the issue of immigration irrevocably to the political legacy of the 1960s. It taught them to raise the spectre of cultural relativism, originally theorized by Leo Strauss in the late 1940s. And it showed them how to reformulate Dutch identity while breaking with traditional pluralist, sceptical and organicist understandings of Dutch national identity. Particularly important was the clash of civilizations theory that served to portray the Netherlands as a front in the global confrontation between Islam and the West. When 9/11 occurred, the Dutch New Right had a narrative in place that could make sense of the new geopolitical constellation. It should be stressed that there were significant differences of opinions among the New Right, on the use of religion to reframe Dutch identity or even on the integration of immigrants. The process of translation was never a smooth, coordinated operation.

In the 1990s, the conservative undercurrent failed to break through politically. As noted before, the conservative wing of the Christian Democrats experienced a powerful defeat in the elections of 1994, taking them out of the game till their resurgence in 2002 under Balkenende. Also the conservative current in the VVD failed, at first, to impose its views within the party. After the publication of the Telders report *Between Permissiveness and Paternalism*, centrist and progressive forces in the VVD once again rebutted the conservative Bolkestein wing of the party. In a party council meeting in 1996, the party cadre rebelled against the proposed conservative turn. The bone of contention was the notion of a moralizing government, as advocated by Bolkestein and the Telders think tank. 'If you mention the word moralism once more, you will leave the building covered in tar and feathers', one member famously snapped at the party leadership.[73] The VVD cadre, historically defined by its cultural opposition to pillarized religiosity, was not ready to embrace conservative morality.

In fact, the party was moving back to the centre also in socio-economic terms, it softened its stance as part of its response to the economic boom of the mid-nineties. Bolkestein became more and more marginalized, and the progressive liberal Dijkstal took over in 1998. Bolkestein left for Brussels to become a European Commissioner and vowed to continue his fight for free markets there. New Right intellectuals such as Kinneging and Cliteur left the VVD in protest. In 2000 they found the Edmund Burke Foundation, an influential conservative think tank that powerfully shaped the Dutch debate in the years to come. Significantly, Hendrik Jan Schoo spoke at its first meeting. Political scientists have argued that this shift to the centre and the failure of the VVD to cover its conservative flank provided the opportunity for the Fortuyn revolt.[74] Paraphrasing Walter Benjamin, one can argue that behind every populism, there is a failed revolution. In this instance, it was a failed palace revolution of the New Right in the mainstream parties.

With regards to the later development of the radical right-wing populism of Fortuyn and Wilders, there is something to be said for the interpretation that the (neo)conservative strand of the Dutch New Right had become so successful that it branched off into an independent (populist) current in the 2000s. Another perspective would be that the populist and establishment elements of the New Right together form one current, whose different components may clash and chafe on some terrains, while reinforcing each other on others. I have had limited opportunity to explore the adjustment of these ideas to the Dutch context. The next chapter deals more extensively with the process of adaptation.

Notes

1 Steinfels, *The Neoconservatives: The Origins of a Movement*. On neoconservatism, see also Jean-François Drolet, *American Neoconservatism: The Politics and Culture of a Reactionary Idealism* (London: Hurst, 2011); Francis Fukuyama, *America at the Crossroads: Democracy, Power, and the Neoconservative Legacy*, The Castle Lecture in Ethics, Politics and Economics (New Haven, CT: Yale University Press, 2006); Irving Kristol, *Neoconservatism: The Autobiography of an Idea* (New York: Free Press, 1995); Peter Steinfels, *The Neoconservatives: The Origins of a Movement* (New York: Simon and Schuster, 2013).

2 Andrew Hartman, *A War for the Soul of America: A History of the Culture Wars* (Chicago, IL: The University of Chicago Press, 2015).

3 Steinfels, *The Neoconservatives*; Vaïsse, *Neoconservatism*.

4 Fukuyama, *America at the Crossroads: Democracy, Power, and the Neoconservative Legacy*; Kristol, *Neoconservatism: The Autobiography of an Idea*.

5 Anne Norton, *Leo Strauss and the Politics of American Empire* (New Haven, CT: Yale University Press, 2004); Shadia B. Drury, *The Political Ideas of Leo Strauss* (New York: Palgrave Macmillan, 2005).

6 On the link between Schmitt and Strauss, see the dissertation by Wout Cornelissen, 'Politics between Philosophy and Polemics: Political Thinking and Thoughtful Politics in the Writing of Karl Popper, Leo Strauss, and Hannah Arendt' (Institute for Philosophy, Faculty of Humanities, Leiden University, 2014).

7 Edmund Burke, *Reflections on the Revolution in France* (London: Penguin, 2004), 118–19. See also Sternhell's discussion of Burke as an underappreciated founder of organic nationalism: Zeev Sternhell, *The Anti-Enlightenment Tradition* (New Haven, CT: Yale University Press, 2010), 422–5.

8 Leo Strauss, *Natural Right and History*, Charles R. Walgreen Foundation Lectures (Chicago, IL: University of Chicago Press, 1953), 318.

9 Fukuyama, *America at the Crossroads*, 30.

10 For an earlier collection of Dutch essays on neoconservatism, see Rob Kroes and Marc Chénetier (eds.), *Neo-Conservatism: Its Emergence in the USA and Europe* (Amsterdam: Free University Press, 1984). At the time of its publication, though, the influence of neoconservative ideas was still quite limited.

11 Sjoerd de Jong, *Een Wereld van Verschil: Wat is er Mis met Cultuurrelativisme?* (Amsterdam: De Bezige Bij, 2008); Huib Pellikaan and Sebastiaan van der Lubben, eds., *Ruimte op rechts? Conservatieve Onderstroom in de Lage Landen* (Utrecht: Het Spectrum, 2006). For a collection of texts written by Dutch supporters of neoconservatism, see Jaffe Vink and Chris Rutenfrans, *De Terugkeer van de Geschiedenis: Letter & Geest* (Amsterdam: Trouw/Augustus, 2005).

12 Jos de Beus, 'De Leegte op Links', *De Volkskrant*, 18 July 2003.

13 Neoconservative ideas are present in all of his books, but perhaps most explicitly in his 2002 lecture on the Dutch 'adversary culture': Frits Bolkestein, *Verzwelgt de Massacultuur de Liberale Democratie?*, Telderslezing; Winter 2001–2002 (Den Haag: Prof. Mr. B.M. Teldersstichting, 2002). See also his aforementioned book *The Intellectual Temptation* (De Intellectuele Verleiding), in which the grand dame of neoconservatism, the historian Gertrude Himmelfarb, has an important role. Finally, there is also his interview with the 'first age' neoconservative Nathan Glazer in *Seizing Control* (*Het Heft in Handen*), where Bolkestein displays an intimate acquaintance with the neoconservative literature of the time. See Frits Bolkestein, *Het Heft in Handen* (Amsterdam: Prometheus, 1995), 135–55.

14 Bart Jan Spruyt, 'In memoriam H.J. Schoo', in *Dwars en bewogen: afscheid van H.J. Schoo (1945–2007)*, ed. Arendo Joustra et al. (Amsterdam: Elsevier/De Volkskrant, 2007), 83–8.

15 Francis Fukuyama, 'The End of History?', *The National Interest*, no. 16 (1989): 3–18.

16 As the British weekly *The Economist* wrote in reaction to Fukuyama: "Islam he dismisses because it has little appeal, yet the faith may already have more true believers among its followers than communism ever had. The clash of gods and the clash of nations may prove just as destructive, and more enduring, than the clash of communism versus liberalism." Cited in Dominique Hope, 'End of History? Not so, Say Critics from Left and Right', *Sydney Morning Herald*, 13 December 1989.

17 Samuel P. Huntington, 'No Exit: The Errors of Endism', *The National Interest*, no. 17 (1989): 3–11.

18 Samuel P. Huntington, 'The Clash of Civilizations?', *Foreign Affairs* 72, no. 3 (1993): 22–49.

19 Ben Knapen, 'Het Einde van de Geschiedenis is Nabij', *NRC Handelsblad*, 12 August 1989.

20 Frits Bolkestein, *De Engel en het Beest* (Amsterdam: Prometheus, 1990), 139–40. Significantly, Bolkestein also expressed the hope that a new conservative ideology would arise in the Netherlands: 'In our restless society, in which freedom can lead to licentiousness, many long for community, spiritual values, social stability, even hierarchy'.

21 Matthew Kaminski, 'Pim's Misfortune', *Wall Street Journal*, 7 May 2002.

22 PVV, 'Een Nieuw-Realistische Visie', 2006, www.pvv.nl/30-visie/publicaties/707-een-nieuw-realistische-visie.html.

23 Ayaan Hirsi Ali, *Nomad: From Islam to America: A Personal Journey through the Clash of Civilizations* (New York: Simon & Schuster, 2010).

24 John Trumpbour, 'The Clash of Civilizations: Samuel P. Huntington, Bernard Lewis and the Remaking of the Post-Cold War World Order', in *The New Crusades: Constructing the Muslim Enemy*, ed. Emran Qureshi and Michael Anthony Sells (New York: Columbia University Press, 2003), 88–130.

25 Bernard Lewis, 'The Roots of Muslim Rage', *The Atlantic*, 1990, 48.

26 Gilles Kepel, *The War for Muslim Minds: Islam and the West* (Cambridge, MA: Belknap Press of Harvard University Press, 2004), 62–3.

27 Frits Bolkestein, 'De Integratie van Minderheden', *De Volkskrant*, 12 September 1991.

28 This is the basic argument of the literature on 'culturism'. On culturism in the Netherlands, see Willem Schinkel, *Imagined Societies: A Critique of Immigrant Integration in Western Europe* (Cambridge: Cambridge University Press, 2017); Marlou Schrover and Willem Schinkel, *The Language of Inclusion and Exclusion in Immigration and Integration*, Ethnic and Racial Studies (London: Routledge, 2014). For the analysis of a similar conservative discourse within the New Right see Amy Elizabeth Ansell, *New Right, New Racism: Race and Reaction in the United States and Britain* (Washington Square, NY: New York University Press, 1997); Anna Marie Smith, *New Right Discourse on Race and Sexuality: Britain, 1968–1990* (Cambridge: Cambridge University Press, 1994).

29 Vaïsse, *Neoconservatism*, 10.

30 Pim Fortuyn, *Tegen de Islamisering van onze Cultuur: Nederlandse Identiteit als Fundament* (Utrecht: Bruna, 1997), 108–9.

31 PVV, 'Klare Wijn', 2006, www.pvv.nl/index.php/component/content/article/30-publicaties/706-klare-wijn.html.

32 Ernst van den Hemel, '(Pro)Claiming Tradition: The "Judeo-Christian" Roots of Dutch Society and the Rise of Conservative Nationalism', in *Transformations of*

Religion and the Public Sphere: Postsecular Publics, ed. Rosi Braidotti et al. (London: Palgrave Macmillan, 2014), 27.

33 Hans Maarten van den Brink, 'VVD-Fractieleider Frits Bolkestein, Gymnasiast in De Politiek', *NRC Handelsblad*, 5 March 1994.

34 Paul Cliteur, 'Neo-Conservatisme en Religie: Irving Kristol als Nieuwe Beschermheer van het Liberale Denken?', *Civis Mundi* 35 (1996): 121.

35 Cliteur, 121.

36 Paul Cliteur, 'Conservatisme', in *De Ideologieën in Grote Lijnen*, ed. J. Weerdenburg (Utrecht: Studium Generale, 1994), 55–70.

37 Bolkestein, *Het Heft in Handen*, 33–46.

38 Frits Bolkestein, 'Hoe Europa zijn Zelfvertrouwen Verloor', *De Volkskrant*, 24 December 2009.

39 Paul Cliteur, 'Op Zoek naar het Bezielend Verband', *Justitiële Verkenningen* 20, no. 6 (1994): 9–37.

40 Paul Cliteur, *Moderne Papoea's. Dilemma's van Een Multiculturele Samenleving* (Amsterdam: Arbeiderspers, 2002), 29.

41 Dick Pels, *Een Zwak voor Nederland: Ideeën voor een Nieuwe Politiek* (Amsterdam: Anthos, 2005), 111.

42 Paul Cliteur, 'Het Europese Conservatisme als Reactie op de Franse Revolutie', in *Opstand Der Burgers: De Franse Revolutie na 200 Jaar*, ed. Servatius W. Couwenberg (Kampen: Kok Agora, 1988), 99–112.

43 Cliteur, *Moderne Papoea's*, 24.

44 Geert Wilders and Ayaan Hirsi Ali, 'Het is Tijd voor een Liberale Jihad', *NRC Handelsblad*, 12 April 2003.

45 Ian Buruma, *Murder in Amsterdam: Liberal Europe, Islam and the Limits of Tolerance* (New York: Penguin, 2007), 29.

46 Daniel Bell, *The Cultural Contradictions of Capitalism* (New York: Basic Books, 1976).

47 Cited in Marshall Berman, *All That Is Solid Melts into Air: The Experience of Modernity* (London: Verso, 1983), 21.

48 Thomas Frank, *What's the Matter with Kansas? How Conservatives Won the Heart of America*, 1st ed. (New York: Metropolitan Books/Henry Holt, 2004), 5.

49 Bolkestein, *Het Heft in Handen*, 132.

50 Dick Pels, 'Een Paar Apart: Fortuyn En Van Doorn Als Publieke Sociologen', in *J. A. A. van Doorn En de Nederlandse Sociologie: De Erfenis, Het Debat En de Toekomst*, ed. Jacques Hoof (Amsterdam: Pallas Publications, 2010), 93.

51 Hans-Georg Betz, *Radical Right-Wing Populism in Western Europe* (Basingstoke: Macmillan, 1994); Herbert Kitschelt and Anthony J. MacGann, *The Radical Right in Western Europe: A Comparative Analysis* (Ann Arbor, MI: The University of Michigan Press, 1995).

52 Karel Groenveld et al., *Tussen Vrijblijvendheid en Paternalisme: Bespiegelingen over Communitarisme, Liberalisme en Individualisering*, Geschrift/Prof. Mr. B.M. Telderstichting; 82 ('s-Gravenhage: Teldersstichting, 1995).

53 Cited in Marcel ten Hooven, 'Het Conservatieve Offensief', 9 September 1995.

54 Ten Hooven.

55 Steinfels, *The Neoconservatives*, 120.

56 Vaïsse, *Neoconservatism*, 77–8.

57 Hendrik Jan Schoo, *Republiek van Vrije Burgers: Het Onbehagen in de Democratie* (Amsterdam: Bert Bakker, 2008), 41.

58 Spruyt, 'In Memoriam, H.J. Schoo', 84.

59 In the introduction of a posthumous collection of Schoo's writings, the leading journalist Marc Chavannes describes Schoo as a 'humane, radical realist'. The label 'realism', also used by Bolkestein, Spruyt, Wilders and Rutte, is often used as a euphemism for conservatism in the Netherlands. See Schoo, *Republiek van Vrije Burgers*, 7.

60 Schoo, 44.
61 See Leo Lucassen and Jan Lucassen: "A crucial element of the Dutch 'pessimistic turn' was the belief broadly shared on both left and right that progressive elites were to blame for the rise of illiberal Islam in the Netherlands and for the problems caused by the descendants of immigrants." Leo Lucassen and Jan Lucassen, 'The Strange Death of Dutch Tolerance: The Timing and Nature of the Pessimist Turn in the Dutch Migration Debate', *Journal of Modern History* 87, no. 1 (2015): 76.
62 Rudolf Koole, 'De Ondergang van de Sociaal-Democratie? De PvdA in Vergelijkend en Historisch Perspectief', in *Jaarboek Documentatiecentrum Nederlandse Politieke Partijen 1992*, ed. Gerrit Voerman and Rudolf Koole (Groningen: Documentatiecentrum Nederlandse Politieke Partijen, 1993), 73–98.
63 Jan Willem Duyvendak, *The Politics of Home: Belonging and Nostalgia in Western Europe and the United States* (Basingstoke: Palgrave Macmillan, 2011); Leo Lucassen and Jan Lucassen, *Winnaars en verliezers: een nuchtere balans van vijfhonderd jaar immigratie* (Amsterdam: Bakker, 2011).
64 Jos de Beus, 'Een Derde Eeuw van Nederlands Conservatisme', in *Ruimte Op Rechts? Conservatieve Onderstroom in de Lage Landen*, ed. Huib Pellikaan and Sebastiaan van der Lubben (Utrecht: Spectrum, 2006), 329.
65 Martin Bosma, the ideologue of Geert Wilders, went on to use the neoconservative 'new class' theory as the core argument of his 2011 book, see Martin Bosma, *De Schijn-Élite van de Valsemunters: Drees, Extreem Rechts, de Sixties, Nuttige Idioten, Groep Wilders en Ik* (Amsterdam: Bert Bakker, 2011).
66 Schoo, *Republiek van Vrije Burgers*, 45.
67 Herman Vuijsje, *Correct: Weldenkend Nederland sinds de Jaren Zestig* (Amsterdam: Contact, 1997).
68 Paul Scheffer, 'Het Multiculturele Drama', *NRC Handelsblad*, 29 January 2000.
69 Scheffer's bestselling book *Land van Aankomst* (*Country of Arrival*) is a discussion of Dutch immigration and integration, through the lens of the debate in the US. Often without mentioning their neoconservative affiliations, the book features an impressive array of neoconservative authors such as Nathan Glazer, Daniel Patrick Moynihan, Dinesh D'Souza, Bernard Lewis, Niall Ferguson, Thomas Sowell, the early Francis Fukuyama, Hirsi Ali and Samuel Huntington. Scheffer has written the book as a dialogue between two camps, positioning himself in the middle, which makes it difficult to properly identify his views. See Paul Scheffer, *Het Land van Aankomst* (Amsterdam: De Bezige Bij, 2007). The book was later reworked into a PhD thesis, see Paul Scheffer, 'The Open Society and Its Immigrants: A Story of Avoidance, Conflict and Accommodation' (Tilburg, Tilburg University, 2010).
70 Schoo, *Republiek van Vrije Burgers: Het Onbehagen in de Democratie*, 66.
71 Piet de historicus Rooy, *Republiek van Rivaliteiten: Nederland sinds 1813* (Amsterdam: Mets & Schilt, 2002), 278.
72 Aukje van Roessel and Mark Kranenburg, 'Een Partij van Amateurpolitici: Het Intellectueel Gehalte van de VVD', *NRC Handelsblad*, 12 May 1990.
73 Tom de Zwart, 'VVD-Partijraad Verwijst Politiek Moralisme naar de Vestmaalt', *De Volkskrant*, 24 June 1996.
74 Huib Pellikaan, Sarah de Lange and Tom van der Meer, 'The Centre Does Not Hold: Coalition Politics and Party System Change in the Netherlands, 2002–12', *Government and Opposition* 53, no. 2 (2018): 231–55.

5   A complex backlash

One of the enduring controversies in European politics is the way progressive values have been mobilized and incorporated in right-wing agendas. The recent wave of radical right-wing movements in Europe has framed its anti-immigration politics as a defence of progressive ideals such as secularism, women's equality and gay rights. In a speech in a Rouen banlieue in 2012, the leader of the French Front National, Marine Le Pen, proposed the creation of a ministry of immigration and secularism, contending that Muslims threatened secularism as a pillar of the French republic. In that same vein, Le Pen quoted the feminist Simone de Beauvoir in a 2016 opinion piece, to support her argument that the European migration crisis could mean the end of hard-won women's rights.[1] In Sweden, a member of the radical right-wing Sweden Democrat party organized an unofficial gay pride parade in two immigrant neighbourhoods of Stockholm. The party leader Jimmie Åkesson contended that the 'Islamisation' of Sweden threatens the rights of sexual minorities.[2] On their part, the German AfD proclaims in their election campaigns 'that women's freedom is not negotiable', the Belgian Vlaams Belang pictured a woman dressed in bikini and burka, inviting voters to choose 'between freedom and Islam', while the current Lega Nord leader Matteo Salvini once asked immigrants applying for Italian citizenship about their views on women's rights.[3] Scholars argue that secularism, women's rights and gay rights have been instrumentalized for nationalist and anti-immigration agendas, a development that has been debated under terms such as sexual nationalism, homonationalism and femonationalism.[4]

The Netherlands has been at the forefront of this development. Politicians such as Frits Bolkestein, Pim Fortuyn, Ayaan Hirsi Ali and Geert Wilders did not express their opposition to Islam, immigration and multiculturalism in the language of traditional right-wing discourse, but rather with an appeal to endangered progressive values.[5] In a now famous interview in 2002, Pim Fortuyn – himself openly gay – declared that he did not want to 'have to repeat the emancipation of women and gays'.[6] His party, the LPF, presented its programme as the defence of Western modernity against Islam – in particular separation of church and state and progressive gender values – stating that 'emancipation is aimed at real freedom of choice for women and men'.[7]

As a result, scholars have had trouble interpreting the politics of Fortuyn. The Dutch political scientist Tjitske Akkermans noted how radical right-wing populists such as Fortuyn 'sometimes even trump the vested liberal parties by posing as the staunch and exclusive defenders of the Enlightenment and its liberal heritage'.[8] The leading populism scholar Margaret Canovan observed how 'his reasons for opposing Muslim immigration and multiculturalism found some echoes on the Left' and concluded that Fortuyn's agenda 'could not simply be dismissed as right-wing xenophobia'.[9] Others would contend that Fortuyn's views on immigration can be described as exactly that: 'we have to close off the country and force those present here to integrate at record speed; no integration means expulsion', Fortuyn once said.[10] Perhaps David Art strikes the right balance when he argues that Fortuyn clearly was the leader of an anti-immigrant party, but his homosexuality and the way he framed his message as a defence of Dutch tolerance shielded him to a certain degree from associations with more traditional radical-right parties.[11]

A similar ambiguity characterizes the major figures of the movement that preceded and accompanied Fortuyn, or that followed in his wake. Ayaan Hirsi Ali presented her criticism of Islam as motivated by the defence of Enlightenment values and the emancipation of Muslim women. Paul Cliteur and Frits Bolkestein argued that the universalism of the Enlightenment, embodied in the Universal Declaration of Human Rights represents a yardstick that allows us to distinguish superior from inferior cultures.[12] The assassinated filmmaker and derisive columnist Theo van Gogh celebrated freedom of speech and attacked Muslim immigrants as 'a fifth column', 'believers that see gays as unclean, just like menstruating women, and unbelievers'.[13] The right-wing Minister of Immigration Rita Verdonk oversaw the introduction of an integration exam that confronted immigrants with pictures of topless women on the beach and kissing gay people on the street. It prompted the remark from philosopher Judith Butler that 'a certain conception of freedom is invoked precisely as a rationale and instrument for certain practices of coercion'.[14] Geert Wilders opposed immigration from Muslim countries since 'it expels Jews and gays and flushes decades of women's rights down the toilet'.[15] As the political scientist Koen Vossen points out in his analysis of the ideology of Geert Wilders' right-wing populist Party for Freedom (PVV):

> The PVV advocates the right to abortion, euthanasia and embryo selection, while the party presents itself as a fierce defender of women and gay emancipation in the face of the advance of an 'intolerant and backward Islam'. It is hard to imagine another national populist party offering a resolution in parliament to allow gay soldiers to wear their military outfit in a gay parade.[16]

The Dutch revolt, legitimated with an appeal to endangered progressive values, was from the very beginning ambiguous in its nature, rendering a clear political characterization more difficult. As a result of which, two completely opposing descriptions of the revolt have been able to peacefully coexist. On the one hand, there are analyses that portray the turnaround as a conservative restoration, while others stress the progressive character of the revolt.

The Dutch revolt: progressive or conservative?

In an essay published in 2006, the Dutch political theorist Jos de Beus wrote of 'the return of conservatism in the Netherlands'. After extensive review of both the intellectual landscape and studies of popular opinion, he attested to 'the implosion of the progressive consensus from the 1960s and the shift towards a new conservative consensus'.[17] De Beus prophesized a 'paradigm change' and a new 'period of conservative hegemony', not seen in the Netherlands since before the Second World War.[18] Chiming in with de Beus, the conservative journalist Hendrik Jan Schoo triumphantly proclaimed in *de Volkskrant* that 'the Netherlands has entered a conservative era'. 'The turnaround came in 2002', Schoo noted, 'when Fortuyn emerged practically out of the blue. Upon closer consideration, his appearance isn't simply an electoral whim, but an event marking the closure of the progressive era after the Second World War'.[19]

Exemplary of the contrasting vision is the prominent sociologist Jan Willem Duyvendak, who has written on the Dutch case in his book on European nativism, *The Politics of Home*.[20] From this point of view, the political polarization in the Netherlands stems from a 'progressive majority' opposing a 'minority seen as conservative-religious'.[21] For scholars departing from this line of reasoning, the rise of populism represents a 'progressive politics of exclusion' and is 'mistakenly analysed as a shift toward conservatism'.[22]

The idea of a purely conservative restoration comes up short because it ignores the innovative progressive elements (or appropriations, depending on one's perspective) that set the discourse of this conservative movement apart from more traditional conservative ideology. Problematic about the progressive reading is that it employs a limited definition of progressiveness, which is confined to 'secularization and the resulting progressive views concerning homosexuality, gender, and family values'.[23] The same is true for Duyvendak's statement that 'the conservative position is not being politically articulated'.[24] Also conservatism is solely considered in terms of sexual morality. The Dutch revolt is thus recast as progressive or secular intolerance towards religious minorities such as Muslims and orthodox Christians.[25] The problem with this view is that ideologies such as progressivism and conservatism cover a much broader terrain than sexual morality. On issues such as law and order, immigration, social security, the environment, cultural policy, internationalism, labour relations and development aid, the Dutch revolt has been more classically conservative in orientation, and actively opposed progressive ideas. While Schoo had a tendency to overstate the conservative character of the revolt, he was certainly right when he wrote in *De Volkskrant* that Fortuyn had been a catalyst, who 'forced a break in the political-intellectual climate' and 'marked an intellectual reassessment' of the progressive legacy of the 1960s.[26]

The conservative moment

In fact, the political breakthrough of Fortuyn formed part of a remarkable conservative intellectual resurgence. Around the turn of the millennium, the intellectuals that formed part of the conservative undercurrent of the 1990s came out of the closet and boisterously presented themselves on the stage of Dutch public opinion. In February 2001, a hotly debated essay appeared in the Dutch newspaper of note, *NRC Handelsblad*. It boldly declared that 'the conservative moment' had come, opening a lively debate on Dutch conservatism that lasted well into 2006. The author was Joshua Livestro, the speechwriter of Frits Bolkestein, then European Commissioner and former leader of the right-wing liberal party (VVD). According to Livestro, the 'ideological legacy of the 1960s' had created a 'superficial political correctness and a deeply felt crisis of old certainties'. The expansion of the welfare state since the 1960s and the resulting individualization had undermined 'core institutions such as marriage, church, voluntary associations, the school and the universities'.[27] Livestro observed that conservatives were spread among the different Dutch political parties, in particular the right-wing liberals (VVD) and the Christian Democrats (CDA). Within these parties, the conservative wing was a minority. For this reason, the conservative mobilization in the 1990s had failed. Livestro called on these divided Dutch conservatives to rally behind a shared banner.

Two months earlier, together with the Reformed conservative Bart Jan Spruyt, former VVD intellectual Andreas Kinneging and the lawyer Michiel Visser, Livestro had founded an influential conservative think tank: the Edmund Burke Foundation. This conservative think tank had close ties to the VVD and the CDA and was founded to promote the New Right agenda in these parties, through 'a politics of ideas'.[28] The foundation was inspired by the model of the American conservative think tank The Heritage Foundation. Prominent conservative Christian Democrat politicians such as former Prime Minister (1977–1982) Dries van Agt, Finance Minister (1982–1989) Onno Ruding and his former aide Hans Hillen were trustees. Paul Cliteur became part of the recommending committee, and his colleague Afshin Ellian an honorary member. Bart Jan Spruyt, then director of the Edmund Burke Foundation, wrote the book *In Praise of Conservatism* (*Lof van het Conservatisme*) in 2003, where he made the case for a conservative movement in the Netherlands. In that same year, Spruyt published the *Conservative Manifesto* (*Het Conservatief Manifest*) with Michiel Visser, amid much consternation. The manifesto did not mince words:

> The 'Left' has brought our country an endless array of problems and now it is time for the 'Right' to rediscover its roots to repair the damage. Only conservatism is capable of that. Conservatism is the archenemy of leftist, progressive thought. It rejects political correctness, multiculturalism, and the moral relativism that the 1960s have brought us.[29]

The text contained the by now familiar New Right formula: the fusion of neoliberal and (neo)conservative views, a strategy centred on a politics of ideas and the indictment of a 'failing political and societal elite'. Echoing the free market aspirations of the conservative wings of the CDA and VVD, Spruyt and Visser called for a minimal state that restricts itself to its 'core tasks': defence and law and order. According to the authors, the welfare state had turned the Dutch people into 'weak, dependent herd animals'. Unemployment benefits sentenced people to 'a life of idleness', the minimum wage needed to be eliminated or lowered, taxes cut and the labour market flexibilized. This free market offensive on the Dutch welfare state and the corporatist labour market was combined with a bold conservative agenda on crime and immigration. The manifesto saw cultural relativism as a principal source of the problem:

> Conservatives choose for Dutch civilization as part of Western civilization, and refuse to capitulate for cultures with values that are fundamentally at odds with ours. Muslims residing here can make use of freedom of religion and the freedom of association that Western civilization, in contrast with Islamic culture, offers to its citizens. But they have to adjust to us, not the other way around. So no sharia in the Netherlands, no subordination of women and girls, no honour killings and blood feuds, no introduction of Islamic holidays.[30]

It would be a mistake, however, to read the manifesto simply as a protectionist impulse to defend Dutch culture as it is. Paradoxically, in the name of defending Dutch culture, the manifesto proposes a sweeping overhaul of Dutch society. A 'radical change of mentality' is needed to combat crime and integrate newcomers. Here the neoliberal and (neo)conservative agenda converge: by retrenching the welfare state, the Dutch will learn to be 'tougher and more mature, and in so doing offer better resistance to enemies'. Eliminating the social support of the state will mean a restoration of Dutch family values and community life. Likewise, when it comes to crime, the authors locate the ultimate source of the problem in the high divorce rate in the Netherlands and the 'crisis in the family' resulting in 'a series of social pathologies'. Similar conservative discontent can be found in the concluding paragraph, where the manifesto called for undoing the 'one-sided upbringing focused on independence and self-assertion, standing up for one's "own opinion", feelings and sentiments, the upbringing that is the legacy of the 1960s and 1970s'.[31]

The ambiguity of the manifesto is typical for Dutch conservative discourse. The same paradox is present in the writings of Bolkestein and Fortuyn. If we scratch the mere surface of conservative appeals to defend Dutch culture, we discover a radical ambition to reform and do away with elements of that very same culture. Also the accusation of cultural and moral relativism levelled at progressive baby boomers should be taken with a grain of salt. As the sociologist Kees Schuyt argued in response to the manifesto, baby boomers were the very opposites of relativists, making them not unlike the 'conservative hotheads' who wrote the manifesto.[32] The protest movements of the 1960s had a very clear conception of Dutch culture and Dutch morality. It just happens to be an egalitarian perspective that Dutch conservatives do not agree with. This is not unknown to conservatives themselves. Schoo has written intelligently on what he considered the 'absolutist' egalitarian ethos of the 1960s and 1970s.[33] The debate on cultural and moral 'relativism' can better be understood as a hegemonic conflict between competing conceptions of Dutch culture and morality. On one side there is a more cosmopolitan, egalitarian and progressive notion of Dutchness stemming from the 1960s and 1970s. On the other, a more nationalist, authoritarian and conservative idea of Dutchness gaining ground in the 1990s. The American conservative Pat Buchanan famously described the US culture wars as a 'battle for the soul of America'. The Dutch culture war, although less grand in scale, has a similar character.[34]

High and low conservatism

There is a close and yet tense relationship between this conservative intellectual current and the right-wing populism of Fortuyn and Wilders. From the mid-1990s onwards, Fortuyn had embraced a comparable New Right fusionist agenda, combining neoliberal with neoconservative views. His 1995 book *The Orphaned Society* (*De Verweesde Samenleving*) was praised by Spruyt in no uncertain terms as 'the most conservative book since the early twentieth century'. Bart Jan Spruyt had regular personal contact with Fortuyn, and visited him at his home on the night that Fortuyn embarked on his political career.[35] Spruyt described Fortuyn as the 'originator of the conservative moment' and the Edmund Burke Foundation hailed Fortuyn as 'conservative of the year' in 2002. At the same time, Spruyt kept his distance from Fortuyn's more liberated views on popular morality in general and sexuality in particular. He described Fortuyn's writing as 'an explosive blend of libertinism, liberalism and socialism'. Fortuyn's populism, Spruyt later commented, was a 'vulgarized' conservatism for the Dutch masses, and it would be a mistake to think that the resurgence of Dutch conservatism could derive from a similar source, filled with 'rancour and resentment'.[36] Spruyt described his engagement with right-wing populism in terms of a tension between 'high' and 'low' conservatism.[37]

A similar tense relationship existed between Bart Jan Spruyt and Geert Wilders. Wilders had contacted Spruyt after the publication of Spruyt's book *In Praise of Conservatism* and the two had met several times to discuss possible cooperation. Wilders referred in 2003 to Spruyt's conservative manifesto as a guideline for a more right-wing course for the VVD, leading ultimately to Wilders' collision with the leadership of the party and his breakaway in 2004.[38] Meanwhile, Bart Jan Spruyt had come to the sobering conclusion that the prospects for a conservative breakthrough in the mainstream parties were limited. The problem was that these parties also had progressive wings that neutralized conservative efforts, a legacy of Dutch pillarization. Traditional party identification prevented a broader realignment of Dutch politics in a single conservative and progressive camp. 'The courage to overcome old differences and to struggle at the front formed by external and internal enemies, is barely present in the Netherlands', Spruyt concluded in an essay from 2005. He concluded with a call to conservatives to ready themselves to support 'an outsider with real credibility'.[39]

The name of that outsider was hardly a secret. In January 2005, Spruyt had accompanied Wilders on a weeklong tour of American (neo)conservative think tanks. Spruyt decided to become the ideologue and number two on the list of Geert Wilders' new Party for Freedom. He wrote the party's first manifesto and political programme. It resulted in a huge crisis at the Edmund Burke Foundation, and the departure of the Christian Democrat trustees. The conservative think tank never really recovered. Spruyt's hope was to create a fusionist conservative party inspired by the Republican Party in the US. When push came to shove, Wilders made a tactical choice for a more populist course. He decided to centre his programme on opposition to Islam and immigration, eliminating references to hierarchy and education while softening his socio-economic profile. In August 2006, Spruyt left the PVV 'heavily disappointed'. His hopes that the PVV could accommodate a broad conservative movement had been thwarted by Wilders' 'egomania'. Martin Bosma, another Dutch conservative with American inspirations, now became the principal ideologue and speechwriter of the PVV.[40]

The breakthrough of Fortuyn and Wilders formed part of a broader conservative resurgence. At the same time, this conservatism had a fundamentally ambivalent character. On the one hand, leading conservative critics blamed the progressive ideals of the 1960s and 1970s for the crisis of authority, for political correctness, for failed immigration and integration policies and for the erosion of Dutch national identity. On the other hand, conservatives presented themselves as the only true defenders of the Dutch progressive legacy against the threat of Islam. Conservatives claimed these accomplishments as proof of Western civilizational superiority. Those disagreeing with that characterization were derided as cultural relativists. As a result, the Dutch revolt cannot simply be portrayed as a conservative attempt to turn back time. Nor is it merely a defence of progressive Dutch culture from the perceived encroachment of conservative Islam, since it is partly a conservative attack on elements of that same progressive culture. In this chapter, an alternative interpretation is proposed.

A complex backlash

The account offered here is inspired to an important degree on Angela McRobbie's work on post-feminism, and elaborates on her thesis of a complex conservative backlash.[41] When the New Right emerged in the US, it took aim against the New Left, against the counterculture and the new social movements: the civil rights movement, the peace movement, the environmentalist movement and the gay rights movement. But above all, it took aim against feminism. It is therefore no coincidence that one of the more extensive analyses of the conservative countercurrent was developed on the terrain of women's rights. American feminist scholars formulated the 'backlash thesis', defined by Susan Faludi as a 'concerted conservative response to challenge the achievements of feminism'.[42] She derived the notion of 'backlash politics' from the political scientist Seymour Martin Lipset. He had used the term to identify a conservative anti-establishment politics, 'a reaction by groups which are declining in a felt sense of importance, influence and power, as a result of a secular endemic change in society', whereupon they 'seek to reverse or stem the direction of change through political means'.[43] A more contemporary and prominent account of this phenomenon is Thomas Frank's *What's the Matter with Kansas*. It describes 'the Great Backlash' as a style of anti-establishment conservatism that manages to garner popular support for free market economics by foregrounding conservative cultural discontent.[44]

Angela McRobbie has attempted to translate the idea of a conservative backlash to the European and British context, where the conservative counter-tendency bears to a lesser degree the stamp of a traditional, Christian conservatism. In her writing, McRobbie proposes a more dialectical understanding of the back-lash, acknowledging its modernizing elements: the conservative countercurrent not only serves as a resistance to feminism and is not simply oriented at turning back time. The conservative response provides its own synthesis, it incorporates the more moderate and generally accepted forms of women's emancipation, in order to be able to more effectively resist the broader claims of the feminist movement as outdated and defunct. McRobbie puts forward 'a complexification of the backlash thesis':

> [It] positively draws on and invokes feminism as that which can be taken into account, to suggest that equality is achieved, in order to install a whole repertoire of new meanings which emphasize that it is no longer needed, it is a spent force. [...] [It] encompasses the existence of feminism as at some level transformed into a form of Gramscian common sense, while also fiercely repudiated, indeed almost hated. The 'taken into accountness' permits all the more thorough dismantling of feminist politics and the dis-crediting of the occasionally voiced need for its renewal.[45]

An illustrative example is the statement on feminism from Margaret Thatcher in 1982: 'The battle for women's rights has been largely won. The days when they were demanded and discussed in strident tones should be gone forever'.[46] Here, the affirmation of women's rights is used to attack feminism. My thesis is that a similar 'complex' conservative backlash has occurred in the Netherlands with respect to the progressive legacy of the 1960s and 1970s. The conservative co-option of progressive values in the Netherlands had the same paradoxical quality that McRobbie ascribes to the backlash against feminism. Conservatives presented progressive values as self-evident and inseparable elements of Dutch culture. Something that could be taken into account. In so doing, progressive accomplishments were disconnected from the political movements that initiated and pushed for these changes. The movements of the 1960s and 1970s and the generation that took part in them, the baby boomers, found themselves, in McRobbie's words, 'fiercely repudiated, indeed almost hated'. While progres-sive values were thus assimilated in a new conservative discourse, the ideal of progress itself was discarded. The idea of a fluctuating but persistent progression on the field of social equality and civil liberties has been replaced with cultural essentialism. The Netherlands, to the very core of its being, was enlightened, tolerant and socially just. Progressive values were culturalized in conservative discourse. They were given a static quality, presented as inbuilt elements of Dutch culture, something that must be conserved and defended from threats from without. In other words, the Dutch emancipatory project was finished. The only ones still in need of emancipation were minorities, who had to adapt to Dutch cultural norms and values, seeing that emancipation is inherent in Dutch culture, and cannot be acquired through another cultural tradition.

A crucial element in the discourse of the Dutch New Right is the idea that emancipation is a done deal, that equality has been achieved. This extends both to the socio-economic and the socio-cultural domain. Fortuyn's plea for neo-liberalism, as we have seen in the previous chapter, is not the classic Hayekian argument that real equality is unachievable (or leads to totalitarianism) and that inequality is a force of nature. To the contrary, Fortuyn argues in his inaugural lecture in 1991 that emancipation is complete: the citizen 'goes his own emancipated way' and no longer needs the welfare state. Fortuyn even references the 1970s slogan the 'political decolonization of the citizen', and proposes that the final hurdle in the project of emancipation is the liberation from welfare state paternalism.[47] His 1992 book *To the People of the Netherlands* (*Aan het Volk van Nederland*) is a celebration of the emancipated citizen, who eagerly embraces the free market as the sign of his liberation.[48] A similar appeal to achieved emancipation can be found in the reports of the VVD think tank. The VVD presented neo-liberalism as following naturally from workers' emancipation:

> The welfare state marks the citizen as weak and dependent. He moves in a climate of state paternalism and welfare patronage. The workers' movement and other emancipatory currents have always seen their historical task as transitory. The switch to a 'guarantor state' is now desirable.[49]

On the socio-cultural domain, the emancipation of women and gays was culturalized by Dutch conservatives. It was increasingly presented as a national achievement lying somewhere in the past, a core value of Dutch culture. The single most important reference is Fortuyn's 1997 book *Against the Islamisation of Our Culture* (*Tegen de Islamisering van Onze Cultuur*). Here, Fortuyn engages in a passionate defence of the emancipation of women and homosexuals, described as a 'cultural achievement' of Dutch society as a whole: 'It should be crystal clear that the equality of men and women, whatever their sexual orientation, is one of the core values of our society, which cannot be tampered with. We have fought hard enough to achieve it'.[50] The challenge that remained was to defend this cultural achievement against the threat of Islamization. This image of emancipation as a cultural achievement did not, in fact, fully concur with Dutch reality at the time. A sizeable element of the Dutch population was still deeply uncomfortable with gay sexuality. Dutch women were still significantly underrepresented in politics, business and culture. Moreover, many politicians on the right were reluctant to embrace progressive sexual morality at the moment of Fortuyn's intervention. Most significantly, the conservative wing of the VVD led by Bolkestein opposed gay marriage in 1996 and

1997.[51] This changed after the spectacular success of Pim Fortuyn. Both conservative Christian Democrats and the conservative wing of the VVD adopted Fortuyn's discourse of achieved emancipation.

In 2003, the Christian Democrat Minister of Social Affairs Aart Jan de Geus declared the emancipation of white Dutch women to be complete. 'The emancipation of women is one of the most important achievements in the 20th century', he said. 'The presence of women on almost all places in Dutch society is self-evident'.[52] An emancipation policy for Dutch women was no longer needed, De Geus declared, only minorities were in need of emancipation. The curious result was that right-wing parties now became the most ardent propagator of emancipation, almost exclusively for Muslim women. This position was epitomized by Ayaan Hirsi Ali's calls for a third wave of feminism.[53] Hirsi Ali framed emancipation as an ideological battle for the minds of Muslims, who needed to convert from Islam and choose for the West as free individuals. The paradoxical result was that Muslim feminists were silenced in the public debate, since they were accused of being controlled by a patriarchal religion. At the same time, white Dutch feminists were told that compared with Saudi Arabia, sexism in the Netherlands did not amount to much, and their feminism was outdated. In the years that followed, the New Right managed to almost seamlessly combine a discourse on the threat of feminization to Dutch society with a patriotic self-image of achieved emancipation.[54]

On the one hand, there is an instrumental quality to this conservative adoption of progressive values. The conservative interest in progressive values such as women's emancipation and gay rights is seen by many as largely a function of their opposition to Islam and does not seem to have much salience on its own. As Tjitske Akkermans argued, 'the paradoxical defence of liberalism is exclusively related to anti-immigration policies'.[55] Internationally, scholars have pointed to a similar political trend in which women's rights and gay rights have been instrumentalized for conservative and nationalist political agendas, a development that has been debated under terms such as sexual nationalism, homonationalism and femonationalism.[56] On the other hand, the depth of the progressive wave of the 1960s and the absence of a convincing conservative reaction in the 1970s and 1980s has made such a contradictory politics almost a necessity for any conservative politics in the Netherlands. Moreover, politicians such as Fortuyn were themselves a product of the sexual revolution. Whether the label conservatism still applies when dealing with such a composite and contradictory form of conservatism is a legitimate question. To answer that question, we will need to consider more extensively the nature of conservatism.

A situational perspective on conservatism

In her book *Backlash*, the feminist and *New York Times* journalist Susan Faludi described the conservative campaign against women's emancipation in the US. She referred to the philosopher Theodor Adorno and his use of the term 'pseudoconservatives' to describe the movement conservatism of the New Right. Rather than defending a prevailing order as conservatives are traditionally wont to do, these anti-establishment movements 'perceive themselves as social out-casts rather than guardians of the status quo', Faludi observed.[57] A prominent school of interpretation of conservative thought, however, argues that such an anti-establishment practice is not the exception within the conservative tradition, but rather the rule.

This 'situational' interpretation of conservatism can be found in the work of authors such as Samuel Huntington, Karl Mannheim, Corey Robin, and the Dutch historians Hermann von der Dunk and Ernst Kossmann. The pre-dominant sentiment of the conservative tradition, according to these authors, is not characterized by a stiff pursuit of conservation. Conservatism is seen as a contingent and innovative politics that annexes and appropriates the ideas of the progressive opponent at regular intervals. With a feeling for dialectics proper to a German emigré, Von der Dunk describes this as 'the dual-aspect of any current of thought, which is always at the same time, continuation and negation of the current that it opposes'.[58] Conserva-tism, according to these authors, is quintessentially a backlash ideology, a philosophy of struggle.

The *locus classicus* of that argument is Karl Mannheim's famous study of conservative thought.[59] Mannheim studied German Romantic conservatism as an intellectual reaction to the perceived threat of the radical Enlightenment thought of the French Revolution. Mannheim made a helpful distinction between traditionalism and conservatism. Traditionalism is the universal psychological tendency to cling to familiar and existing modes of life. In a similar way, one can develop a psychological attachment to an old pair of jeans, or a piece of fur-niture: it is largely intuitive and does not have an elaborate logic to it. (In fact, the Dutch *Van Dale* dictionary defines conservatism as 'the attachment to that what exists', which in Mannheim's terms would be traditionalism rather than conservatism.)

Conservatism, in contrast, represents a politicization of traditionalism. Con-servatism is the product of a specific historic situation, the moment when a perceived threat arises to established ways of life. In the late eighteenth century, that threat is formed by the progressive, rationalist thought of the French Revolution and bourgeois capitalism. Old traditions among the nobil-ity, the peasants and the petty bourgeois are now taken up and inscribed on the banner of counter-revolutionary forces: community against society, family against contract, intuition against reason, spiritual against material experience. What was largely intuitive and submerged is now laid bare by reflection and fought for. 'Conservatism first becomes conscious and reflective when other ways of life and thought appear on the scene, against which it is compelled to take up arms in the ideological struggle', Mannheim writes.[60] Paradoxically, in this process, Romantic conservatism developed from an inarticulate sentiment to a rationally elaborated doctrine. It became increasingly disconnected from its feudal, agrarian social origins, and developed over time into a modern, urban current of thought. Mannheim stresses the contradictory aspects of this countermovement:

> No antithesis escapes conditioning by the thesis it sets out to oppose, and Romanticism suffered the same paradoxical fate; its structure was fundamentally conditioned by the attitudes and methods of that very movement of Enlightenment in opposition to which it originally developed.[61]

Crucial to Mannheim's argument is that conservative philosophy is a tactical style of thought, a highly flexible ideology, defined more by what it opposes than by what it positively stands for. This tactical flexibility has allowed for a wide variety of responses to political challenges, ranging from prudent reform to counter-revolutionary agitation.

The American conservative Samuel Huntington expanded on Mannheim in his 1957 essay *Conservatism as an Ideology*. Writing in a time when the New Deal reigned supreme and the conservative movement was condemned to the margins of US political life, Huntington was brooding on a new conservative strategy. Building on the argument of Karl Mannheim, Huntington defined conservatism as 'the ideology arising out of a distinct but recurring type of historical situation in which a fundamental challenge is directed at established institutions and in which the supporters of those institutions employ the conservative ideology in their defense'.[62] The author was not merely making a scholarly point. The essay contained a critique of the then emerging US conservative movement – 'New Conservatism' – for being too traditional and alienated from modern US institutions: 'Their rejection of the existing American political and social system makes it impossible for them to be truly conservative', Huntington suggested.[63]

Because of the overwhelming political consensus of the 1950s, progressives could not be portrayed as a political threat giving rise to a conservative politics. Huntington was convinced of 'the sterility of a conservative defence of one segment of American society against another segment'. Only an external threat would provide the conditions for a conservative rebirth: 'The only threat extensive and deep enough to elicit a conservative response today is the challenge of communism and the Soviet Union to American society as a whole'.[64] Naming, accentuating and exaggerating this threat would make it possible for conservatives to appoint themselves as defenders and spokespersons for US society as a whole. For that to occur, it would be necessary for conservatives to co-opt and defend progressive values, and vice versa:

> As an island of plenty and freedom in a straitened world, America has much to defend. American institutions however, are liberal, popular and democratic. They can best be defended by those who believe in liberalism, popular control and democratic government. Just as aristocrats were the conservatives in Prussia in 1820 and slave-owners were the conservatives in the South in 1850, so the liberals must be the conservatives in America today.[65]

For Huntington, this conservative defence of liberalism implies that liberalism in the American sense (progressivism in the European sense) must discontinue its emancipatory agenda, and become conservative:

> Historically, American liberals have been idealists, pressing forward toward the goals of greater freedom, social equality, and more meaningful democracy. The articulate exposition of a liberal ideology was necessary to convert others to liberal ideas and to reform existing institutions continuously along liberal lines. Today, however, the greatest need is not so much the creation of more liberal institutions as the successful defense of those which already exist. This defense requires American liberals to lay aside their liberal ideology and to accept the values of conservatism for the duration of the threat. [...] To continue to expound the philosophy of liberalism simply gives the enemy a weapon with which to attack the society of liberalism.[66]

Huntington concludes by stating that 'current conflict, rather than ancient dogma, will yield a "New Conservatism" which is truly conservative'.[67] The essay is a powerful exposition of the modernizing element within US conservatism, which Huntington claims to be the 'true' spirit of conservatism.

The godfather of neoconservatism, Irving Kristol, defined neoconservatism in very similar situational terms. He would famously characterize the movement as 'liberals mugged by reality'. In a retrospective essay from 2003 titled *The Neoconservative Persuasion*, Kristol defined the 'historical task and political purpose of neoconservatism' as the conversion of 'the Republican party, and American conservatism in general, against their respective wills, into a new kind of conservative politics suitable to governing a modern democracy'.[68] In his view, neoconservatism is an intellectual undercurrent that surfaces only intermittently, not an ideologically consistent movement but rather a conjunctural response to a specific historical situation. He presented it as an attempt at modernizing conservatism. This conservatism was in 'the American grain': 'hopeful not lugubrious; forward-looking, not nostalgic; and its general tone is cheerful, not grim or dyspeptic'. Kristol added that there 'is nothing like neoconservatism in Europe', and that 'Europeans think it absurd to look to the United States for lessons in political innovation'. On these last two points, Kristol was clearly mistaken.

A conservatism 'in the Dutch grain'

Neoconservative inspirations were at the basis of a comparable renewal of conservatism in the Netherlands, albeit in a rather diffused and chaotic manner. Dutch conservatives have appointed themselves as the militant defenders of progressive values and liberal Western civilization. They portrayed progressive elites – hesitant to claim 'the superiority of Western civilization' and unable to identify its 'core values' – as incapable of defending themselves. Bart Jan Spruyt has formulated the argument for a conservative takeover of liberalism most clearly. In *The Future of the Polis* (*De Toekomst van de Stad*), an essay inspired by a book by Leo Strauss, Spruyt endorses the plea of the neoconservative Hillel Fradkin for a 'newer and stronger liberalism', able to protect liberal society from external and internal threats. Spruyt argued that liberalism is not able to generate a moral framework to defend itself. The 'premodern' contribution of conservatism is needed 'to prevent liberalism from suicide'. While 'liberalism has brought the world great achievements', while it 'is a dominant political current' and 'has provided our society an unambiguous consensus', a recourse to conservative principles is needed to safeguard it.[69]

Dutch conservatives in the 1990s and 2000s were presented with a very similar predicament as the American conservatives in the 1950s and 1960s. To paraphrase Huntington: Dutch institutions are progressive, secular and egalitarian. They can best be defended by those who believe in progressive values, secularism and egalitarianism. The conservative social democrat Jos de Beus forcefully presented this argument. De Beus criticized Dutch conservatives inspired by US neoconservatism – such as Spruyt and Kinneging – for not being American enough. They were still too traditional and sceptical in their views, too far removed from the dominant values of Dutch society. Their conservatism with its

> gloomy vision of man, its tragic philosophy of history, its sceptical approach to politics and human reason, its fear of the tyrannical state, its preference for a hierarchical society, held together as an organic community by religion, authority and discipline,

could never succeed in the Netherlands. The 'optimism, commercialism and even democratic participation' of American conservatism were needed. Even though De Beus acknowledged there were limits to 'this [American] renewal of conservatism', he insisted that Dutch conservatism 'could only gain ground in the Netherlands by discarding certain elements of European conservatism, and incorporating certain elements of American neoconservatism'.[70]

Also other Dutch conservatives pointed to neoconservative inspirations as a way to modernize Dutch conservatism. Hendrik Jan Schoo, as editor-in-chief of the right-wing weekly *Elsevier*, an important influence on Fortuyn in the mid-nineties, noted approvingly that the Fortuyn revolt 'can well be compared with American neoconservatism'.[71] In both the US and the Netherlands, Schoo observed a modernized, adapted conservatism that resisted the ideals of the 1960s, stresses the agency of ordinary people to determine their own fate without the welfare state, while pleading for a moral revival. In similar fashion, Paul Cliteur pointed out that in the Dutch 'post-revolutionary' context where progressive values were dominant, a moderate Burkean conservatism was rather unconvincing:

> Burkean thought is at its most convincing when one can still avert impending catastrophe. It is a wholly different matter when one writes and thinks in a post-revolutionary phase in which the revolution has brought things that are

not to be considered an improvement. In Europe, just like in the United States, we live in a post-revolutionary phase. May '68 is in power. [...] That is the context in which American neoconservatives such as Irving Kristol, Norman Podhoretz, but also the Dutch Edmund Burke Foundation have had to operate.[72]

Neoconservative ideas had been circulating among Dutch conservative intellectuals throughout the 1990s, but they gained dramatically in visibility in the 2000s. While politics in the Netherlands is traditionally considered dull and uneventful, this changed after 9/11. The attacks on the Twin Towers played a large role in providing the idea of an external threat to Dutch society, in addition to the internal threat posed by the Dutch elite culture of accommodation. As Bart Jan Spruyt argued: 'There is the outside threat of the anti-Western ideology of Islam and its political-theological effects. There is the paralysing relativism that threatens us from within, and that always results in containment and accommodation'.[73] Pim Fortuyn, who introduced himself to an American journalist as 'the Samuel Huntington of Dutch politics', had declared a 'cold war against Islam' in a column published in the week before 9/11. 'The role of communism' in serving as a threat to Western norms and values, Fortuyn argued, had been 'taken over by Islam'.[74] Fortuyn called for

a war with arguments and words; not a hot, armed conflict – an ideological battle with Islam, with the goal of convincing its adherents that they are better off when they loyally and royally embrace the core norms and values of modernity.[75]

After the 9/11 attacks, Fortuyn's electoral fortunes took flight and he successfully campaigned on a platform to forcefully assimilate Muslim immigrants.

During this period, neoconservatism attained influential adherents in the Dutch press. From 2001 till 2006, journalists Jaffe Vink and Chris Rutenfrans used a weekly opinion section of the national newspaper *Trouw* to promote what they called 'the neoconservative revolution'. Vink described the neoconservatives as 'the revolutionaries of our time' who 'have taken over the banner of the progressives'.[76] Meanwhile, Paul Cliteur had developed into an influential commentator on television, and had a major impact with his critique of cultural relativism and Islam, in his 2002 book *Modern Papuans* (*Moderne Papoea's*). His colleague Afshin Ellian started writing columns for *NRC Handelsblad,* where he popularized the neoconservative critique of Islam. Their befriended writer and columnist Leon de Winter published typically unsubtle neoconservative pamphlets, such as *The Enemy: An Essay* (*De Vijand: Een Opstel*) in 2004.[77] In this period, Schoo became first sub-editor and then columnist at the social democrat leaning newspaper *de Volkskrant*. Following in his wake, an influential circle of conservative (former) social democrat journalists and intellectuals such as Martin Sommer, Herman Vuijsje, Hans Wansink, Jos de Beus and Paul Scheffer would take up neoconservative ideas.

But the star that burnt brightest was that of the Somalian-born Islam critic Ayaan Hirsi Ali. After 9/11 she was catapulted in the public limelight, to become one of the most influential and controversial political figures of the decade. The ideas of Hirsi Ali – often ignored in the Netherlands or conflated with her personal history – were formed in the same circle of Dutch (neo) conservative intellectuals mentioned above. In her biography, Hirsi Ali calls Frits Bolkestein her 'intellectual mentor' and thanks Chris Rutenfrans, Afshin Ellian, Paul Cliteur and Jaffe Vink for their guidance. As shown in the next chapter, Hirsi Ali's views on Islam were inspired by the work of Bernard Lewis and Samuel Huntington. When Hirsi Ali switched from the PvdA to the VVD, and entered parliament in January 2003 with a huge preferential vote, Ayaan Hirsi Ali and Geert Wilders campaigned together against Islam, smoothly adopting Huntington's clash of civilizations framework. In a 2003 opinion piece by Ayaan Hirsi Ali and Geert Wilders, they called for a 'liberal jihad': 'To defend a tolerant and liberal Netherlands, elementary rights and laws have to be put aside to effectively handle those people that abuse them and want to eliminate them as the foundation of our society'.[78]

With the dramatic assassinations of Fortuyn and Van Gogh, the political situation escalated. In May 2002, Fortuyn was assassinated by a Dutch animal rights activist, leading to a national outcry and a landslide election victory for his now leaderless party. When in 2004, the controversial filmmaker, columnist and Islam critic Theo Van Gogh was brutally killed by a Dutch-Moroccan jihadist, the Netherlands came to perceive itself as a frontline in the global War on Terror.[79] In this context, the neoconservative message of an epic struggle against a civilizational enemy could count on a warm reception. In these polarized years, the eclectic coalition of Dutch conservative intellectuals powerfully shaped the public debate.

Pim Fortuyn and the Dutch adaptation

The most important difference with US (neo)conservatism is that Dutch conservatives perceived the struggle to uphold traditional sexual and religious morality as a lost cause. The conservative law scholar Wim Couwenberg observed that conservatism in the Netherlands

> had been undermined since the 1960s by left-libertarian influences, which have predominated for years, with far-reaching liberalization of public morals as a consequence, leading to sexual liberty, legalization of abortion, homosexuality, prostitution and euthanasia, the introduction of gay marriage, and a policy of toleration with regards to coffee shops and so on.[80]

Leading empirical studies have characterized the value patterns of the Dutch population since the 1970s in terms of a 'prudent progressivism': a self-evident progressive morality regarding social issues and public authority, connected with a widespread belief in the necessity of redistribution of wealth. This prevailing progressive mentality is a clear challenge to any conservative politics in the Netherlands, as De Beus notes:

> The progressive vision of man, society, government and history has apparently pervaded the common sense opinions of all sorts of sectors of the population so deeply, that conservatives in the CDA, VVD, LPF, ChristenUnie, SGP and possibly a new conservative formation, need to sustain a radical cultural politics that can only acquire broad popular support in the long term.[81]

That is most likely what Cliteur referred to with his reference to a 'post-revolutionary phase'. 'In terms of conservatism, in the Netherlands it is not five to twelve but quarter past three in the night', Spruyt argued.[82] While more traditional conservatives such as Kinneging, Spruyt, Verbrugge and Livestro argued for the undoing of progressive morality, Fortuyn perceived this to be both impossible and undesirable. As a child of the 1960s, Fortuyn chose to integrate certain progressive values in his programme, creating a rather unique and ambiguous synthesis. After Bolkestein's gradual marginalization within the VVD, Fortuyn was the first to force an electoral breakthrough and achieve popular support for conservative ideas. Fortuyn articulated that strategy in a series of books and pamphlets.

The most illustrative example of Fortuyn's ambiguous conservatism is *The Orphaned Society*, published in 1995. His previous books had been neoliberal tributes to the *homo economicus*, the calculating and emancipated citizen who happily entered the globalized marketplace and no longer needed the welfare state. *The Orphaned Society*, in contrast, is introduced as a 'religious-sociological treatise', a plea for the reappraisal of community and authority. In the book, Fortuyn portrays the 1960s and 1970s as a generational rebellion against parental authority. The consequence of this progressive revolt is the erosion of 'the pattern of norms and values' that binds society.[83] The authority of the father figure has ceased to exist and, similarly, women's emancipation has led to the decline of the attention-giving role of the symbolic mother. Emancipation and individualization resulted in the corrosion of the integrity of the family.[84] Lacking authority figures establishing norms, without the old ideological certainties, decadence and relativism proliferate. Without mothers who give attention, children feel orphaned. The result is a young generation adrift who 'lavish their pleasure at house parties with XTC'.[85] So far, *The Orphaned Society* reads as a classic conservative polemic. Fortuyn goes on to state, however, that he does not want to go back to the old pillarized system, since this would be impossible and not fitting with the modern world. The author feels he has 'to contort himself, to not be relegated to the corner of neoconservatism'.[86]

Fortuyn argues for the restoration of the family, for a return of the Father who decrees the Law and the Mother who gives attention. But at the same time, he decouples these figures from traditional gender roles: 'Fruit of emancipation and individualization could be that the care-giving role of the mother, and the law-function of the father, do not have to be linked to the biological position of men and women'.[87] The symbolic father could very well be a woman or gay. It is a strange synthesis between the conservative appeal to a moral order founded on traditional family values, and progressive sexual norms popular-ized in the 1960s and 1970s. Fortuyn distances himself from the more traditional position of then VVD leader Frits Bolkestein, claiming that his appeal to the spiritual bond of Christian values would mean a return to an outdated system:

> Such a badly considered recommendation, reminds us too much of the time that the minister and the priest kept the common believers quiet and the rich businessman kept them poor. In this case, a system of norms and values is no more than an instrument of discipline in the hands of the ruling elite. This is not only undesirable but, considering the degree of emancipation of ordinary citizens in western societies, also unrealistic. People have learned to think for themselves, to decide for themselves concerning their per-spective on life, and will not be told what to do, not even by such a decent gentleman as Bolkestein.[88]

Fortuyn does not want to go back to the past: 'society must be reinvented'.[89] Crucial here is that he has a social constructionist view of Dutch identity. For Fortuyn, Dutch identity is not something that is simply out there, something that needs to be conserved. Identity is a work in progress, it needs to be actively con-structed and requires social engineering. This argument comes to full fruition in *Against the Islamisation of Our Culture: Dutch Identity as Foundation*, his 1997 anti-Islam pamphlet:

> What is past, is over and done with and cannot simply be recalled. The modern, open information society does not allow it, not counting the fact that no one wants to go back to that relatively closed and socially controlled society of the era of pillarization.[90]

In a turbulent and globalizing cultural and economic world order, Fortuyn states:

> [C]ollectively experienced norms and values, Dutch identity and history, the notion of the maakbare samenleving [untranslatable Dutch term, expressing the progressive belief that society can be shaped by politics], and the need to occupy ourselves more than ever with social engineering, meaning the design, creation and maintenance of social relations in which the 'human scale' is front and centre, will be of decisive importance.[91]

Fortuyn shares this constructionist view with neoconservatives such as Leo Strauss and Samuel Huntington in the US and Bart Jan Spruyt in the

Netherlands. As Samuel Huntington suggested in a famous passage in *The Clash of Civilizations*, identities and ethnicities can be reinvented: 'For peoples seeking identity and reinventing ethnicity, enemies are essential, and the potentially most dangerous enmities occur across the fault lines between the world's major civilizations'.[92] Neoconservatives conceive of political identities as relational, and enemy images are seen as a crucial resource for the reinvention of community. A case in point is Bart Jan Spruyt's essay *The Future of the City* from 2005, inspired by Leo Strauss's *The City and Man*. In this short book, Spruyt wrote about Carl Schmitt's famous contention that the crucial distinction in politics is that between friend and enemy.[93] Spruyt argued that the political assassinations had shown that 'Western civilization now had an enemy' in the Schmittian sense. While pointing to Islam and citing Carl Schmitt, he advised his readers that the relation to the enemy must be construed as 'irreconcilable'. It is the enemy that provides the answer to the identity crisis of the West. 'In battle with the enemy we learn who we are', Spruyt noted hopefully.[94] More concretely: through confrontation with Islam, Dutch national identity can be reinforced and reinvented. Fortuyn appears to adopt the same neoconservative approach in *Against the Islamisation of Our Culture*:

> The loss of the enemy, state socialism, leaves us behind like an emperor without clothes. Our own energy, positive attitude, and identity had become too closely intertwined with the image we had constructed of that country. We were everything they were not. It appears to be difficult, when that image disappears, to create an image of ourselves, in which we can articulate who we are in a positive and a negative sense, what we want, what drives us, and where we come from.[95]

The problem that Fortuyn starts his analysis with is not Islam; it is the West. We recognize Fukuyama's bleak portrait from *The End of History*. The Western citizen after the Cold War is condemned to a life without meaning, like Nietzsche's last man.[96] Similarly, Fortuyn depicts life in capitalism after the collapse of communism as 'one big party, without tragedy, contemplation and ideals that surpass personal wellbeing'.[97] The emancipation of the workers and the lack of an ideological opponent had led to an amoral individualism. What is lacking is a collective bond, a shared set of consciously experienced norms and values. In this context, ironically enough, Islam fulfils a Western need. Fortuyn identifies Islam as the new enemy image, providing the West with renewed identity and purpose. Fortuyn praises Reagan's 'cultural definition' of the Soviet Union as 'the Great Satan'. And he calls it a 'very successful strategy which definitely bears repeating' with Islam.[98] These constructionist motivations of Fortuyn's campaign against Islam have received little attention. The most astute analysis of this strategy is by Dick Pels, who describes the idea of a clash of civilizations as a 'political myth in which the domestic *need* of an enemy is projected on a real but limited terrorist threat'.[99]

For Fortuyn, the threat to the West lies in Islam's inherent fundamentalism, which he defines as the idea that 'norms and values stemming from ideology or religious outlook, prescribe behaviour in the public domain'.[100] But fundamentalism is not necessarily bad. We can learn something from the fundamentalism inspired on Christian values found in the US, namely that secularization can lead to decadence and the denial of one's norms and values. In a context where networked capitalism is eroding the social bond, making community more 'temporary' and 'fluid', a counterweight is needed. Fundamentalism can serve a positive function by providing a source of security, in response to the economic anxieties created by globalization:

> Everywhere in the world one can observe a revival of fundamentalism. Partly it is caused by internationalization of the world in cultural and economic terms. That creates a large degree of freedom and a large expansion of choice, but also fears especially among those that do not stand to profit as much from globalization. Fundamentalism provides a medium to canalize these fears, a medium that is often theological-political in nature.[101]

In this context, the meaning of the subtitle 'Dutch Identity as Foundation' becomes clear: Fortuyn is constructing a fundamentalist notion of Dutch identity that can canalize the fears of the Dutch 'losers of globalization'. Not for nothing, *The Orphaned Society* was introduced as a 'religious-sociological treatise'. What Fortuyn proposes is a civil religion, a secular fundamentalism that can serve as a foundation for Dutch identity in opposition to Islam. Put differently, Fortuyn uses the term fundamentalism in the same way that Bolkestein and Cliteur appeal to a 'spiritual bond'. Does this mean that the Dutch core values, like Islamic fundamentalism, prescribe behaviour in the public domain? Not yet, or rather, not yet for the native Dutch population: 'At this point I do not wish to go so far as to demand that people conform to these essential values of our culture, but I make an exception for newcomers'.[102] Fortuyn ends the book with a call for an ideological campaign against Islam, which has 'irreconcilable' differences with the West. Yet he frames that struggle with Islam in a progressive manner, as a reiteration of Dutch secularization and emancipation.

Fortuyn's ideas constitute an at times eclectic, chaotic and inconsistent – but nevertheless influential – attempt to reformulate a conservative position on a terrain marked by the dominance of progressive values. Seen from Huntington's situational definition of conservatism, it is Fortuyn who channels the true conservative spirit. Other Dutch conservatives were simply too far removed from dominant Dutch social mores to be able to position themselves as credible defenders of Dutch institutions against external threats. After the breakthrough of Fortuyn, Dutch conservatives would come around to champion women's rights and gay rights as an expression of Western civilizational superiority. In so doing, Dutch conservatives came to embrace progressive values.

Notes

1 Marine Le Pen, 'Un Réferendum Pour Sortir de La Crise Migratoire', *L'Opinion*, 13 January 2016.
2 Alexander Sehmer, 'Sweden Right-Wingers Plan LGBT March through Stockholm's Muslim-Majority Neighbourhoods', *Independent*, 25 July 2015.
3 Sara R. Farris, *In the Name of Women's Rights: The Rise of Femonationalism* (Durham, NC: Duke University Press, 2017), 39.
4 Farris, *In the Name of Women's Rights: The Rise of Femonationalism*; Paul Mepschen and Jan Willem Duyvendak, 'European Sexual Nationalisms: The Culturalization of Citizenship and the Sexual Politics of Belonging and Exclusion', *Perspectives on Europe* 42, no. 1 (2012): 70–6; Jasbir K. Puar, *Terrorist Assemblages: Homonationalism in Queer Times* (Durham, NC: Duke University Press, 2007).
5 Paul Mepschen, Jan Willem Duyvendak and Evelien H. Tonkens, 'Sexual Politics, Orientalism and Multicultural Citizenship in the Netherlands', *Sociology* 44, no. 5 (2010): 962–79; Samira van Bohemen, Roy Kemmers and Willem de Koster, 'Seculiere Intolerantie', *Sociologie* 8, no. 2 (2012): 199–218.
6 Hans Wansink and Frank Poorthuis, 'De Islam is een Achterlijke Cultuur', *De Volkskrant*, 9 February 2002.
7 LPF, *Politiek is Passie: Verkiezingsprogramma Lijst Pim Fortuyn 2003–2007* (Rotterdam: Lijst Pim Fortuyn, 2002).
8 Tjitske Akkerman, 'Anti-Immigration Parties and the Defence of Liberal Values: The Exceptional Case of the List Pim Fortuyn', *Journal of Political Ideologies* 10, no. 3 (1 October 2005): 341.
9 Margaret Canovan, *The People* (Oxford: Polity, 2005), 76.
10 Pim Fortuyn, *Droomkabinet: Hoe Nederland Geregeerd Moet Worden* (Uitgeverij Van Gennep, 2001), 102.
11 David Art, *Inside the Radical Right: The Development of Anti-Immigrant Parties in Western Europe* (New York: Cambridge University Press, 2011), 180.
12 Frits Bolkestein, *De Intellectuele Verleiding* (Amsterdam: Prometheus, 2012); Paul Cliteur, *Moderne Papoea's. Dilemma's van Een Multiculturele Samenleving* (Amsterdam: Arbeiderspers, 2002).
13 Theo van Gogh, 'Uitspraken van Theo van Gogh', *De Volkskrant*, 3 November 2004.
14 Judith Butler, 'Sexual Politics, Torture, and Secular Time', *British Journal of Sociology* 59, no. 1 (2008): 3.
15 PVV, 'Een Agenda van Hoop en Optimisme: Een Tijd om te Kiezen: PVV 2010–2015' (Den Haag: PVV, 2010), 6.
16 Koen Vossen, *Rondom Wilders: Portret van de PVV* (Amsterdam: Boom, 2013), 187.
17 Jos de Beus, 'De Terugkeer van het Conservatisme', *De Helling*, 21 June 2006, https://wetenschappelijkbureaugroenlinks.nl/artikel-tijdschrift/de-terugkeer-van-het-conservatisme.
18 Jos de Beus, 'Een Derde Eeuw van Nederlands Conservatisme', in *Ruimte Op Rechts? Conservatieve Onderstroom in de Lage Landen*, ed. Huib Pellikaan and Sebastiaan van der Lubben (Utrecht: Spectrum, 2006), 237.
19 Hendrik Jan Schoo, 'Het Nieuwe Conservatisme', *De Volkskrant*, 10 December 2005. Schoo referred in his article to an unpublished version of the essay of De Beus, who had personally sent it to him before its publication.

20 Jan Willem Duyvendak, *The Politics of Home: Belonging and Nostalgia in Western Europe and the United States* (Basingstoke: Palgrave Macmillan, 2011), 87.

21 Dick Houtman and Jan Willem Duyvendak, 'Boerka's, Boerkini's En Belastingcenten: Culturele en Politieke Polarisatie in en Post-Christelijke Samenleving', in *Polarisatie: Bedreigend En Verrijkend*, ed. Raad voor Maatschappelijke Ontwikkeling (Amsterdam: SWP Publishers, 2009), 96.

22 The authors define neoculturalists by their view of the world as 'divided into different, inimical cultures', and by their opposition to 'cultural relativism'. In practice, neoculturalists are seen to combine a progressive sexual discourse with an anti-Muslim and anti-immigration agenda. See Justus Uitermark, Paul Mepschen and Jan Willem Duyvendak, 'Populism, Sexual Politics, and the Exclusion of Muslims in the Netherlands', in *European States and Their Muslim Citizens: The Impact of Institutions on Perceptions and Boundaries*, ed. John R. Bowen et al., Cambridge Studies in Law and Society (New York: Cambridge University Press, 2013), 88–130.

23 Houtman and Duyvendak, 'Boerka's, Boerkini's En Belastingcenten', 4

24 Jan Willem Duyvendak, *Een Eensgezinde, Vooruitstrevende Natie: Over de Mythe van 'de' Individualisering en de Toekomst van de Sociologie*, Oratiereeks/Faculteit der Maatschappij- en Gedragswetenschappen (Amsterdam: Vossiuspers UvA, 2004), 11.

25 Samira van Bohemen, Roy Kemmers and Willem de Koster, 'Seculiere Intolerantie', *Sociologie* 8, no. 2 (2012): 199–218.

26 Hendrik Jan Schoo, *Een Bitter Mensbeeld: De Transformatie van een Ontregeld Land* (Amsterdam: Bakker, 2004), 51.

27 Joshua Livestro, 'Het Conservatieve Moment Is Gekomen', *NRC Handelsblad*, 3 February 2001.

28 In September 2002, Edwin van de Haar and Joshua Livestro, members of both the VVD and the Edmund Burke Foundation, published the manifesto *Helder Liberaal en Duidelijk Rechts* (Cearly Liberal and Firmly on the Right). The manifesto pleaded for a New Right course, combining free market and conservative themes. The leadership of the VVD responded negatively to the report. See: Joop Hippe et al., *Kroniek 2002: Overzicht van Partijpolitieke Gebeurtenissen van het Jaar 2002* (Documentatiecentrum Nederlandse Politieke Partijen, 2004), 166–80. Similar discussions took place between the Edmund Burke Foundation and the CDA. See Thijs Jansen, 'CDA Moet Conservatieve Verleiding Weerstaan', *Christen Democratische Verkenningen*, Winter (2004): 5–18. Spruyt's work for the PVV came to overshadow these more mainstream affiliations of the Edmund Burke Foundation.

29 Bart Jan Spruyt and Michiel Visser, 'Conservatief Manifest', *Trouw*, 18 October 2003.

30 Spruyt and Visser.

31 Spruyt and Visser.

32 See, for instance, Kees Schuyt's response to the manifesto, in which he argues that baby boomers were the very opposites of relativists, making them not unlike the 'conservative hotheads' who wrote the manifesto. Kees Schuyt, 'Conservatieve Geschiedvervalśing', *De Volkskrant*, 22 October 2003.

33 Hendrik Jan Schoo, *De Verwarde Natie: Dwarse Notities over Immigratie in Nederland* (Amsterdam: Prometheus, 2000).

34 Andrew Hartman, *A War for the Soul of America: A History of the Culture Wars* (Chicago, IL: The University of Chicago Press, 2015).

35 Guus Valk, 'Het Conservatieve Moment is Voorbij', *NRC Handelsblad*, 26 August 2006.

36 Bart Jan Spruyt, *Lof van het Conservatisme* (Amsterdam: Balans, 2003), 9–10, 205–8.

37 Bart Jan Spruyt, 'De Verdediging van het Westen: Leo Strauss, Amerikaans Neo-conservatisme en de Kansen in Nederland', in *Ruimte op rechts? Conservatieve onderstroom in de Lage Landen*, ed. Huib Pellikaan and Sebastiaan van der Lubben (Utrecht: Het Spectrum, 2006), 286, 295.

38 More precisely, Wilders referred to a publication of the Edmund Burke Foundation (Spruyt and Visser, 2004), titled *The Crisis in the Netherlands and the Conservative Response*. The conservative manifesto was a synthesis of that publication. See Bart Jan Spruyt and Michiel Visser, *De Crisis in Nederland en het Conservatieve Antwoord* (Den Haag: Edmund Burke Stichting, 2004). For Wilders' reference to this publication see Elaine de Boer and Theo Koelé, 'Een Rechtse Directe', *De Volkskrant*, 20 November 2003.

39 Bart Jan Spruyt, 'De Zuilen Staan nog Fier Overeind', *Historisch Nieuwsblad*, 2005, www.historischnieuwsblad.nl/nl/artikel/6608/de-zuilen-staan-nog-fier-overeind.html.

40 Valk, 'Het Conservatieve Moment is Voorbij'.

41 Angela McRobbie, 'Post-feminism and Popular Culture', *Feminist Media Studies* 4, no. 3 (2004): 255–64.

42 Susan Faludi, *Backlash: The Undeclared War against American Women*, First Anchor books ed. (New York: Anchor Books, 1992); Lisa Duggan and Nan D. Hunter, *Sex Wars: Sexual Dissent and Political Culture* (New York: Routledge, 2006); Judith Stacey, 'The New Conservative Feminism', *Feminist Studies* 9, no. 3 (1983): 559–83.

43 Seymour Martin Lipset and Earl Raab, *The Politics of Unreason: Right Wing Extremism in America, 1790–1970*, Patterns of American Prejudice Series, 5 (New York: Harper & Row, 1970), 29.

44 See: Thomas Frank, *What's the Matter with Kansas? How Conservatives Won the Heart of America*, 1st ed. (New York: Metropolitan Books/Henry Holt, 2004), 5.

45 Angela McRobbie, *The Aftermath of Feminism: Gender, Culture and Social Change* (London: SAGE, 2009).

46 Sidney Blumenthal et al., 'Margaret Thatcher in Her Own Words', *New York Times*, 8 April 2013.

47 Pim Fortuyn, *Zonder Ambtenaren. De Ondernemende Overheid*, 1e dr. (Amsterdam: Van Veen, 1991).

48 Pim Fortuyn, *Aan het Volk van Nederland: de Contractmaatschappij, een Politiek-Economische Zedenschets* (Amsterdam: Contact, 1992).

49 Karel Groenveld et al., *Tussen Vrijblijvendheid en Paternalisme: Bespiegelingen over Communitarisme, Liberalisme en Individualisering*, Geschrift/Prof. Mr. B.M. Telderstichting; 82 ('s-Gravenhage: Teldersstichting, 1995).

50 Pim Fortuyn, *Tegen de Islamisering van Onze Cultuur: Nederlandse Identiteit als Fundament* (Utrecht: Bruna, 1997).

51 Uitermark, Mepschen and Duyvendak, 'Populism, Sexual Politics, and the Exclusion of Muslims in the Netherlands'.

52 NRC Handelsblad, 'De Geus: Post Emancipatie Is Overbodig', *NRC Handelsblad*, 17 November 2003.

53 Trouw, 'Hirsi Ali Roept op tot een Derde Feministische Golf', *Trouw*, 10 March 2003.

54 See Dick Pels on the machismo of the Dutch New Right: Dick Pels, *Een Zwak voor Nederland: Ideeën voor een Nieuwe Politiek* (Amsterdam: Anthos, 2005), 40.
55 Akkerman, 'Anti-Immigration Parties and the Defence of Liberal Values', 341.
56 Farris, *In the Name of Women's Rights: The Rise of Femonationalism*; Mepschen and Duyvendak, 'European Sexual Nationalisms: The Culturalization of Citizenship and the Sexual Politics of Belonging and Exclusion'; Puar, *Terrorist Assemblages: Homonationalism in Queer Times*.
57 Faludi, *Backlash: The Undeclared War against American Women*, 243.
58 Hermann von der Dunk, *Conservatisme* (Haarlem: Fibula- Van Dishoeck, 1976), 89.
59 Karl Mannheim and Kurt Wolff, *From Karl Mannheim* (New Brunswick, NJ: Transaction Publishers, 1993).
60 Mannheim and Wolff, 173.
61 Mannheim and Wolff, 147.
62 Samuel P. Huntington, 'Conservatism as an Ideology', *American Political Science Review* 51, no. 2 (1957): 455.
63 Huntington, 471
64 Huntington, 472.
65 Huntington, 472.
66 Huntington, 472–3.
67 Huntington, 473.
68 Irving Kristol, 'The Neoconservative Persuasion', *The Weekly Standard* 8, no. 47 (2003): 23–5.
69 Bart Jan Spruyt, *De Toekomst van de Stad: Over Geschiedenis en Politiek.* (Zoetermeer: Boekencentrum, 2005), 73.
70 Jos de Beus, 'Een Derde Eeuw van Nederlands Conservatisme', 236.
71 Hendrik Jan Schoo, *Republiek van vrije burgers: het onbehagen in de democratie*, 2e dr. (Amsterdam: Bert Bakker, 2008), 264.
72 Paul Cliteur, 'Van Burke Naar Bork', in *De Conservatieve Uitdaging: De Scepsis van J.L. Heldring*, ed. Marcel ten Hooven (Amsterdam: Prometheus, 2003), 37.
73 Spruyt, 'De Verdediging van het Westen', 294.
74 Pim Fortuyn, 'Koude Oorlog Met Islam', *Elsevier*, 25 August 2001. For a similar Cold War comparison of communism and Islam, see: Geert Wilders, *Marked for Death: Islam's War against the West and Me* (Washington, DC: Regnery, 2012).
75 Pim Fortuyn, *De Islamisering van Onze Cultuur: Nederlandse Identiteit als Fundament* (Uithoorn Rotterdam: Karakter Uitgevers, 2001), 9.
76 Jaffe Vink, 'De Neoconservatieve Revolutie', *Trouw*, 12 February 2006.
77 Leon de Winter, *De Vijand: Een Opstel* (Amsterdam: De Bezige Bij, 2004).
78 Geert Wilders and Ayaan Hirsi Ali, 'Het Is Tijd Voor Een Liberale Jihad', *NRC Handelsblad*, 12 April 2003.
79 Ian Buruma, *Murder in Amsterdam: Liberal Europe, Islam and the Limits of Tolerance* (New York: Penguin, 2007).
80 Servatius W. Couwenberg, 'Heeft Conservatisme in Nederland Geen Voedingsbodem?', *Civis Mundi Digitaal* 19, no. 6 (2011).
81 Beus, 'Een Derde Eeuw van Nederlands Conservatisme', 224.
82 Bart Jan Spruyt, 'De Verdediging van het Westen', 292–3.
83 Pim Fortuyn, *De Verweesde Samenleving: Een Religieus-Sociologisch Traktaat* (Uithoorn Rotterdam: Karakter Uitgevers, 2002), 17.
84 Fortuyn, 37.
85 Fortuyn, 17.

86 Fortuyn, 37.
87 Fortuyn, 17.
88 Fortuyn, 85.
89 Fortuyn, 206.
90 Fortuyn, 56.
91 Fortuyn, 56.
92 Samuel P. Huntington, *The Clash of Civilizations and the Remaking of World Order* (New York: Simon & Schuster, 1996), 20.
93 Bart Jan Spruyt, *De Toekomst van de Stad: Over Geschiedenis en Politiek* (Zoetermeer: Boekencentrum, 2005). Parts of Spruyt's 2005 essay appeared in the PVV's 2006 party manifesto *A Neo-Realist Vision* (it is worth repeating here that 'realism' in the Dutch context often denotes conservatism). This philosophical manifesto of the PVV has clearly been written by Spruyt and contains quite explicit references to Leo Strauss. It references the passage on cannibalism and cultural relativism from *Natural Right and History*. See PVV, 'Een Nieuw-Realistische Visie', 2006, www.pvv.nl/30-visie/publicaties/707-een-nieuw-realistische-visie.html.
94 Spruyt, *De Toekomst van de Stad*, 59.
95 Pim Fortuyn, *Tegen de Islamisering van onze Cultuur: Nederlandse Identiteit als Fundament* (Utrecht: Bruna, 1997), 10.
96 Francis Fukuyama, 'The End of History?', *The National Interest*, no. 16 (1989): 18.
97 Fortuyn, *De Verweesde Samenleving*, 12.
98 Fortuyn, *Tegen de Islamisering van onze Cultuur*, 37.
99 Dick Pels, *Een Zwak voor Nederland*, 15.
100 Fortuyn, *Tegen de Islamisering van onze Cultuur*, 32.
101 Fortuyn, 108.
102 Fortuyn, 109.

6   The double life of Ayaan Hirsi Ali

After the fall of the Berlin Wall, Krzysztof Kieślowski's *The Double Life of Veronique* poetically portrayed a deeper, underlying unity connecting East and West, divided for almost half a century by the Iron Curtain. In Kieślowski's film, this connection is symbolized by the deep, unconscious bond between two female figures with identical appearance, whose trajectories cross only for a fleeting moment: Weronika in Poland and Véronique in France. The double life of Hirsi Ali epitomizes a more troubling similitude between East and West, in a time when the idea of a clash of civilizations came to replace the divisions of the Cold War. In her personal history, Ayaan Hirsi Ali embodies the oppositions of this new era and the remarkable parallels between the two ideological currents that positioned themselves at the forefront of that conflict, seen by both as a civilizational clash. As in Kieślowski's film, the two lives of Ayaan Hirsi Ali hide a deeper underlying unity, even though the parallel is ultimately one of confrontation, not reconciliation.[1]

Two political movements came to play a leading role in the life of Ayaan Hirsi Ali: Islamic fundamentalism and neoconservatism. The two currents are remarkably co-joined in the personal history of Ayaan Hirsi Ali, as chronicled in her bestselling autobiography *Infidel*, which is divided into two parts, echoing the divisions in her personal trajectory: 'My Childhood' and 'My Freedom'.[2] In the first section is recounted how Hirsi Ali's family, a prominent clan in Somalia, fled the country in 1976 during the dictatorship of Siad Barré, before the ensuing civil war. The first place of refuge was Saudi Arabia, followed by sojourns in Ethiopia and finally Kenya, where she would stay for 12 years. There, Hirsi Ali came in contact with the *Sahwa*, the puritan religious revival that emanated from the Muslim Brotherhood and Saudi Wahhabism, onto the broader domain of Sunni Islam. Hirsi Ali describes how she became part of this movement through the religious education she received at the age of 16 in Kenya, given by a certain 'Sister Aziza'. Hirsi Ali recounts her subsequent conversion, how she started to veil herself in a hidjab, and read Islamist texts with a community of like-minded believers.

In the process of escaping from an arranged marriage and coming to the Netherlands as a political refugee in 1992, Hirsi Ali slowly started repudiating her Islamic belief. She describes the day of her arrival as her 'real birthday': 'the birth of me as a person, making decisions about my life on my own'.[3] From 1995 to 2000, Hirsi Ali studied political science in Leiden. Amongst others, she was taught by Paul Cliteur, a prominent New Atheist inspired by US neoconservatism. Cliteur was part of a circle of Dutch intellectuals who devoted themselves to the propagation of a Dutch clash of civilizations theory, while critiquing religion in general and Islam specifically. After her studies, Hirsi Ali joined the think tank of the Dutch social democrats (PvdA), the Wiarda Beckman Stichting (WBS), where she started writing on Islam and immigration. As we will see, Hirsi Ali's writing at the WBS was inspired by the work of Bernard Lewis. In the months after 9/11, Hirsi Ali's critique of Islam could count on a receptive audience. While still working at the WBS, Hirsi Ali was adopted as their protégé by the neoconservative intellectual circle surrounding Cliteur. The group is described in her autobiography as the 'Gent's Club': the journalists Chris Rutenfrans, Jaffe Vink, Hans Wansink, the columnist Sylvain Ephimenco, the writer Leon de Winter and the New Atheist professors Herman Philipse and Paul Cliteur. She refers to Frits Bolkestein, the former leader of the conservative liberal party (VVD) and arguably the most prominent Dutch exponent of neoconservatism, as her 'intellectual mentor' in the acknowledgements.[4]

After calling Islam a 'backward religion' on Dutch public television in September 2002, on the occasion of the anniversary of 9/11 and only months after the assassination of Fortuyn, Hirsi Ali started receiving death threats. She became an instant celebrity in the heated debate on freedom of speech, women's emancipation and Islam that followed. Her status as an endangered feminist public intellectual paved the way for her broad appeal, with prominent progressive Dutch politicians, intellectuals and feminists (justifiably) rallying to her defence. After a short period hiding from the threats in the US, Hirsi Ali exchanged the social democrat think tank for a position as parliament member for the VVD. In the following years, she engaged in a spectacular, contentious and short-lived political career. After a huge political controversy surrounding her reception as a refugee in the Netherlands, Hirsi Ali moved to the US in 2006 where she started working for the American Enterprise Institute, a prominent neoconservative think tank. She subsequently married the conservative historian Niall Ferguson.

With this remarkable course of life, Ayaan Hirsi Ali is one of the few people to have been part of both the Islamic fundamentalist and the neoconservative movement. In this itinerary of contrasting conversions and opposing allegiances, the strategic use of enemy images and essentialism that is inherent to both currents provides a connecting thread. In his book *War for Muslim Minds: Islam and the West*, the French Middle East scholar Gilles Kepel described the ascendency of these movements and famously argued that both are to a certain degree each other's mirror image, feeding and reinforcing each other.[5] 'You're either with us, or against us', would become a shared mantra of both George W. Bush and Osama Bin Laden. Both movements are seen to derive strength and legitimacy from an aggressive opponent. Both movements share an essentialist view of Islam, in which the fundamentalist perspective is seen as the true nature of Islam. *Infidel* is a remarkable account of this confluence.

In her autobiography, Hirsi Ali has transposed the fundamentalist image of Islam, known to her from her teenage years, unto the Islamic world as a whole. This fundamentalist image – defined by a literalist approach to Koran and Hadith; the idea of the timelessness of Islam; the stress on Islam's inherent hostility to modernity and the West; and the view of Islam as an all-embracing societal system – bears a striking resemblance to the perspective on Islam developed by neoconservatives, which has its roots in the Western tradition of Orientalism. As the Middle East scholar Olivier Roy writes: 'Critics of Islam and Muslim fundamentalists are mirrors of each other, and each corroborates the other in the view of Islam that they share, merely with the signs reversed'.[6]

Hirsi Ali has made ample use of these analytical tools of Orientalism, a long tradition of western colonial scholarship regarding Islam and the Orient. As Edward Said wrote in *Orientalism*, in this tradition Islam is reduced to 'tribe and tent'.[7] Olivier Roy summarized Orientalism succinctly as the view that a time-less and pervasive 'Islamic culture' structures the whole of society from politics to law and architecture, and prohibits access to political modernity.[8] As we will see, these Orientalist themes characterize Ayaan Hirsi Ali's views on Islam. An observation that is not surprising if we consider that her views are largely inspired by the work of the Orientalist Bernard Lewis, a principal target of Said's critique. Hirsi Ali fits the category of the 'native informant', a term used by Edward Said to describe a Middle Eastern scholar sitting 'at the feet of American Orientalists', who uses her Western training 'to feel superior to [her] own people', because she 'is able to "manage" the Orientalist system'.[9] Oriental-ism, according to Said, has a theatrical quality, and he describes that learned system of viewing the Orient as a 'stage on which the whole East is confined':

> On this stage will appear figures whose role it is to represent the larger whole from which they emanate. The Orient then seems to be, not an unlim-ited extension beyond the familiar European world, but rather a closed field, a theatrical stage affixed to Europe.[10]

Ayaan Hirsi Ali can be seen as an actor on that theatrical stage, representing the Orient to a Western audience. What is specific to Hirsi Ali is that she uses the Orientalist paradigm, not so much to study Islam or her society of origin, but to make sense of her own personal story, and to adapt that experience so as to fit into the public role she has crafted for herself on the confined space of the stage. Hirsi Ali has offered her personal story as an illustration of the clash of civiliza-tions thesis developed by Bernard Lewis and Samuel Huntington, referring to her life as 'a personal journey through the clash of civilizations'.[11] This chapter retraces that intellectual journey.

Qutb and political Islam

The Sunni Islamist part of the story has its crystallization point in the figure of Sayyid Qutb. Born in 1906 in a traditional rural context in Egypt, Qutb first became a teacher, then a prominent intellectual, and finally the most important voice of modern Sunni Islamism.[12] The Sunni Islamist movement has its origins in the 1930s. Hassan al-Banna, the Egyptian founder of the Muslim Brotherhood, and Abul-Ala Maududi, the leader of the Indian-Pakistani Jamaat-i-Islami party, founded a new political movement that aimed to reinvent Islam as a political order. Qutb would build on the work of al-Banna and Maudadi, with the goal of developing Islam into a holistic alternative for modern twentieth century ideologies. The leading Middle East scholar Olivier Roy – whose interpretation I will follow here, with the aid of John Calvert's probing intellectual biography of Qutb – defines this movement as Islamism or political Islam, because it redefines Islam as a political ideology.[13] This attempt at modernizing Islam was paradoxically given legitimacy by presenting it as a restoration, a return to the source, to the original texts and the original inspirations of the first community of believers under the Prophet Mohammed. Islamism, Roy argues, is a movement that denies its own historicity.

The core proposition in Olivier Roy's work is that Islamism, both sociologically and intellectually, is a product of modernity, a result of the rapid modernization process in the Muslim world. Like Qutb himself, the vanguard of adherents and disseminators of political Islam did not originate from traditional Islamic clergy (the *ulamas*). They did not write in the ancient Arabic, the learned language of the Koran, but in national popular languages. The Islamists 'are a product of the modern education system', Roy writes, 'where they took classes together with militant Marxists, whose concepts they used, and translated in the terminology of Koran'.[14] Special attention was devoted to organizational form, reminiscent of Leninist vanguard parties on the one hand and the Sufi brotherhoods on the other.[15]

Like other Muslim intellectuals of his generation, Sayyid Qutb searched for a formula to modernize Islam, in such a way that Western technological and scientific knowledge could be assimilated without the accompanying liberal values. For that to occur, Islam had to be developed into a fundamentalist and all-embracing societal 'ideology' (*fikra*), a term derived from European progressive thought. For Qutb, a reinvented Islamic ideology had to function as an alternative to Third World nationalism, communism, capitalism and liberal democracy.

The titles of Qutb's most popular books, published around 1950, are a good indication of the worldly character of his religious thought: *Social Justice in Islam* (1949), *The Battle between Capitalism and Islam* (1951), and *Islam and World Peace* (1951). The central idea in these books is holism: Qutb describes Islam as *nizam*, an integrated order that encapsulates economy, society and politics.[16] This fundamentalist vision needed to be realized by the creation of an Islamic state, starting at the national level. This was an important innovation. In traditional Islam, Roy writes:

> The state is never considered in terms of a territorialized nation-state: the ideal is to have a power that would rule over the entirety of the *umma*, the community of the faithful, while actual power is exercised over a segment of the *umma* whose borders are contingent, provisional, and incomplete.[17]

The term *nizam* is also a modern invention, and is not to be found in the Koran.[18] The break with Islamic tradition is that the idea of divine unity (*tawhid*) is now applied to society, while before it only referred to God. Society needs to be a reflection of God's unity. But where God's unity is natural, in society it will have to be created. A holistic society does not tolerate intrinsic segmentation, be it social, ethnic, tribal or national, or a political order that claims autonomy from divine order.[19] Therein lies the fundamentalist aspect of Islamism. Before the twentieth century, Islam was used as a verb describing a practice of personal belief and dedication. Only after the creation of the Muslim Brotherhood by Hasan al-Banna does the word attain the meaning that Qutb bestows upon it: an integrated societal system.[20]

Following the military coup of Nasser and the Free Officers in 1953, Qutb joined the Muslim Brotherhood and became the intellectual leader of the movement. The Brotherhood saw Nasser's regime as an opportunity to implement their ardently desired Islamic state in Egypt. But Nasser decided on a path of secular modernization and relations with the Brotherhood turned sour. After an attempt by the Muslim Brotherhood to overthrow the Nasser government, the regime decided to eliminate the Brotherhood and arrest hundreds of its most prominent members. Qutb was among them. In the years of imprisonment that followed, Qutb was tortured and his views radicalized. His writings in prison were oriented at formulating an Islamic doctrine that would legitimate a revolt against sovereign power (as in Christian faith, obedience to God-given authority is required in Islam). Qutb does that, on the one hand, by placing divine authority (*hakimiyya*, again a term that does not exist in the Koran) above state sovereignty and popular sovereignty. And on the other, by stating that Muslim societies in which this godly sovereignty is not recognized, in which there is no attempt to implement divine law (*sharia*) are in reality in a state of unbelief. Under Western influence, a form of bad faith had developed amongst the political elites of Muslim countries, as in society more broadly. Qutb called this *jahiliyya* (a state of unbelief), a Koranic concept that refers to the situation in the Arabic world before the arrival of Islam. For Qutb, obedience to secular authorities implied disobedience to divine authority:

> God (limitless is He in His glory) says that this whole issue is one of faith or unfaith, Islam and non-Islam, Divine law or human prejudice. No compromise or reconciliation can be worked out between these two sets of values. Those who judge on the basis of the law God has revealed, enforcing all parts of it and substituting nothing else for it, are the believers. By contrast, those who do not make the law God has revealed the basis of their judgement, are unbelievers, wrongdoers and transgressors.[21]

Qutb's views form a mirror image to the friend-enemy distinction employed by the neoconservatives, as we shall see later on. Qutb makes a black-and-white distinction between true Islam and the enemies of Islam, compounded by essentialist views of Jews, communists, westernized elites, Orientalists and other opponents of true Islam. In spite of the fact that Qutb saw his modernized version of Islam as relying on 'Western ways of thought', he portrayed Western thinking as especially hostile to Islam, due to the fact that Western science had developed historically in opposition to (Christian) religion:

> The Western ways of thought and all the sciences started on the foundation of these poisonous influences with an enmity towards all religions, and in particular with greater hostility towards Islam. This enmity towards Islam is especially pronounced and many times is the result of a well thought out scheme, the object of which is first to shake the foundations of Islamic beliefs and then gradually to demolish the structure of Muslim society.[22]

In the eyes of Qutb, belief and religion are the only dignified and legitimate bonds that can keep people together. Jihad is for Qutb an offensive expansionist struggle in the name of a universal Islamic revolution, not unlike the universal American hegemony that neoconservatives aimed for. Qutb took aim against those that defined jihad as a spiritual struggle or a defensive practice, arguing that it went against Islam's universal mission.[23] Qutb's revolution involved an existential struggle between good and evil that needed to be prepared by a professional revolutionary vanguard (*tali'a*), able to extract itself from the false consciousness of depraved *jahili* culture. Qutb attributed to conflict and strife an important formative role, leading to a deeper consciousness of one's values.

An important contradiction in the thought of Qutb is the conviction that it is possible to have unmediated access to divine teachings. Islam, according to Qutb, is a doctrine that exists outside of human consciousness, as objective truth. Interpretation must be avoided as much as possible, so that human igno- rance, individual desire, or group interests will not contaminate the purity of the doctrine. When confronted with an explicit text in the Koran or the Hadith, there is no space for *ijtihad* (personal appraisal).[24] In the case of uncertainty, interpretation only serves to ascertain divine truth. A scenario in which several interpretations come to coexist, a normal situation given the diversity of Islamic jurisprudence, is not deemed possible; there is only right and wrong. Since the assessment of clarity already requires human judgement, and there is no basis for assessing the correctness of an interpretation in the case of uncertainty, that vision is tautolo- gical. Ultimately, Qutb's method requires a personal (and political) decision on the interpretation of divine truth, a decision that remains veiled behind the appeal to unmediated access. But the advantage of this approach is that it allowed Qutb and the Islamist movement to marginalize the traditional Islamic clergy such as the Egyptian Al-Azhar University. The Islamists contested their monopoly on interpreting the religious texts and criticized the clergy's loyalty to existing political regimes.

Qutb interpreted and innovated to an important degree, by introducing new concepts, or by giving new meaning to existing terms. Denying the innovative aspects of his approach allowed Qutb to articulate a political programme in the name of Islam, while cementing his vision in an appeal to divine truth. When

Qutb is released from prison in 1964, members of the Muslim Brotherhood are working on the creation of an underground military organization. Qutb takes personal charge of the operation. When the organization is discovered, the Nasser regime decides to round up the Muslim Brotherhood, and to sentence Qutb to death.

Qutb would go down in history as a martyr. The Muslim Brotherhood distanced itself from the more radical aspects of his legacy, rejecting the revolutionary *jahiliyya* doctrine. The vanguardist strategy of catastrophic revolution was abandoned for reformism and missionary work from the ground up. Only God has the authority to judge the veracity of the belief of other Muslims, Hudaybi argued, then Brotherhood leader. This continues to be the majority position in the Sunni world: failures in practice, be they crimes or omissions of worship, do not exclude a person from the community of believers, only the confession of the faith matters. Nonetheless, in the following years, Qutbism inspired radicals all over the world of Sunni Islam. From that moment on, the Sunni Islamist movement is seen as divided between a reformist and a revolutionary pole.[25]

The reformist pole is exemplified by Mohammed Qutb, the brother of Sayyid Qutb. He was invited by the Saudi monarchy – and with him many other Muslim Brothers – to integrate Islamism with the Saudi tradition of Wahhabism, an ultra-conservative, fundamentalist interpretation of Islam. At the time, the Saudi monarchy saw the Muslim Brotherhood as an appropriate tool to form an international counterweight to the appeal of secular pan-Arabism, and from 1979 on, revolutionary Shiism from Iran. On a domestic level, it was inspired by strategic concerns to limit the influence of Wahhabi clerics on Saudi society, by providing them with a competing doctrine. As a result, the kingdom of Saudi Arabia became a site of refuge for the radical religious movements that arose in opposition to secular Arab regimes, often aligned with the Soviet Union. This development was actively encouraged by the US as part of its Cold War strategy. Large amounts of Saudi oil-dollars were invested to facilitate this new religious movement. From the convergence of the activist impulse of the Muslim Brotherhood and the literalist, strict and puritanical approach of the Wahhabi tradition, also described as Salafism, the *Sahwa* (the awakening) emerged.[26] Both Islamists and Salafists can be described as fundamentalist, although they differ in the nature of their fundamentalism, with Islamists more prone to challenge the political status quo and Salafists more focused on personal piety. This movement became very prominent in the 1980s and would take up the young Hirsi Ali in its sweep.[27]

One of the younger Muslim Brothers, and a scion of the Egyptian elite, Ayman al-Zawahiri, continued the revolutionary tradition of Islamism, and radicalized the ideas of Qutb further. He became part of the group Islamic Jihad that assassinated Sadat in 1981, basing themselves on the revolutionary ideas Qutb had formulated. Heavy repression followed, and when Zawahiri was released from prison, he continued his activities as part of the Afghan Mujahideen, where he met Bin Laden. Here, Salafist and Islamist radicals successfully mingled, as the guerrilla fighters were trying to live their lives (and fight) according to a very literal interpretation of scripture. After the success of the guerrilla war against the Soviet Union, Zawahiri took up the plan to take aim, not at the corrupt Arabic regimes (the nearby enemy), but directly at the puppet player itself: the United States (the faraway enemy). He became the mentor of Bin Laden and the second in command of Al-Qaeda.

Mohammed Bouyeri, the Dutch-Moroccan killer of Theo van Gogh who also threatened Hirsi Ali, belonged to this latter revolutionary pole. Together with a group of friends and acquaintances, dubbed the *Hofstadgroep* by Dutch police, Bouyeri had become radicalized by reading and translating radical Islamist texts downloaded from the internet. They became acquainted with this tradition through the former Syrian army officer Abu Khaled, who spoke at informal meetings throughout Europe. Abu Khaled introduced them to the thought of Sayyid Qutb and Al Maududi. As described by Rudolph Peters in his account of Bouyeri's political radicalization, Qutb's ideas were a crucial reference point: 'An inventory of the documents found on his and other computers shows that he and the group were ideologically heavily indebted to the Egyptian Sayyid Qutb and the Indian/Pakistani Aba al-A la al-Mawdudi'.[28]

Neoconservatism and the clash of civilizations

The neoconservatives, like the Islamists, have championed an image of the world as divided by a dramatic conflict of starkly contrasted forces of good and evil. The philosophy of Leo Strauss provided an important theoretical reference point. Amongst the Straussians were many neoconservatives who would later acquire positions of power in government, in military and foreign policy circles, and in neoconservative think tanks.[29] Elaborating on the thesis of the German jurist Carl Schmitt that friend-enemy distinctions form the essence of politics, Strauss saw the struggle against an enemy – portrayed as an absolute moral evil – as a necessary precondition for the construction and maintenance of a healthy and hierarchical political community. Strauss defined and defended such sentiments as 'patriotism'. 'The most potent opinion regarding justice', Strauss argued in *The City and Man*,

is the opinion according to which justice means public-spiritedness or concern with the common good, full dedication to one's city as a particular city which as such is potentially the enemy of other cities, or patriotism. Justice thus understood consists indeed in helping one's friends, i.e. one's fellow citizens, and in hating one's enemies, i.e. the foreigners.[30]

In a personal letter to Carl Schmitt, Strauss expressed this philosophy thusly:

The ultimate foundation of the Right is the principle of the natural evil of man; because man is by nature evil, he therefore needs dominion. But dominion can be established, that is man can be unified, only in a unity against – against other man. Every association of men is necessarily a separation from other men. The tendency to separate (and therewith the grouping of humanity into friends and enemies) is given with human nature; it is in this sense destiny, period.[31]

The clear identification of enemies in the Schmittian sense of the word became a hallmark of US neoconservatism. As Irving Kristol argued: 'statesmen should, above all, have the ability to distinguish friends from enemies'.[32] A new conservative politics, Samuel Huntington would argue at the end of the 1950s, could only succeed if there was a credible external threat that allowed conservatives to take up a position as defenders of US institutions. That enemy was first identified as communism.[33] Naming, accentuating and exaggerating this threat would make it possible for neoconservatives to appoint themselves as defenders of American institutions. For that to occur, the détente in the Cold War that came into being in the late 1960s had to be undone.

The pragmatist outlook of foreign policy 'realists' like Kissinger and especially the CIA provided the biggest obstruction. They had little reason, given the available information on Soviet military expenditures, to see the Soviet Union as an existential threat. The neoconservative movement, aligned with foreign policy hawks and organized around organizations such as the *Committee for a Democratic Majority* and the bipartisan *Committee on the Present Danger*, moved to marginalize the realist tendency.[34] Neoconservatives and hawks such as Paul Wolfowitz, Albert Wholstetter and Richard Perle, aided by the California governor Ronald Reagan, managed to circumvent the CIA by lobbying for an independent revision of the confidential CIA assessment of the Soviet threat. The recently appointed CIA director Bush senior complied in 1976. He created a commission of three separate teams of analysts – all lavishly staffed by neoconservatives and hawks – which became known as TEAM B. Richard Pipes, a conservative Harvard professor, led the most famous of the three. The commissions created a range of reports in which an exaggerated and threatening image was presented of the military power and intentions of the Soviet Union. Strategic leaks to the media were instrumental in fomenting a culture of anxiety amongst the wider US population, resulting in popular support for an expanded military budget and a more aggressive foreign policy. Trying to accommodate the hawks, President Carter appointed Samuel Huntington to author a report and revise government policy. Although somewhat more moderate, Huntington presented an equally intimidating portrait of the military threat of the Soviet Union in 1977. Like the TEAM B reports, these assessments were later found to be consciously exaggerated.[35]

In July 1979, Carter approved a large CIA operation funding the Mujahideen revolt in Afghanistan. It helped to provoke the Soviet intervention in December that year, in what is commonly seen as a decisive escalation of the Cold War. The Soviet invasion turned US popular opinion and emboldened hawks and neoconservatives. In the elections of 1980, many neoconservatives joined the victorious Reagan campaign, resulting in a large neoconservative presence among the Reagan staff. Reagan's election victory led to an intensification of the Cold War and the accompanying arms race. In subsequent years, the CIA campaign to fund the Mujahideen became the largest covert operation in American history. An important leader among the Mujahideen was the Saudi prince Osama Bin Laden, whose network geared to funding and recruiting jihadists to fight in Afghanistan, and went on to become Al-Qaeda. In the Middle East, the US either supported or acquiesced in the rapid growth of the Islamic right. The neo-conservative ascendency to political power under Reagan thus coincided with the rise of the jihadist movement.

In the beginning of the 1990s, after the fall of the Berlin Wall, many in the US establishment were convinced that a new rationale for conflict – and therefore a new enemy – needed to be identified. The initial impetus in that effort was given by the Princeton-based Orientalist Bernard Lewis.[36] In 1990, a month after the beginning of the First Gulf War, Lewis published the essay *The Roots of Muslim Rage* in *The Atlantic*. It was not Western intervention in Muslim countries, or Western support for dictatorial regimes that led to virulent anti-Americanism in the Middle East. The hatred of Muslims against the West, Lewis wrote,

> goes beyond hostility to specific interests or actions or policies or even countries and becomes a rejection of Western civilization as such, not only what it does but what it is, and the principles and values that it practices and professes. These are indeed seen as innate evil, and those who promote them or accept them as the 'enemies of God'.[37]

The author came to this startling conclusion by presenting Islamic fundamentalism as an authentic return to 'the classic Islamic view'. In this way Lewis equated fundamentalist Islam with the Islamic religion as a whole. Lewis' thesis became an important mantra of the Bush administration after 9/11: 'Why do they hate us? […] They hate our freedoms'.[38]

Samuel Huntington took up Lewis' thesis in a groundbreaking essay titled *The Clash of Civilizations?*, published in 1993 in the journal of the US foreign policy establishment, *Foreign Affairs*.[39] Since the end of the Cold War, Huntington suggested, people defined their identity increasingly in ethnic and religious terms, making them prone to observe an us-versus-them opposition between themselves and members from another ethnicity or religion. Secular ideology was losing ground, and elites would now attempt to garner support by appealing to the religion and cultural identity of their particular civilization. In the opening pages of his famous book *The Clash of Civilizations and the Remaking of World Order*, Huntington did not mince words:

> One grim Weltanschauung for this new era was well expressed by the Venetian nationalist demagogue in Michael Dibdin's novel, Dead Lagoon: 'There can be no true friends without true enemies. Unless we hate what we are not, we cannot love what we are. These are the old truths we are painfully rediscovering after a century and more of sentimental cant. Those who

deny them deny their family, their heritage, their culture, their birthright, their very selves! They will not lightly be forgiven'. The unfortunate truth in these old truths cannot be ignored by statesmen and scholars. For peoples seeking identity and reinventing ethnicity, enemies are essential, and the potentially most dangerous enmities occur across the fault lines between the world's major civilizations.[40]

To the attentive reader, Huntington's clear-cut prose provides an artful blend of what is and what ought to be. Written in a style of sober factual description, it equally serves as political and strategic prescription. After reading the book and going over the above passage several times, it becomes clear that this is not a message of caution, but one of instruction. Huntington pointed especially towards Islam as a possible source of enmity for the West and a touchstone for reinventing Western identity. Carl Schmitt's definition of the political as the distinction between friend and enemy looms large in Huntington's writing:

> It is human to hate. For self-definition and motivation people need enemies: competitors in business, rivals in achievement, opponents in politics. They naturally distrust and see as threats those who are different and have the capability to harm them. The resolution of one conflict and the disappearance of one enemy generate personal, social, and political forces that give rise to new ones. 'The 'us' versus 'them' tendency is', as Ali Mazrui said, 'in the political arena, almost universal'. In the contemporary world the 'them' is more and more likely to be people from a different civilization.[41]

Controversially, Huntington defined Islam (and secondarily China, or the Confucianist civilization) as the primary source of civilizational conflict for the West. The 'centuries-old military interaction between the West and Islam is unlikely to decline. It could become more virulent', Huntington proposed. As Gilles Kepel observed, Cold War enmity towards the Soviet Union was now transposed onto Islamic civilization as a whole.

> [T]he comparison was misleading since it suggested that the world of Islam is as centralized as the Soviet bloc once was (Chinese dissidence notwithstanding) and the Mecca really constitutes the Moscow of Islam. But the Muslim world is neither monolithic nor homogeneous. It has many centers, all of which compete for hegemony over political and religious values. Islam's relation to the West, and to the modernity the West invents and disseminates, is more complex, historically fraught, and intimate than the clear-cut ideological and military antagonism that prevailed between the United States and the USSR.[42]

The 1990s offer a startling similarity to the neoconservative campaign for intensification of the Cold War in the 1970s. In 1996, the neoconservatives Bill Kristol and Robert Kagan published an article in *Foreign Affairs*, 'Toward a

Neo-Reaganite Foreign Policy'. It argued for a massive investment in advanced weaponry, allowing Washington, now the sole superpower, to aggressively pursue a 'benevolent' world hegemony in defiance of rogue states: a *Pax Americana*. The article signalled the beginning of a larger campaign. In this, the neoconservatives were sustained by the powerful organized interests of the American defence industry.

An influential neoconservative think tank was founded one year later, the Project for a New American Century (PNAC), to pressure the Clinton Administration. Among the signers of the PNAC petitions were neoconservative intellectuals such as Francis Fukuyama and Norman Podhoretz, but also future Vice-President Dick Cheney, future Secretary of Defense Donald Rumsfeld, future assistant Secretary of Defense Paul Wolfowitz, future Undersecretary of Defense Douglas Feith and future Department of Defense Policy Board Chairman Richard Perle, famously referred to by colleagues as 'the prince of darkness'.[43] In 1998, the PNAC published an open letter to Bill Clinton, calling for pre-emptively 'removing Saddam Hussein and his regime from power'.[44] However, it wasn't until the attacks on 9/11 that these ambitions became policy.

The manipulated evidence of weapons of mass destruction that led to the Iraq War is a faithful copy of the imaginative portrait painted by neoconserva-tives of the Soviet threat in the 1970s. The problem was, again, the scepticism of the CIA and foreign policy realists like Colin Powell, unconvinced of the ties between Saddam Hussein and Al-Qaeda, or the acuteness of the threat posed by Saddam's regime. Rumsfeld and Wolfowitz created the Office of Special Plans, headed by Abram Shulsky, a scholarly expert on the work of Leo Strauss.[45] There were also other, more personal lines of continuity. George W. Bush, the son of Bush senior (who as CIA director had an important role in facilitating TEAM B) was now in charge. Daniel Pipes, the son of TEAM B president Richard Pipes, became one of the most important anti-Islam hawks. In 2003, Bush appointed him to the board of the US Institute of Peace, a foreign policy think tank originally founded under Reagan. Richard Pipes also became one of the most important inspirations and fundraising conduits for Geert Wilders.[46]

It is this political history that forms the background for the development of a neoconservative perspective on Islam. Neoconservative Islam critics such as Daniel Pipes and Bernard Lewis used the fundamentalist myth of a return to a pure Islam, in order to equate the religion as such with fundamentalism, describ-ing it as the 'true nature' of Islam. Ayaan Hirsi Ali became one of the most prominent exponents of that perspective.

Deconstructing Ayaan

The task of reconstructing the personal intellectual history of Hirsi Ali is com-plicated by the fact that her very first articles are already the finished product of an intellectual conversion whose precise origin and nature are withheld from us in her writing. A commonly held opinion is that Hirsi Ali's ideas have

developed and radicalized gradually over time in reaction to real-life occur-
rences such as 9/11, the death threats she received, her switch to the VVD and
the brutal assassination of her collaborator on the film *Submission*, Theo van
Gogh. That is also how Hirsi Ali has presented her political trajectory in her
writing. In *Infidel*, she depicts her views on Islam as formed in response to 9/11,
an event described as a moment of political awakening: 'the little shutter at the
back of my mind, where I pushed all my dissonant thoughts, snapped open after
the 9/11 attacks, and it refused to close again'.[47] She retrospectively portrays
herself in the weeks after the attacks as a deeply confused Muslim:

> War had been declared in the name of Islam, my religion, and now I had to
> make a choice. Which side was I on? I found I couldn't avoid the question.
> Was this really Islam? Did Islam permit, even call for, this kind of
> slaughter? Did I, as a Muslim, approve of the attack? And if I didn't, where
> did I stand on Islam? I walked around with these questions for weeks; I
> couldn't get them out of my head.[48]

None of that confusion is apparent, however, in those very same first weeks
after 9/11, when Hirsi Ali's first published article appeared. It was published in
the monthly journal of the think tank of the social democrat party where she then
worked as a researcher, bearing the title *In Between Confrontation and Reconciliation: The Netherlands and Islam*.[49] The short essay analyses the Dutch
debate on Islam in the wake of 9/11, a discussion between those proposing a
more confrontational approach and those advocating tolerance. After some
deliberation, Hirsi Ali sides with those opting for a more confrontational
approach, in order to 'force Muslims to debate Islam'.[50] That force is necessary
because 'in the perception of a Muslim, the Koran contains the truth and this
truth is of all times and places. That makes it impossible for moderate Muslims
to express doubts about the religion'.

Especially regarding three Islamic dogmas there is no substantive discussion
possible, not between Muslims, nor between Muslims and non-Muslims. First,
in Islam, 'the individual and the community are inextricably bound up with each
other. The will of Allah, as revealed in the Koran, determines ideology, politics,
law, individual identity and his relation to the community'. Second,

> the loyalty of a Muslim to other Muslims is obligatory: in a conflict between
> Muslims and non-Muslims, sympathy and support will always go to
> Muslims first. Who violates this rule is a traitor and, according to the Koran,
> worse than unbelievers.

The demand towards Muslims to 'clearly distance themselves from acts of terror
and radical Islam again and again faces the opposition of this loyalty principle'.

> Finally, there is the significance of the hereafter. Life on earth only counts
> as a passage towards eternal life after death [...]. When one doubts the unity

of God or his words in the Koran, then you spoil your chances on a place in the hereafter.[51]

Muslims are not allowed to doubt or ask questions concerning their faith, Hirsi Ali concludes.

To be clear, these are not empirical observations about the reality of Muslim life; they are statements that primarily serve a political purpose. To take only the most obvious example: in the immediate aftermath of 9/11, the attacks were widely and explicitly denounced by leading Muslim organizations around the world. On 14 September 2001, the following communiqué was published. Its signatories included leaders of the Muslim Brotherhood in Egypt, Sudan, Syria and Jordan, Pakistan's Jamaat-e-Islami, Palestine's Hamas movement, Tunisia's Nahda movement, Malaysia's PAS, Indonesia's PKS, Morocco's PJD, and scholars from al-Azhar University:

> The undersigned, leaders of Islamic movements, are horrified by the events of Tuesday 11 September 2001 in the United States which resulted in massive killing, destruction and attack on innocent lives. We express our deepest sympathies and sorrow. We condemn, in the strongest terms, the incidents, which are against all human and Islamic norms. This is grounded in the Noble Laws of Islam which forbid all forms of attacks on innocents. God Almighty says in the Holy Qur'an: 'No bearer of burdens can bear the burden of another'.
>
> (Surah al-Isra 17:15)[52]

The logical consequence of Hirsi Ali's propositions on Islam is that of implicitly tying together Al-Qaeda and the 9/11 attacks with the whole of Islam, seeing that all Muslims are divinely ordained to be loyal to one another. She thus divides the world into two monolithic blocs, Islam versus the West, and questions the loyalty of Muslim immigrants in the West, who are pressed to choose sides – as individuals – against their own communities. In a typical case of textual determinism, Hirsi Ali reduces the everyday reality of contemporary Muslim life to the Koran, depicted as a body of closed norms, beyond discussion, governing all aspects of life. Olivier Roy aptly characterized this type of Western criticism of Islam:

> [T]o define Islam as a body of closed norms and Muslims as making up a community excluding membership in any other group is precisely to adopt the fundamentalists' definition of Islam. This is a reference to an imaginary Islam, not to the real Muslim world, and the fundamentalists are made into authentic representatives of Islam, even if this means speaking with benevolent condescension about the poor [Muslim] liberals who cannot make themselves heard.[53]

In that same very first article, Hirsi Ali writes how 'moderate, benevolent Muslims' are hopelessly uninformed about the true nature of their religion. The goal of the Western 'dialogue' with moderate Muslim immigrants, the aim of forcing them to debate Islam, is to make Muslims more informed about the inherent radicalism and violence of their religion.[54] Only by secularizing their faith – accepting scripture as man-made and Mohammed as a human, fallible figure – and only by extracting themselves from their communities can Muslims become acceptable to the West. This is the binary vision that Ayaan Hirsi Ali started out with, inspired by the views of Bernard Lewis. And it is this vision that she would consistently continue to defend right up to her latest book, *Heretic*, where the ideas of Bernard Lewis again figure prominently.[55]

Hirsi Ali's writing, right from the very beginning, is a well-thought-out clash of civilizations narrative, drawing on Dutch New Atheists inspired by neoconservatism, such as Paul Cliteur and Herman Philipse on the one hand, and Orientalist authors such as Bernard Lewis and Lewis Pryce-Jones on the other. Put differently, Ayaan Hirsi Ali's ideas on Islam are of decidedly Western extraction, and these ideas are – at times – in open contradiction with Hirsi Ali's own life story, as we shall soon see.

Her first public contact with the wider circle of Dutch neoconservatives was in November 2001. The editors of the neoconservative opinion section of *Trouw*, Jaffe Vink and Chris Rutenfrans, had organized a debate with the appropriate Manichean title 'The West or Islam: Who Needs a Voltaire?' in the Amsterdam cultural centre De Balie. In *Infidel*, Ayaan Hirsi Ali describes how she intervened from the stand exclaiming: 'Allow us a Voltaire, because we are truly living in the Dark Ages'.[56] At this occasion Hirsi Ali met Afshin Ellian, the Iranian refugee who had become one of the country's fiercest Islam critics. Hirsi Ali compared him to Salman Rushdie.[57] Vink and Rutenfrans invited her to write her first opinion piece on the theme of her intervention at cultural centre De Balie. From that point on, Jaffe Vink claimed Hirsi Ali as his discovery and protégé, publishing a series of Hirsi Ali's opinion pieces in *Trouw*.[58] Rutenfrans and Vink were the editors of Hirsi Ali's first book, *The Factory of Little Sons* (*De Zoontjesfabriek*), published in 2002, launching Hirsi Ali's career as one of the most influential and controversial Dutch public figures of the decade.[59]

The Orientalist lens

The role of Orientalist authors in forming Hirsi Ali's view of Islam can be deduced from her first more elaborate and theoretical text, published in the yearbook of the social democrat think tank in the autumn of 2002 and translated and reprinted in *The Caged Virgin*. In the article *What Went Wrong? A Modern Clash of Cultures*, titled after the well-known book by Bernard Lewis, Hirsi Ali lays out her ideas on Islamic culture.[60] Basing herself on Lewis and Pryce-Jones, Hirsi Ali argues that 'the religious-cultural identity' of Muslims is characterized by:

- A hierarchical-authoritarian mentality: 'The boss is almighty; others can only obey'.

- Group identity: 'The group always comes before the individual'; if you do not belong to the clan/tribe you will be treated with suspicion or, at best, not be taken seriously.
- A patriarchal mentality and a culture of shame: The woman has a reproductive function and must obey the male members of her family; failure to do so brings shame on the family.[61]

Here we find the classic Orientalist theme of timelessness, abstraction and uniformity. From the skyscrapers in Istanbul and Teheran to the villages in rural Pakistan and Somalia, from the Indonesian archipelago to Muslim immigrants on the European mainland: there is a single, unchanging Islamic 'religious-cultural identity' that can be known in the abstract. 'The Islamic identity (view of mankind and the world)', Ayaan Hirsi Ali writes, 'is based on groups, and its central concepts are honour and disgrace, or shame'.[62] The principal group is the family and then the clan.

According to Hirsi Ali, the values of traditional Islam collide with the principal norms and values of Dutch society and explain 'for a large part' the socio-economic backwardness that Muslims in the Netherlands suffer from. In other words, Hirsi Ali frames integration primarily as a socio-cultural problem, a view that came to dominate the Dutch integration debate. The 'cultural expressions of the majority of Muslims' in the Netherlands, we learn, 'are still at a premodern stage of development'.[63]

Drawing on Pryce-Jones, Hirsi Ali's reasoning concerning the inherent 'backwardness' and traditionalism of Islam revolves around its connection with tribal norms. The argument is as follows: the Koran consists of a set of rules that are adopted from tribal customs, specifically designed to organize the tribes in a coherent tribal system. Warring tribes were convinced to accept laws assuaging them to direct their animosity to unbelievers, leading to Islam's inherently expansionist character and its hostility to the West. Tribal values are thus ingrained in the Koran, reproducing premodern practices, even in modern urban societies: 'the ideas and traditions of Muhammad's tribal society are adopted straight into the industrial and urban society of today'.[64]

Is there any way out of this vicious circle for Muslims? Hirsi Ali wavers between Lewis and Pryce-Jones. She is appreciative of Lewis' argument that either the lack of secularism or the patriarchal nature of Arab societies is responsible for their backwardness. Muslims can undertake the painful process of modernization once they 'relinquish their most substantial values'.[65] Pryce-Jones, on the other hand, believes that secularism and other Western developments cannot be truly understood by people living in an eternal tribal society. Ayaan Hirsi Ali chose Lewis' vision, critiquing the Islamist idea of emancipation and equating emancipation with the escape from religious community:

[E]mancipation doesn't mean the liberation of the community of the faithful or its safeguarding from the power of evil outside forces, such as colonialism,

capitalism, the Jews and the Americans. It means the liberation of the individual from that same community of the faithful.[66]

Finally, she concludes her article in the yearbook of the social democrat think
tank by proposing to 'interpret the concept of "integration" as a process of civilization for groups of Muslim immigrants living in Western societies', and so
'render superfluous the pseudo-debate about the equality of cultures'.[67] Here, the
colonial 'civilizing mission' is turned inwardly, towards the immigrants in
the West. Considering integration to be a process of civilization is also good for the
immigrants themselves since it allows them to 'develop an awareness of their
level of achievement in relation to others', and to 'see that in order to progress
they need to behave according to the values and standards of their newly
adopted home country'.[68] Making immigrants aware of their backwardness will
make them happier to adjust.

Stark contradictions

Tactically choosing to adopt the Orientalist imaginary of Islam, instead of
describing modern-day Muslim reality, Ayaan Hirsi Ali had to work around a
set of stark contradictions from the outset. In the essay *Why Can't We Take a
Critical Look at Ourselves?*, published in the neoconservative opinion section of
newspaper *Trouw* in March 2002, Ayaan Hirsi Ali uses the father of Mohammed
Atta, the lead organizer of the 9/11 attacks, as a metaphor for the state of the
Islamic world. Confronted with the terrible acts of his son, the father enters a
state of denial, blaming everyone – the Jews, the CIA – but his son. That father,
Hirsi Ali argues, is like Islam: his offspring is Islamic radicalism, but he denies
his responsibility. Like the father of Mohammed Atta who was wholly unaware
of the dark streak in his son, Muslims refuse to see the dark and violent side of
their religion. At this point the reader is confronted with a large contradiction. If
Islam is really a deeply communal, patriarchal and authoritarian culture where
loyalty to one's family and clan comes first, then Mohammed Atta not only
rebelled against his father, the patriarch of the family; he rebelled against Islam.
If power and authority are absolute and unassailable for the 'primitive' minds of
Muslims, as Hirsi Ali has written before, then what explains the revolt of
Islamic fundamentalists against the Islamic establishment, sidelining the clerics,
killing Sadat and denouncing the Saudi monarchy?

Another important contradiction concerns Muslims' lack of knowledge about
the Koran. How can contemporary Muslim life be completely determined by the
Koran, when the average Muslim 'does little with his faith', and 'knows little of
the Koran'?[69] According to Hirsi Ali 'most Muslims never delve into theology',
and 'rarely read the Koran'; 'it is taught in Arabic, which most Muslims can't
speak'.[70] Here, Hirsi Ali wrestles with what Said has described as the second
dogma of Orientalism: the notion that abstractions about the Orient based on
ancient texts are preferable to direct evidence drawn from modern realities. She
resolves that problem by introducing a tautology: 'for many non-practising

Muslims, the essence of their identity and the system of values and morals by which they live remain Islamic'.[71] Moroccan and Turkish immigrants have somehow assimilated the seventh-century tribal values embedded in the Koran, which are 'adopted straight into the industrial and urban society of today', without ever having had contact with the text itself.

The most delicate question, however, is whether Hirsi Ali also used these Oriental motifs to frame the story of her own brutal and traditionalist upbringing. Critics have suggested that there is a tendency in her writing to 'exoticise and Islamicise' her Somalian background.[72] Accusations of deceit regarding an earlier fake story she concocted to enter the Netherlands as a refugee, continue to haunt her later writing as well. Most notably, the Dutch documentary *The Holy Ayaan* (screened on Dutch public television on 11 May 2006) raised a series of doubts concerning her personal story.[73] First of all, did Hirsi Ali really escape to the Netherlands because of a forced marriage and the fear of an honour killing by her family, as Hirsi Ali had told the Dutch public? The people Ayaan Hirsi Ali had stayed with in the Netherlands during her asylum procedure raise legitimate doubts; her family and Somalian acquaintances have denied knowledge of the entire practice of honour killings. Second, in a Dutch television programme, Ayaan Hirsi Ali explained that she was absent during her own wedding, because a woman's presence was not required in Islam. Confronted with opposite testimonies from her family in the documentary claiming she was present, Ayaan Hirsi Ali is shown in the documentary rejecting these as lies, part of what she called the 'Islamic honour-shame complex'. Not long after, however, Hirsi Ali quietly changed her story and in the narrative of her autobiography *Infidel* she is present at her wedding.[74]

Third, in her writing, Ayaan Hirsi Ali depicts her mother as a deeply traditional and religious figure, who 'flourished' in Saudi Arabia, 'a country with such a strict religious climate' and did not want her and her sister to attend school: 'we were going to be married off in a few years anyway, so what good would all that knowledge be to us?'[75] In the documentary, the very opposite is told by her brother: her mother did not want her to marry too early, before finishing her university education. A university-educated woman would be more independent in case of a divorce. The documentary shows how Hirsi Ali was sent to one of the best schools in Kenya, and her brother was sent to a Christian school, because the education was better there. The mother's purported concern about divorce is understandable, since she divorced Hirsi Ali's father when Hirsi Ali was 12, because of his long absences. This, of course, is in clear violation of the religious culture sketched by Hirsi Ali:

> To maximize their potential as producers of sons, girls are taught from early on always to conform – to God, to their father and brothers, to the family, to the clan. The better a woman seems at this, the more virtuous she is thought to be. You should always be patient, even when your husband demands the most dreadful things of you. You will be rewarded for this in the hereafter.[76]

Which is all the more surprising, considering that these codes were suppos-edly strictly observed by Hirsi Ali's family: 'Islam dominated the lives of our family and relations down to the smallest detail. It was our ideology, our politi-cal conviction, our moral standard, our law, and our identity. We were first and foremost Muslim and only then Somali'.[77]

The motivation to raise these issues is not to challenge or downplay the ser-iousness of the mistreatment Ayaan Hirsi Ali is said to have experienced. The pertinent question here is how much of her experiences can be explained by the Orientalist ideas that Hirsi Ali has used to frame her history. Hirsi Ali seems to consciously confound traditional habits of Somali tribal culture with Islam as a religion. And it is unclear to what degree her life story conforms to either. Having grown up with divorced parents, and considering her father's relatively modern ideas in some areas at least, her personal life seems far more complex, multilayered and contradictory than her representation of it. To quote the remarks of the Dutch feminist scholar Bosch in her sharp analysis of *Infidel*:

> Did she not choose herself to wear the hijab and to attend meetings of the Muslim Brotherhood, even though one of her housemates regarded her mode of dress as 'a complete joke' and fellow students avoided her as a 'religious freak in a black tent'? Did she not have a whole line of boyfriends in spite of this, including an imam she used to kiss in secret after prayers? And how many self-confident and independent aunts and female cousins are not featured in the book, who – like her mother in fact – first build up inde-pendent lives of their own, marry, get divorced on their own initiative, and sometimes remarry and sometimes not. Even her relationship with her father and brother is not unequivocal, and her account certainly does not give the impression that they tried hard to restrict her freedom.[78]

Infidel

These contradictions come to a head in *Infidel*, where Hirsi Ali's personal experiences openly contradict the views she adopted from Bernard Lewis. The paradoxical nature of fundamentalist Islam, as described by Roy, a modernizing break with tradition that represents itself as a return to tradition, is also to be found in Hirsi Ali's autobiography:

> A new kind of Islam was on the march. It was much deeper, much clearer and stronger – much closer to the source of the religion – than the old kind of Islam my grandmother believed in, along with her spirit ancestors and djinns. It was not like the Islam in the mosques, where imams mostly recited by memory old sermons written by long-dead scholars, in an Arabic that barely anyone could understand. It was not a passive, mostly ignorant, acceptance of the rules: Insh'Allah, 'God wills it'. It was about studying the Koran, really learning about it, getting to the heart of the nature of the Prophet's message. It was a huge evangelical sect backed massively by

Saudi Arabian oil wealth and Iranian martyr propaganda. It was militant, and it was growing. And I was becoming a very small part of it.[79]

Of course, the very notion of a 'new' kind of Islam contradicts her earlier Orientalist statement that Islam is 'an unchanging, fossilized culture'.[80] In *Infidel*, Hirsi Ali stresses the innovative, modernizing aspects of fundamentalist Islam, the break with old traditions and existing forms of religiosity: 'Traditional ways of practicing Islam had become corrupted, diluted with ancient beliefs that should no longer have currency'.[81] Fundamentalist Islam represents a break with the quietist passivity of mainstream Islam:

> We were not like the passive old school, for whom Islam meant a few rules and more or less devoutly observed rituals, and who interlaced their Koran with tribal customs and magical beliefs in amulets and spirits. We were God's shock troops.[82]

She writes about her immersion in political Islam:

> We read Hasan al-Banna, who set up the Society of Muslim Brothers to oppose the rise of Western ideas in the lands of Islam and promote a return to the Islam of the Prophet. We read Sayyid Qutb, another Egyptian, who said preaching was not enough, that we must stage a catastrophic revolution to establish the kingdom of God on Earth. We thrilled to new movements called Akhwan (Brotherhood) and Tawheed (the Straight Path); they were small groups of true believers, as we felt ourselves to be. This was the True Islam, this harking back to the purity of the Prophet.[83]

Many of Olivier Roy's observations concerning the modern character – in the sociological sense – of political Islam can also be found in Hirsi Ali's writing. The we-form that Ayaan Hirsi Ali employs in the quotations above refers to an Islamic debating group in a local neighbourhood centre in Nairobi that Hirsi Ali joins in her late teens. The group consists mostly of highly educated urban Pakistani and Somalian youth, dressed in western clothing. They were 'dissatisfied with the intellectual level of the teaching at the madrassahs', and Hirsi Ali portrays them as 'very bright, deeply committed older students'. Whereas in the mosque, sermons were often just a recitation of old texts in Arabic, here the debates were in English, they 'were lively, and often clever, as well as much more relevant to our lives than the mosque'.[84] An image that raises questions about Hirsi Ali's earlier claim that Muslims are not allowed to debate their religion. It corresponds with how Roy describes the religious revival in the 1970s and 1980s, the emergence of which is a consequence of the disembedding of Islam from the local, traditional culture.[85]

Hirsi Ali writes disparagingly of the local Islamic traditions of believers who 'interlaced their Koran with tribal customs' and points to the 'universal character' of the Brotherhood: 'In contrast to the clan warfare of Somalia, the Brotherhood seemed to have a more universal character because it included people of every clan'.[86] Here the Brotherhood's Islamism seems to go against the very clan culture that Hirsi Ali has argued to be quintessential to Islam. It is in line with Roy's argument, that Islamist radicals are westernized youth who now see Islam as a universal and global phenomenon, decoupled from local traditions. The loss of cultural identity – 'the old Islam my grandmother believed in', in the words of Hirsi Ali – is the condition for the rise of new forms of fundamentalism.

The modern aspects – on an intellectual level – of the Islamism of Sayyid Qutb and the Muslim Brotherhood are also present in the writing of Ayaan Hirsi Ali. There is the dismissal of the authority of the mosques and existing Islamic jurisprudence (*fiqh*), described as 'old sermons written by long-dead scholars'. There is the aversion to Arabic and the idea of studying the Koran independently in modern languages: 'I bought my own English edition of the Koran and read it so I could understand it better'.[87] There is the notion of 'a catastrophic revolution', alien to the Islamic tradition, and closer to Lenin than Mohammed. There is the ideal of Islam as a universal government, to be realized not by God, but by the movement itself: 'Our goal was a global Islamic government, for everyone'. There is the idea of a revolutionary vanguard, which we see expressed in terms like 'small groups of true believers' and 'God's shock troops', and finally there's the radical Islamist distinction between 'active' and 'passive' Muslims and the 'true' and 'untrue' faith, when she describes their intention 'to awaken passive Muslims to the call of the true, pure belief'.[88]

At the same time, Hirsi Ali stays true to the theme of the return to the source, the notion of a pure Islam. In her autobiography, Sister Aziza tells the teenager Hirsi Ali that it is 'not permitted for one second to imagine that perhaps the Koran's words could be adapted to a modern era. The Koran had been written by God, not by men'. Surprisingly, Hirsi Ali seems to agree with this statement. At times, a more sceptical tone is present in the text. When Hirsi Ali for example writes how 'the Muslim Brotherhood believed that there was a pure, original Islam to which we all should return'.[89] Or when she describes how 'the Islam that we were imbibing stemmed from the hard, essentialist beliefs of thinkers seeking to revive the original Islam of the Prophet Muhammad and His disciples in the seventh century'.[90] Her scepticism is even more explicit in *The Caged Virgin*, where she writes of 'a return to a largely imaginary past as occurred in the Iranian Revolution and in other fundamentalist movements and regimes in Muslim countries'.[91] In these passages, Hirsi Ali seems to be conscious of the fact that the appeal to a return to a true, pure Islam needs be taken with a few grains of salt.

Nothing of that scepticism remains, however, when Ayaan Hirsi Ali writes about her response to 9/11 in a later chapter of *Infidel*. It is the assault on the Twin Towers, we learn, that gave the decisive impetus for her break with her belief. The attacks on the World Trade Center took place in the period that Hirsi Ali worked at the Wiarda Beckman Foundation, the think tank of the Dutch social democrats (PvdA). She recounts how she exits the train, on the morning of the attacks, heading for the office. On the way, she encounters Ruud Koole, then party chairman, who asks her why everybody seems to connect Islam with the attacks, when it is nothing but a 'lunatic fringe'.[92] Ayaan Hirsi Ali answers: 'This is Islam' and recounts her thoughts, walking into the office as having 'to wake these people up'.[93] When she describes the letter from Mohammed Atta with the instructions to the hijackers, how they are to die as good Muslims, she recognizes it as originating in the fundamentalist movement she herself had been part of. She concludes: 'This was not just Islam, this was the core of Islam'.[94]

The recurring essentialist qualifications in Hirsi Ali's autobiography *Infidel* – true Islam, the core of Islam, pure Islam, genuine Islam, timeless Islam, the source of Islam, the essence of Islam, the real Islam – are deeply significant. Take the following passage:

> I first encountered the full strength of Islam as a young child in Saudi Arabia. It was very different from the diluted religion of my grandmother, which was mixed with magical practices and pre-Islamic beliefs. Saudi Arabia is the source of Islam and its quintessence. It is the place where the Muslim religion is practiced in its purest form, and it is the origin of much of the fundamentalist vision that has, in my lifetime, spread far beyond its borders.[95]

Hirsi Ali is aware that these fundamentalist views originate from the *Sahwa* mentioned before, the religious revival in the 1970s and 1980s that she became part of, a combination of Islamism and Wahhabism. She presents the fundamentalist perspective as the timeless essence of the entire Islamic religion. Here it is useful to return to Olivier Roy's remark that Islamic fundamentalism is a movement that denies its own historicity. Hirsi Ali uses that myth of timelessness as a weapon against her former religion.

According to Hirsi Ali, it is scripture and not Bin Laden that is responsible for the attacks: 'The Prophet Muhammad was the moral guide, not Bin Laden, and it was the Prophet's guidance that should be evaluated'.[96] She mentions seeing interviews with Bin Laden, and she is impressed by his references to the Koran, such as 'You who believe, do not take the Jews and Christians as friends; they are allies only to each other. Anyone who takes them as an ally becomes one of them'.[97] She then describes finding these quotations in the Koran:

> I didn't want to do it, but I had to: I picked up the Koran and the Hadith and started looking through them, to check. I hated to do it, because I knew that I would find Bin Laden's quotations in there, and I didn't want to question God's word.[98]

The problem, however, is that the interpretation of the Koran does not function like that. It is not like the Bible or the Gospels, it does not tell a readily understandable story of a person or a people. While the Koran alludes to stories, events and situations that occurred during the time of its inception in Mecca and Medina, it does not provide that context to its readers.[99] To understand the meaning of a verse in the Koran, it is necessary to understand what particular historical situation statements in the Koran refer to. The verse cited above by Bin Laden, for example, refers to a religious conflict in Mohammed's time, in which some Muslims in Medina were considering siding with Jewish tribes. Only when Bin Laden can make clear that the present situation is comparable to that of Medina during the time of Mohammed, does the above quote have relevance. And that is widely contested by other Muslim scholars. It is very unlikely that Hirsi Ali, having studied the Koran herself, is unfamiliar with that basic exegetic logic.

Yet, in her biography she seems convinced that quotations from the Koran can be taken literally: 'All these statements that Bin Laden and his people quote from the Koran to justify the attacks – I looked them up; they are there. If the Koran is timeless, then it applies to every Muslim today'.[100] 'Did the 9/11 attacks stem from true belief in true Islam?', Hirsi Ali asks rhetorically.[101] The answer is clearly confirmative. It is difficult not to wonder whether she *really* believes that. In other parts of her writing she criticizes the people who 'interpret the holy texts' in a 'literal vein', blaming the number of Islamic 'word-Nazis' for the sad state of women in Islam. She associates the literalist reading with fundamentalist Islam.[102] One can only guess that to retaliate against Islam, she has decided to become a 'word-Nazi' too, and pretend the fundamentalists are right and that it is possible to take the Koran literally.

The consequence of Hirsi Ali's assumed literalist position is that she opposes any reform of Islam that centres on interpretation. Edward Said described this paradox succinctly: 'If Islam is flawed from the start by virtue of its permanent disabilities, the Orientalist will find himself opposing any Islamic attempts to reform Islam, because, according to his views, reform is a betrayal of Islam'.[103] Likewise, Hirsi Ali has voiced her opposition to a reform of the interpretation of Islam: 'I have read books written by Muslim "feminists" who seek to reinterpret the Koran.... Yet the works of these so-called moderate interpreters of the Muslim faith are not helpful in their attempt to present a moderate Islam'.[104] She pleads to finally reject the idea that scripture is sacred, and take out entire parts of the text, since the literal text itself is the real culprit:

> What is striking about this tortuous struggle to reinterpret Muslim scripture is that none of these intelligent and well-meaning men and women reformers can live with the idea of rejecting altogether the troublesome parts of scripture. Thus, in their hands, Allah becomes a God of ambiguity rather than of clarity.[105]

In reality, the Koran is full of ambiguities, like any religious text. Clarity resides in the mind of the fundamentalists. Hirsi Ali follows in the footsteps of Bernard Lewis, by describing the friend-enemy logic employed by jihadists, and by subsequently equating Islamic jihadism with scripture as such. In this way, she portrays the whole of Islam as an enemy that needs to be vanquished. 'The greatest advantage of Huntington's civilizational model of international relations is that it reflects the world as it is – not as we wish it to be', Hirsi Ali wrote in

2010 in an opinion piece in the *Wall Street Journal*.[106] 'It allows us to distinguish friends from enemies', she added. The friend-enemy distinction employed by Hirsi Ali closely mirrors the worldview of the 9/11 hijackers she had described in *Infidel*: 'Their world is divided between "Us" and "Them"'.[107]

Notes

1 An earlier and shorter version of this chapter was published as: M. Oudenampsen, 'Deconstructing Ayaan Hirsi Ali: On Islamism, Neoconservatism, and the Clash of Civilizations', *Politics, Religion and Ideology* 17, no. 2–3 (2016): 227–48.

2 Ayaan Hirsi Ali, *Infidel* (New York: Free Press, 2007). The Dutch edition appeared as *Mijn Vrijheid* (*My Freedom*) in 2006. See Ayaan Hirsi Ali, *Mijn Vrijheid* (Amsterdam: Augustus, 2006).

3 Hirsi Ali, 188.

4 Hirsi Ali, 352.

5 Gilles Kepel, *The War for Muslim Minds: Islam and the West* (Cambridge, MA: Belknap Press of Harvard University Press, 2004).

6 Roy, *Secularism Confronts Islam* (New York: Columbia University Press), 43.

7 Edward W. Said, *Orientalism* (London: Penguin, 2003), 105.

8 Roy, *Secularism Confronts Islam*, 7.

9 Said, *Orientalism*, 323–4.

10 Said, 63.

11 Ayaan Hirsi Ali, *Nomad: From Islam to America: A Personal Journey through the Clash of Civilizations* (London: Simon & Schuster, 2010).

12 For reasons of brevity, the focus of this chapter is restricted to the Sunnite tradition, which has been central to Hirsi Ali's development. While the Shiite tradition is of equal political significance in general terms, it occupies a more marginal role in the life and writings of Hirsi Ali.

13 John Calvert, *Sayyid Qutb and the Origins of Radical Islamism* (Cairo: The American University in Cairo Press, 2011).

14 Olivier Roy, *The Failure of Political Islam* (Cambridge, MA: Harvard University Press, 1996), 40.

15 Roy, 3.

16 Calvert, *Sayyid Qutb*, 130.

17 Roy, *The Failure of Political Islam*, 13.

18 Calvert, *Sayyid Qutb*, 130.

19 Roy, *The Failure of Political Islam*, 40–1.

20 Calvert, *Sayyid Qutb*, 130.

21 Cited in Calvert, *Sayyid Qutb*, 216. Qutb stopped short of calling individual Muslims unbelievers (kafirs): 'Whereas the kafir is a person who intentionally disbelieves in God, the jahili individual sees himself as a believer yet dismisses Islam's prerogative to govern all aspects of life'. See: Calvert, *Sayyid Qutb*, 220.

22 Sayyid Quṭb, *Milestones* (Cedar Rapids, Iowa: Unity Pub. Co., 1981), 128.

23 Calvert, *Sayyid Qutb*, 222.

24 Sayyid Quṭb, *Milestones*, 43.

25 Roy, *The Failure of Political Islam*, 24.

26 While all Wahhabists are Salafists, not all Salafists are Wahhabists, which could roughly be described as the Saudi current in Salafism.

27   Calvert, *Sayyid Qutb*, 276.
28   Rudolph Peeters, 'Dutch Extremist Islamism: Van Gogh's Murderer and His Ideas', in *Jihadi Terrorism and the Radicalisation Challenge in Europe*, ed. Rik Coolsaet (Aldershot: Ashgate, 2008), 119.
29   Shadia B. Drury, *The Political Ideas of Leo Strauss* (New York: Palgrave Macmillan, 2005); Anne Norton, *Leo Strauss and the Politics of American Empire* (New Haven, CT: Yale University Press, 2004).
30   Leo Strauss, *The City and Man* (Chicago, IL: University of Chicago Press, 1964), 79.
31   Heinrich Meier, ed., *Carl Schmitt & Leo Strauss: The Hidden Dialogue*, trans. J. Harvey Lomax (Chicago, IL: University of Chicago Press, 1995), 125.
32   Irving Kristol, 'The Neoconservative Persuasion', *The Weekly Standard* 8, no. 47 (2003): 23–5.
33   Samuel P. Huntington, 'Conservatism as an Ideology', *American Political Science Review* 51, no. 2 (1957): 472.
34   Justin Vaïsse, *Neoconservatism: The Biography of a Movement* (Cambridge, MA: Belknap Press of Harvard University Press, 2010), 149.
35   Anne Hessing Cahn, *Killing Detente: The Right Attacks the CIA* (Penn State Press, 2007); Tom Gervasi, *The Myth of Soviet Military Supremacy* (New York: Harper & Row, 1986).
36   Emran Qureshi and Michael Anthony Sells, *The New Crusades: Constructing the Muslim Enemy* (New York: Columbia University Press, 2003).
37   Bernard Lewis, 'The Roots of Muslim Rage', *The Atlantic*, 1990, 48.
38   George W. Bush, 'Speech to Joint Session of Congress' (United States Congress, Washington, DC, 20 September 2001). After 9/11, Bernard Lewis would become the Bush administration's preferred academic expert on the Middle East, visiting Washington six times in the weeks after 9/11. See Nicholas Lemann, 'The Next World Order: The Hawks' Plan to Reshape the Globe', *The New Yorker*, 2002, 42–8.
39   Samuel P. Huntington, 'The Clash of Civilizations?', *Foreign Affairs* 72, no. 3 (1993): 22–49.
40   Samuel P. Huntington, *The Clash of Civilizations and the Remaking of World Order* (New York: Simon & Schuster, 1996), 20. Notable scholars, such as the political theorist Etienne Balibar, have pointed to the similarities between the basic framework of *The Clash of Civilizations* and the work of Carl Schmitt, in particular *Nomos of the Earth*. Writing about Huntington's notion of irreducible civilizational conflict, Balibar concludes: "This idea clearly derives from the geopolitical notions that were theorized around World War II by the German (pro-Nazi) jurist and philosopher Carl Schmitt, who explained that every political institution was based on the absolute primacy of the 'friend versus foe' divide and sought to transfer this notion to the new 'spatial distribution of power' (*Nomos of the Earth*) emerging after the Second World War.'" See Etienne Balibar, We, the People of Europe? Reflections on Transnational Citizenship (Princeton University Press, 2009), 231.
41   Huntington, The Clash of Civilizations, 130.
42   See Kepel, *The War for Muslim Minds*, 60.
43   Kepel, 61.
44   Kepel, 67.
45   Seymour Hersh, 'Selective Intelligence', *The New Yorker*, 4 May 2003.
46   When Wilders was prosecuted in the Netherlands on the grounds of inciting hatred, Daniel Pipes asserted to have raised an amount of six numbers: "Another American support pillar for Wilders, the conservative de Daniel Pipes of the pro-Israel Middle

East Forum, had a year income of 235,000 dollars. Pipes, who is set against a Palestinian state and campaigns for a military attack on Iran, says that in the past year he has collected 'an amount of six numbers' for Wilders in the US." See Tom-Jan Meeus and Guus Valk, 'De Buitenlandse Vrienden van Geert Wilders', *NRC Handelsblad*, 15 May 2010

47 Hirsi Ali, *Infidel*, 272.

48 Hirsi Ali, 269.

49 Ayaan Hirsi Ali, 'Tussen Confrontatie en Verzoening: Nederland en de Islam', *Socialisme & Democratie* 58, no. 10 (2001): 446–51. The article originally appeared in the journal of the Dutch social democrat think tank WBS. It was published on 10 October 2001, and included in *De Zoontjesfabriek* (*The Factory of Sons*), Hirsi Ali's first book published in 2002.

50 Hirsi Ali, *Infidel*, 451.

51 Hirsi Ali, 450–551.

52 Cited in Quintan Wiktorowicz and John Kaltner, 'Killing in the Name of Islam: Al-Qaeda's Justification for September 11', *Middle East Policy* 10, no. 2 (2003): 77.

53 Roy, *Secularism Confronts Islam*, 42.

54 Hirsi Ali, *Infidel*, 451.

55 Margriet Oostveen, 'Paniek en Roem', *NRC*, 12 October 2002.

56 Hirsi Ali, *Infidel*, 275.

57 'Very few Muslims are actually capable of looking at their faith critically. Critical minds like those of Afshin Ellian in the Netherlands and Salman Rushdie in England are exceptions'. Ayaan Hirsi Ali, *The Caged Virgin: An Emancipation Proclamation for Women and Islam*, 1st Free Press ed. (New York: Free Press, 2006), 32.

58 Margriet Oostveen, 'Paniek en Roem', *NRC*, 12 October 2002.

59 Ayaan Hirsi Ali, *De Zoontjesfabriek: Over Vrouwen, Islam en Integratie*, ed. Chris Rutenfrans (Amsterdam: Augustus, 2002).

60 Bernard Lewis, *What Went Wrong? Western Impact and Middle Eastern Response* (Oxford: Oxford University Press, 2002).

61 Hirsi Ali, *The Caged Virgin*, 46.

62 Hirsi Ali, 47.

63 Hirsi Ali, 56.

64 Hirsi Ali, 52.

65 Hirsi Ali, 52–3.

66 Hirsi Ali, 32.

67 Hirsi Ali, 56.

68 Hirsi Ali, 56.

69 Hirsi Ali, *Infidel*, 450.

70 Hirsi Ali, 272.

71 Hirsi Ali, *The Caged Virgin*, 44.

72 Mineke Bosch, 'Telling Stories, Creating (and Saving) Her Life. An Analysis of the Autobiography of Ayaan Hirsi Ali', vol. 31 (Women's Studies International Forum, Elsevier, 2008), 143.

73 Kees Driehuis, 'De Heilige Ayaan', *Zembla*, 11 May 2006. The documentary attempted to fact-check the story that Hirsi Ali had told of her flight to the Netherlands, leading to a famous incident around the false name and story that Hirsi Ali invented to enter the Netherlands as a political refugee. When her officially reported name was shown as false in this Dutch documentary, it became the reason for the hard-line Minister of Immigration Rita Verdonk to revoke Hirsi Ali's Dutch

passport. Since Ayaan Hirsi Ali was at the time MP of the same party as Verdonk, the right-wing liberal party VVD, it led to a political crisis and the fall of the second Balkenende cabinet in 2006. Ayaan Hirsi Ali became a victim of the anti-immigrant agenda of the party she herself had been MP of, prompting her departure to the US. For our purposes here, the political scandal itself is not that significant. Ayaan Hirsi Ali had been quite open about the fact that she had lied about her name and country of provenance in her asylum procedure, and she had understandable reasons to do so.

74 Hirsi Ali, *Infidel*, 176.
75 Hirsi Ali, *The Caged Virgin*, 137.
76 Hirsi Ali, *Infidel*, 74.
77 Hirsi Ali, *Infidel*, ix.
78 Bosch, 'Telling Stories', 143.
79 Hirsi Ali, *Infidel*, 88.
80 Hirsi Ali, *The Caged Virgin*, 153.
81 Hirsi Ali, *Infidel*, 215.
82 Hirsi Ali, 220.
83 Hirsi Ali, 108.
84 Hirsi Ali, 109.
85 Roy, *Secularism Confronts Islam*, vi.
86 Hirsi Ali, *Infidel*, 36.
87 Hirsi Ali, 104.
88 Hirsi Ali, 109.
89 Hirsi Ali, 105.
90 Hirsi Ali, 108.
91 Hirsi Ali, 51.
92 Hirsi Ali, 268.
93 Hirsi Ali, 268.
94 Hirsi Ali, 269.
95 Hirsi Ali, 675–6. Italics mine.
96 Hirsi Ali, 271.
97 Hirsi Ali, 271.
98 Hirsi Ali, 271.
99 Suleiman Mourad, 'Riddles of the Book', *New Left Review*, no. 86 (2014): 15–52.
100 Hirsi Ali, *Infidel*, 273.
101 Hirsi Ali, 271.
102 Hirsi Ali, *The Caged Virgin*, 160, 171.
103 Said, *Orientalism*, 106.
104 Hirsi Ali, *Nomad*, 196.
105 Hirsi Ali, 197.
106 Rogier van Bakel, ' "The Trouble Is the West": Ayaan Hirsi Ali on Islam, Immigration, Civil Liberties, and the Fate of the West', *Reason*, 10 October 2007.
107 Hirsi Ali, *Infidel*, 272.

7 The dawn of an online counterculture

No analysis of the rightward turn in Dutch society can be complete without considering the effervescent movement of 'keyboard warriors' populating the internet. The wave of anti-establishment sentiment that brought Pim Fortuyn to political stardom happened to coincide with the emergence of the internet as a prominent factor in shaping public opinion. The Dutch blogosphere became the natural habitat of a peculiar conservative counterculture that took the country by storm in the decade to come. A key role in that development was reserved for a controversial weblog called *GeenStijl* (literally: No Style). It quickly developed into the flagship of the Dutch right-wing blogosphere and continues to be influential today. Its editors combine irony with derisive attacks on the Dutch political and media establishment, amid a flurry of sexist and racist jokes, all with the professed larger aim of mocking Dutch decency and political correctness. With between half a million and one-and-a-half million unique visits a month, the internet juggernaut serves a significant part of the Dutch population of 17 million. It can claim the downfall of a minister, the establishment of its own public television franchise, and a successful campaign for a national political referendum on an association treaty between the EU and the Ukraine. All in all, no minor feats.

From an international viewpoint, *GeenStijl* is perhaps best described as a Dutch forerunner to the alt-right in the United States. The American online radical-right movement quickly acquired international fame due to its prominent role in Donald Trump's campaign in the 2016 elections. As outlined in Angela Nagle's *Kill All Normies*, the American alt-right is known for its online jargon, its weaponization of irony, its love of transgression for its own sake and its peculiar relation to the counterculture of the 1960s:

> This was unlike the culture wars of the 60s or the 90s, in which a typically older age cohort of moral and cultural conservatives fought against a tide of cultural secularization and liberalism among the young. This online backlash was able to mobilize a strange vanguard of teenage gamers, pseudonymous swastika-posting anime lovers, ironic South-Park conservatives, anti-feminist pranksters, nerdish harassers and meme-making trolls whose dark humour and love of transgression for its own sake made it hard to know what political views were genuinely held and what were merely, as they used to say, for

the lulz. What seemed to hold them all together in their obscurity was a love of mocking the earnestness and moral self-flattery of what felt like a tired liberal intellectual conformity.[1]

As we will see, the online subculture surrounding the weblog *GeenStijl* contains striking similarities to the American alt-right. As one *GeenStijl* editor wrote on the occasion of the weblog's ten-year anniversary: 'The basis of *GeenStijl* remains lol'.[2] Yet there are also significant differences. *GeenStijl* emerged almost a decade earlier, in a very different context. Its political orientation is arguably more mainstream than its American counterpart, which contains, by its own admission, openly extreme right and neo-Nazi strands. *GeenStijl* prefers to ridicule the Dutch extreme right as *kaalkopjes* (baldies). Moreover, the discourse of GeenStijl has its own peculiar political roots. The weblog has popularized a critique of the progressive *Gutmensch* – a sarcastic insult referring to someone who dogmatically seeks to impose morality on others. As shown by the Austrian political scientist Katrin Auer, the term *Gutmensch* – traced back to the philosophy of Friedrich Nietzsche – emerged in the 1990s in Germany and Austria as part of the larger radical right opposition to 'political correctness'.[3] There is no apparent equivalent in the American debates and the English language.

Two dominant frames have served to explain the emergence of *GeenStijl* and the Dutch online counterculture. On the one hand, there is the more technological determinist view, which maintains that the medium is the message. It sees phenomenon like *GeenStijl* as a logical expression of a new generation formed by the conventions of the internet. The nihilism and cynicism of *GeenStijl*, in this perspective, is 'a cultural spin-off from blogging software' and the 'techno-mentality of users'.[4] On the other hand, there is the cultural pessimist view that portrays *GeenStijl* as part of a broader societal trend of declining manners and increasing impudence. Drawing on a larger tradition of mass culture theory, this explanation focuses on the declining confidence of Dutch elites and the crisis in morality caused by consumer capitalism.

Both of these perspectives fail to capture an important fact: *GeenStijl*'s effective countercultural assault on the *Gutmensch* draws on a prominent and long-established Dutch intellectual and literary tradition. The cultural critique popularized by *GeenStijl* cannot be properly understood if we assume that it simply oozed out of the 'digital underbelly'.[5] Rather, its origins lie in the very cultural revolution of the 1960s and 1970s that *GeenStijl* so effectively vilifies. What follows is an attempt to situate the phenomenon of *GeenStijl* in this larger intellectual context. In so doing, the analysis serves to illustrate the complex backlash thesis and the broader argument concerning the manifold, often contradictory manifestations of anti-establishment conservatism.

Tendentious, unfounded and needlessly offensive

The weblog *GeenStijl* was founded in a highly polarized context. The website's humble beginnings can be traced back to 2003, when it started out as a hobby project of Dominique Weesie, a journalist originally born in Rotterdam in a family of Christian entrepreneurs. At that point in time, Weesie still worked at the largest Dutch newspaper: the popular, lowbrow and right-leaning *Telegraaf*. The website *GeenStijl* first achieved prominence as a digital sinkhole, publishing news, videos and opinions that were deemed too controversial or simply unseemly by the conventions of established journalism. Its initial popularity was built on reporting on leaked nude photos, small-town scandals, security footage of burglaries, celebrity gossip or personal videos of fighting couples, drunk students or a soccer player being anally pleasured by his girlfriend. Anyone doing anything wildly embarrassing on video could end up on *GeenStijl*. A particularly popular subject was small-time crime and public misbehaviour, more so when committed by non-white perpetrators. The weblog was no exception to a more general trend of the online world starting to function as both free state and virtual pillory.[6]

While optimistic views concerning the democratizing potential of digital technology resonated loudly in the 1990s, in the wake of 9/11 a darker strain of online culture came to the fore. The digital domain, due to its accessibility, anonymity and libertarian ethos, turned out to be an ideal refuge for extremist and violent views. After the assassination of Fortuyn in 2002, the internet functioned as an outlet for pent up emotions and antagonism. Extremist views concerning Islam, minorities and asylum seekers were vented online by various shades of right-wing populists, extremists and neo-nationalists. At the other end, a number of Muslim immigrant youth radicalized on the internet: an Amsterdam circle of jihadists organized online, translating texts, sharing videos and calls for jihad. As the sociologist Albert Benschop noted in a report for the multicultural foundation *Forum*, the internet played a vital role in the political polarization that resulted in the murder of the Dutch polemical columnist, filmmaker and *enfant terrible* Theo van Gogh in November 2004:

> The rise of populist Fortuynism in the Netherlands went hand in hand with a strong hardening of the political debate and a coarsening in the style of discussion. It was difficult not to notice that many people who make use of the internet contributed to this polarized hardening. Many discussion forums have degenerated into refuges for people who deeply insult and slander each other, and even threaten each other with death.[7]

Around the same time, Theo van Gogh had set up his own website, *De Gezonde Roker* (The Healthy Smoker). Van Gogh prided himself on insulting as many people as possible, reserving particular scorn for Muslim immigrants. He perceived the internet as the only place where he could speak without censorship altogether. Unlike many other online authors, however, Theo van Gogh did not write anonymously and quickly became the target of online hatred. In April 2004, four months before his assassination, Van Gogh was threatened with death on a forum site visited by Moroccan youth.[8] Not for nothing, Benschop's report bears the title *Chronicle of a Political Murder Foretold* (*Kroniek van een Aangekondigde Dood*). In this turbulent and polarized context, *GeenStijl* was born.

Politically, both the editors of the website and its online community were deeply marked by the assassinations of Pim Fortuyn and especially that of Theo Van Gogh. As Dominique Weesie later explained in a prominent newspaper interview, *GeenStijl* functioned as a refuge of sorts for all those who were rendered politically homeless by the murders of Fortuyn and Van Gogh:

> I don't want to be identified with anyone. But I don't deny that around Fortuyn something happened and that GeenStijl came to function as a sort of refuge. The murder of Theo van Gogh ... that impacted me a lot. The comments on the site were so serious, at the time everybody was out of their minds for a while. We have had to close down the site for a period of time.[9]

Omitted from this personal account is the fact that Dominique Weesie had played a prominent role in this dynamic himself, calling for violence in the week after the murder of Van Gogh, under his digital alter ego *Fleischbaum*: 'No dialogue, it is time to avenge violence with violence. An eye for an eye, a tooth for a tooth!'[10] After reopening the site, the editors adopted a policy of disassociating themselves both from (calls to) violence and from the Dutch extreme right, ridiculing Dutch neo-Nazis as 'baldies'. *GeenStijl* hired staff with the specific task of deleting comments that were deemed too violent or right-wing extremist.

GeenStijl's peculiar style and rhetoric stood out from the beginning. The website became notorious for its ironical, cynical, hyperbolic and abusive language. Not for nothing, the motto of the blog, still prominently displayed on the site banner, reads: 'Tendentious, unfounded and needlessly offensive'. Over the years, *GeenStijl* developed its own political subculture, a special vernacular by now part of the cultural mainstream. Some of the internet slang coined by *GeenStijl* entered into common usage and eventually found its way into Dutch dictionaries. Another prominent feature was the thousands of committed followers of the website, described as *reaguurders* (a Dutch neologism, roughly equivalent to an internet troll), or *toetsenbordkrijgers* (keyboard warriors). They present the editors with scoops, help to manipulate internet polls, assist in digital investigations of theft and robberies, and more importantly: bombard the comment sections, Twitter accounts or contact forms of political opponents with remarks, insults and in the worst case, death threats. In some prominent cases, the *GeenStijl* editors published addresses and telephone numbers of the people they happened to disagree with, a technique known as doxxing, a way of intimidating and silencing opponents.

After the assassination of Theo van Gogh, the website and its followers could increasingly be described in terms of a social movement. In short opinionated pieces and video reports, the editors campaigned on familiar Fortuynistic themes such as the threat of Islam, the problems of multiculturalism, the hypocrisy of Dutch political elites, the laxness of authorities and the need for law and order, the redundancy of what it called the 'reserve' of 'dead-tree' newspaper media and the incestuous nature of Dutch public broadcasting. For their online video reports, *GeenStijl* perfected the technique of the ambush-interview. Its notoriously insolent reporters aimed to provoke, mock and embarrass. Following a couple of successful *GeenStijl* ambushes that grew out to become true PR-disasters, Dutch politicians started receiving special training on how to deal with *GeenStijl*'s reporters, responding to their provocations with a smile. Despite its cultivated style of political unpredictability and irreverence, *GeenStijl* soon became seen as the voice of the Fortuyn revolt.

The weblog became the flagship of a rapidly growing armada of right-wing blogs in the Netherlands, and a central node in a tightly networked online conservative counterculture. The rallying cry of the movement was not '*a las barricadas!*', but rather: 'to the comment sections!' In this way, *GeenStijl* managed to unlock the potential of a right-leaning segment of the electorate historically known for its political passivity. A demographic that never had been prone to demonstrate or engage in traditional forms of political activity. As newspapers increasingly took their content online, journalists who had never had a large audience talking back to them were suddenly confronted with a virtual people in the comment sections. And an angry people at that: a vast audience of overwhelmingly right-wing commenters, voicing the by now familiar Fortuynistic talking points. In this way, the online world had a prominent role in contributing to the alarming sentiment that Dutch politics and media were hopelessly out of touch after the Fortuyn revolt, setting the scene for a broad rightward shift in public opinion in the years that followed.

Mirroring political developments, in particular the accommodation of Geert Wilders' Party for Freedom (PVV) after the 2010 elections, institutionalization of *GeenStijl* set in after 2010. *GeenStijl* had successfully campaigned for programming slots on Dutch public television, and some of its most successful columnists went on to write for national newspapers, or started their own opinion sites. In 2016, *GeenStijl* entered yet a new phase, launching and finally winning a controversial national referendum on an EU association treaty with Ukraine. What was once a marginal and rebellious boys' club, now became an established part of the opinion landscape. In the words of cultural studies godfather Raymond Williams, we could say that *GeenStijl* is an indispensable element of the 'structure of feeling' of the last decade.[11]

Technological determinism and cultural pessimism

To proceed with the analysis, a broader understanding is needed of the relationship between communication technology, cultural form and social change. The development of such a conception has been central to cultural studies and more specifically, the writing of Raymond Williams. It can be said that Raymond Williams and British cultural studies more generally, underwent a parallel development in relation to Marxism in the 1960s and 1970s as Mannheim's sociology of knowledge had in the 1930s. While underlining the relative autonomy of the cultural field, Williams analysed cultural artefacts by situating them in a larger historical, societal and economic context.

His 1972 book *Television: Technology and Cultural Form* marked a seminal debate on the subject.[12] Williams contrasted his approach to the technological determinism of McLuhan, who argued that the intrinsic formal properties of media such as type, print, radio and television were in and of themselves responsible for their social effects. At the same time, Williams distanced himself from cultural pessimism: the dismissive and often panic-ridden attitude of traditional cultural elites towards emerging technologies. In the mind of the pessimist, new technologies such as radio, television, and later the internet, were associated with the advent of mass man and mass culture, threatening both political stability and the established cultural domains administered by traditional intellectuals. In cultural studies, this perspective on the advent of mass culture became known as the 'mass culture thesis'; it has been criticized for its one-dimensional conception of both 'the masses' and the effects of technology on the audience.[13]

In fact, technological determinism and cultural pessimism are the dominant frames in the Dutch debate on *GeenStijl*. Technological determinism expresses itself in the mainstream view that *GeenStijl* is somehow a natural expression of a new internet-savvy generation, commonly dubbed the '*GeenStijl*-generation'.[14] It is expressed more poignantly by the well-known Dutch media theorist Geert Lovink, who describes *GeenStijl* as a logical result of blogging as a 'techno-social condition' leading to a 'nihilist impulse'.[15] On the other hand, cultural pessimism is to be found in the way prudent-progressive thinkers such as Dick Pels or Bas van Stokkum analyse *GeenStijl* as the quintessential form of so-called *verhuftering* (literally: boorification), a modern variation on the timeless intellectual theme of the moral decline of the masses.[16] According to Dick Pels, 'the vitriolic tone of internet-trolls' should be seen in connection with the 'discontent of those left behind by society', with 'boorishness in traffic, and indecency in public space'.[17] Let's shortly expand on these two frames.

In his book *Zero Comments*, Lovink develops a helpful typology of blogging as technological form. A blog is defined as a frequent chronological publication of personal opinions and web links, often in response to the mainstream media. Blogging is the product of a period of massification of the internet at the end of the 1990s, made possible by automated software with user-friendly interfaces. Bloggers position themselves on the borders of the news industry, framing and commenting on news rather than fully adopting the role of journalists themselves. In this way, Lovink argues convincingly, bloggers transform news from a lecture into a conversation and incorporate rumour and gossip, mixing the logic of public and private realms. *GeenStijl* is characterized by Lovink as the epitome of a radical subgenre of the blog, namely the 'shocklog' that 'use shock and slander to sling mud at current affairs, public individuals and institutions'.[18]

According to Lovink, the character of blogs is determined by a combination of software functionalities and the attitudes of the generation of early adopters, who go on to dominate the politics and aesthetics of a particular communication medium for decades after its emergence. Consequently, the cynical and/or nihilist character of shocklogs such as *GeenStijl* is a logical outcome of blogging as a 'techno-social condition' described by Lovink in exceedingly McLuhanesque terms:

What is important to note is the Zeitgeist into which blogging as a mass practice emerged. Internet cynicism in this case is a cultural spin-off of blogging software, hardwired in a specific era; it is the result of procedures such as login, link, edit, create, browse, read, submit, tag and reply.[19]

Proceeding to compare bloggers to the characters in Michel Houellenbecq's work, who project their coldness and loneliness to the world, Lovink sees bloggers as driven by a 'nihilist impulse'. The hegemonic truths presented by the mainstream media have increasingly been undermined due to the rise of the internet. Yet the revolution promised by new communication technology has never been realized. The certainty that the old, top-down media paradigm will be overthrown has dissipated, leading to nihilism. Lovink ends his analysis with a passionate defence of blogging: 'As a micro-heroic, Nietzschean act of the pyjama people, blogging grows out of a nihilism of strength, not of out of the weakness of pessimism'.[20]

Interesting enough, Lovink's analysis chimes with how *GeenStijl* went on to identify itself at a later point in time, as the expression of the 'cynicism' and 'modern nihilism' of the 'network-generation'. In a 2012 column written by Van Rossem, the online moniker of *GeenStijl* editor Bart Nijman, he argued that the baby-boomer generation had betrayed its own cultural revolution by wresting itself free from the Calvinistic mores of their parents, only to impose their own (failed) morality on the generations after them. (Here we recognize the basic thesis of Herman Vuijsje's book *Correct.*) The transparency of the internet had burst the bubble of baby-boomer idealism, a generation whose high aspirations ended with prosaic concerns about lining their own pockets, culminating in cynicism. The tendentious journalism of *GeenStijl* was seen by the mainstream as 'aggressive' and 'indecent', and some discarded it as 'modern nihilism', but Nijman saw that as preferable to the baby boomer's denial of reality. The older generations blame the young for their lack of idealism and their failure to take to the streets in defence of a cause. But the network-generation has discovered that 'banners and mass demonstrations are powerless in the digital age':

> The real protest is to be found on the internet, where boorish precision bombardments destroy the sacred totems called 'decency' and 'respect'. Only when these are fully obliterated, something new can arise from the ashes. The network-generation demonstrates, and does so non-violently, with verbal and digital cynicism.[21]

This notion of a nihilist and cynical 'network-generation' fits seamlessly into how political change is commonly conceptualized in the Dutch consensual tradition: not as the uncertain outcome of a struggle for dominance between opposing ideological camps, but rather as a historical succession of generations, who somehow apolitically and spontaneously incarnate the *Zeitgeist* into which they are born and raised. There is no better way to advocate a certain political agenda in the Netherlands, than to give out that your politics is that of an entire young generation who embody the future. Of course, this generational narrative of *GeenStijl* is a self-aggrandizing origin myth, as any social movement is wont to manufacture. As we will see later, the nihilism and cynicism of *GeenStijl* is neither principally a generational nor a technological phenomenon, but builds on an older – and rather bookish – Dutch nihilist tradition.

Cultural pessimism: 'Boorification'

A very different view on *GeenStijl* is to be found among the cultural pessimists. According to this broad current of opinion, the shockblog is merely the most visible exponent of a much larger societal trend. In the eyes of sociologist Dick Pels, the 'abusive language of internet trolls' should be seen in connection with the 'malaise of the societal discontents' and the 'boorishness in traffic and indecency in public space'.[22] The basic thesis in Dick Pels' 2009 manifesto against 'boorification', is that the excessive success of the individualistic and democratic ideals of the 1960s have led to an absence of social norms, and a rampant egoism facilitated by commercialization and consumerism. This provided the breeding ground for the right-wing populist revolt. For Dick Pels, *GeenStijl* serves as illustration of the fact that the emancipation of the popular classes has simply gone too far:

> In the Netherlands, a group of licentious and assertive citizens has emerged that think they have a right to everything, while they have little sense of solidarity, easily blame others for their own anxieties and failures, and overload the government with their demands, even though at the same time they deeply mistrust it. These new individualists with their 'big egos' and 'mouthiness' comport themselves as citizen-kings whose opinions and desires simply need to be heard by politicians.[23]

In an intriguing reversal of roles, Dick Pels, a card-carrying member of the Dutch left who worked as director of the think tank of the GreenLeft party, opposes emancipation and defends authority and moral order. While the right, in a rather unusual historical conjunction, becomes the voice of the disenfranchised, 'pseudoconservatives' in Adorno's words, fighting against the established moral order. This role reversal can be explained by two different developments: on the one hand, the growing embourgeoisement of Dutch progressive politics since the 'cultural revolution' of the 1960s and 1970s, which contained from the very beginning a strong antipopular sentiment.[24] The central reference is Herbert Marcuse's portrait of the worker as a 'one-dimensional man', corrupted by consumerism.[25] In the Netherlands, Marcuse's analysis was taken up by the famous leftist writer Harry Mulisch in his novel *Message to the Rat King*.[26] It also inspired the activist Roel van Duijn, who was the leader of the Provo's – the rebellious youth movement of the 1960s – and founder of the Dutch Green Party. Both Mulisch and Van Duijn used the term *klootjesvolk* (± hoi polloi).

The term was originally coined by the late nineteenth century Romantic poet Willem Kloos to (pejoratively) refer to the lower classes, those deemed merely suitable for reproducing themselves. After the paternalistic and conservative Dutch elites, the *klootjesvolk* formed the main antagonist for the progressive youth revolt of the 1960s. The term referred to the materialistic, hardworking, authoritarian and boring petty bourgeoisie. In the words of Roel van Duijn: 'the masses who we can't and barely want to convince'.[27]

In a short period of time, the young radicals of the 1960s and 1970s were absorbed and accommodated by Dutch institutions, a strategy famously described as 'repressive tolerance'. Many of the student radicals soon became part of the establishment and changed their thinking accordingly, mixing a progressive outlook with more traditional, conservative ideas on 'prudence' and 'moderation'. This is the 'prudent progressive' synthesis, the 'Burkean progressivism' represented by intellectuals such as Bas van Stokkom and Dick Pels. The other development is the birth of a conservative anti-establishment politics, a backlash against the institutional sediments of the 1960s and 1970s. *GeenStijl* is no exception to the observation that this backlash is at the same time a revolt and an echo. Indeed, *GeenStijl* has been described as a contemporary, right-wing incarnation of the Provo youth movement, with very similar tactics of teasing and provoking the established authorities.[28]

These tactics were prominently on display when *GeenStijl* began to actively intervene in the discussion on *boorification*. The occasion was the publication in 2010 of a book by the sociologist and philosopher Bas van Stokkom titled *What a Boor!* (*Wat een Hufter!*). Politically, the book's publication coincided with the dramatic electoral breakthrough of Geert Wilders' Party for Freedom (PVV). Wilders' party grew from nine to 24 seats (16 per cent of the vote) in Dutch parliament. Wilders was given a powerful supporting role in the right-wing minority government led by Mark Rutte (2010–2012). Van Stokkom's book linked this populist breakthrough with a more general narrative of moral decline, sparking a national debate on 'boorification'.

According to Bas van Stokkom, whose analysis was grounded on the writings of a series of prominent Dutch social scientists, the country suffered from a severe moral crisis. The cause was particularly Dutch and could be traced back to the country's history of pillarization. Emancipation and depillarization in the 1960s had cast suspicion on elite authority and attempts to edify of the masses. In the 1990s a second, even more sizeable wave of emancipation from paternalism occurred, as the commercialization of the media took hold. From this point on, Dutch elites simply gave up on the ambition to enlighten the larger populace, retreating into their own lofty subculture. Only when cosmopolitan elites would once again engage in a civilizing mission, could the rightward shift in Dutch society be halted, to make way for a 'prudent progressive spirit'.[29] In fact, Van Stokkom did not single out the lower classes or the electorate of the PVV as the main culprit. He presented Dutch moral decline as a more generalized phenomenon. But he did, in passing, criticize the shockblog *GeenStijl* for 'its abundance of loveless and disdainful comments' and its nihilism. For him, its 'impetuous use of freedom of expression' and its 'destructive, abusive online language' were symbolic of the larger moral crisis.[30]

In a confrontation that has achieved somewhat of a cult status, *GeenStijl* visited Bas van Stokkom for a surprise interview at a book presentation of *What a Boor!* After being prodded for examples illustrating his criticism of *GeenStijl*, the philosopher came up empty and had to guiltily admit that he had not really studied the website very thoroughly. When Van Stokkom, visibly uncomfortable and embarrassed, walked away in the middle of the interview with the pretext that he needed to go and present his book, the *GeenStijl* interviewer reprimanded him: 'We do give each other a hand, don't we?' After the handshake, the interviewer finished the job by subtly calling Van Stokkom a *hufter*. No Dutch professor had ever been humbled in this way by the media. From that moment on, *GeenStijl* took a lively interest in the matter. It eagerly devoted a series of blog-posts to their favourite 'fake scientist' and decided to appropriate the term *hufter* (boor) as a nickname for their movement. A month after the interview, *GeenStijl* published the *Boor Manifesto* (*Hufter Manifest*) that embraced and redefined boorishness as a form of transparency and progression (more on the manifesto shortly). Dick Pels responded to the manifesto in an article describing Geert Wilders from the PVV as 'the boss of the boors':

> The old Provo Roel van Duijn is right: 'With Wilders the klootjesvolk has seized power'. Modern populism is the rebellion of the boors, and Wilders is their boss. Always aggressive, always angry, always indignant, always teasing, nagging, pulling, barking, pestering and intimidating. Always blowing things out of proportion, screaming as loudly as possible. Wilders is the perfect embodiment of the 'Boor Manifesto' of GeenStijl that praises verbal extremism as an expression of brave recalcitrance, while calling decency the 'cancer of society'.[31]

GeenStijl fired back by stating that the 'GreenLeft-nerd' had not properly understood the manifesto and advised Pels (born in 1948) to ask his mother 'what her generation thought about the 1960s, when his generation were seen as boors'.[32] Here, *GeenStijl* positioned itself as the rightful heir of the 1960s and 1970s rebellion. Originally, the term Provo was coined by the conservative criminologist Wouter Buikhuisen in 1965, to describe a growing current of anti-authoritarian youths, driving around on scooters, hanging out in public space, listening to rock and roll and harassing passers-by. Provo leader Roel van Duijn subsequently appropriated the word with the intention of politicizing the youth, which he aimed to magically transform into the 'revolutionary provotariat'.

Van Stokkom and Dick Pels, both former members of the 1960s and 1970s student generation, now found themselves in the position of Buikhuisen, defending established authority against youth rebellion. It allowed *GeenStijl* to proverbially take on the mantle of Roel van Duijn and appropriate the word *hufter* as a point of pride. A similar provocative tactic had been pursued when newspaper *de Volkskrant* condemned *GeenStijl* in 2008 for its effect on youth culture. A prominent journalist connected *GeenStijl* with the increased amount of death threats to politicians. 'A big supplier of the rapidly grown amount of threats that Ministers and MPs receive, is the high school circuit of the uninhibited *GeenStijl*-generation, accustomed to react in primordial fashion to anything that is unwelcome'.[33] *GeenStijl* responded in style by filing a complaint at the Dutch Press Council, ironically accusing *de Volkskrant* of being 'tendentious, unfounded and needlessly offensive', while dismissing the Press Council at the same time as 'a club of windbags without real authority'.[34]

The rhetoric and textuality of GeenStijl

There is a degree of truth to both the cultural pessimist frame (*GeenStijl* as epitome of a larger moral crisis) and the technological determinist frame (*GeenStijl* as the logical product of uninhibited cynicism of the network-generation). Pels and Van Stokkom are right to stress the continuities and causal connections between *GeenStijl* and the anti-authoritarian protest movements of the 1960s. And as Benschop argued, technological form did play a role in facilitating an almost unconditional and absolutist notion of freedom of speech. At the same time, these frames simplify and distort our understanding, and preclude a more substantive engagement with the peculiar discourse of *GeenStijl*.

In contrast to technological determinism, Raymond Williams stressed that 'the moment of any new technology is a moment of choice'. Of course, technological form has specific effects. But there is no such thing as a culture that is 'hardwired' into technological form.[35] Rather, soft and malleable forces such as the intentions of the broadcaster, institutional practices and power dynamics decide how a technology is put to use. Communication technology is not a mere transmission belt for a pre-existing culture that is already somehow out there; it is a creative and social constructionist force. In order to understand and make use of its power, Williams argued, it is indispensable to analyse the rhetoric and textuality of new cultural forms. In contrast to the cultural pessimists, Raymond Williams stated that one 'cannot be satisfied with the older formula: enlightened minority, degraded mass'.[36] Black-and-white distinctions between elite and mass culture fail to do justice to the versatility of culture. Williams insisted that the intellectual and literary tradition is a common inheritance, and not the product of any single class or sector. The importance of Williams' approach is that it gives room for cultural and political agency, and does not draw too decisive a boundary between high and popular culture.

What is missed by both of the interpretative frames we have analysed is the fact that the cultural critique championed by *GeenStijl* builds on a much larger and older tradition in the Netherlands. When we look more closely at the writings on the website of *GeenStijl*, two elements stand out. First, the blog is characterized by a nihilist orientation that is Nietzschean in inspiration. Second, the use of satire and ironic humour by *GeenStijl* draws on the provocative use of irony in the Romantic literary tradition. These elements have not been concocted or even assembled by *GeenStijl* itself. They are derived from a larger nihilist and ironic tradition in the Netherlands, that runs from literary luminaries such as W.F. Hermans and Gerard Reve to Theo van Gogh, Theodor Holman, the literary journal *Propria Cures* and finally *GeenStijl*.

Nietzsche for the masses

GeenStijl's Nietzschean inspiration is most clearly expressed in the *Boor Manifesto* that has by now acquired the status of a programmatic statement. In this ironically written text, an epic battle is sketched between the 'boors' and the 'decency terrorists', in which the boors are the heroes and the moral censors represent the evil to be vanquished: 'Boors create transparency and progress. It's the decency terrorists who are the true anti-socials, by trying to contain the Netherlands in their status quo'. According to the manifesto, boors are people that dare to ask controversial questions, who are not afraid to think for themselves and tread outside of given conventions. When we think of boors, we should think of scientists like Copernicus and Darwin who have made progress possible by ignoring the religious 'decency terrorists'. According to the editors of *GeenStijl*, the boorification described by Pels and Van Stokkom is a positive trend to be heartily embraced. 'Being a boor is disregarding the critique or compliments of others. Being a boor is a road trip to the land of unlimited possibilities. Being a boor is discovering, demonstrating and constantly doubting the foundations of one's world'.[37]

The attentive reader is by now becoming suspicious. Yes, the shockblog *GeenStijl*, notorious for being home to the darkest dregs of the digital underbelly, writes on (metaphysical) foundations that need to be called into question. Scrolling further, one discovers that the *Boor Manifesto* contains obvious parallels to the moral philosophy that Nietzsche penned down in books such as *Beyond Good and Evil* and *On the Genealogy of Morality*.[38] In these texts, Nietzsche polemicizes against what he calls 'slave morality' or 'herd animal morality'. He opposes the values that derive from the weak, the oppressed and the dependent, ingrained in Christian ethics and socialist egalitarianism. On the opposite pole, Nietzsche identifies master morality – 'the elevated, proud states of soul' of the noble and powerful that dare to take themselves as point of departure. As Nietzsche writes:

> The noble type of person feels that he determines value, he does not need anyone's approval, he judges that 'what is harmful to me is harmful in itself', he knows that he is the one who gives honour to things in the first place, he creates values.[39]

The manifesto reads as a paradoxical translation of these Nietzschean themes to the realm of popular (online) culture. The 'boors' equal master morality, the 'decency terrorists' represent slave and herd morality. Where Nietzsche states that the aristocratic man needs no approval from others, engaging in experiment and transgression of norms, *GeenStijl* writes of boors that break loose from the herd, 'to jump over the fence and explore the wilderness'. Nietzsche jeers at the group conformism that characterizes herd morality. *GeenStijl* describes 'decency terrorists' as a 'herd of cows that loudly moo NOT ALLOWED! to the cow that has broken loose, while they allow themselves to be meekly led to the slaughterhouse. In the name of decency. Decency is the cancer of society'. Also the Christian character of slave morality comes to the fore in the figure of the 'decency terrorist' in the manifesto, who 'preaches hell and damnation or brings in God or Godwin to reinforce his mistaken view'.

Nietzsche's critique of religion and slave morality is that it denies life in this world in the name of another, morally righteous and heavenly world. In so doing it tames and civilizes the beast of prey 'man', leading to a world of mediocrity. There is an essential role for the priest in Nietzsche's philosophy, whose remedy for the suffering of the weak is the ascetic ideal that interiorizes suffering as feelings of guilt, fear and punishment. In this way, the pain of the weak is turned inwardly, into self-discipline, self-surveillance and self-overcoming. Whereas the cruelty and punishment of the noble, aristocratic type is directed towards an external enemy, the ascetic finds it inside himself, the 'enemy' within. The ascetic derives pleasure from denouncing pleasure, from not harming the other but rather himself.[40] This is clearly what progressive political correctness amounts to for *GeenStijl*: self-denial in the name of an unnatural and in the end illusory progressive moral order. This stance leads to an aversion to altruism, another striking Nietzschean theme:

The noble and brave types of people, are the furthest removed from a morality that sees precisely pity, actions for others, and *désintéressement* as emblematic of morality. A faith in yourself, pride in yourself, and a fundamental hostility and irony with respect to 'selflessness' belong to a noble morality just as certainly as does a slight disdain and caution towards sympathetic feelings and 'warm hearts'.[41]

A similar sentiment resounds in the manifesto:

Decency terrorists feel at their best when they can passionately feel offended on behalf of a group of people they do not belong to. 'I do not have red hair myself, but I find it indecent of you to say that red-haired people do not have a soul. These type of remarks touch my heart!' That type of people. Not only because they believe it is decent to stand up for everyone, but also because they sincerely think that insulted groups have the resistance of an HIV patient with pulmonary emphysema.[42]

Even the militant tone of *GeenStijl* assumes new meaning, when we look at it in the context of the qualities that Nietzsche attributed to master morality: finding 'subtlety in retaliation' and 'a certain need to have enemies (as flue holes, as it were, for the affects of jealousy, irascibility, arrogance)'.[43] The most significant paradox here is that Nietzsche's elitist lamentations against the herd mentality of lowly plebeians is reproduced in this manifesto for an audience that is itself often described as a resentful digital herd: the *GeenStijl* commenters. The *GeenStijl* editors seem content to inhabit this contradiction.

This negative or radical nihilism of *GeenStijl* is of course far from consistent and a very selective phenomenon, as it ultimately serves to reinstitute a petit-bourgeois conservative morale. Especially when it comes to crime or lax author-ities, *GeenStijl* turns out to be a fervent defender of the existing moral order. Just as well, the weblog then shouts NOT ALLOWED! to the cow that has broken loose, especially when the perpetrator's skin colour happens to be not white.

It is mostly the negative, destructive qualities of nihilist philosophy that *GeenStijl* has mastered in order to provoke and bring down a moral order per-ceived as too egalitarian. Here, nihilism is the figurative paint stripper that serves to disintegrate the progressive layers of lacquer that have been applied to Dutch morality over the decades. In terms of its positive programme, *GeenStijl* advocates a secular, conservative politics oriented at the hardworking white Dutch male. It is focused on a restoration of authority, on an aversion to immigration and Islam and a restored masculinity in opposition to the perceived feminization of Dutch society. Here an excerpt from one of the many semi-ironic posts dedicated to feminization:

> Stop the feminisation of society! Time for the first Mannarchist Wave. Men that do what they have been built for: churning meat, not giving a shit and taking the lead. Living from our Mars-DNA. Check the history of humanity: a million years of MANnarchie. Let's bring it back. Stop the genuflection for the vaginal jihad that is DESTROYING men. Turn the tide! Hetero or gay, who has a dick is the boss.[44]

Nietzschean parallels are again present. In the eyes of Nietzsche, being a man is being able to conquer and command, to say: 'I like that, I'll take it for my own and protect it and defend it against everyone'. The compassion preached by Christian and progressive morality is therefore seen as unmanly:

> A man who can conduct business, carry out a resolution, be faithful to a thought, hold on to a woman, punish and defeat someone for being insolent; a man who has his anger and his sword, and whom the weak, the suffering, the distressed, and even the animals like to come to and, by nature, belong to; in short, a man who is naturally *master* – if a man like this has pity, well then! *This* pity is worth something! But what good is the pity of the sufferer! Or particularly, the pity of those who preach it! The *unmanliness* of what is christened 'pity' in the circles of these enthusiasts is always, I think, the first thing that strikes your eye.[45]

When *GeenStijl* opposes the feminization of Dutch society, it is above all these vitalist Nietzschean themes that come to the fore, instead of a more conventional pol-itics of sexuality as promoted by traditional or religious conservatives. *GeenStijl* believes that a real man is proud of his lack of restraint, and revels in the breaking of taboos. Inextricably bound up with his enjoyment of life are the typical incorrect jokes about Muslims with goats on their balcony, opponents that one would wish dead, and the intelligence of blonde women. A real man openly shows his virility, tells everyone that wants to hear it that he likes to watch porn, and judges all female beauty by asking whether she is 'doable'. This virile, vitalist masculinity is contrasted with colourful language to the repressed masculinity of progressives, the so-called *linksmensch* (literally: left-human), *deugmensch* (literally: decent man), *Gutmensch* (a Germanism, literally: good man), 'moral fag' or 'decency terrorists'.

A good example of the genre is a *GeenStijl* blogpost that introduces itself as a 'SAS survival-guide' on how to 'recognize, isolate and undermine' the 'decency-wanker' at birthday parties, namely by covering said person under 'an avalanche of sarcasm and irony'.[46] The decent type, we learn, serves organic fair trade peanuts on his birthday party, and foregoes flirting with the 'hot babe' in attendance out of political correctness. He fails to enjoy life because he represses his inner drives. Secretly he would prefer to live out those desires, but that is not considered correct by his peers. This is the assumed hypocrisy of politically correct, higher educated progressives that *GeenStijl* loves to crusade against. In a paradoxical sense, *GeenStijl* follows in the footsteps of the libertine 1960s and 1970s slogan 'it is forbidden to forbid' and the connected idea of emancipation and progress as the breaking of taboos. It uses these notions as artillery in the *Kulturkampf* against the baby-boomer generation that once championed them.

The weaponization of irony

This use of nihilism is accompanied by a particular form of ironic humour. *GeenStijl* employs irony to transgress the moral order, and write about the Moroccan-Dutch minority as 'Rif Monkeys', women as 'fuck objects', refugees as 'floatnegroes' and to publicly wish their opponents dead, all with a wink and a smile. Bas Heijne, the acclaimed intellectual and columnist of *NRC Handelsblad*, wrote incisively on the subject. He linked the rise of right-wing populism and *GeenStijl* to the work of the canonical Dutch writer Gerard Reve (1923–2006, more on Reve in the next chapter):

> When the history of new-right populism will be written, then its greatest influence should not be forgotten: Gerard Reve. The language of the current political revolt is pervaded with the irony of Reve – that half-ironic, half seriously teasing of those brave progressive bien pensants with their lack of humor and moral self-righteousness. 'They should ride a burning doll's pram into your twat', is one of the favourite sentences of many Reve adepts. It's all there – the hyperbolic aggression that expresses real anger, but at the same time comical impotence. The irony of Reve, always only half-ironic, has now lodged itself in the public domain. Theo van Gogh, allowed to

whisper to 'the Divine Bald One' Fortuyn, was a great fan of Reve. Martin Bosma finds Reve to be the greatest writer. The best of GeenStijl is steeped in Revian irony.[47]

Indeed, *GeenStijl* often refers to Reve. An illustrative example is a blogpost by *GeenStijl* that deals with commenting on social media. The post starts out as follows: 'Internet comments: axe at the root of civilization or finger in the arse of society?' It discusses the investigation by the Dutch Public Prosecutor of a policeman who voiced Islamophobic comments online and wished Muslims dead. After lamenting the fact that one cannot speak freely anymore, the *GeenStijl* blogpost refers with wistfulness to the time when we could still laugh about Gerard Reve's famous words of abuse: 'They should ride a burning doll's pram into your twat'.[48]

The text of the blogpost is followed by a short video. A man called 'René Lambswool Jumper' – who happens to wear a lambswool jumper – appears on screen, seated in a comfortable armchair. He is 'close reading' a selection of insulting and racist Facebook comments, posted in response to an incendiary video shared by *GeenStijl* some time ago. The soft-spoken, formal delivery of the comments is accompanied by kitschy piano music. While the item is obviously a statement in favour of freedom of speech, the irony has the effect of leaving the viewer uncertain as to whether it is the censors or the abusive commenters that are being ridiculed. It is exactly this combination of making political statements while confusing the audience that is deemed typical of Revian irony.

The occasion for Bas Heijne's comments on irony was a small political scandal that revolved around the use of the Dutch *prinsenvlag* by Geert Wilders' Party for Freedom (PVV). The *prinsenvlag* – a historical flag with orange, white and blue colours – stems from the anti-Spanish revolt and the birth of the Dutch Republic in the sixteenth century. It has since acquired a controversial status, because of its use by the Dutch National Socialist Party in the 1930s, the NSB. The Party for Freedom started to display the flag in their parliamentary office in 2011, causing a public controversy. To complicate matters, the party had hung it next to a flag of Israel and publicly denied the flag's extreme right connotation. According to Bas Heijne, it allowed the PVV to flirt with the extreme-right subtext of the flag, trolling the Dutch political establishment. The response was a predictable, concerned reaction: some spoke of the return of fascism.

For Heijne, the incident epitomized the complex, often half-ironic posturing of the PVV and the Dutch right-wing populist revolt more in general. He saw this political use of irony as setting Dutch populism apart from other European right-wing populist movements, who are more straightforward in their intolerance. Perhaps that is a bit overstated: playful intolerance is certainly not limited to the Dutch.[49] But Heijne is certainly right to argue that the political use of irony in Dutch populism is poorly understood internationally, if only for the fact that irony is difficult to translate. Referring to the anti-Muslim slur that Theo van

Gogh popularized and the incendiary proposal by the PVV to tax Muslim women for wearing headscarves ('head-rags'), Heijne observed: 'Goatfucker, head-rag-tax – one never succeeds in explaining the correspondents of foreign newspapers that it sounds really intense, but at the same time has an ironic undertone. Well, half-ironic; or, a little bit ironic'.[50]

A very similar political use of irony was pioneered by Gerard Reve in response to the immigration wave from the former Dutch colony Surinam, which became independent in 1975. In August 1974, Reve published the poem *For Our Estate* (*Voor Eigen Erf*) in *Propria Cures*, a famous satirical literary weekly, run by students. 'Throw out all that black scum, our country for us. Onwards, towards White Power!', the ironic and hyperbolic poem ended. Despite its inflammatory content, the poem did not elicit much response. That changed when Reve presented the poem in a theatrical manner on the yearly Poetry Night in Kortrijk, Belgium. A scandal was born.

A historical documentary of the Dutch television programme *Andere Tijden*, titled The Riddle of Reve (*Het Raadsel van Reve*), shows archival footage of the Surinam-Dutch lawyer Haakmat. He walked up to Reve after his performance to confront him with the criticism that he deployed 'despicable racism'. The reaction of Reve is striking: the ironic mask is suddenly gone. 'Because those niggers were slaves in Surinam 125 years ago, is it their right that their great-grandchildren come to Amsterdam to live off welfare?', Reve answers visibly agitated.[51] In fact, Reve used irony to make serious political statements. Further confirmation is a letter sent by Reve to the newspaper *Het Parool*, in response to the consternation caused by his performance. He described his poem as a 'primitive cry of alarm, probably posited in too vulgar terms':

> I do not literally mean what is said in the poem, because I am no racist and the negro, in my opinion, has a right to a place under the sun that is equal to the white man. I have in this brutish way, found an audience of millions for my plea, stating that the migration policy of the Dutch government that allows massive entry of migrants, for whom in the Netherlands, there is no work, no accommodation and no future, except pauperization and criminality, will lead to disaster.[52]

A similar potent combination of irony and anti-immigrant politics has been popularized by *GeenStijl*. In a 2017 interview with *NRC Handelsblad*, former *GeenStijl* writer Annabel Nanninga said that her recurring use of the (self-invented) word 'float-negro', to refer to drowning refugees in the Mediterranean, was meant ironically. The same was true for her statement 'Let's hope that Ebola continues to do its work'. The occasion for the interview was the fact that Annabel Nanninga had become a city councillor in Amsterdam for the radical right-wing party Forum voor Democratie. She concluded the interview by stating that 'what Amsterdam needs right now, is a sturdy dose of Revian irony'.[53]

Notes

1 Angela Nagle, *Kill All Normies: The Online Culture Wars from Tumblr and 4chan to the Alt-Right and Trump* (Winchester: Zero Books, 2017), 10.
2 Johnny Quid, 'Gefeliciteerd! GeenStijl bestaat 9 jaar!', *GeenStijl*, 10 April 2012, www.geenstijl.nl/2951751/gefeliciteerd_geenstijl_bestaa/.
3 Katrin Auer, '"Political Correctness" – Ideologischer Code, Feindbild Und Stigmawort Der Rechten', *Österreichische Zeitschrift Für Politikwissenschaft* 31, no. 3 (2002): 291–303.
4 Geert Lovink, *Zero Comments: Blogging and Critical Internet Culture* (New York: Routledge, 2008), 12–13.
5 For the Dutch debate on the *Gutmensch*, see: Joost de Vries, 'Reaguurders in de Digitale Onderbuik', *De Groene Amsterdammer*, 12 December 2008; Thijs Kleinpaste, 'Wie is die Gutmensch? Of Misschien Beter: Wat is de Gutmensch?', *De Groene Amsterdammer*, 16 December 2015; Haro Kraak, 'Gutmensch Groeit Langzaam uit tot Geuzennaam', *De Volkskrant*, 21 December 2015.
6 Clyde Haberman, 'Mob Shaming: The Pillory at the Center of the Global Village', *New York Times*, 19 June 2016.
7 Lovink, *Zero Comments*, xvi.
8 Lovink, xvii.
9 Toine Heijmans, 'Ik Heb Altijd Overal een Mening over, Maar die Is Genuanceerder dan de Mensen Denken', *De Volkskrant*, 23 July 2011.
10 Albert Benschop, 'Kroniek van een Aangekondigde Politieke Moord: Jihad in Nederland' (FORUM Instituut voor Multiculturele Ontwikkeling, 2005).
11 The term 'structure of feeling' is inspired by Gramsci's concept of hegemony. It refers to a dominant formation of thought in a particular time and place that is dynamic, fragmented and not yet fully articulated, emerging in the gap between official policy documents and cultural texts. See: Raymond Williams, *Marxism and Literature* (Oxford: Oxford University Press, 1977).
12 Raymond Williams and Ederyn Williams, *Television: Technology and Cultural Form* (London: Routledge, 2003).
13 See John Storey, *Cultural Theory and Popular Culture: A Reader* (Harlow, England; Pearson/Prentice Hall, 2006), 189–97.
14 Sheila Sitalsing, 'GeenStijlgeneratie Bedreigt erop los', *De Volkskrant*, 18 July 2008.
15 Geert Lovink, 'Nihilism and the News', in *Open! Key Texts 2004, 2012: Art, Culture & the Public Domain*, ed. Jorinde Seijdel, Liesbeth Melis and Pierre Bouvier, Open, 1570–4181 (Rotterdam: Nai010 Publishers, 2012), 90–8.
16 Bas van Stokkom, *Wat een Hufter! Ergernis, Lichtgeraaktheid en Maatschappelijke Verruwing* (Amsterdam: Boom, 2010).
17 Dick Pels, 'Tegen de Verhuftering: Het Nieuwe Nationaal-Individualisme', *De Groene Amsterdammer*, 4 November 2009.
18 Lovink, 'Nihilism and the News', 94–5.
19 Lovink, *Zero Comments*, 12–13.
20 Lovink, 17.
21 Van Rossem, 'Rutger Castricum Is Een HELD', *GeenStijl*, 1 March 2012, www.geenstijl.nl/2903861/rutger_castricum_is_een_held/.
22 Pels, 'Tegen de Verhuftering'.
23 Dick Pels, *Het Volk Bestaat Niet: Leiderschap en Populisme in de Mediademocratie* (Amsterdam: De Bezige Bij, 2011), 42.
24 There was also an opposite tendency of 'workerism', as some leftist students, under the influence of Maoism, for example, went to work in the factories to meet workers, with the ostensible aim of partaking in their revolutionary consciousness.
25 Herbert Marcuse, *One Dimensional Man* (London: Sphere Books Ltd., 1968).
26 Harry Mulisch, *Bericht aan de Rattenkoning* (Amsterdam: De Bezige Bij, 1966).

27 Cited in Trouw, 'Het is Weer Amsterdam Tegen de Provincie', *Trouw*, 20 November 2004.
28 Carel Brendel, 'De Republikein van 1980 is nu Loyale Oranjeklant', *de Volkskrant*, 1 February 2013.
29 Bas van Stokkom, 'Het Klimaat in Nederland is Wel Degelijk Intoleranter Geworden', *NRC Handelsblad*, 14 January 2011.
30 Stokkom, *Wat een Hufter!*, 14–15.
31 Dick Pels, 'De Hoofdman der Hufters', *Joop*, 5 October 2011, https://joop.bnnvara.nl/opinies/de-hoofdman-der-hufters.
32 Johnny Quid, 'GL-nerd Dick Pels Snapt Huftermanifest niet', *GeenStijl*, 6 October 2011, www.geenstijl.nl/2725881/glnerd_dick_pels_snapt_hufterm/.
33 Sitalsing, 'GeenStijlgeneratie Bedreigt Erop Los'.
34 NRC Handelsblad, 'GeenStijl: Klacht tegen Volkskrant', *NRC Handelsblad*, 22 July 2008.
35 Williams and Williams, *Television*, 133.
36 Cited in Storey, *Cultural Theory and Popular Culture*, 49.
37 GeenStijl, 'Het Hufter Manifest', *GeenStijl*, 20 October 2010, www.geenstijl.nl/2260821/het_hufter_manifest_work_in_pr/.
38 In their equally delighted and disdainful responses to journalistic or academic think pieces written about their weblog, the editors of *GeenStijl* are keen to establish their theoretical credentials, even if the tone is ironic. Responding to the critique of a literature professor that the language of its commenters is the direct stylistic expression of raw, unprocessed emotions, the editors of *GeenStijl* defend the opposite: "At *GeenStijl*, a lot of thought is put into comments. Primary emotions are foreign to us. Really, even the biggest banalities are the result of deep philosophical reflection. One on one, Nietzsche is no match for necrosis [the nickname of a *GeenStijl* commenter, MO]. Kierkegaard is not even close to pius." Nietzsche and Kierkegaard, the godfathers of nihilism and Romantic irony, could well serve as the philosophical figureheads of the site, if it was in need thereof. See Johnny Quid, 'Meest Debiele Kritiek Op GeenStijl Ooit', *GeenStijl*, 11 August 2013, www.geenstijl.nl/3592341/het_begint_met_tahahaha_hahaha_haha_hahahaha_hahaha/.
39 Friedrich Nietzsche, *Beyond Good and Evil: Prelude to a Philosophy of the Future* (Cambridge: Cambridge University Press, 2002), 154.
40 Bülent Diken, *Nihilism*, Key Ideas (London: Routledge, 2009).
41 Nietzsche, *Beyond Good and Evil*, 155.
42 *GeenStijl*, 'Het Hufter Manifest'.
43 Nietzsche, *Beyond Good and Evil*, 155.
44 Johnny Quid, 'GeenStijl: MANNARCHISME! GeenStijl Gaat de Man Redden', 5 March 2011, www.geenstijl.nl/2477271/mannisme_geenstijl_gaat_de_man/.
45 Nietzsche, *Beyond Good and Evil*, 174.
46 Johnny Quid, 'GeenStijl: Hoe Herken je de Moraalneuker op een Feestje?', 12 April 2011, www.geenstijl.nl/2516421/hoe_herken_je_de_linkschmensch/.
47 Bas Heijne, 'Vieze Vingers', *NRC Handelsblad*, 14 May 2011.
48 Brusselmans, 'Facebookreacties Lezen met Van Leeuwen', 24 October 2014, www.geenstijl.nl/4176051/gstv_facebookreacties_lezen_met_van_leeuwen_af/.
49 A similar use of irony and exaggeration, for instance, has been observed in the Italian Lega Nord party. See Lynda Dematteo, *L'idiotie en Politique: Subversion et Néo-Populisme en Italie* (Paris: Les Éditions de la Maison des sciences de l'homme, 2014).
50 Heijne, 'Vieze Vingers'.
51 Ad van Liempt, 'Het Raadsel van Reve', *Andere Tijden*, 16 December 2003.
52 Cited in Laura van Hasselt, 'Het Raadsel van Reve', Andere Tijden, 16 December 2003, https://anderetijden.nl/aflevering/484/Het-raadsel-van-Reve.
53 Reinier Kist, 'Nanninga Kwetst Om een Punt te Maken', *NRC Handelsblad*, 24 October 2017.

8   Rebels without a cause

The intellectual roots of the nihilist and ironic discourse of *GeenStijl* can be traced back to the Dutch 1960s, when a peculiar right-wing intellectual figure emerged on the scene, epitomized by leading writers such as Willem Frederik Hermans and Gerard Reve. In his 1964 book *Commentaries on Chaos*, the leading essayist Henk Hofland spelled doom for the leftist intellectual. Referencing the American end of ideology debate, Hofland observed the slackening of political passions on the Dutch left, due to the build-up of the welfare state and the rise of a powerful technocracy. He described this development as 'mass humanism':

> The enemy of the radical is modern mass humanism that has deprived him of his identity as a member of the resistance. [...] His biggest opponents are the allies of the past, who have cultivated this mass humanism and now sit enthroned as Buddhas in their limitless political virtuousness.[1]

As Hofland noted, the post-war intellectuals with their oppositional mentality had thus far been linked with the left in some way or other. The emerging welfare state technocracy, however, made it increasingly difficult for leftist intellectuals to persevere in their anti-establishment attitude. A new radical figure entered the scene, this time from the other side of the political spectrum. Hofland described these radicals as 'desperate insurgents that protest fiercely in the name of Nothing':

> Those that made a name for themselves as the true radical and active opposition did not want to reform anything. They answer exactly to the description that is given of rebels without a cause. [...] For those that work with traditional political distinctions it is clear, that they are positioned far on the right, in a psychological or sociological sense they are rebels without a cause.[2]

While Hofland does not mention them explicitly, the Dutch writers Willem Frederik Hermans and Gerard Reve gained notoriety in the 1950s and 1960s for their bleak post-war novels offering merciless and amoral portrayals of Dutch society. Both were described as cynics and nihilists by commentators and literary critics, due to their sharp critiques of the Dutch post-war moral order.[3] The prevailing perspective on the literary nihilism and irony of Hermans and Reve has long been to consider these predominantly as literary themes, neatly confined to the fictional world of their novels. But there has always been a worldlier and more political character to this peculiar intellectual current.

W.F. Hermans used his nihilism as a weapon to fight progressive Dutch writers and intellectuals who moralized over the legacy of the Second World War. In this capacity as a critic of Dutch post-war progressivism, Hermans has been described as the intellectual godfather of the conservative campaign against political correctness that gathered pace in the 1990s. In his insightful study on W.F. Hermans and the Second World War, the Dutch historian Ewoud Kieft portrays Hermans as the principal 'trailblazer of Dutch populism':

> If there is anyone that has tried to snatch from the 'leftist church' its most 'exclusive possession', it was him. Few others have so doggedly and lengthily tried to decouple the Second World War from the moral claims that the proponents of multiculturalism have attached to it. And that is nothing less than the core of the ideological battle that the PVV had to pursue in the Netherlands: 'We've been talked into accepting mass-immigration with reference to the Holocaust', Martin Bosma writes in his book.[4]

The use of the term 'leftist church' requires some elaboration. The concept was introduced by Pim Fortuyn in the 1990s to refer (pejoratively) to the moralizing tone of progressive politicians and intellectuals. The idea of 'the leftist church' became a leitmotif in the right-wing backlash of the 2000s and has become a staple of Dutch political discourse ever since. Significantly, the concept has deeply Nietzschean undertones in the way that it opposes moralizing (which is exceptional for a conservative discourse) and conflates the egalitarianism of the left with Christianity.

Similarly, Gerard Reve has been described as an intellectual godfather of sorts to the right-wing backlash of the 2000s. As we've seen in the last chapter, the intellectual Bas Heijne identified Gerard Reve as the 'greatest influence' on the 'part ironic, part pestering, part deadly serious' tone of Dutch populism.[5] This view of Hermans and Reve as the intellectual godfathers of the conservative backlash clashes with the conventional historical image of the 1960s as singularly progressive in character. In his classic interpretation of the progressive turn in Dutch society in the 1960s and 1970s, James Kennedy reserves a central role for literary iconoclasts such as Hermans and Reve:

> Already in the fifties, a talented 'realist' tradition emerged, with Anna Blaman, Willem Frederik Hermans, and Gerard K. van het Reve in the vanguard. These realists presented themselves as iconoclasts; Hermans was indicted (and acquitted) for insulting Dutch Catholics in 1951, and Van het Reve was sued in 1966 in a trial for blasphemy.[6]

On the one hand it is logical that Reve and Hermans are seen as part of the progressive wave of the 1960s. Both authors were at the forefront of the post-war struggle for artistic autonomy. Hermans and Reve engaged in famous judicial battles to defend their ability to insult or mock Christians and God in their books, in defiance of established Christian opinion. There is a real sense that this post-war struggle for artistic and literary autonomy was coterminous with the expanded personal autonomy that was being wrested from the old pillarized order by the protesting youth. This link between the artistic avant-gardes and the youth counterculture of the 1960s and 1970s has been a prominent topic of sociological debate. In *The Cultural Contradictions of Capitalism*, the neocon- servative Daniel Bell famously portrayed the 1960s youth culture in the US (dubbed 'counterculture' or 'adversary culture') as a product of the populariza- tion of the anti-bourgeois, taboo-breaking mindset of the artistic avant-gardes to ever-larger parts of the educated middle classes. Similarly, in his classic account of the Dutch 1960s, the Dutch historian Hans Righart drew on Bernice Martins' *A Sociology of Contemporary Cultural Change* (1981), to make an analogous point.[7] The Dutch counterculture of the 1960s, he argued, copied artistic themes: the radical bohemian, the individual as artist striving towards self-expression, the centrality of experiment in the process of renewal, the employment of shock tactics to break taboos and transgress cultural and personal barriers.

On the other hand, the relationship between iconoclastic literary figures such as Hermans and Reve and the broader progressive youth movement is deeply ambig- uous. When we look more closely at the political views of Hermans and Reve, we find that they were declared adversaries of progressivism in both a more political and a more philosophical sense. Both authors were notorious right-wing polemi- cists, vehemently opposed to the left and the protest generation. On major themes such as the 1960s youth movements, democratization, immigration, the Cold War, decolonization, and apartheid in South Africa, Hermans and Reve found them- selves at loggerheads with the progressive protest generation. Hermans opposed the boycott of South Africa and defended apartheid as 'the only solution for the South-African problem, on the condition it is applied in a humane manner'.[8] On the Vietnam War, Reve opposed the peace movement and declared that he stood 'behind Johnson, behind America'.[9] Reve repeatedly spoke out against the spirit of 1968 and positioned himself firmly on the (secular) right:

> When it comes to politics: I vote for the Vereniging voor Vrijheid en Democratie (VVD) because it is the only non-religious party who dares to raise its voice against the mounting terror of the rabble, against the veneration of imbecilic youth-gangsterism.[10]

In a more philosophical and intellectual sense, Hermans and Reve were inspired by conservative thought, in particular German Romanticism, the intellectual and artistic counter-reaction to progressive Enlightenment thought and the French Revolution. Some of the major themes of the Romantic-conservative tradition – scepticism concerning the ability of man to acquire knowledge of history, society and self; the pessimistic vision of man as inherently prone to evil; cynicism when it comes to the ability of politics to effect change – pervade the novels and public statements of Hermans and Reve. Following Karl Mannheim's description of the Romantic-conservative tradition mentioned earlier in this book, it is fair to say that the views of man and society espoused by Hermans and Reve can be placed in this school of thought.[11]

Important here is that the opposition to pillarization and Christian religion in the 1960s and 1970s was a politically heterogeneous phenomenon. There is no denying that the Dutch 'cultural revolution' of the 1960s and 1970s was predominantly progressive in character. But perhaps it was less singularly progressive than is commonly assumed in historical accounts. Progressives and right-wing intellectuals such as Hermans and Reve had common cause in their opposition to the stifling dominance of religion in Dutch public life. But after the 1960s, when depillarization and secularization set in, progressive morality became the new target of choice for Hermans and Reve.

The divided national self-image of pillarization – Protestants, Catholics, liberals, socialists – started to give way in the 1960s to a reconstituted, unitary Dutch identity, built on the moral lessons of the Second World War. Dutch national identity was reconstructed in opposition to German occupation, to fascism and National Socialism. On the basis of this all-important reference point, a progressive moralism developed in the 1960s and 1970s that was seen by many as a secular continuation of Christian morality. Where the Italians had Catho-Communism, it can be argued that the Dutch developed a Protestant Progressivism.[12] It is the central thesis of the German sociologist Ernest Zahn: Dutch secularization did not change the Christian thought pattern as such in the Netherlands; it merely transformed in a secular, progressive direction.[13]

This idea was a central reference point for Dutch right-wing intellectuals, long before Fortuyn coined the term 'leftist church'. Gerard Reve was 'convinced that the consciously rejected myth of original sin [...] lives on subconsciously in the myth of 'Western guilt' towards the poor former colonial peoples' while in reality, their indolence was to blame for their backwardness.[14] Frits Bolkestein referred to Dutch progressive politics as a 'theological vision', a 'secularized messianism', and a 'social gospel' preaching 'consensus, social justice and a satisfactory existence for everyone'.[15] Karel van het Reve, the brother of Gerard Reve and a prominent Cold War liberal intellectual, portrayed progressivism in similar religious terms in 1983 as the General Progressive Worldview (*Algemene Vooruitstrevende Levensbeschouwing*, AVL):

> The AVL states the following: the society in which we live is sinful, because it is a consumption society, a society that pollutes the environment, a society with millions of unemployed, a profit-driven capitalist society, a society run by Jews – sorry – I mean of course multinationals, a society that is actively leading the entire world to its demise.[16]

While the descriptions above are somewhat of a caricature, it is true that such a post-religious progressive moralism formed the backbone of the protest movements of that time. Hermans and Reve formed the main intellectual opposition from the right. Eventually, their anti-moralist position came to inspire the backlash against political correctness in the 1990s. What follows is a more extensive exploration of the core themes of their work: nihilism and irony.

Dutch nihilism

The Dutch history of nihilism begins with the leading Dutch interwar critic and essayist Menno ter Braak (1902–1940). He introduced the philosophy of Nietzsche to the Dutch literary field in the 1920s and 1930s, as he struggled to free himself from his own Christian beliefs. In the post-war period the nihilist tradition was continued by W.F. Hermans (1921–1995), considered by some as the greatest post-war Dutch writer.[17] Hermans became the most prominent exponent of nihilist philosophy, a worldview that he popularized through novels such as *I Am Always Right* (*Ik Heb Altijd Gelijk*, 1952) and *The Darkroom of Damocles* (*De Donkere Kamer van Damokles*, 1958). With his distaste for literary engagement and his pitch-black vision of man and society, W.F. Hermans originally occupied an exceptional position both nationally and internationally. But eventually, nihilism developed into the single most important intellectual current of the Dutch literary field, in a similar way as Sartre's existentialism did in post-war France. As the comparative literature scholar Aukje van Rooden observes in her comparison of Hermans and Sartre: while his 'disillusioned attitude' initially found a chilly reception, 'presently it seems to have become the common literary mentality'.[18] This doesn't seem to be an exaggeration, considering that nihilism is a central motif in the work of leading contemporary authors in the Netherlands such as Arnon Grunberg, Herman Koch, and P.F. Thomése.[19]

Even if nihilist ideology is rarely lengthily or explicitly debated in the Netherlands, it has nestled itself deeply into the Dutch intellectual field and is reproduced by many prominent writers and journalists.[20] Some of the defining themes of this deeply sceptical worldview are as follows: the inherent hypocrisy of any form of idealism or lived morality; Bildung as disillusionment; the impossibility of interpersonal connection and empathy; the failure to understand reality or to be understood; and the dominance of primary drives (sex, power and ego).

The question why nihilism became such an important intellectual theme in the Netherlands is difficult to answer in a conclusive way. Significant is that nihilist thought took hold in the Netherlands as a response to pillarization, the organization of Dutch society into Protestant, Catholic, socialist and liberal organizational subcultures, generally portrayed as lasting from 1919 to 1967. The dominant Christian pillars formed the heart of this constrained moral order, which was overseen by priests and Protestant ministers, and maintained by what many described as stifling forms of social control. For subsequent generations of

Dutch artists and especially literary authors, nihilist philosophy provided an escape route. Due to the absence of a prominent bourgeois elite, the pursuit of artistic autonomy did not manifest itself as it did in France, in the form of *épater les bourgeois*.

As the sociologist Pierre Bourdieu observed in his classic *Distinction*, the principal way to shock the bourgeois was by 'proving the extent of one's power to confer aesthetic status' on objects and themes outside of established conventions, and to 'transgress ever more radically the ethical censorships', concerning sex, racism, sacrilege or violence. For the artist to assert autonomy and to privilege the aesthetic above conventional societal norms implied 'moral agnosticism'.[21] Here we are merely only a small step away from nihilism. The difference with France is that in the Netherlands, artistic autonomy had to be achieved, first and foremost, in confrontation with religious elites, rather than the bourgeoisie.

The first Dutch literary avant-garde of the late nineteenth century still attacked the bourgeoisie in classic fashion. In his famous book *Max Havelaar*, Multatuli (Eduard Douwes Dekker) immortalized the conservative hypocrisy of the Dutch bourgeois elite in the figure of *Droogstoppel*. The Romantic writer Lodewijk van Deyssel portrayed the ladies and gents of Dutch high society as soulless robots, or 'unconscious outgrowth'.[22] The ascendency of the Christian parties in the twentieth century changed that dynamic. The segmented class structure of pillarization and the dominance of religion in public and intellectual life, meant that not the bourgeoisie but rather the Catholic and Protestant Church and their petty-bourgeois base became the principal target for those aiming to transgress and expand the boundaries of artistic autonomy. Nietzsche's eloquent critique and conflation of Christian morality and socialist egalitarianism had a particular pertinence in the Netherlands, considering the socio-economically emancipatory role of the Dutch Christian currents.

The meaning of nihilism

Before we continue, it is necessary to elaborate on the meaning of nihilism. As Bülent Diken has noted, nihilism is perhaps 'the most misunderstood concept in history'.[23] We can add that it is one of the most complex and contradictory concepts, too. For Friedrich Nietzsche, nihilism originates as an inability to accept the world as it is, with all of its conflicts, suffering and pain. An inability to endure the fact that the world is devoid of a goal, lacking unity or meaning. Nihilism refers to the invention of another, imaginary world where these blemishes cease to exist, where reason, justice and truth reign supreme. The origin of nihilism is the invention of a transcendent God bestowing meaning on life. This 'negative' or 'religious nihilism' posits certain moral values as superior to life and makes this life subservient to another *after*life. Therefore, Nietzsche describes the three monotheistic religions, Judaism, Christendom and Islam, as nihilistic religions. But progressive ideology can also be a form of nihilism. Nihilism here is escapism, a form of false consciousness. It refers more to a historical condition than a distinct doctrine. When W.F. Hermans, as we shall soon see, blames the 'nihilistic hordes' for the rise of the Nazis, he means negative or religious nihilism. Hermans used the term nihilism only in this negative or religious sense, to refer to the necessity of the masses to belief in something.

After 'the death of God' however, with modernity, nihilism becomes something rather different. It divides in two. There is an attempt at overcoming nihilism, moving beyond escapism and false consciousness. This is what is called 'radical nihilism': a wilful attempt to passionately negate the existing moral order. Nietzsche is a radical nihilist. This is how the term is commonly understood in common parlance when we refer to someone as being a nihilist, or when we refer to nihilism as a doctrine, rather than a historical condition. When *GeenStijl* proposes to obliterate the existing moral order, so that something new might arise from its ashes, we are talking about radical nihilism. When Geert Lovink discusses the 'nihilist impulse' of blogging as a 'nihilism of strength', he means radical nihilism. But there is also a passive nihilism, blandly accepting the world as it is, and its inherent meaninglessness. This complacent nihilism does not have a will, a passion or a programme. In sum, there are three forms of nihilism: negative, radical and passive.

The political character of Nietzsche's nihilism is a matter of much scholarly controversy. While it is often argued that Nietzsche's thought is so protean that it allows a wide diversity of readings, a series of political thinkers have argued that Nietzsche can (and should) be read as part of the conservative or Counter-Enlightenment tradition. The benefit of this perspective on Nietzsche as one of the foremost critics of egalitarian and progressive ideals is that it helps explain the contemporary radical right-wing interest in Nietzsche's work. The political project of Nietzsche, Fredrick Appel argues in *Nietzsche Contra Democracy*, can be cast in terms of an aristocratic revolt against egalitarianism. For Nietzsche, the problem is that Christian and progressive ideals have become dominant in the Western world and have indoctrinated the aristocracy in a levelling, egalitarian ethos, exemplified by the French Revolution. The aim of Nietzsche is to contest this herd morality and restore human excellence.[24] As Nietzsche writes in *Beyond Good and Evil*:

> [T]he essential feature of a good, healthy aristocracy is that [...] it accepts in good conscience the sacrifice of countless people who have to be pushed down and shrunk into incomplete human beings, into slaves, into tools, all *for the sake of the aristocracy*. Its fundamental belief must always be that society *cannot* exist for the sake of society, but only as the substructure and framework for raising an exceptional type of being up to its higher duty and to a higher state of *being*. In the same way, the sun-seeking, Javanese climbing plant called the *sipo matador* will wrap its arms around an oak tree so often and for such a long time that finally, high above the oak, although still supported by it, the plant will be able to unfold its highest crown of foliage and show its happiness in the full, clear light.[25]

For this reason, Nietzsche is described by intellectual historians as part of the Romantic-conservative reaction against the universalist, egalitarian and rationalist thought of the French Enlightenment. As Zeev Sternhell argues in *The Anti-Enlightenment Tradition*, Nietzsche – who lent 'the stamp of genius to anti-rationalism and anti-universalism' – was at the core of that intellectual revolt.[26] Perhaps the political character of Nietzsche's work has been masked to a degree by his appeal to nature. In Nietzsche's philosophy, man is propelled by a will to power, located in natural instincts and subconscious drives. These natural instincts do not lead to cooperation or egalitarianism. For Nietzsche, what is natural is hierarchy and usurpation:

> Mutually refraining from injury, violence, and exploitation, placing your will on par with the other's: in a certain, crude sense, these practices can become good manners between individuals when the right conditions are present (namely, that the individuals have genuinely similar quantities of force and measures of value, and belong together within a single body). But as soon as this principle is taken any further, and maybe even held to be the *fundamental principle of society*, it immediately shows itself for what it is: the will to *negate* life, the principle of disintegration and decay. Here we must think things through thoroughly, and ward off any sentimental weakness: life itself is *essentially* a process of appropriating, injuring, overpowering the alien and the weaker, oppressing, being harsh, imposing your own form, incorporating, and at least, the very least, exploiting – but what is the point of always using words that have been stamped with slanderous intentions from time immemorial?[27]

Now establishing what life *essentially* is, necessarily entails a form of projection and metaphysical speculation. Nietzsche's travail of destroying false gods has always been a selective endeavour. Like the conjuror that tricks his audience by enticing them to look in the wrong direction, Nietzsche never really destroyed his idols. By dextrous sleight-of-hand he concealed them in the appeal to natural, subconscious drives. The best way to defend a hierarchical ideology or morality is to pretend that it is not an ideology or morality at all, but rather what Nietzsche calls an 'instinct for rank' that is beyond good and evil.[28] A similar appeal to natural inequality can be found in Burke:

> We fear God, we look up with awe to kings; with affection to parliaments; with duty to magistrates; with reverence to priests; and with respect to nobility. Why? Because when such ideas are brought before our minds, it is natural to be so affected.[29] .

As the Dutch historian Ernst Kossmann argued in his Huizinga-lecture on conservatism, conservative thought often presents itself as empirical and realist, but in reality, it is an abstract form of thought. The conservative defence of a 'natural' order, Kossmann argued, is in fact deeply metaphysical. It 'departs from an analogy between nature and society, an analogy that cannot be observed, it can only be thought'.[30] Such an analogy between nature and society is also central to Nietzsche's philosophy.

At first glance, Nietzsche and Burke seem to occupy the opposite extremes when it comes to their appreciation of prejudice, morality and virtue. On a deeper level, Nietzsche's writing contains obvious parallels to Burke, who similarly camouflaged his metaphysical claims in an appeal to nature. Nietzsche stayed true to the major theme of conservatism, which has over hundreds of years consistently confronted progressive ideology with an appeal to nature, instinct and tradition. In this sense, radical nihilism and conservatism can go hand in hand, if nihilism means a return to 'natural' instincts that happens to agree with the conservative defence of human inequality. If Nietzsche is the dawn of the counterculture, as French philosopher Gilles Deleuze wrote, it seems pertinent to specify we are dealing with a conservative counterculture.[31]

W.F. Hermans' nihilism

These Nietzschean themes characterize the work of W.F. Hermans, the foremost nihilist on the Dutch literary and intellectual scene. Hermans positioned himself on the one hand against Menno ter Braak, the leading Dutch intellectual in the interwar period, and the most prominent Dutch exponent of Nietzschean nihilism. Confronted with the rise of National Socialism, Ter Braak faced the problem that Nietzsche's will to power was not a very effective intellectual defence against the Nazis. Ter Braak became increasingly politically active. He joined the Committee of Vigilance, a coalition of intellectuals that spoke out against growing anti-Semitism in Dutch public opinion and raised consciousness concerning the dangers of National Socialism.

Eventually, Ter Braak saw himself forced to abandon his nihilism by adopting a humanist position. He made an appeal to 'human dignity' and called for a 'struggle against the cynical contempt for humanity of fascism and National Socialism in general'.[32] This improvised alarm against fascism was Ter Braak's last effort, until the invasion of the Nazis, when he decided to commit suicide. In the post-war period, Ter Braak's figure loomed large in the Dutch intellectual scene. Many saw him as the heroic archetype of the independent, politically engaged intellectual.

W.F. Hermans, who had remained passive in the course of the war, like the vast majority of the Dutch population, launched a frontal attack on both Ter Braak and the Dutch resistance in his post-war novels. Hermans engaged in merciless polemics against the legacy of Ter Braak and political commitment. In his eyes, Ter Braak had never been Nietzschean enough:

> In fact, Ter Braak yearned for an ideology, a doctrine; he was not a- and immoral enough. It was not sufficient for him to say: we must fight the Germans because they are our enemies, or: we must watch the Nazis closely because they will betray us. No, it had to be founded on something, he wanted to write, he wanted to 'think'.[33]

For Hermans, Ter Braak's appeal to human dignity was a form of religious nihilism, a denial of life as is.[34] He argued that from a proper Nietzschean perspective on nihilism, it did not really matter for the masses what form their escapist ideology took:

> Ter Braak did not know that the nihilist hordes are satisfied with everything that masks their nihilism. They have no special preference for a racial theory or a leader, often they are equally satisfied with dialectical claptrap, psalms, de VARA [the Dutch social democratic broadcaster], democracy, Christianity, the American Way of Life, the Third Way, peace missions, the welfare state. What they choose depends on circumstances that no one knows exactly and that Ter Braak has never inquired after.[35]

In his many essays and novels, Hermans expounded his interpretation of nihilism, turning it into a rather absolutist anti-ideological and anti-moralist position. Hermans argued that it was useless for Ter Braak to speak out against National Socialism, since ideas do not really matter; only power does. That the Americans and the Russians chose to fight Hitler was primarily because their armies were stronger and they knew they could win. Why would anyone try to unmask Nazism, when there is nothing to unmask? Hermans considered it to be a great historical error that Ter Braak and his close collaborator Du Perron were seen by many as nihilists and cynics, while they had no idea what 'true cynicism, true immoralism, true godlessness' meant.[36] Ter Braak failed to take Nietzsche's philosophy to its logical conclusion. Hating Hitler or the Church, necessarily means one hates the people that fall for it, the 'beastly stupidity' of the masses, it meant 'total misanthropy'. Shortly before, in his novel *The Great Compassion* (*Het Grote Medelijden*), Hermans had identified his programme with the triad: 'creative nihilism, aggressive compassion, total misanthropy'. He defended his authorship as an outlet for religious or negative nihilism: literature could satisfy the human longing for meaning and mythology while at the same time recognizing these as mere stories.[37] Hermans is often described as an intellectual opponent of Ter Braak and Du Perron, but perhaps it would be more correct to argue that Hermans took it upon himself to more consistently expound Ter Braak's Nietzschean inspirations.

The other reference point and nemesis of Hermans was Jean-Paul Sartre. Like Sartre, Hermans used his novels as an exposition of his political philosophy. At the same time, he refined his nihilist convictions in opposition to Sartre and existentialist philosophy. As Otterspeer observes in his thorough intellectual biography, Hermans had extensively familiarized himself with Sartre's existentialism during his visits to Brussels shortly after the war.[38]

Sartre departed from the notion that man, after the death of God, is responsible for creating his own values and acting in accordance with them. During the war, Sartre had been active in the resistance, and this experience was vital to the existentialist idea that passivity or neutrality is also a choice; man is burdened with the responsibility to act, and failure to do so is a denial of the self. One of Sartre's central concepts is *mauvaise foi*, or bad faith. Sartre explained it in *Being and Nothingness* using the metaphor of a woman on a date, who is the subject of romantic advances by a man. He touches her hand and she faces the choice of either refusing or accepting the flirtation. When the woman chooses not to act at all, and to pretend that the hand being touched is not part of her body, she acts in bad faith.[39] Sartre's existentialism became the dominant current in post-war French intellectual life and this implied, for intellectuals and authors, a responsibility to act and to engage themselves politically.

The ideas that Hermans championed, and that came to dominate the Dutch literary scene eventually, were the very mirror image of Sartre's existentialism. From a Sartrean perspective, Hermans project revolves around the defence of *mauvaise foi*: the denial of the possibility to act and to make moral choices. Again, why France opted for Sartrean existentialism and the Netherlands eventually for Hermans' nihilism is difficult to determine. Certainly, Hermans' passive conception of man concurred with the dominant political culture of passivity that Lijphart saw as characteristic for Dutch politics at the time.[40] Hermans' most famous book, *The Darkroom of Damocles*, is a powerful exposition of his dark and sceptical vision of man. The main character, Osewoudt, is active in the Dutch resistance. Until the very end of the novel, it remains unclear whether the person he is working for, Dorbeck, is an authentic resistance fighter or a double agent for the Germans. The moral of the story is that it is not possible to distinguish good and evil and act accordingly. Osewoudt cannot make a moral judgement and choose which side he is on, because he never fully understands who is who. When Osewoudt is caught and put in jail because he is accused of collaborating with the Germans, this nihilist philosophy is expressed by a cellmate of Osewoudt: 'for those who know they have to die, no absolute moral can exist, for him goodness and charitableness are nothing but disguises of fear'.[41]

This is a passive nihilism – a nihilism that, in contrast with the radical nihilism that Nietzsche proposed, is not interested in overcoming nihilism and giving form to new values.[42] In his novels, Hermans construed a passive subject, who is politically paralysed and cannot change the world for the better. 'You don't even have the choice to leave things as they are in the Netherlands and in the world', he told his literary opponent Harry Mulisch in a famous double interview. 'The world changes without anyone knowing exactly how or through what'. All societal changes, Hermans proposed, did not result from ideas and ideals, but rather from technological development. In that same interview, however, Hermans went on to rapidly contradict himself, when he stated with equal decisiveness that Nietzsche provided the main inspiration for the Nazis, and that ideas which cannot be empirically proven, like those of Mulisch, 'are the cause of all those societal convulsions, revolutions, that will lead to nothing. Only to useless bloodshed, noise, and wastefulness'. Ideas suddenly appear to have great influence, albeit only in a negative sense.[43]

The power of political ideas remains one of the central paradoxes in Hermans' worldview. Hermans was a very political author, even if his message as a sceptical conservative was the defence of political passivity and an opposition to political commitment. As Hermans explained in interviews and essays, he had an explicitly ideological perspective on literature: 'A writer, a poet, a novelist puts a certain worldview on stage with his characters, those people live according to the rules of that worldview'. Or even more explicit: 'I consider a novel actually as a sort of parable that matches with a certain philosophy, a certain worldview'.[44] But Hermans denied that the worldview he was offering to his readers affected them in any way. 'Oh, they will read a book of mine', he said to Mulisch, 'in terms of their deeds and daily mechanisms, they will keep plodding along'. Literature, Hermans argued, is not capable of 'reaching beyond its confines and have meaning for anything whatsoever'.[45] At the same time, in the same interview, in a remarkably different tone, Hermans would describe it as his 'calling' and lifelong 'mission', to fight the 'starry-eyed idealists' of the left and to defend the status quo, a classically conservative statement:

> Perhaps I too have a sort of mission. I mean, the situation is not only terrible, but the situation is terrible according to my view, because the human psyche is not all that the do-gooders imagine it to be. In fact, in my books I want to point to the limited psychological capabilities of man. I am convinced that a human being is not suitable to love others, and that means things should stay as they are.[46]

Yet Hermans' nihilism is often interpreted in an apolitical fashion and described by scholars as a form of 'realism', 'neutrality' or 'factuality'. Take the prominent Flemish literary critic Frans Boenders, who describes Hermans in glowing terms as 'the only writer with a consistent vision of man and society', who is 'lucidly focused on facts and the unmasking of all ideologies'.[47] A similar perspective is offered by the philosopher Fons Elders: 'His worldview is that of the geologist, who forces earth dwellers to a mental striptease – willingly or not, because he is almost always right – returning them to their natural state they have disavowed'.[48] Even the historian Ewoud Kieft, who presents Hermans as the single most important intellectual forefather of right-wing populism, goes on to qualify Hermans' nihilism as an attempt at 'being as neutral as possible'. In the eyes of Kieft, Hermans is an anti-ideological and realistic thinker, teaching 'true lessons, by taking away preconceived prejudices and misunderstandings'.[49]

This perspective on Hermans is puzzling, since there is nothing 'factual' or 'realistic' about Hermans' deeply metaphysical views on human nature. Hermans himself would never have described his authorship in those terms. He publicly proclaimed his novels were mythological and he explicitly distanced himself from realism and pedagogical intentions. The aforementioned authors are exemplary of the uncritical nature of much of the secondary literature on Hermans, which treats his nihilism as an objective critique of all forms of political ideology, politely exempting Hermans' own worldview from such scrutiny. What is omitted in these commentaries is that to accept Hermans' sceptical conservative worldview as 'realism' ultimately depends on an ontological decision of the reader, who needs to embrace his dark and sceptical vision of man as 'natural'.

It is this nihilist and anti-moralistic current of thought that continues to inspire right-wing opposition to progressives today. The sizeable influence of what we can call 'the Nietzschean right' has led to a remarkable turnaround. Traditionally, conservatives were the ones to insist on virtuousness and decency. Currently it is progressives that find themselves subject to the odd right-wing accusation of being a *Gutmensch* and a 'decency terrorist'.

Reve and Romantic irony

The influence of Willem Frederik Hermans on the Dutch literary scene is only paralleled by that of Gerard Reve (1923–2006). His 1947 debut *The Evenings* (*De Avonden*) became a Dutch classic. It is a nihilistic portrait of a young man living with his family in Amsterdam at the end of 1946, spending his seemingly futile days desperately trying to simply pass the time. A scathing ironic humour seems to be his only relief. Characteristically, the war is never mentioned, heated post-war debates on collaboration and resistance, the fate of the Jews or the colonial war in Indonesia seem to have been consciously erased from the picture, which seems to contradict the 'realism' that is commonly ascribed to the novel.

Parallels to Hermans' bleak nihilist worldview are also present in Reve's work: the pitch-black vision of man, the meaninglessness of life, the assumed uselessness and unsocial nature of art, and the aversion to the left as a secular continuation of a religious morality. But Reve was a radically different author, in that he chose to explore questions surrounding his own public persona as a writer, rather than construing impersonal systems in his novels, like Hermans did. Reve's open homosexuality, his ironic conversion to the Catholic Church, his racist pronouncements and his play with artistic conventions by flirting with commerciality, mass media and popular culture, made him into a celebrity, equally provocateur, show master and jester.

In his study of Gerard Reve, the literary scholar Edwin Praat explored the subject in a brilliant fashion. His central focus is the self-reflexive manner in which Reve started to confuse his – increasingly autobiographical – literary universe with that of his public persona. Similar to Hermans, Reve's first opponent in his pursuit of symbolic transgression was the Catholic Church. In 1966, Reve had to appear in court on blasphemy charges, for describing in one of his books a sex scene with God incarnated as a donkey. The trial became an iconic reference in the secularization process that started to take hold in those years. More important for our purposes here, however, is the controversy surrounding Reve's racist statements. In a personal letter to a fellow writer included in *The Language of Love* (*De Taal der Liefde*), a book from 1972, Reve pleaded to deport immigrants from the former Dutch colonies, who had arrived in the Netherlands in large numbers, in the process of decolonization:

> Now we still have to get rid of that trash from Surinam, Curacao and the Dutch Antilles. I am much in favour of those beautiful peoples becoming

fully independent as soon as possible, and no longer costing us anything, so we can send them all with a big bag of little beads and mirrors on the Tjoekie Tjoekie steamer, single way to the Takki Takki jungle, Sir![50]

It led to a sharp reaction from Harry Mulisch, who condemned Reve for hiding sincere racism behind irony.[51] It was not the first time that Mulisch and Reve confronted each other. With his communist sympathies, his affiliation with the Provo youth movement, and his belief in authenticity and literary engagement, Mulisch embodied everything that Reve (and Hermans) opposed. During his trial defence on the donkey controversy, Reve had called Mulisch a 'motorized riot voyeur' and, in interviews, he suggested that Mulisch should be beaten to death and put into a communist prison camp. In the same letter in *The Language of Love*, Reve portrayed Mulisch, son of an Austrian-Hungarian father and a German-Jewish mother, as an (artistically) infertile product of miscegenation. He also stated that an earlier personal accusation of racism by Mulisch had allowed him to sell more books:

> As you know, due to the accusation of 'racism', directed at my person some years ago, the sale of my books has multiplied. I am not single minded enough of spirit, and also far too intelligent, to be a racist. But those accusations, and their lucrative effect, have made me think. I only need to stage some character, uttering degrading things concerning all sorts of inferior coconut pickers, who defends the honour of 'our young girls and women', and Money comes flooding in. Black gold.[52]

In an elaborate polemical essay, Mulisch argued that the irony of Reve's irony was that Reve was being sincere in his opinions:

> The irony leads to parody, parody leads to identification – that is the infallible law that Reve is beholden to above all. [...] In this way, play becomes serious. The fraternity student plays the man with the filthy mouth, to the point where he becomes his role. That is the irony of irony: that it suddenly stops being ironic. He has, so to say, fallen through the double bottom of irony. Who speaks ironic, says the opposite of what is intended, but in such a way that the other sees it. Van het Reve says what he means, but in such a way, that the other doesn't get it and thinks he is still being ironic. When he writes: 'I believe that the workers should live in separate neighbourhoods, that they are only allowed to exit when commuting to work, and beyond that only with special permit-passes' – that is simply his opinion, no joke, no fantasy.[53]

As Edwin Praat makes clear, two different visions on irony collide in this confrontation. Mulisch departs from classical irony, which is based on a notable discrepancy between what is said and what is intended. Even if people can momentarily be misled, in the end, this type of irony leads to closure. Mulisch accuses Reve of using irony the wrong way around: Reve is sincere while pretending to be ironic, and thus falls through 'the double floor' of irony.

It is debatable whether Mulisch fully does justice to Reve's use of irony. Following the lead of Ernst Behler's study of irony, Edwin Praat argues that Reve stands in the Romantic tradition of literary irony, which was introduced by Friedrich Schlegel and the German Romantics at the end of the eighteenth century. Romantic irony implies a playful, subjective, seemingly non-committal, suspended and sceptical pose. It does not restrict itself to a single ironical statement, but encompasses an entire philosophical attitude, in which the boundaries between art and life, between author, narrator and characters are increasingly dissolved, in accordance with the Romantic mission to aestheticize life and make it subservient to artistic play.

In this way, the confrontation extended to the very character of literary autonomy itself. In his critique of Reve, Mulisch distinguished between the fictional world of the novel, and the world of everyday reality. Characters in a novel are free to say anything because they are fictional, and their words can never be ascribed to real people. In everyday reality, however, people are not free to say anything they like; they have a responsibility for the consequences of their words and can be called to account. In public appearances, the author needs to present him or herself in an authentic manner, so that his or her statements can be judged accordingly. Mulisch accused Reve of consciously confusing his audience, first by mixing his literary work with autobiographical elements, for example by publishing a seemingly authentic (racist) personal letter in a fictional work such as *The Language of Love*. And second, by being ironic and insincere in his public interventions, fictionalizing his public persona. When Mulisch wrote that for the reader, Reve is 'less of an author than a fictional character', that is meant as a critique. It allows Reve to play hide and seek, and make racist statements pretending to be engaged in artistic play. But from a Romantic perspective, the accusation is a compliment, testament to the superiority of art over life.

Revian irony distinguishes itself from Romantic irony in one important respect that isn't mentioned by Praat. In his writings on the tradition of Romantic irony, Kierkegaard portrayed it as an inherently elitist and exclusive form:

> It looks down, as it were, on plain and ordinary discourse immediately understood by everyone: it travels in an exclusive incognito. [...] [It] occurs chiefly in the higher circles as a prerogative belonging to the same category as that bon ton requiring one to smile at innocence and regard virtue as a kind of prudishness, although one still believes in it to a certain extent.[54]

For Kierkegaard, irony is like a masked ball, aristocratic and refined. In comparison, Revian irony is more popular and crasser. Reve continuously mocked artistic conventions in a way that the Romantics never would, by portraying himself as a 'writer of the people' or 'everyman's writer' and brutishly promoting his work as a commercial enterprise.

Revian irony seems to also draw on another literary tradition. It contains strong parallels to what Bakhtin once called the carnivalesque: a literary form that aims at breaking conventions through humour and confusion.[55] Bakhtin formulated his theory of carnival as a way to interpret the work of the French humanist Francois Rabelais (1494–1553) and other writers of his time (Shakespeare, Boccaccio, Dante, Cervantes). Particular to carnivalesque humour is that it does not place itself above or outside the object of mockery. The joker himself is an integral part of the world that is being mocked. Likewise, in his many public performances, Reve continuously satirizes himself and the aura surrounding the figure of the writer.

In parallel to Mulisch, many critiqued Reve for his clownesque behaviour and his camp television performances, in short, for playing the joker to the point where the real Gerard Reve disappeared behind a smokescreen of poses and fictional storylines. When Reve received the most important Dutch literature prize in 1969, the P.C. Hooft prize, the award ceremony was held in a Catholic church in Amsterdam, and broadcast on Dutch public television. After a night of circus-like performances and interviews, in which he likened the church to a puppet theatre in need of a Punch like Reve, causing great consternation among the Catholic community, Reve ended with an expression of gratitude:

> To those who might think differently of me, who always say, whether they are my enemies I don't know, he is an actor, a charlatan, a comic, he is a clown; to these people I would like to say: yes, that is true. I am an actor, I am a comic, I am a charlatan, and a clown. But the crazy thing is, that I am the role that I play, and that tonight, I sincerely believe, I haven't actually said anything that I did not mean.[56]

Again, there is an interesting role reversal taking place here. Mulisch is the emblematic figure of the politically engaged author, with his belief in sincerity and his leftist sympathies. At the same time, Edwin Praat accuses Mulisch of seeing the literary world as a cage, a confined space in which literary characters have to be restrained.[57] Only when exiting the literary world, in serious public interventions, can a writer be politically engaged. The paradox here is that it is Reve, the man who argued that all art is quite useless, amoral and incapable of influencing society in any way, who seems to believe in the power of literature to transcend its artistic confines.[58] Similar to Hermans, it is by denying that he has an effect on the world that Reve legitimates his ability to do so. In his pleas against immigration, Reve adopts the position of the politically engaged author, all the while denying that this is what he is doing.

Closing the circle: From Hermans and Reve to Van Gogh and *GeenStijl*

In the 1990s the iconoclastic right-wing repertoire of Hermans and Reve was picked up by a new generation whose activities no longer restricted themselves to the confines of the literary field. The judicial battles of Hermans and Reve surrounding their liberty to mock and insult a religion were returning references in the debate on Islam and freedom of expression. More so after Salmon Rushdie became the victim of a fatwa due to his book *The Satanic Verses*. The 1960s literary rebellion against the priests of the religious and progressive moral order proved a formative inspiration for the right-wing counterculture that accompanied the Fortuyn backlash.

The murdered Dutch filmmaker and columnist Theo van Gogh is perhaps one of the most intriguing examples of this development. Theo van Gogh first achieved fame in a long crusade against columnists and antiracist organizations that mobilized the memory of the Second World War to curb racism and hate speech. In fact, Van Gogh's first protracted battle in the 1980s and the beginning of the 1990s revolved around the liberty to insult Jewish people with references to the Holocaust and Anne Frank. As Theo van Gogh was taken to court seven times in that period, he defended himself by referring to the genre of the 'sick joke', introduced by the surrealist avant-garde.[59] He explicitly placed himself in the tradition of Reve and in particular Hermans, who had been sued with the accusation of 'insulting the Catholic part of the nation' in the 1950s. In his columns, Van Gogh made repeated references to Hermans, writing about being prosecuted for insulting the 'Jewish part of the nation'. He made sarcastic jokes about insulting epileptics and being prosecuted for insulting 'the epileptic part of the nation'.[60] And when Van Gogh achieved fame for insulting Muslims as 'goat fuckers', many forgot to mention that Reve was the first to coin the term.[61]

Theo van Gogh was not merely being recalcitrant, his insults were part of a deliberate campaign against political correctness and the Dutch law section 137c prohibiting insults to groups on the basis of race, sexuality, religion, physical ability, etc. Semi-ironically, Theo van Gogh described freedom of speech in religious terms as absolute, one and indivisible. More generally, Van Gogh's politics were informed by a nihilist aversion to consensus and social justice as leading to mediocrity. 'I'm a preacher of the Nihilist Congregation, more particularly of its reactionary wing', Van Gogh stated in interviews.[62] For Nietzsche, profound suffering is at the root of nobility and creativity. The attempt to abolish suffering, to seek comfort, leads to mediocrity and boredom as exemplified by Nietzsche's last man. Van Gogh's critique of Dutch politics is Nietzschean in nature:

> Here people do not starve to death on the streets, here the trade unions bend the knee, here the police is corrupt but not unreasonable. I stand with empty hands, since the true paradise is an idyll for the mediocre who smother their lack of passion in reasonableness. [...] Dutch politics listlessly proceeds in an endless drizzle, constructing the most just society ever created by man. We will die of boredom.[63]

Like Reve, Theo van Gogh is often described as the figure of the jester: an anti-authoritarian rebel, a nihilist, a provocateur and a self-proclaimed village idiot. In the spirit of Reve, Van Gogh played the role of Punch in the puppet theatre of the Dutch media landscape of the 1990s and early 2000s. In what is probably the single most accomplished analysis of the political context of Van Gogh's assassination, the Yale sociologist Ron Eyerman portrays Theo van Gogh as a child of the 1970s: 'In many ways Van Gogh was perfectly placed to absorb the anti-bourgeois, anticlerical revolutionary atmosphere that ran through significant parts of Dutch society during his teenage years'.[64] The leading Dutch anthropologist Peter van der Veer describes Van Gogh in a similar vein: 'He was fat, purposefully unkempt, antiauthoritarian, satirical, and immoderate in his language – in short, a personification of the Dutch cultural ethos since the 1970s'.[65]

But it would be a mistake to characterize Van Gogh as a progressive figure. Returning to the more ambiguous view of the 'cultural revolution' introduced earlier, Van Gogh was clearly drawing on the right-wing undercurrent in that 1960s and 1970s ethos. Like Hermans and Reve, Van Gogh's political affinities were firmly on the right, as a self-declared fan of Frits Bolkestein and Pim Fortuyn. And if, as his close friend and kindred spirit Theodor Holman argued, the remembrance of the Second World War shaped his entire artistic production, we should add that it was very much in the nihilist, anti-moralist and anti-progressive spirit of Hermans and Reve.[66]

Two weeks after the brutal murder of Theo van Gogh, the literary critic Arnold Heumakers published a landmark essay in *NRC Handelsblad*. It identified a 'literary genealogy' of a form of polemic where arguments no longer seem to matter. The offensive, foul-mouthed writing style of Theo van Gogh, Heumakers observed, drew on the polemical techniques employed in the Dutch literary field and the privileges accorded to the domain of aesthetic play. He identified the style of Van Gogh, 'vicious, lively, course, funny, overblown, always in opposition and always ad-hominem' as part of the Romantic tradition of the polemic 'that doesn't focus on reasonable arguments, but rather on style, aggression and exaggeration, in which play and sincerity are difficult to distinguish'.[67]

Heumakers credits W.F. Hermans, who prided himself on the aesthetic, non-argumentative quality of his polemics in the book *Mandarins in Vitriol* (*Mandarijnen op Zwavelzuur*), as the initiator of that style. In a famous 1955 polemic against the left-wing writer J.B. Charles, author of an award-winning book on the Dutch resistance in the Second World War, Hermans pestered him for his baldness. He went on to ironically suggest visiting his house one evening, 'throw a bomb through the window, tie J.B. Charles to the Christmas tree, and carve up his wife and children'.[68] This abrasive style became a defining influence on the Dutch public debate in the decades after. A polemic had to entertain and preferably offer malicious delight in the victim being rhetorically ripped apart. We have seen the same register employed by Reve in his personal attacks on Mulisch.

For Heumakers, the case of Theo van Gogh is that of the literary polemic gone rogue. While Hermans and Reve claimed the freedom to shock and insult in a literary setting, that abrasive style increasingly expanded itself beyond the literary domain in the 1990s and 2000s. Unlike Hermans and Reve, Theo van Gogh had no literary background and did not write in a literary context. He was a columnist. The media platforms used by Van Gogh further enhanced the dynamic of an originally literary genre progressively transgressing the limits of the literary field. Through television and above all the internet, Van Gogh's interventions were no longer understood by his audience in the context of the literary rules of the game; they were taken seriously. And in fact, when Van Gogh turned on Muslims and Islam, he himself became increasingly sincere in his attacks. As Heumakers concluded, the ability to pursue literary polemics is dependent on the willingness to recognize a confined literary space, regulated by certain conventions. 'Uninhibited, the citizen pours out his heart in the digital jungle, if needed anonymous or under a fake name'. To Heumakers, the murder of Van Gogh was a cruel reminder to the world of aesthetic play that it should know its proper place. Of course, the opposite occurred. Following the assassination of Van Gogh, his abrasive style of writing and his semi-ironic, semi-religious crusade for freedom of speech was taken up by friends and followers, including some leading columnists.

At the same time, when compared to Hermans and Reve, a qualitative change had taken place in the target of provocation. While the Catholic and Protestant Church in the 1950s and 1960s could still be described as a dominant institution, and literary autonomy a subordinate phenomenon, this had radically changed after the 1960s due to rapid secularization. The polemics of Van Gogh and his contemporaries were targeted at minorities in the name of a dominant, secular order that fully accepted the autonomy of the artistic field. These developments were accompanied at the end of the 1990s by the emergence of the internet. In his columns for newspapers and weeklies Van Gogh still experienced occasional censorship, and he welcomed the internet as the ultimate haven of freedom of speech:

> Internet is a revolution that can only be compared with the Enlightenment: a stream of information that threatens to reach all sensible citizens without any form of censorship. [...] Seldom have I made such a self-evident statement, but the strange thing is that if you ask the ordinary proponent of 'protective measures' and 'decency', you are confronted with an abyss of misunderstandings. No censorship, no form of prohibition will be to the advantage of our ignorant humanity. To the contrary, only in the greatest possible freedom of expression lies the saviour of humanity. And only the terrorists who want to safeguard the internet from sinful opinions are afraid of that.[69]

At this point, we have come around full circle and we are back at the origins of *GeenStijl*'s rhetorical attacks on 'decency terrorists'. There is also a direct link connecting Reve, Hermans, Van Gogh and one of the editors of *GeenStijl*. All partook in the student-run satirical literary magazine *Propria Cures*. A magazine that is renowned for the many Dutch writers and journalists who started their careers there. At *Propria Cures*, Reve published his racist poem *Voor Eigen Erf* (For Our Estate). At *Propria Cures*, Hermans' polemics were covetously imitated by new generations of writers in the 1970s and 1980s. While the magazine had shifting political affinities over the years, it acquired fame for its rebellious stance against political correctness, insulting as many people as possible, including Jewish, Surinam and Turkish minorities.[70] Reve praised the magazine as follows:

> The tendency of PC has always been strictly negative. God, the Nation and the Monarchy, Parliament, princess Beatrix, Renate Rubinstein, the University, the United Nations, the struggle against Fascism and Communism, Jews, Christians, Mohammedans, the First World, the Second World, the Third World, the Ten Commandments – for this magazine nothing is holy, everything is fondly poked fun at.[71]

This description would not be unfitting for *GeenStijl*, even if PC is firmly part of the Dutch cultural establishment and *GeenStijl* is commonly seen as engaged in cultural guerrilla warfare against that very establishment. Together with his kindred spirit Theodor Holman, Theo van Gogh became guest editor of *Propria Cures* in 1987. The journal was proud to be sued for publishing an incendiary anti-Semitic illustration of Jewish writer Leon de Winter. In typical unsubtle fashion, Van Gogh accused him of exploiting the Holocaust to sell his books. From 1995 to 1997, Marck Burema served as editor of *Propria Cures*, depicted in the journal's 125th anniversary publication while making an ironic Hitler salute.[72] Burema, nicknamed *Pritt Stift*, became one of the editors of *GeenStijl*.

GeenStijl is a result of a process in which a literary culture is popularized, politicized and transposed onto the digital domain. The writers of *GeenStijl* perceive the internet as an autonomous space, and their relationship to their online identity has surprising parallels to the way literary authors relate to the fictitious characters in their novels. In media interviews, the editors of *GeenStijl* take particular pleasure in sowing confusion regarding the sincerity of their online identities. The founder of *GeenStijl*, Dominique Weesie, used the online alter ego *Fleischbaum*, a name he adopted in online gaming. 'We were so-called Germans and had all taken Germans names for that purpose, ending in -*baum*. Then we would be in the German team and shoot these guys in the back. Very lame'. Friends describe Weesie as a very well behaved and decent guy, his nihilism supposedly merely a front for his petty-bourgeois character. 'You will never get to see my real me', Weesie stated in an interview in *de Volkskrant*.

> Imagine what happens when I say publicly that 'I spend every evening snugly on the couch with my girlfriend watching [the popular Dutch soap series] *Goede Tijden, Slechte Tijden*'. It is not true of course, but it would be the end of the cool Fleischbaum.[73]

Former *GeenStijl* editor Bert Brussen, dubbed 'the monster of Blog Ness', or 'figurehead of the online bully-generation', presented his online persona in a similar manner, as belonging to another, autonomous dimension. In a prominent interview in the Dutch weekly *Vrij Nederland*, Brussen explained his motives. 'The moment I get behind my computer, I immediately enter my own universe. There is no one in front of you. You do not see any facial expressions, if you get angry, there is nothing to temper it'. In everyday reality, Brussen asserts, he is well behaved: 'In normal human interrelations I have been raised as any other person. If I get emotional, I apply the brakes, I will not start cursing or use big words'. In the digital world, it is different. Brussen compares the expression of opinions to urinating: 'It is like being toilet trained. In real life you will visit the toilet when peeing, on the internet, you just let it loose; because you know, it does not matter, there are no borders'. The internet is a giant toilet for Bert Brussen, an autonomous domain where one can do everything that is not allowed in everyday life:

> It was a subculture of provocation, of saying really intense things, and espe-
> cially in the beginning there was little consciousness of the outside world.
> The idea was: the internet, it is ours, it is for the boys who enjoy it. The old
> media are there for the official, decent stories, on the internet one can let fly,
> there are no limits.[74]

But it is not merely an observation of a technological mindset that Brussen describes. It is literary nihilism gone rogue and digital. Brussen talks of his strict Christian upbringing in the provincial town of Bennekom and his discussions with the minister on the existence of God. Nietzsche called the death of God and the absence of moral certainties a 'metaphysical wound' that can never be healed. Brussen presents his life, and that of his nihilist circle, as an attempt at coping with that condition:

> He lives 'within a wound', Brussen says. And that is what he proposes to have
> in common with the circle he regularly hangs out with. The circle of friends of
> [comedian] Hans Teeuwen, people such as [columnist] Theodor Holman,
> [writer] Jonathan van het Reve and [illustrator] Gummbah. They gather in the
> house of Teeuwen, dubbed 'the Palace of Freedom'. 'We often have a lot of
> fun, we have great nights. An open house. But a certain nihilism, a realization
> that this life is quite miserable in the end, that is something that binds us'.[75]

Notes

1 Henk Hofland, *Opmerkingen over de Chaos* (Amsterdam: Bezige Bij, 1964), 9.
2 Hofland, 9.
3 Elly Kamp, *Iedereen Zei, Dat Is Pornografie: Willem Frederik Hermans en de Ont-vangst van de Tranen der Acacia's* (Amsterdam: Aksant, 2005).
4 Ewoud Kieft, *Oorlogsmythen: Willem Frederik Hermans en de Tweede Wereldoorlog* (Amsterdam: De Bezige Bij, 2012), 229.
5 Bas Heijne, 'Vieze Vingers', *NRC Handelsblad*, 14 May 2011.
6 James Kennedy, 'Building New Babylon: Cultural Change in the Netherlands during the 1960s' (PhD thesis, Iowa, Iowa University, 1995), 123.

7 See the foreword of historian Niek Pas in Hans Righart, *De Eindeloze Jaren Zestig: Geschiedenis van een Generatieconflict* (Amsterdam: Amsterdam University Press, 2006).

8 Hans Serfontijn, 'Apartheid Enige Oplossing, Mits Menselijk Toegepast', *Trouw*, 8 March 1983.

9 Harry Mulisch, *Het Ironische van de Ironie: Over het Geval G.K. van het Reve* (Brussels: Manteau, 1976), 29.

10 Cited in Theodor Holman, 'Gerard – 49 de Politiek', *Groene Amsterdammer*, 31 August 1994.

11 Karl Mannheim, 'Conservative Thought', in *From Karl Mannheim*, ed. Kurt Wolff (New York: Oxford University Press, 1971), 132–222.

12 Catho-communism is neutrally defined as the combined commitment to Catholic values and leftist politics. It is often used in a pejorative sense to describe a dangerous combination of two absolutist, dogmatic doctrines. See: Zygmunt G. Barański and Rebecca J. West, 'The Cambridge Companion to Modern Italian Culture', *Modern Italy* 8, no. 1 (2003): 109–45.

13 Ernest Zahn, *Regenten, Rebellen en Reformatoren: Een Visie op Nederland en de Nederlanders*, trans. Dik Linthout (Amsterdam: Contact, 1989).

14 Cited in: Holman, 'Gerard – 49 de Politiek'.

15 Frits Bolkestein, *De Engel en het Beest* (Amsterdam: Prometheus, 1990), 17, 23, 66, 238.

16 Karel van het Reve cited in Hans Wansink, *De Conservatieve Golf* (Amsterdam: Prometheus, 1996), 136.

17 Bart Tromp, *Tegen het Vergeten: Degenstoten en Sabelhouwen* (Nieuwegein: Aspekt, 1997), 178.

18 Aukje van Rooden, 'Het Gelijk van de Schrijver – Willem Frederik Hermans' Fictieve Discussie Met Jean-Paul Sartre', *Nederlandse Letterkunde* 17, no. 3 (2012): 159–77.

19 Literary critic Arnold Heumakers once described the worldview of Arnon Grunberg, often considered the single most influential Dutch writer today, as a copy of Hermans or 'nihilism-on-the-cheap'. See Arnold Heumakers, 'Nihilisme op een Koopje', *NRC Handelsblad*, 27 April 2001.

20 It is surprising that (to my knowledge) no studies exist of Dutch nihilism as a current of thought. An academic search query on 'Dutch nihilism' returns no results. Perhaps a Romantic tendency in the Dutch literary field to accord each author their own unique and deeply personal worldview has prevented more general accounts of this influential intellectual current. On the post-war reception of the novels of Reve and Hermans, in which they were frequently referred to as nihilists by leading literary critics, see Kamp, *Iedereen zei, dat is pornografie*. For a more general attempt to sociologically situate the pessimist worldview of Hermans and Reve, see Ido Weijers, *Terug naar het Behouden Huis: Romanschrijvers en Wetenschappers in de Jaren Vijftig* (Amsterdam: SUA, 1991).

21 Pierre Bourdieu, *Distinction: A Social Critique of the Judgement of Taste* (London: Routledge, 1984), 40.

22 Lodewijk van Deyssel, *De Scheldkritieken*, ed. Harry Prick (Amsterdam: De Arbeiderspers, 1979), 103.

23 Bülent Diken, *Nihilism*, Key Ideas (London: Routledge, 2009), 2.

24 Fredrick Appel, *Nietzsche Contra Democracy* (Ithaca, NY: Cornell University Press, 1999), 1–2. For other studies of Nietzsche as a conservative/Counter-Enlightenment thinker, see Isaiah Berlin, *Against the Current: Essays in the History of Ideas* (Random House, 2012); Malcolm Bull, *Anti-Nietzsche* (London: Verso, 2014).

25 Friedrich Nietzsche, *Beyond Good and Evil: Prelude to a Philosophy of the Future* (Cambridge: Cambridge University Press, 2002), 152.

26 Zeev Sternhell, *The Anti-Enlightenment Tradition* (New Haven, CT: Yale University Press, 2010), 344.

27 Nietzsche, *Beyond Good and Evil*, 152.

28 Nietzsche, 160.

29 Edmund Burke, *Reflections on the Revolution in France* (London: Penguin, 2004), 182–83.

30 Ernst Kossmann, *Politieke Theorie en Geschiedenis: Verspreide Opstellen en Voordrachten* (Amsterdam: Bert Bakker, 1987), 20.

31 Gilles Deleuze, 'Nomad Thought', in *The New Nietzsche: Contemporary Styles of Interpretation*, ed. David B. Allison (New York: Delta/Dell, n.d.), 142.

32 Menno Ter Braak, 'Antisemitisme in Rok', *De Blaasbalg*, 1939.

33 Willem Frederik Hermans, *Mandarijnen op Zwavelzuur* (Amsterdam: Thomas Rap, 1973), 60.

34 Hermans interpreted Nietzsche selectively, reducing the meaning of nihilism to negative or religious nihilism. Here I differ in opinion from Kieft, who argues that Hermans' interpretation of Nietzsche's nihilism is essentially correct, and who portrays Hermans as giving Ter Braak a 'beginner's course' in nihilism. See Kieft, *Oorlogsmythen*, 118.

35 Hermans, *Mandarijnen op zwavelzuur*, 61.

36 Hermans, 63.

37 Kieft, *Oorlogsmythen*, 96–139.

38 Willem Otterspeer, *De Mislukkingskunstenaar Deel 1: Willem Frederik Hermans biografie (1921–1952)* (Amsterdam: De Bezige Bij, 2014).

39 Jean-Paul Sartre, *Being and Nothingness: An Essay on Phenomenological Ontology* (London: Methuen, 1943).

40 Thinkers such as Bülent Diken connect passive nihilism with the post-political order, the end of ideological conflict since 1989, when politics was increasingly reduced to technocratic management. Of course, there was also an earlier end of ideology debate in the 1960s. The work of Hermans can be seen as an expression of that political reality. See Diken, *Nihilism*.

41 Willem Frederik Hermans, *De Donkere Kamer van Damocles* (Amsterdam: Van Oorschot, 1967), 361.

42 At times, Hermans appears to employ Nietzsche's nihilism to defend a *l'art pour l'art* position. In the eyes of Hermans, the big problem of the religious nihilists, and the major error of Ter Braak's appeal to human dignity, is that they 'were opposed to l'art pour l'art [...], opposed to entartete kunst, against surrealism'. Hermans, *Mandarijnen op Zwavelzuur*, 60. But for Nietzsche, the function of art was to beautify life. In this way, it would allow us to cope with the truth of life's inherent ugliness and meaningless. Hermans does the very opposite in his literary practice. Rather than beautifying life, his novels are an expression of Nietzsche's bleak vision.

43 See Frans A. Janssen, *Scheppend Nihilisme: Interviews met Willem Frederik Hermans* (Amsterdam: Loeb & Van der Velden, 1979), 170–89.

44 Fons Elders and Jan Aler, *Filosofie als Science-Fiction: Interviews en een Enquête* (Amsterdam: Polak & Van Gennep, 1968), 132–56.

45 Janssen, *Scheppend Nihilisme*, 177.

46 Janssen, 179.

47 Frans Boenders, 'Willem Frederik Hermans en Ludwig Wittgenstein', *Freddy de Vree (ed.), W.F. Hermans, Speciaal Nummer van Bzzlletin* 13 (1985): 60.

48 Elders, *Filosofie als Science-Fiction*, 132.

49 Kieft, *Oorlogsmythen*, 229–30.

50 Laura van Hasselt, 'Het Raadsel van Reve', Andere Tijden, 16 December 2003, https://anderetijden.nl/aflevering/484/Het-raadsel-van-Reve.

51 Mulisch, *Het Ironische van de Ironie*.

52 Cited in Van Hasselt, 'Het Raadsel van Reve'.

53 Mulisch, *Het Ironische van de Ironie*, 20.

54 Denise Riley, *The Words of Selves: Identification, Solidarity, Irony, Atopia* (Stanford, CA: Stanford University Press, 2000), 149.

55 Michael Bakhtin, *Rabelais and His World* (Bloomington, IN: Indiana University Press, 1984).
56 Edwin Praat, *Verrek, het is geen Kunstenaar: Gerard Reve en het Schrijverschap* (Amsterdam: Amsterdam University Press, 2014), 175.
57 Praat, 145.
58 Praat, 72–3.
59 Theo van Gogh wrote he 'had been acquitted, partly thanks to Hofland's view on the function of the sick joke ("making the unspeakable visible")'. See Theo van Gogh, *Er Gebeurt Nooit Iets* (Amsterdam: Veen, 1993), 105. More specifically, Theo van Gogh mentioned Hofland's writings on the subject in *Opmerkingen over de Chaos* (*Commentaries on Chaos*). See Hofland, *Opmerkingen over de Chaos*, 37.
60 Van Gogh, *Er Gebeurt Nooit Iets*, 93. For Van Gogh's references to Hermans' 'Catholic part of the nation' (Katholieke volksdeel), see Van Gogh, 75, 118.
61 Max Pam, another leading Dutch columnist in the tradition of Hermans and Reve, has written a useful historical overview of the use of the term 'goatfucker'. See Max Pam, *Het Bijenspook: Over Dier, Mens en God* (Amsterdam: Prometheus, 2009).
62 Maarten van Hinsberg, 'Theo van Gogh, Aso van Het Jaar', *Essensie*, March 1998.
63 Theo van Gogh, *De Gezonde Roker* (Baarn: De Prom, 2000).
64 Ron Eyerman, *The Assassination of Theo Van Gogh: From Social Drama to Cultural Trauma* (Durham, NC: Duke University Press, 2008).
65 Peter van der Veer, 'Pim Fortuyn, Theo van Gogh, and the Politics of Tolerance in the Netherlands', *Public Culture* 18, no. 1 (2006): 111–24.
66 Eyerman, *The Assassination of Theo Van Gogh*, 94.
67 Arnold Heumakers, 'De Grenzen van het Spel: Over Literaire Polemiek en de Moord op Theo van Gogh', *NRC Handelsblad*, 12 November 2004.
68 Willem Frederik Hermans, *Het Geweten van de Groene Amsterdammer, of: Volg Het Spoor Omhoog* (Amsterdam: GA Van Oorschot, 1955), 9–10.
69 Gogh, *Er Gebeurt Nooit Iets*, 32.
70 Lucas Ligtenberg and Bob Polak, *Een Geschiedenis van Propria Cures, 1890–1990* (Amsterdam: Nijgh en Van Ditmar, 1990), 325.
71 Cited in Ligtenberg and Polak, 386.
72 Bob Polàk, *Het Gezicht van Propria Cures, 1890–2015* (Amsterdam: Stichting Propria Cures, 2015).
73 Maud Effting and Wilco Dekker, 'Eerlijke Jongen Met Een Flinke Onderbuik', *De Volkskrant*, 26 August 2008.
74 Sander Donkers, 'Interview Met Bert Brussen: "Ik Werd Ziek van de Verzuring in Mezelf"', *Vrij Nederland*, 25 April 2013.
75 Donkers.

Conclusion
Both a revolt and an echo

This study is an interpretation of the swing to the right in Dutch politics in the years surrounding the Fortuyn revolt. In seeking to make sense of this political shift, this book has foregrounded two major points of reference. On the one hand, I have argued that the political transformation of the 1990s and 2000s cannot be understood in separation from the profound political changes of the 1960s and 1970s. The analysis in this book builds on the analytical framework set out by the historian James Kennedy to understand the exceptional consensual nature of the progressive paradigm shift of the 1960s and 1970s. Kennedy famously argued that the accommodating attitude of traditional Dutch elites made them comply with the progressive protest generation of the 1960s, rather than resisting it wholesale, mobilizing a conservative countertendency. As a result, the Dutch experience of the 1960s and 1970s differs strikingly from countries such as the US and the UK, where the New Right emerged as a conservative backlash movement contesting the advances of the New Left. Kennedy attributed this difference to the importance attached to consensus in the Netherlands. In a political culture where ideological conflict is seen as undesirable, opposing visions do not clash but succeed one another in time. The conservative reaction against the progressive wave of the 1960s did not occur in the 1970s or 1980s in the Netherlands. It first emerged in the 1990s, when the progressive wave had fully ebbed away. The profundity of the changes surrounding the Fortuyn revolt can be explained, as in the 1960s and 1970s, by the accommodating attitudes of Dutch elites. Even though in this instance, the roles have been reversed. It is the prudent-progressive elites who are doing the accommodating and a conservative backlash movement that has taken over the historic role of the protest generation.

On the other hand, I have tried to make sense of Dutch reality by placing it against the background of Anglo-American developments. In the 1990s, a conservative undercurrent emerged in Dutch politics and public opinion that drew inspiration from the New Right movements in the US and the UK. These Dutch conservatives, present in all major parties, became the social critics of the 1990s, lamenting the atomization, permissiveness and moral decline in Dutch society. They appointed themselves as the spokespersons of a broadly felt anxiety surrounding the erosion of community through globalization, deindustrialization, individualization and immigration. These critics portrayed the baby-boomer generation and the progressive legacy of the 1960s as a primary cause of Dutch distress. The central thesis of this study is that this conservative wave of the 1990s and 2000s can be understood as a belated iteration of the New Right backlash that occurred overseas. The New Right has been described as a tactical fusion consisting of neoliberal and (neo)conservative currents. I believe it makes analytical sense to look at the politics of Dutch New Right figureheads such as Bolkestein, Fortuyn, Wilders and Hirsi Ali in the light of a similar framework. To a large degree, these figures derived their ideas from their Anglo-American counterparts. By setting Dutch developments against an Anglo-American background, I have been able to discuss ideological currents in Dutch politics that have thus far received little scholarly attention.

The process of translation has not been a simple copy and paste from the Anglo-American source. The import of New Right ideas formed part of a complicated negotiation with the existing Dutch context, marked by its exceptional progressivism, due to the unusual length and breadth of the progressive wave of the 1960s. The New Right backlash in the Netherlands distinguished itself from its Anglo-American counterparts by both its belated occurrence and by the greater degree to which it has absorbed progressive values. I have drawn on Angela McRobbie's notion of a 'complex' conservative backlash, to make sense of this phenomenon. It refers to a conservative countercurrent that incorporates a select series of progressive attainments, while contesting the progressive agenda in a broader sense. McRobbie introduced that notion in the field of women's rights; she called this conservative tendency 'post-feminism'. The Dutch New Right has a broader scope, and extending on McRobbie's analysis, we could qualify this conservative movement as a 'post-progressive' politics.

The contradictory nature of the revolt

A current of thought is always, at the same time, a continuation and negation of the current that it opposes. Following this dialectical logic described by the Dutch historian Von der Dunk, the complex New Right backlash against the 1960s and 1970s is best described as both a revolt and an echo. In part, this double character is due to the fact that some of the standard-bearers of the New Right were politically formed by the movements of the 1960s and 1970s, as was Dutch society more broadly. And in part it is a logical result of the fact that ideological contestation never implies a wholesale and clean-cut replacement of one body of ideas for another. Rather, it involves a reordering of existing elements into a new synthesis. This contradictory character is particularly visible in five key themes from the 1960s and 1970s that were embraced by the conservative countercurrent in contradictory fashion and mobilized against the progressive legacy of that period.

The discourse of emancipation

Rather than bitterly opposing the emancipatory project of the long 1960s as such, the Dutch New Right came to present its politics as a further extension thereof. In his books, Fortuyn appealed to the emancipated citizen, and sought to complete the process of emancipation by ridding Dutch citizens of the welfare state. The right-wing liberals (VVD) argued that the emancipatory project of the workers' movement had been such a great success that the workers could now be relieved from the burden of the existing social security system. It needed to be replaced by a basic income on subsistence level, inspired by Milton Friedman.

The same curious contradictions can be seen on the social-cultural level. In a short period of time, the conservative currents within the Dutch right, who had never been the most joyous supporters of women's emancipation and gay rights, revealed themselves as the most strident defenders of that progressive legacy, in the face of the challenge posed by conservative Islam. The discourse of emancipation became a central element in the Dutch version of the clash of civilizations theory. That theory was expressed by Fortuyn in terms of a cold war: an 'ideological battle' with Islam to convince Muslims to 'embrace the norms and values of modernity', with the goal of making 'prosperity, development, self-fulfilment and emancipation' for them achievable.[1] In so doing, the legacy of emancipation became an important pawn in the cultural politics revolving around Dutch Muslim minorities.

Ayaan Hirsi Ali became the most important expression of this paradoxical embrace of emancipation by the New Right. Like Fortuyn, she offered Muslims a choice between the West and Islam. She equated emancipation with the escape from (Muslim) community, requesting Dutch Muslims to turn their backs on their families and friends. One of the many curious side effects of this new discourse of emancipation was that the emancipation of the white Dutch population was now considered complete. Dutch feminism was seen as a largely defunct phenomenon. A more conservative neo-masculine rhetoric could increasingly be heard. These paradoxes would eventually come to a head in the New Right critiques of the feminization of Dutch society. The supposed prevalence of 'feminine values' was seen as a dangerous weakness preventing the Dutch from defending their emancipated norms and values from the macho-culture of Islam. As *Elsevier* editor Syp Winia wrote: 'The "feminine" Dutch values are no challenge for a collectivistic, masculine culture focused on shame and honour that has the eternity as its horizon'.[2] The implication is that Dutch femininity needs to be curtailed to protect Dutch femininity.

The notion of progress as the breaking of taboos

In the writings of Fortuyn, Schoo and Vuijsje, the legacy of the 1960s was described in terms of a campaign to break the totems and taboos of the Christian, pillarized order. Emancipation meant liberation from the religious taboos on sexuality. The most powerful complaint of Dutch conservatives against the baby boomers was that they had betrayed their own ideals by installing a series of new taboos, in particular on the issue of race and immigration. Also more traditionalist conservatives eventually adopted this discourse. The conservative law professor Couwenberg, who at earlier moments had railed against the 'hedonism' of the 1960s, is a good example of this shift:

> The repressive and controlling sexual morality of pillarization that leftist elites from the rebellious 1960s generation rose up in resistance against was under their supervision swiftly replaced by a new repressive and controlling morality, with political correctness as its guideline.[3]

In so doing, the conservative countercurrent evoked a metonymical connection between sexual liberation and the liberation from political correctness. The Romantic motif of sexual liberation as the authentic expression of self was now mobilized to promote an almost absolute version of freedom of expression. Contained implicitly in this notion, as defended by Fortuyn and Van Gogh, there is an image of the Dutch discursive order as fundamentally free, open and equal, once the taboos have been cast aside. It is a utopian image unspoilt by any Foucauldian insights concerning the way discourse is always saturated with power, or more common concerns about unequal access to the public sphere. We can speak freely about race, sexuality and religion in the Netherlands, because we are all equal. We have the right to offend, because the Netherlands is an emancipated country.

The conservative campaign against political correctness was framed as a paradoxical reiteration of the secularization of the 1960s. It involved emancipation for the white Dutch majority, who were liberated from the 'leftist Church' and could now speak freely. And it (ostensibly) meant emancipation for Dutch Muslims, who were freed from protective paternalism, whose religion needed to be criticized and mocked as the Dutch had criticized Christian religion in the 1960s. Free and uninhibited discussion of immigration and race, even if it involved and encouraged open racism, came to be seen as a sign of Dutch progress with regards to other countries with more restrictive public debates, for instance Germany. The abolition of anti-racism was thus incorporated in the progressive national imaginary of the Netherlands, as a *Gidsland*, a pioneering country.

The critique of Dutch political culture

The 1960s critiques of Dutch democracy and political culture were a crucial inspiration for the conservative countercurrent. Leading lights of the movement, such as Bolkestein, Fortuyn and Spruyt, criticized the Dutch political culture of consensus, depoliticization and accommodation, referencing Daalder, Lijphart and Hofland. Pim Fortuyn was one of the first to enact a change in the political character of these critiques. In the beginning of the 1990s, Fortuyn connected the critique of consensus politics with a radical neoliberal programme that would serve as the lever to break open the closed Dutch political system. Plans originally formulated in the 1960s to introduce more competition into Dutch democracy were now taken up by the New Right under the banner of Fortuyn's 'new politics'. The election of Mayors and the introduction of referenda, the instruments with which the progressive-liberal D66 sought to bring down the closed political order in the 1960s, were now propagated by the other side of the political aisle. The ambition to introduce a more competitive Anglo-American election system in the Netherlands, first discussed by social democrat luminaries in the 1960s and 1970s such as Ed van Thijn, were proposed by Bart Jan Spruyt and Geert Wilders in the first political programme of the PVV.

Accusations of sweeping contentious issues under the rug had been a prominent theme of the critiques of the 1960s and 1970s, such as Hofland's astute commentary on decolonization.[4] What Lijphart called the 'icebox policy', the tendency of Dutch elites to agree to disagree and allow 'a vexatious issue to be temporarily frozen' originally referred to both decolonization and the controversies surrounding the Monarchy. In the 1990s, a similar attitude seemed to prevail on the issue of immigration, as Dutch elites were again criticized for sweeping things under the rug.[5] The widely documented inability of Dutch political culture to deal with conflict and emotionally contentious topics functioned at the same time as a break and a catalyst for the New Right. It functioned as a break, because debate on hot-button issues such as immigration and integration was preferably suppressed. After the initial efforts of Bolkestein to gain acceptability for a New Right discourse on immigration and race, it still took a long time before the issues became an acceptable topic of conversation. The publication of Vuijsje's *Correct* in 1997 was widely seen as one of the milestones.[6] At the same time, the Dutch culture of consensus functioned as a catalyst for the New Right because once the ban had been lifted, it was seen as polarizing to oppose the New Right position on these issues. The inability to deal with conflict meant that after wholesale exclusion from the debate proved untenable, accommodation was the only other option in the playbook. The alternate option of accepting the legitimacy of political positions outside of the given consensus, while ideologically contesting them, still seems quite foreign to Dutch political culture.

The appeal to accommodation and toleration

Despite these radical critiques of Dutch consensual politics, the Dutch New Right did appeal to a distinct element of that same political culture. In the 1960s, the protest movements were famously co-opted by accommodating elites. Bolkestein, Fortuyn and Wilders consciously made a plea for a similar accommodating treatment of the New Right backlash in the 1990s and 2000s, in particular on the issue of race and immigration. They presented their politics as a therapeutic escape valve, a way to relieve tension and prevent extremism. And they evoked the fear of polarization, radicalization and even civil war, Lijphart's foundational myth of Dutch political culture. The Dutch argument for toleration and accommodation can perhaps best be compared with the toleration of soft drugs: you accommodate or tolerate something with the idea of keeping it under control. Toleration prevents drug use from going underground, where the step from soft drugs to hard drugs is easier to take. The New Right discourse on racism in the 1990s appealed to this Dutch tradition. Allowing people to express their feelings on immigration, even if these feelings were racist, would forestall political radicalization. It would prevent people from radicalizing, going underground, resorting to extremism or violence. Politicians needed to politically represent anti-immigrant sentiments, to prevent people from turning to the extreme right.[7]

Before, the scapegoat mechanism had been an important frame in the understanding of racism and the public debate, leading to some degree of suppression of the debate on these issues. As the French theorist René Girard famously explained, the scapegoat mechanism is a classic and recurring dynamic in which societal tensions and frustrations are projected on a subordinate group.[8] With the memory of the Second World War in the back of the mind, Dutch politicians viewed the issue of immigration implicitly through this frame. The unspoken rule was that politicians and journalists should not stir up anti-immigrant sentiments. This began to change in the late 1990s, when the escape valve frame became more and more dominant. Fortuyn (and many others on the New Right) defended civic nationalism, as a way to prevent ethnic nationalism:

> If we continue to ignore the essential human need to distinguish oneself, and to experience identity, then we pave the way for an experience of identity that excludes outsiders. Concretely, we open the door for nationalist and ethnically 'pure' ideas. We leave the expression and formulation of our identity to extreme right political organisations.[9]

Of course, Fortuyn's civic nationalism is less exclusionary and violent than ethnic nationalism, and therefore preferable. But the way he formulated and expressed Dutch identity did have an exclusionary effect. As part of his 'cold war' against Islam, Fortuyn argued that Muslims were condemned by their culture to backwardness and could not leave their culture behind. This more subtle form of cultural discrimination – 'culturalism' – became normalized in the years after Fortuyn in Dutch politics, policy and public opinion, and have been discussed by Dutch scholars in terms of the 'culturalization of citizenship'.[10] As these scholars have argued, the lines between culture and race cannot be clearly drawn; culturism and racism have historically been deeply intertwined. In that sense, the civic nationalism of the New Right is not harmless and can in itself serve as a 'gateway drug' if left unchecked.

The adversary culture

The New Right in the US opposed the New Left counterculture of the 1960s, referring to it as the 'adversary culture', the 'counterculture' or the 'new class'. The neoconservatives, in particular Daniel Bell, argued that the hedonism, normlessness and licentiousness of the counterculture undermined American norms and values. While Dutch New Right intellectuals such as Schoo, Vuijsje and Bosma were explicitly inspired by the New Right analysis of the 1960s counterculture, the critique was taken in a remarkably different direction. Schoo, Vuijsje and Bosma criticized the Dutch baby boomers for their 'conformism', their unwillingness to break taboos on all terrains. The charge was not that baby boomers were too hedonistic and licentious. It was that they were not rebellious enough; they had failed to live up to their non-conformist image. In fact, the 1990s saw the emergence of a conservative counterculture that embodied many of the characteristics Daniel Bell had attributed to the adversary culture. Theo van Gogh, Theodor Holman and the website *GeenStijl* are the most prominent examples. This conservative counterculture celebrated the breaking of taboos and the freedom provided by the internet, in terms of pornography and freedom of speech. It even explicitly mirrored itself, at times, to the counterculture of the 1960s. Ironically, 'prudent progressive' intellectuals such as Dick Pels and Bas van Stokkum came to occupy the traditionalist position of decrying the degeneration of norms and values among the wider population in general and *GeenStijl* in particular.

A politics of ideas

This study has looked at the role of ideas in the swing to the right in Dutch politics. That choice of focus has sometimes led to raised eyebrows, since the right is not commonly associated with the power of thought in the Netherlands. A prominent motivation of this study has been to dispel a long, established tradition of intellectual disdain for right-wing politics. Perhaps a verse by the leftist writer Harry Mulisch is the most significant Dutch expression of this pervasive prejudice. In May 1970, Harry Mulisch presented his vision on the political difference between left and right at the manifestation *Writers for Vietnam* in the Amsterdam Frascati theatre:

> The left has opinions.
> The right has interests.
> The left needs to have opinions because it has no interests.
> The right can do without opinion because it has interests.
> The left has its opinion as interest.
> The right has its interest as opinion.
> The left is therefore in good faith.
> The right is therefore in bad faith.[11]

This distinction between idea and interest is of course overblown. Mulisch has a rather intellectualist understanding of politics. Historically, the left tends to defend the interests of the workers and the underprivileged. And the right needs to formulate opinions to understand how its interests are best served in the first place. But even if this is clearly an oversimplified and partisan view, it resonates with a more common perspective on politics: the left is the faction of idealism and ideas, the right is the faction of power and interests. As the American political theorist Corey Robin argues in his study of US conservatism, 'it has long been an axiom on the left that the defence of power and privilege is an enterprise devoid of ideas'.[12] In fact, that point of view is not restricted to the left: liberal intellectuals have equally underlined the thoughtless nature of right-wing politics. Thomas Paine described the counter-revolution as an 'obliteration of knowledge'. To Lionel Trilling, American conservatism was a collection of 'irritable mental gestures which seek to resemble ideas'. Robert Paxton saw fascism as an 'affair of the gut', not 'of the brain'.[13]

Similar perspectives can be heard in the Netherlands, where Menno ter Braak claimed that the essence of fascism resided in its resentful surface rather than its romantic depths. Treading in the footsteps of Ter Braak, prominent Dutch intellectuals such as Henk Hofland, Rob Hartmans and Kees Schuyt have explained the rise of Fortuyn as a comparable knee-jerk expression of the resentment of the masses.[14] As a result of this still common perspective, confusion surrounding Fortuyn's political ideas continues to abound, even if Fortuyn's ideology has achieved semi-mythical proportions in the wake of his assassination. When asked about Pim Fortuyn in a television programme dedicated to the ten-year anniversary of Fortuyn's election victory, then social democrat leader Wouter Bos confessed that he couldn't make heads or tails of his ideas.[15] The same preconceptions appear to prevail when it comes to more established forms of right-wing politics. As we have seen, the Dutch newspaper of note, *NRC Handelsblad*, wrote of the VVD at a moment of peak intellectual activity that 'intellectual laziness and poverty are catchwords that seem to cling to the party'.[16] Dutch political journalists certainly cannot be accused of exhibiting a vivid interest in political ideas.

In fairness, this preconception of a thoughtless right-wing politics has often been reinforced by the right itself. As Corey Robin points out, it was the nineteenth century aristocrat Palmerston, when he was still a Tory, who introduced the famous nickname of the Conservative Party: the stupid party. Republicans have taken to describing themselves in similar terms, as part of their populist charm and common appeal. That self-image, Corey Robin contends, should not be taken too seriously.[17] When not playing the role of the dull-witted country squire, the right engages as much in an idea-driven politics as its left-wing contestants. Part of the confusion arises from the fact that the right tends to dress up its politics as a form of sober realism. From Burke to Hayek, from Nietzsche to Strauss, the right has traditionally clothed its ideas in an appeal to human nature and historical tradition. For the right, understanding historical and natural laws – which conveniently tend toward a conservative agenda – is a matter of hard-boiled realism, mere common sense. Inequality is natural, redistribution artificial; cultural homogeneity is natural, diversity artificial; the market is natural, the welfare state artificial; authority is natural, dissent artificial. The seemingly self-evidential nature of this political appeal allows for a broad anti-intellectual repertoire. But when progressive movements and revolutions change the natural order of things, what was self-evident becomes curiously contingent. It leads the right to profound intellectual remunerations on how to restore order and lend it once again its lost aura of taken-for-grantedness. That is the argument of Robin, and some of it certainly seems to apply to the New Right backlash in the Netherlands too.

The Dutch right-wing liberal party (VVD, the party closest to Anglo-American conservatism) has cherished a comparable anti-intellectual self-image. As the journalist Sheila Sitalsing writes in a recent book on the VVD:

> You can try to have an endless discussion on Popper and Hayek and who fits in what liberal tradition, but many within the VVD find that deep in their heart, to be the pursuit of a hobby by a handful of people.

And she cites the former chairman of parliament, Frans Weisglas: 'At a certain moment the Dixieland band starts playing and then for the VVD, the blabbering is over'.[18] Former party leaders unanimously affirm: for the VVD, the game of politics revolves solely around the players, not ideas or ideology. This is the practical image that the party prefers to present to the outside world, but it is a rather deceptive self-image. After all, it has been the VVD that has functioned as a biotope for a political figure some consider to be un-Dutch: ideologically driven, intellectually developed, combative, sharp, eager to engage in controversy. Figures such as Frits Bolkestein, Geert Wilders, Ayaan Hirsi Ali, Andreas Kinneging, Gerry van der List or Paul Cliteur, who have all made their mark on Dutch public opinion. To be sure, we are talking about a passionate minority; of whom many have since left the party, but in retrospect it has been a remarkably influential current.

When we expand our horizon beyond the VVD, arguably the most remarkable and – frankly – admirable quality of the Dutch New Right is the movement's widely shared belief in the power of ideas. Pim Fortuyn saw the 'clash of ideas' as central to politics. He lamented the fact that political debates in the Netherlands were marked by pragmatism and consensus. He proposed an alternative form of conflict management, namely through lively public debate, in which opposing parties respectfully expressed and explored their ideological differences, instead of seeking consensus. Fortuyn framed his conflict with Islam explicitly as a battle of ideas that had to be pursued with 'the word as a weapon'. He strongly admonished his readers that violence was a form of cowardice.[19] For Bart Jan Spruyt and the other members of the Edmund Burke Foundation, ideas are the principal drivers of change: •

> Who wants to change political decision-making should not in the first place strive to acquire power, to represent interests or to form parties. One should use ideas to acquire influence over the public debate – for instance through a real think tank – because a change of culture precedes political transformation.[20]

For Bolkestein, the long-term Hayekian 'battle of ideas' has been central to his entire political career. For Wilders, it was the principal lesson he learned as Bolkestein's 'sorcerer's apprentice'. Hirsi Ali described herself as engaged in a battle of ideas with Islamic fundamentalism, to win over the hearts and minds of

Muslims. Paul Cliteur presented himself as a freethinker, who could dispel religion through the force of his arguments. Theo van Gogh believed in ideas as a means to bring down the politically correct establishment, through shock, provocation and transgression. *GeenStijl* presented its ideas in a glorified manner as 'boorish precision bombardments', 'verbal and digital cynicism' aimed at destroying the sacred totems called 'decency' and 'respect'.

This eclectic alliance has been a dominant force in Dutch intellectual life since the 1990s, while Dutch progressives became increasingly intellectually moribund, expressed in Jos de Beus' critique of 'the lacuna on the left'.[21] What the New Right philosophy lacked in consistency, it amply made up in its fidelity to the Gramscian ideal of the socialization of political thought:

> Creating a new culture does not only mean one's own individual 'original' discoveries. It also, and most particularly, means the diffusion in a critical form of truths already discovered, their 'socialisation' as it were. [...] For a mass of people to be led to think coherently and in the same coherent fashion about the real present world, is a 'philosophical' event far more important and 'original' than the discovery by some philosophical 'genius' of a truth which remains the property of small groups of intellectuals.[22]

The New Right has consciously sought to fundamentally change Dutch politics through a battle of ideas, contesting the legacy of '1968'. Even though its victories have been partial and the battle far from finalized, its impact has been considerable. This study tells the story of that battle.

Notes

1 Pim Fortuyn, *Tegen de Islamisering van onze Cultuur: Nederlandse Identiteit als Fundament* (Uithoorn/Rotterdam: Karakter Uitgevers, 2001).
2 Syp Wynia, 'Meebuigen met de Moslims: Hoe de Islam Nederland Verandert', *Elsevier Weekblad*, 14 April 2017.
3 Servatius W. Couwenberg, *Opstand Der Burgers: De Fortuyn-Revolte En Het Demasqué van de Oude Politiek* (Damon, 2004), 23.
4 Henk Hofland, *Tegels Lichten of Ware Verhalen over Autoriteiten in het Land van de Voldongen Feiten* (Amsterdam: Contact, 1973).
5 Arend Lijphart, *The Politics of Accommodation: Pluralism and Democracy in the Netherlands* (Berkeley, CA: University of California Press, 1968), 125.
6 Herman Vuijsje, *Correct: Weldenkend Nederland sinds de Jaren Zestig* (Amsterdam: Contact, 1997), 80.
7 Already in 1992, Bolkestein had argued that speaking out on immigration would lead to a dampening of resentment. See Frits Bolkestein, *Woorden Hebben Hun Betekenis* (Amsterdam: Prometheus, 1992), 199.
8 René Girard, *The Scapegoat* (Baltimore, MD: Johns Hopkins University Press, 1989).
9 Pim Fortuyn, *Tegen de Islamisering van Onze Cultuur: Nederlandse Identiteit als Fundament* (Utrecht: Bruna, 1997).
10 Jan Willem Duyvendak, Peter Geschiere and Evelina Hendrika Tonkens, *The Culturalization of Citizenship: Belonging and Polarization in a Globalizing World* (London: Palgrave Macmillan, 2016).

11 Cited in Piet Piryns, *Er is nog Zoveel Ongezegd: Vraaggesprekken met Schrijvers* (Antwerpen Baarn: Houtekiet, 1988), 6.
12 Corey Robin, *The Reactionary Mind: Conservatism from Edmund Burke to Sarah Palin* (New York: Oxford University Press, 2011), 17.
13 Robin, 20.
14 Merijn Oudenampsen, 'De Dubieuze Psychologie van de Boze Burger', *De Groene Amsterdammer*, 25 June 2014.
15 Pauw & Witteman, 'Het Gedachtegoed van Pim Fortuyn', *Pauw & Witteman*, 6 March 2013.
16 Aukje van Roessel and Mark Kranenburg, 'Een Partij van Amateurpolitici: Het Intellectueel Gehalte van de VVD', *NRC Handelsblad*, 12 May 1990.
17 See also Michael Freeden's discussion of conservative ideology, who notes that 'proponents of conservatism have shared this deep-rooted self-image of anti-intellectualism' and concludes that 'this line of argument cannot be adopted'. Michael Freeden, *Ideologies and Political Theory: A Conceptual Approach* (Oxford: Oxford University Press, 1996), 318.
18 Sheila Sitalsing, *Mark: Portret van een Premier* (Amsterdam: Prometheus, 2016), 30–1.
19 Fortuyn, *Tegen de Islamisering van Onze Cultuur*.
20 Bart Jan Spruyt, *Lof van het Conservatisme* (Amsterdam: Balans, 2003), 204.
21 Jos de Beus, 'De Leegte Op Links', *De Volkskrant*, 18 July 2003.
22 Antonio Gramsci, *Selections from the Prison Notebooks of Antonio Gramsci*, trans. Quintin Hoare and Geoffrey Nowell-Smith (New York: International Publishers, 1973).

Postscript
The next generation: Postscript on Thierry Baudet

The Dutch regional elections are generally a rather dull affair. In 2019, they turned into a massive political upset. The radical right party Forum for Democracy (FvD, or Forum), led by the conservative intellectual Thierry Baudet, participated for the first time. It won 16 per cent of the vote which, given the very fragmented nature of the Dutch political landscape, meant that it had bested all the established parties. While Forum at the time of writing still has only two seats in the Dutch House of Representatives, it often outperforms Geert Wilders' Party for Freedom (PVV) in the polls and is widely seen as the new standard-bearer of the radical right in the Netherlands.[1]

Ever since the establishment of his party in 2015, Baudet has become a permanent fixture in the Dutch media, stealing Geert Wilders' thunder as the country's most provocative anti-establishment politician. Due to the fact that this book has largely been written from 2014 till 2018, the rise of Forum for Democracy falls outside of the scope of its argument. Still, it is worthwhile to shortly reflect on the rise of Forum for Democracy in this postscript, since Baudet and his party are very much the offspring of the conservative intellectual movement described in this book. Moreover, the rise of Forum for Democracy is a compelling illustration of two central contentions of this book: that political ideas matter, and that conservatism and radical right-wing populism are deeply intertwined.

The origins of Forum for Democracy can be traced back to a campaign against the European Union. When David Cameron announced the Brexit referendum in January 2013, an eclectic group of Dutch Eurosceptic intellectuals founded the EU Citizens' Forum that pleaded for a similar Dutch referendum.[2] In January 2014, Thierry Baudet presented a petition in Dutch parliament, declaring that the sovereignty that Dutch politicians were yielding to Brussels was not theirs to give away; it belonged to the Dutch people. It was an argument that Baudet had developed in his controversial PhD thesis, *The Significance of Borders*.[3] In the thesis, Baudet claimed the existence of a long-term campaign by international elites and institutions to do away with the democratic (and culturally homogenous) nation state.

When the Dutch parliament voted against holding an EU referendum, it prompted Baudet to found the conservative think tank Forum for Democracy in

2015, housed in a basement in an Amsterdam canal house. A new opportunity presented itself when the Dutch parliament needed to decide on the trade association between the EU and Ukraine. Together with the right-wing website *GeenStijl*, Forum for Democracy successfully campaigned and won a referendum against the trade association, mobilizing nationalist sentiment against the EU. When Dutch politicians largely ignored the results, Forum for Democracy was transformed into a political party. It won two seats (out of 150) in the parliamentary elections of 2017, and soon the Dutch media found itself drawn to the polemical interventions of Forum for Democracy, like moths to a flame. Baudet came to be seen as the new Fortuyn.

The rise of Forum for Democracy represents an important transformation of the Dutch radical right, in both organizational, demographic and ideological terms. Geert Wilders deliberately abstained from building a party organization. His party PVV is a closed association with only one member: Geert Wilders himself. Forum for Democracy, in contrast, boasts a massive membership drive: with its 45,000 members, it now has the largest membership of any Dutch political party. While decision-making remains centralized and authoritarian, the party has a large youth wing, lots of local chapters and its own ideological infrastructure. Moreover, while the electorate of Geert Wilders tend to be lower educated, Forum for Democracy has managed to expand the radical right demographically. The party appeals to cultural and economic elites as much as to the lower educated. The candidate list of Forum consists of lawyers, businessmen, surgeons, retired military officers and managers. While the youth wing of the party is very popular with law and history students in the Netherlands.

Perhaps the most significant change is on the ideological front. The ideology of right-wing populists such as Fortuyn and Wilders had always been quite eclectic and underdeveloped. While Fortuyn and Wilders began their careers combining a free market agenda with cultural conservatism, they have been far from consistent, prioritizing a populist focus on Islam and immigration above other concerns. Forum for Democracy is much more coherent and consciously ideologically driven. It espouses an explicit conservative philosophy, which can ultimately be traced back to the books of Baudet.

The political programme of Forum for Democracy could be described as a New Right fusionist agenda, combining a free market platform of lowering taxes, cutting welfare and flexibilizing the labour market with a conservative cultural agenda focused on limiting immigration, defending 'Western civilization', reclaiming national sovereignty and countering feminism and environmentalism. Baudet is also more radical than Wilders and Fortuyn; he openly flirts with far-right and racist thinkers such as the German conservative revolutionary Oswald Spengler, the French fascist Pierre Drieu de la Rochelle and the alt-right race-thinker Jared Taylor.

In his speeches, Baudet has called to maintain a 'dominantly white Europe', while denouncing attempts to 'homeopathically dilute the Dutch population' with people from other cultures. In Dutch parliament and on his Twitter account, he has popularized the extreme-right conspiracy theory of the Great Replacement, which contends that European elites aim to substitute the white European population with Muslim immigrants.[4] These extremist ideas are not supported, however, by the entire party cadre. Baudet's interventions have led to a major schism in the summer of 2019 with the more pragmatic business wing of his party. But all in all, Forum has been able to enlarge the political space rightwards, mainstreaming conservative and extremist ideas that were considered out of bounds just a few years ago.

Formative years

It is no exaggeration to state that Baudet is the offspring of the conservative intellectual resurgence of the 2000s. To properly understand the roots of Baudet and his party Forum for Democracy, we have to go back to that other major political upset in recent Dutch history: the breakthrough of Pim Fortuyn in the so-called 'voter revolt' of 2002. As I've shown in this book, the spectacular rise of Fortuyn formed part of a larger conservative intellectual resurgence. Dutch conservatives founded the influential think tank the Edmund Burke Foundation in December 2000, in an attempt to strengthen the conservative factions in the different Dutch parties. The long-term aim was to establish a Dutch conservative party modelled on the broad-tent conservatism of the US Republican Party. In early 2001, the intellectuals of the Edmund Burke Foundation – Bart Jan Spruyt, Joshua Livestro, Paul Cliteur, Michiel Visser and Andreas Kinneging – boldly proclaimed that the 'conservative moment' had come and called for a 'conservative revolution' against progressive baby boomers and the legacy of 1968. They saw in Pim Fortuyn a conservative ally, not in the least due to his book *The Orphaned Society*, which blamed the '68 generation for having bereft Dutch society of its paternal and maternal authority figures.

For Thierry Baudet, this 'conservative moment' was a formative experience. He was an 18-year-old student at the time, and attested to having been struck by Fortuyn's *The Orphaned Society*. What drew Baudet to conservatism was its insistence on the importance of community and the norms and values that bind society, a consideration that he found lacking in liberalism:

> It started with concrete experiences. September 11, the rise of Fortuyn, his ideas of an orphaned society. Those events kickstarted the debate on immigration and Dutch identity. I thought, damn, he is right. Liberals don't have any appreciation of the need for 'community'.[5]

While studying law and history at the University of Amsterdam, Baudet founded the reading group Winfried, where he got together with other students interested in conservatism. He invited the Edmund Burke Foundation members Bart Jan Spruyt, Joshua Livestro and Paul Cliteur to come and speak, and attended a summer school of the Edmund Burke Foundation. After a personal invitation from Cliteur, who is a professor in legal philosophy at Leiden University, Baudet went on to pursue his PhD at the Leiden law faculty from 2007 till 2012.

Baudet credits Cliteur for having 'opened his eyes' politically.[6] If it weren't for Cliteur, Baudet suggested, he would have become a lawyer or a banker. In accordance with his status as a key conservative ideologue, Cliteur was named head of the think tank of Forum for Democracy.

A second defining influence was the British conservative philosopher Roger Scruton, who co-supervised Baudet's PhD thesis. Baudet popularized many of Scruton's ideas in the Netherlands, in particular the concept of Oikophobia (aversion to one's own culture, as opposed to xenophobia, fear of what is foreign). The term was used by Scruton to critique the ideological (leftist/liberal) tendency to prefer other cultures, while being (too) critical of the western tradition. Baudet published a collection of his newspaper columns under the title *Oikophobia*, claiming that multiculturalism, atonal music and modernist architecture were signs of the self-hatred of western progressive elites.[7] When Scruton passed away in January 2020, Baudet wrote an in memoriam attesting that Scruton had been a crucial influence on his worldview. The political programme of Forum for Democracy, Baudet declared, had been based on Scruton's ideas.[8]

During his PhD, Baudet edited two Dutch volumes on conservative thinkers, together with Michiel Visser, a lawyer and co-founder of the Edmund Burke Foundation. *Conservative Progress* was published in 2010, featuring contributions from Roger Scruton, Andreas Kinneging and Theodore Dalrymple.[9] The book was a surprising success and showed there was a sizeable audience for conservative ideas in the Netherlands. The sequel *Revolutionary Decay* was published in 2012, again with contributions from Cliteur, Scruton and Dalrymple.[10] Thierry Baudet thus established himself as a leading conservative voice by building on the foundations laid by the conservative networks around the Edmund Burke Foundation and the Leiden law faculty. While the tone of these edited volumes was surprisingly moderate ('conservatism cannot be described as neither left nor right', Baudet and Visser claimed in the introduction of *Conservative Progress*), Baudet would soon opt for a more open radical right-wing stance.

By the time Baudet had finished his PhD thesis *The Significance of Borders* (published in Dutch as *The Assault on the Nation State*), he had a weekly column at the newspaper *NRC Handelsblad* and was an established commentator. His PhD thesis contained many of the key nationalist themes that Forum for Democracy would later mobilize on. In *The Significance of Borders*, Baudet argued that the territorial sovereignty of the democratic nation state faced a twofold threat from supranationalism and multiculturalism: 'Supranationalism dilutes sovereignty, and so brings about the gradual dismantling of borders from the outside; multiculturalism weakens nationality, thus delegitimizing their existence altogether from the inside'.[11] For Baudet, political legitimacy derives from cultural affinity: citizens will recognize the legitimacy of political elites when they share the same culture and language. Because Baudet's definition of democratic legitimacy hinges on a shared national culture, he rejects supranational institutions and human rights treaties as an undemocratic constraint upon the nation state, in particular the European Union and the European Court of Human Rights. The problem is that current political and academic elites are in thrall to supranationalism and multiculturalism. The defence of the nation state therefore requires new (conservative) elites to come forward.

Continuity and change

Baudet's radical conservatism obviously builds on the ideas of the Edmund Burke Foundation. Already in 2001, the intellectuals of the Edmund Burke Foundation had made a plea for a new conservative radicalism. Paul Cliteur, writing in *NRC Handelsblad*, distinguished two forms of conservatism. On one side, there is a moderate 'procedural' conservatism, which seeks to prevent radical and revolutionary breaks with the past by enacting moderate reforms. On the other, there is a more radical 'substantive' conservatism, which is based on a series of values that are seen as fixed and eternal. For Cliteur, moderate conservatism was useless in the Netherlands. Since 1968, the progressive baby-boomer generation – 'former revolutionaries who have succeeded completely in their revolution' – had taken over the institutions. At this point in time, moderate conservatism only played into the hands of the baby boomers. Pleas for moderation and warning against revolutionary challenges were clearly to the advantage of the progressives status quo. In reality, conservatives needed a revolution to dethrone the baby boomers. At the time, Cliteur saw Fortuyn as the catalyst of that revolution.[12]

Baudet describes his political mission as a continuation of that legacy. Like the intellectuals of the Edmund Burke Foundation, Baudet believes in a 'politics of ideas': true transformation is not achieved through practical politics, but by way of a continuous 'battle of ideas'. Like his mentors, Baudet contends that progressives have taken over the political, academic and media institutions since 1968, undermining society from within. And like Cliteur, he believes in the necessity of a conservative revolution, stating in interviews that 'there is an enormous opportunity to make the conservative revolution really succeed this time'.

In an infamous victory speech at the provincial elections of 2019, Baudet invoked Oswald Spengler and Carl Schmitt to claim that his electoral victory represented a growing consciousness of western civilization decline. 'And here we stand, at the eleventh hour, in the midst of the ruins of the greatest and most beautiful civilization the world has ever known'. The problem is that conservatives only become aware of the threat against traditional certainties when it is already too late to merely conserve. What is needed, in this context, is restoration of an order that has already been lost. 'Our boreal civilization', he asserted, 'is being wrecked by the people who should be protecting us'. Baudet described his movement as a 'new political theology' which will bring about a 'renaissance' by reconnecting the country to its 'ancient roots and make it blossom again'.

An important difference is that Cliteur, Spruyt and Livestro appealed to American (neo)conservatism, while Baudet clearly also draws on the far-right conservative tradition that existed in Europe in the 1920s and 1930s. It is an inspiration he shares with the American alt-right, the French Front National, the Spanish party VOX, the German AfD and the Italian Lega Nord. Baudet is also more radical than the first-generation Dutch conservatives, flirting openly with fascist ideas and racist conspiracy theories and claiming that the emancipation of Dutch women has made them unhappy and alienated. For some of the first-generation conservatives, like Joshua Livestro, Baudet has gone too far. Others, such as Paul Cliteur and Bart Jan Spruyt, see in Forum for Democracy the long-awaited fulfilment of their desire for a conservative party. Illustrative of that generational connection was an event in the summer of 2019, where Baudet and Spruyt spoke on the relation between conservatism and Christianity. Spruyt revealed that Baudet had once, in an informal personal message, addressed him as John. 'It took some time before I understood what you meant', Spruyt said at the event, half-jokingly. 'But then the penny dropped. I was, like John the Baptist once, in your eyes the trailblazer. And you a messiah of sorts'.[13]

Notes

1 For journalistic articles in English, see: Joost de Vries, 'Meet Thierry Baudet, the Suave New Face of Dutch Rightwing Populism', *Guardian*, 3 April 2019; Sebastiaan Faber, 'Is Dutch Bad Boy Thierry Baudet the New Face of the European Alt-Right?', 5 April 2018; Alex de Jong, 'The Decline of the Low Countries', *Jacobin Magazine*, 25 March 2019; Thijs Kleinpaste, 'The New Face of the Dutch Far-Right', *Foreign Policy*, 28 March 2019.
2 Pim van den Dool, 'Onherroepelijk Richting een Federale Unie. Ook Wij Eisen een Referendum!', *NRC Handelsblad*, 26 January 2013.
3 Thierry Baudet, *The Significance of Borders: Why Representative Government and the Rule of Law Require Nation States* (Leiden: Martinus Nijhoff Publishers, 2012).
4 Bas Tierolf et al., *Zevende rapportage racisme, antisemitisme en extreemrechts geweld in Nederland: Incidenten, aangiftes, verdachten en afhandeling in 2017* (Utrecht: Verwey-Jonker Instituut, 2018).
5 Floor Rusman, 'Over Tien Jaar Zeggen We: In 2014 Kantelde het Debat', *NRC Handelsblad*, 24 May 2014.
6 Thomas Rueb and Floor Rusman, 'Zonder Paul Cliteur Was Baudet Bankier Geworden', *NRC Handelsblad*, 16 October 2017.
7 Thierry Baudet, *Oikofobie: De Angst Voor Het Eigene* (Amsterdam: Prometheus, 2013).
8 Thierry Baudet, 'Baudet: Scruton Heeft Als Leermeester Mijn Wereldbeeld Beslissend Gevormd', *NRC Handelsblad*, 13 January 2020.
9 Thierry Baudet, *Conservatieve Vooruitgang* (Amsterdam: Prometheus, 2012).
10 Thierry Baudet, *Revolutionair Verval en Conservatieve Vooruitgang in de 18e En 19e Eeuw* (Amsterdam: Prometheus, 2012).
11 Baudet, *The Significance of Borders: Why Representative Government and the Rule of Law Require Nation States*, 3.
12 Paul Cliteur, 'Conservatieven Hebben Een Revolutie Nodig', *NRC Handelsblad*, 5 May 2001.
13 Merijn Oudenampsen, 'Revolutionairen van Deze Tijd', *De Groene Amsterdammer*, 7 March 2019.

Bibliography

Achterhuis, Hans. *De Erfenis van de Utopie*. Amsterdam: Ambo, 1998.

Achterhuis, Hans. 'Verkwanseling van Het Conservatisme'. *Trouw*, 25 October 2003.

Achterhuis, Hans. *De Utopie van de Vrije Markt*. Rotterdam: Lemniscaat, 2010.

Achterhuis, Hans. 'De Armoede van Het Neoliberalisme'. In *De Open Samenleving Onder Vuur*, edited by Dirk Verhofstadt, 103–26. Amsterdam: Lemniscaat, 2012.

Akkerman, Tjitske. 'Anti-Immigration Parties and the Defence of Liberal Values: The Exceptional Case of the List Pim Fortuyn'. *Journal of Political Ideologies* 10, no. 3 (1 October 2005): 337–54. https://doi.org/10.1080/13569310500244354.

Akkerman, Tjitske, Sarah L. de Lange, and Matthijs Rooduijn. *Radical Right-Wing Populist Parties in Western Europe: Into the Mainstream?* London: Routledge, 2016.

Albeda, Wil. 'De Droom van een Humaan Kapitalisme'. *Maandschrift Economie* 63, no. 6 (1999): 406–26.

Andeweg, Rudy, and Galen A. Irwin. *Governance and Politics of the Netherlands*. Basingstoke: Palgrave Macmillan, 2009.

Andrews, Geoff. *New Left, New Right and Beyond: Taking the Sixties Seriously*. Basingstoke: Palgrave Macmillan, 1999.

Ansell, Amy Elizabeth. *New Right, New Racism: Race and Reaction in the United States and Britain*. Washington Square, NY: New York University Press, 1997.

Appel, Fredrick. *Nietzsche Contra Democracy*. Ithaca, NY: Cornell University Press, 1999.

Art, David. *Inside the Radical Right: The Development of Anti-Immigrant Parties in Western Europe*. New York: Cambridge University Press, 2011.

Audier, Serge. *Néo-Libéralisme(s): Une Archéologie Intellectuelle*. Mondes Vécus. Paris: Bernard Grasset, 2012.

Auer, Katrin. '"Political Correctness" – Ideologischer Code, Feindbild Und Stigmawort Der Rechten'. *Österreichische Zeitschrift Für Politikwissenschaft* 31, no. 3 (2002): 291–303.

Baalen, Carla van. *Waar Visie Ontbreekt, Komt Het Volk Om*. Jaarboek Parlementaire Geschiedenis 2011. Amsterdam: Boom, 2011.

Bakel, Rogier van. '"The Trouble Is the West": Ayaan Hirsi Ali on Islam, Immigration, Civil Liberties, and the Fate of the West'. *Reason*, 10 October 2007.

Bakhtin, Michael. *Rabelais and His World*. Bloomington, IN: Indiana University Press, 1984.

Balibar, Etienne. *We, the People of Europe? Reflections on Transnational Citizenship*. Princeton University Press, 2009.

Barański, Zygmunt G., and Rebecca J. West. 'The Cambridge Companion to Modern Italian Culture'. *Modern Italy* 8, no. 1 (2003): 109–45.

Baudet, Thierry. *Conservatieve Vooruitgang*. Prometheus, 2010.

Baudet, Thierry. *Revolutionair Verval en Conservatieve Vooruitgang in de 18e En 19e Eeuw*. Prometheus, 2012.

Baudet, Thierry. *The Significance of Borders: Why Representative Government and the Rule of Law Require Nation States*. Leiden: Martinus Nijhoff Publishers, 2012.

Baudet, Thierry. *Oikofobie: De Angst Voor Het Eigene*. Amsterdam: Prometheus, 2013.

Baudet, Thierry. 'Baudet: Scruton Heeft Als Leermeester Mijn Wereldbeeld Beslissend Gevormd'. *NRC Handelsblad*, 13 January 2020.

Bell, Daniel. *The Radical Right*. New York: Routledge, 1964.

Bell, Daniel. *The Cultural Contradictions of Capitalism*. New York: Basic Books, 1976.

Bell, Daniel. *The End of Ideology: On the Exhaustion of Political Ideas in the Fifties: With 'The Resumption of History in the New Century'*. Harvard University Press, 2000.

Belt, Christophe van der. ' "Fortuyn Is Aanwinst, Maar Geen Behoudende Bondgenoot": Het Reformatorisch Dagblad over de Opkomst van Een Populistisch Fenomeen'. In *Theocratie En Populisme: Staatkundig Gereformeerden En de Stem van Het Volk*. Houten: Den Hertog, Forthcoming.

Benschop, Albert. 'Kroniek van Een Aangekondigde Politieke Moord: Jihad in Nederland'. FORUM Instituut voor Multiculturele Ontwikkeling, 2005.

Berlin, Isaiah. *Against the Current: Essays in the History of Ideas*. Random House, 2012.

Berman, Marshall. *All That Is Solid Melts into Air: The Experience of Modernity*. Verso, 1983.

Betz, Hans-Georg. *Radical Right-Wing Populism in Western Europe*. Basingstoke: Macmillan, 1994.

Beus, Jos de, Jacques van Doorn, and Piet de Rooy. 'De Ideologische Driehoek'. *Nederlandse Politiek in Historisch Perspectief*, 1989.

Beus, Jos de. 'De Europese Sociaal-Democratie: Politiek Zonder Vijand'. *Socialisme & Democratie* 57, no. 1 (2000).

Beus, Jos de. 'De Leegte Op Links'. *De Volkskrant*, 18 July 2003.

Beus, Jos de. 'De Terugkeer van het Conservatisme'. *De Helling*, 21 June 2006. https://wetenschappelijkbureaugroenlinks.nl/artikel-tijdschrift/de-terugkeer-van-het-conservatisme.

Beus, Jos de. 'Een Derde Eeuw van Nederlands Conservatisme'. In *Ruimte Op Rechts? Conservatieve Onderstroom in de Lage Landen*, edited by Huib Pellikaan and Sebastiaan van der Lubben, 221–37. Utrecht: Spectrum, 2006.

Blumenthal, Sidney, A. Dant, H. Ingber, A. Mainland, S. Sinha, and R. Taylor. 'Margaret Thatcher in Her Own Words'. *New York Times*, 8 April 2013.

Blyth, Mark. *Great Transformations: Economic Ideas and Institutional Change in the Twentieth Century*. Cambridge University Press, 2002.

Boenders, Frans. 'Willem Frederik Hermans En Ludwig Wittgenstein'. Freddy de Vree et al. (ed.), *W.F. Hermans, Speciaal Nummer van Bzzlletin* 13 (1985): 58–62.

Boer, Elaine, and Theo Koelé. 'Een Rechtse Directe'. *De Volkskrant*, 20 November 2003.

Bohemen, Samira van, Roy Kemmers, and Willem de Koster. 'Seculiere Intolerantie'. *Sociologie* 8, no. 2 (2012): 199–218.

Bolkestein, Frits. *De Engel en Het Beest*. Amsterdam: Prometheus, 1990.

Bolkestein, Frits. 'De Integratie Van Minderheden'. *De Volkskrant*, 12 September 1991.

Bolkestein, Frits. *Woorden Hebben Hun Betekenis*. Amsterdam: Prometheus, 1992.

Bolkestein, Frits. *Het Heft in Handen*. Amsterdam: Prometheus, 1995.

Bolkestein, Frits. 'The EU's Economic Test: Meeting the Challenges of the Lisbon Strategy'. Presented at the 17th Annual State of the International Economy Conference, London, 19 November 2001.

Bolkestein, Frits. *Verzwelgt De Massacultuur De Liberale Democratie?* Telderslezing Winter 2001–2002. Den Haag: Prof. Mr. B.M. Teldersstichting, 2002.

Bolkestein, Frits. 'Hoe Europa Zijn Zelfvertrouwen Verloor'. *De Volkskrant*, 24 December 2009.

Bolkestein, Frits. *De Intellectuele Verleiding*. Amsterdam: Prometheus, 2012.

Bos, Wouter. 'De Derde Weg Voorbij. 21e Den Uyl-Lezing'. Presented at the Rode Hoed, Amsterdam, 25 January 2010.

Bosanquet, Nicholas. *Economics: After the New Right*. Kluwer Academic Pub., 1983.

Bosch, Mineke. 'Telling Stories, Creating (and Saving) Her Life. An Analysis of the Autobiography of Ayaan Hirsi Ali'. *Women's Studies International Forum* 31, no. 2 (2008): 138–47.

Bosma, Martin. *De Schijn-Élite van de Valsemunters: Drees, Extreem Rechts, de Sixties, Nuttige Idioten, Groep Wilders En Ik*. Amsterdam: Bert Bakker, 2011.

Boucher, David. *Texts in Context: Revisionist Methods for Studying the History of Ideas*. Springer Science & Business Media, 2012.

Bourdieu, Pierre. *Distinction: A Social Critique of the Judgement of Taste*. London: Routledge, 1984.

Bracke, Sarah. '"Niet in Onze Naam!" Een Hartenkreet tegen de Inzet van het Feminisme in de "Beschavingsoorlog"'. *Ethiek en Maatschappij* 7, no. 4 (2004): 112–28.

Braidotti, Rosi. *Transformations of Religion and the Public Sphere: Postsecular Publics*. New York: Palgrave Macmillan, 2014.

Breevaart, Piet van de. 'Liberalen: Bestek Op de Schroothoop'. *Reformatorisch Dagblad*, 28 May 1988.

Brendel, Carel. 'De Republikein van 1980 is nu Loyale Oranjeklant'. *de Volkskrant*, 1 February 2013.

Brink, Hans Maarten van den. 'VVD-Fractieleider Frits Bolkestein, Gymnasiast in De Politiek'. *NRC Handelsblad*, 5 March 1994.

Brubaker, Rogers. 'Between Nationalism and Civilizationism: The European Populist Moment in Comparative Perspective'. *Ethnic and Racial Studies* 40, no. 8 (2017): 1191–1226.

Brusselmans. 'Facebookreactie's Lezen met Van Leeuwen', 24 October 2014. www. geenstijl.nl/4176051/gstv_facebookreacties_lezen_met_van_leeuwen_af/.

Brussen, Bert. 'Interview Met Bert Brussen: "Ik Werd Ziek van de Verzuring in Mezelf"'. *Vrij Nederland*, 25 April 2013.

Bull, Malcolm. *Anti-Nietzsche*. Verso Trade, 2014.

Buma, Sybrand van Haersma. *Tegen Het Cynisme: Voor Een Nieuwe Moraal in de Politiek*. Prometheus, 2016.

Burgin, Angus. *The Great Persuasion: Reinventing Free Markets since the Depression*. Harvard University Press, 2012.

Burke, Edmund. *Reflections on the Revolution in France*. London: Penguin, 2004.

Buruma, Ian. *Murder in Amsterdam: Liberal Europe, Islam and the Limits of Tolerance*. New York: Penguin, 2007.

Bush, George W. 'Speech to Joint Session of Congress'. Presented at the United States Congress, Washington, DC, 20 September 2001.

Bussemaker, Jet. 'Pim Fortuyn: De Eerste Politieke Postmodernist'. *Socialisme & Democratie* 59, no. 4 (2002): 8–9.

Butler, Judith. 'Sexual Politics, Torture, and Secular Time'. *The British Journal of Sociology* 59, no. 1 (2008): 1–23.

Butt, Ronald. 'Interview with Margaret Thatcher'. *Sunday Times*, 3 May 1981.

Cahill, Damien, Melinda Cooper, Martijn Konings, and David Primrose. *The SAGE Handbook of Neoliberalism*. Los Angeles, CA: SAGE Reference, 2018.

Cahn, Anne Hessing. *Killing Detente: The Right Attacks the CIA*. Penn State Press, 2007.

Calvert, John. *Sayyid Qutb and the Origins of Radical Islamism*. Cairo: The American University in Cairo Press, 2011.

Campbell, Angus, and Philip E. Converse. *The Human Meaning of Social Change*. Russell Sage Foundation, 1972.

Canovan, Margaret. 'Trust the People! Populism and the Two Faces of Democracy'. *Political Studies* 47, no. 1 (1999): 2–16.

Canovan, Margaret. *The People*. Oxford: Polity, 2005.

Cliteur, Paul. 'Het Europese Conservatisme Als Reactie Op de Franse Revolutie'. In *Opstand Der Burgers: De Franse Revolutie Na 200 Jaar*, edited by Servatius W. Couwenberg, 99–112. Kampen: Kok Agora, 1988.

Cliteur, Paul. 'Conservatisme en Cultuurrecht'. *Over de Fundering van Recht in Rechtsbeginselen. Drukkerij Cliteur, Amsterdam*, 1989.

Cliteur, Paul. 'Conservatisme'. In *De Ideologieën in Grote Lijnen*, edited by J. Weerdenburg, 55–70. Utrecht: Studium Generale, 1994.

Cliteur, Paul. 'Op Zoek Naar Het Bezielend Verband'. *Justitiële Verkenningen* 20, no. 6 (1994): 9–37.

Cliteur, Paul. 'Neo-Conservatisme en Religie. Irving Kristol Als Nieuwe Beschermheer van Het Liberale Denken?' *Civis Mundi* 35 (1996): 6.

Cliteur, Paul. 'Conservatieven Hebben een Revolutie Nodig'. *NRC Handelsblad*, 5 May 2001.

Cliteur, Paul. *Moderne Papoea's. Dilemma's van Een Multiculturele Samenleving*. Amsterdam: Arbeiderspers, 2002.

Cliteur, Paul. 'Van Burke Naar Bork'. In *De Conservatieve Uitdaging: De Scepsis van J.L. Heldring*, edited by Marcel ten Hooven, 35–41. Amsterdam: Prometheus, 2003.

Cockett, Richard. *Thinking the Unthinkable: Think-Tanks and the Economic Counter-Revolution 1931–1983*. Rev. ed. London: HarperCollins, 1995.

Cornelissen, Wout. 'Politics between Philosophy and Polemics: Political Thinking and Thoughtful Politics in the Writing of Karl Popper, Leo Strauss, and Hannah Arendt'. PhD thesis, Institute for Philosophy, Faculty of Humanities, Leiden University, 2014.

Couwenberg, Servatius W. *Op de Grens van Twee Eeuwen: Positie En Perspectief van Nederland in Het Zicht van Het Jaar 2000*. Kok Agora, in samenwerking met Stichting Civis Mundi, 1989.

Couwenberg, Servatius W. *Opstand Der Burgers: De Fortuyn-Revolte En Het Demasqué van de Oude Politiek*. Damon, 2004.

Couwenberg, Servatius W. 'Heeft Conservatisme in Nederland Geen Voedingsbodem?' *Civis Mundi Digitaal* 19, no. 6 (2011).

Crouch, Colin. *The Strange Non-Death of Neo-Liberalism*. Cambridge: Polity, 2011.

Daalder, Hans. 'The Netherlands: Opposition in a Segmented Society'. In *Political Oppositions in Western Democracies*, edited by Robert Dahl, 188–236. New Haven, CT: Yale University Press, 1966.

Daalder, Hans. *Politisering En Lijdelijkheid in de Nederlandse Politiek*. Assen: Van Gorcum, 1974.

Daalder, Hans. 'The Consociational Democracy Theme'. *World Politics* 26, no. 4 (1974): 604–21. https://doi.org/10.2307/2010104.

Daalder, Hans. 'On the Origins of the Consociational Democracy Model'. *Acta Politica* 19, no. 1 (1984): 97–116.

Daalder, Hans. *Politiek en Historie: Opstellen over Nederlandse Politiek en Vergelijkende Politieke Wetenschap.* Edited by J.T.J. van den Berg. Amsterdam: Bakker, 1990.

Daalder, Hans. *Van Oude en Nieuwe Regenten: Politiek in Nederland.* Amsterdam: Bakker, 1995.

Daalder, Hans. *State Formation, Parties and Democracy: Studies in Comparative European Politics.* Colchester: ECPR Press, 2011.

Dardot, Pierre, and Christian Laval. *The New Way of the World: On Neoliberal Society.* London: Verso, 2013.

Daudt, Hans, and Ernst van der Wolk, eds. *Bedreigde Democratie? Parlementaire Democratie En Overheidsbemoeienis in De Economie.* Assen; Amsterdam: Van Gorcum; Intermediair, 1978.

De Koster, Willem, Peter Achterberg, Jeroen Van der Waal, Samira Van Bohemen, and Roy Kemmers. 'Progressiveness and the New Right: The Electoral Relevance of Culturally Progressive Values in the Netherlands'. *West European Politics* 37, no. 3 (2014): 584–604.

De Vries, Bèrt. *Overmoed en Onbehagen: Het Hervormingskabinet-Balkende II.* Amsterdam: Bert Bakker, 2005.

Dematteo, Lynda. *L'Idiotie en Politique: subversion et néo-populisme en Italie.* Online resource (276 pages). Chemins de l'ethnologie. Paris: Les Éditions de la Maison des sciences de l'homme, 2014.

Den Uyl, Joop. *Inzicht en Uitzicht: Opstellen over Economie en Politiek.* Amsterdam: Bakker, 1978.

Den Uyl, Joop. 'Tegen de Stroom In'. Presented at Paradiso, Amsterdam, 3 May 1981.

Deyssel, Lodewijk van. *De Scheldkritieken.* Edited by Harry G.M. Prick. Synopsis. Amsterdam: De arbeiderspers, 1979.

Diken, Bülent. *Nihilism.* Key Ideas. Abingdon, Oxon: Routledge, 2009.

Dool, Pim van den. 'Onherroepelijk Richting Een Federale Unie. Ook Wij Eisen Een Referendum! – NRC'. *NRC Handelsblad*, 26 January 2013.

Driehuis, Kees. 'De Heilige Ayaan'. *Zembla*, 11 May 2006.

Drolet, Jean-François. *American Neoconservatism: The Politics and Culture of a Reactionary Idealism.* London: Hurst, 2011.

Drury, Shadia B. *The Political Ideas of Leo Strauss.* Updated ed. Online resource (lxv, 256 pages). New York: Palgrave Macmillan, 2005.

Duggan, Lisa, and Nan D. Hunter. *Sex Wars: Sexual Dissent and Political Culture.* New York: Routledge, 2006.

Dunk, Hermann von der. 'Conservatisme in Vooroorlogs Nederland'. *BMGN – Low Countries Historical Review* 90, no. 1 (1975): 15. https://doi.org/10.18352/bmgn-lchr.1851.

Dunk, Hermann von der. *Conservatisme.* Haarlem: Fibula Van Dishoeck, 1976.

Dunk, Hermann von der. 'Conservatism in the Netherlands'. *Journal of Contemporary History* 13, no. 4 (1978): 741–63. https://doi.org/10.1177/002200947801300407.

Duyvendak, Jan Willem. *Een Eensgezinde, Vooruitstrevende Natie: Over de Mythe van 'de' Individualisering en de Toekomst van de Sociologie.* Oratiereeks/Faculteit der Maatschappij- en Gedragswetenschappen. Amsterdam: Vossiuspers UvA, 2004.

Duyvendak, Jan Willem. *The Politics of Home: Belonging and Nostalgia in Western Europe and the United States.* Basingstoke: Palgrave Macmillan, 2011.

Duyvendak, Jan Willem, Peter Geschiere, and Evelina Hendrika Tonkens. *The Culturalization of Citizenship: Belonging and Polarization in a Globalizing World.* Online resource (XII, 231 pages). London: Palgrave Macmillan, 2016.

Duyvendak, Jan Willem. 'Zijn We Dan Niet Altijd Modern Geweest?: Over Collectief Geheugenverlies in Nederland En de Overwinning van de Jaren Zestig'. *Socialisme & Democratie* 73, no. 1 (2016): 13–19.

Eagleton, Terry. *Ideology*. London: Longman, 1994.

Effting, Maud, and Wilco Dekker. 'Eerlijke Jongen Met Een Flinke Onderbuik'. *De Volkskrant*, 26 August 2008.

Elders, Fons, and Jan Aler. *Filosofie als Science-Fiction: Interviews en een Enquête*. Amsterdam: Polak & Van Gennep, 1968.

Etty, Elsbeth. 'Liegen over Je Identiteit Is Noodzaak'. *NRC Handelsblad*, 26 May 2005.

Eyerman, Ron. *The Assassination of Theo Van Gogh: From Social Drama to Cultural Trauma*. Politics, History, and Culture. Durham, NC: Duke University Press, 2008.

Faber, Sebastiaan. 'Is Dutch Bad Boy Thierry Baudet the New Face of the European Alt-Right?', *The Nation*, 5 April 2018.

Faludi, Susan. *Backlash: The Undeclared War against American Women*. First Anchor books edition. New York: Anchor Books, 1992.

Farris, Sara. *In the Name of Women's Rights: The Rise of Femonationalism*. Durham, NC: Duke University Press, 2017.

Fennema, Meindert. *Geert Wilders: Tovenaarsleerling*. Amsterdam: Bakker, 2010.

Fiske, John. *Media Matters: Everyday Culture and Political Change*. Routledge, 1994.

Fortuyn, Pim. *Een Toekomst Zonder Ambtenaren*. Den Haag: SDU Juridische & Fiscale Uitgeverij, 1991.

Fortuyn, Pim. *Zonder ambtenaren. De ondernemende overheid*. Amsterdam: Van Veen, 1991.

Fortuyn, Pim. *Aan het Volk van Nederland: De Contractmaatschappij, een Politiek-Economische Zedenschets*. Amsterdam: Contact, 1992.

Fortuyn, Pim. *Het Zakenkabinet Fortuyn*. Utrecht: Bruna, 1994.

Fortuyn, Pim. *Uw Baan Staat op de Tocht! De Overlegeconomie Voorbij*. Utrecht: Bruna, 1995.

Fortuyn, Pim. *Tegen de Islamisering van Onze Cultuur: Nederlandse Identiteit Als Fundament*. Utrecht: Bruna, 1997.

Fortuyn, Pim. 'Koude Oorlog Met Islam'. *Elsevier*, 25 August 2001.

Fortuyn, Pim. 'Heer van Stand in de Politiek'. *Reformatorisch Dagblad*, 8 September 2001.

Fortuyn, Pim, and Abdullah Haselhoef. *De Islamisering van Onze Cultuur: Nederlandse Identiteit als Fundament*. Uithoorn/Rotterdam: Karakter Uitgevers, 2001.

Fortuyn, Pim. *De Puinhopen van Acht Jaar Paars: Een Genadeloze Analyse van de Collectieve Sector en Aanbevelingen voor een Krachtig Herstelprogramma*. Uithoorn: Karakter uitgevers, 2002.

Fortuyn, Pim. *De Verweesde Samenleving: Een Religieus-Sociologisch Traktaat*. Uithoorn Rotterdam: Karakter; Speakers Academy Uitgeverij, 2002.

Fortuyn, Pim. *Droomkabinet: Hoe Nederland Geregeerd Moet Worden*. Uitgeverij Van Gennep, 2004.

Frank, Thomas. *What's the Matter with Kansas?: How Conservatives Won the Heart of America*. 1st ed. New York: Metropolitan Books/Henry Holt, 2004.

Freeden, Michael. *Ideologies and Political Theory: A Conceptual Approach*. Oxford; New York: Clarendon Press; Oxford University Press, 1996.

Freeden, Michael. *Ideology: A Very Short Introduction*. Oxford: Oxford University Press, 2003.

Freeden, Michael, Lyman Tower Sargent, and Marc Stears. *The Oxford Handbook of Political Ideologies*. Oxford: Oxford University Press, 2013.

Friedman, Milton. 'Neo-Liberalism and Its Prospects'. *Farmand* 17 (1951): 89–93.

Friedman, Milton, and Rose D. Friedman. *Capitalism and Freedom*. Chicago, IL: University of Chicago Press, 1962.

Fukuyama, Francis. 'The End of History?' *The National Interest*, no. 16 (1989): 3–18.

Fukuyama, Francis. *America at the Crossroads: Democracy, Power, and the Neoconservative Legacy*. The Castle Lecture in Ethics, Politics, and Economics. New Haven, CT: Yale University Press, 2006.

Fukuyama, Francis. *The End of History and the Last Man*. 20th anniversary ed. London: Penguin Books, 2012.

Gamble, Andrew. 'Thatcherism and Conservative Politics'. In *The Politics of Thatcherism*, edited by Stuart Hall and Martin Jacques, 109–31. Lawrence & Wishart, 1983.

Gamble, Andrew. *The Free Economy and the Strong State: The Politics of Thatcherism*. 2nd ed. Basingstoke: Macmillan, 1994.

Gana, Nouri. 'Introduction: Race, Islam, and the Task of Muslim and Arab American Writing'. *PMLA* 123, no. 5 (2008): 1573–80.

GeenStijl. 'Het Hufter Manifest', 20 October 2010. www.geenstijl.nl/2260821/het_hufter_manifest_work_in_pr/.

Gervasi, Tom. *The Myth of Soviet Military Supremacy*. 1st ed. New York: Harper & Row, 1986.

Ghorashi, H. 'Ayaan Hirsi Ali: Daring or Dogmatic? Debates on Multiculturalism and Emancipation in the Netherlands'. *Focaal*, no. 42 (2003): 163–9.

Ghorashi, H. 'Benauwd Door de Verlichting'. *Eutopia*, no. 10 (2005): 31–7.

Girard, René. *The Scapegoat*. Johns Hopkins paperbacks ed. Baltimore, MD: Johns Hopkins University Press, 1989.

Girvin, Brian. *The Right in the Twentieth Century: Conservatism and Democracy*. London; New York: Pinter, 1994.

Girvin, Brian. *The Transformation of Contemporary Conservatism*. London: SAGE, 1988.

Global Axess. 'Ayaan Hirsi Ali Meets Tariq Ramadan'. *Global Axess*, 2013. www.youtube.com/watch?v=f0MezyDEHyw.

Gogh, Theo van. *Er Gebeurt Nooit Iets*. Amsterdam: Veen, 1993.

Gogh, Theo van. 'Theo van Gogh, Aso van Het Jaar'. *Essensie*, March 1998.

Gogh, Theo van. *De Gezonde Roker*. Baarn: De Prom, 2000.

Gogh, Theo van. 'Uitspraken van Theo van Gogh'. *De Volkskrant*, 3 November 2004.

Goudsblom, Johan. *Dutch Society*. Studies in Modern Societies; 31. New York: Random House, 1967.

Graaf, Ton de. 'Entree Fortuyn in de Politiek Is Bedenkelijk Voor Leefbaarheid'. *De Volkskrant*, 13 November 2001.

Gramsci, Antonio. *Selections from the Prison Notebooks of Antonio Gramsci*. Translated by Quintin Hoare and Geoffrey Nowell-Smith. New York: International Publishers, 1973.

Gray, John. *Beyond the New Right: Markets, Government and the Common Environment*. London: Routledge, 1993.

Grewal, Kiran. 'Reclaiming the Voice of the "Third World Woman" but What Do We Do When We Don't Like What She Has to Say? The Tricky Case of Ayaan Hirsi Ali'. *Interventions* 14, no. 4 (2012): 569–90.

Groenveld, Karel, Paul Cliteur, Andreas Kinneging, Gerry van der List, and Rolf Hansma. *Tussen vrijblijvendheid en paternalisme: bespiegelingen over communitarisme, liberalisme en individualisering*. Geschrift/Prof. Mr. B.M. Telderstichting; 82. 's-Gravenhage: Prof. Mr. B.M. Teldersstichting, 1995.

Groenveld, Karel, and Andreas Kinneging. *Liberalisme en politieke economie*. Geschrift; 54. 's-Gravenhage: Prof. Mr. B.M. Teldersstichting, 1985.

Haar, Edwin van de, and Joshua Livestro. *Helder Liberaal, Duidelijk Rechts: Voorstellen Voor Een Inhoudelijke Heroriëntatie van de VVD*, 2002.

Haar, Edwin van de. 'De Ideeënoorlog van Friedrich Hayek'. *Trouw*, 12 June 2004.

Haberman, Clyde. 'Mob Shaming: The Pillory at the Center of the Global Village'. *New York Times*, 19 June 2016.

Habermas, Jürgen. 'Neoconservative Culture Criticism in the United States and West Germany: An Intellectual Movement in Two Political Cultures'. *Telos* 1983, no. 56 (1983): 75–89. https://doi.org/10.3817/0683056075.

Hall, Peter A. 'Policy Paradigms, Social Learning, and the State: The Case of Economic Policymaking in Britain'. *Comparative Politics* 25, no. 3 (1993): 275–96.

Hall, Stuart, and Martin Jacques. *The Politics of Thatcherism*. London: Lawrence and Wishart, 1983.

Halsema, Femke. *Nergensland: Nieuw Licht op Migratie*. Amsterdam: Ambo Anthos, 2017.

Hartman, Andrew. *A War for the Soul of America: A History of the Culture Wars*. Chicago, IL: The University of Chicago Press, 2015.

Hasselt, Laura van. 'Het Raadsel van Reve'. *Andere Tijden*, 16 December 2003. https://anderetijden.nl/aflevering/484/Het-raadsel-van-Reve.

Hayek, Friedrich A. *The Road to Serfdom: With the Intellectuals and Socialism*. London: Institute of Economic Affairs, 2005.

Heijmans, Toine. 'Ik Heb Altijd Overal Een Mening over, Maar Die Is Genuanceerder Dan de Mensen Denken'. *De Volkskrant*, 23 July 2011.

Heijne, Bas. 'Vieze Vingers'. *NRC Handelsblad*, 14 May 2011.

Hellema, Duco. *Nederland En de Jaren Zeventig*. Boom Amsterdam, 2012.

Hemel, Ernst van den. '(Pro)Claiming Tradition: The "Judeo-Christian" Roots of Dutch Society and the Rise of Conservative Nationalism'. In *Transformations of Religion and the Public Sphere: Postsecular Publics*, edited by Rosi Braidotti, Bolette Blaagaard, Tobijn de Graauw, and Eva Midden, 53–76. London: Palgrave Macmillan, 2014. https://doi.org/10.1057/9781137401144_4.

Hemerijck, Anton. 'The Historical Contingencies of Dutch Corporatism'. PhD thesis, Oxford University, 1992.

Hendriks, Frank, and Mark Bovens. 'Pacificatie En Polarisatie: Kentering En Continuïteit in Politiek En Bestuur in Nederland Post 2002'. *Bestuurskunde* 17, no. 3 (2008): 56–63.

Hermans, Willem Frederik. *Het Geweten van de Groene Amsterdammer, of: Volg Het Spoor Omhoog*. Amsterdam: GA Van Oorschot, 1955.

Hermans, Willem Frederik. *Mandarijnen op zwavelzuur*. Amsterdam: Thomas Rap, 1964.

Hermans, Willem Frederik. *De Donkere Kamer van Damocles*. Amsterdam: Van Oorschot, 1967.

Hersh, Seymour. 'Selective Intelligence'. *The New Yorker*, 4 May 2003.

Heumakers, Arnold. 'Nihilisme op een Koopje'. *NRC Handelsblad*, 27 April 2001.

Heumakers, Arnold. 'De Grenzen van het Spel: Over Literaire Polemiek En de Moord Op Theo van Gogh'. *NRC Handelsblad*, 12 November 2004.

Heynders, Odile. *Writers as Public Intellectuals: Literature, Celebrity, Democracy*. Palgrave Studies in Modern European Literature. Basingstoke: Palgrave Macmillan, 2016.

Heywood, Andrew. *Political Ideologies: An Introduction*. London: Macmillan, 1992.

Hippe, Joop, Gerrit Voerman, Joop Hippe, and Paul Lucardie. *Kroniek 2002: Overzicht van Partijpolitieke Gebeurtenissen van het Jaar 2002*. Documentatiecentrum Nederlandse Politieke Partijen, 2004.

Hirsi Ali, Ayaan. 'Tussen Confrontatie En Verzoening: Nederland En de Islam'. *Socialisme & Democratie* 58, no. 10 (2001): 446–51.

Hirsi Ali, Ayaan. *De zoontjesfabriek: over vrouwen, islam en integratie*. Edited by Chris Rutenfrans. Amsterdam: Augustus, 2002.

Hirsi Ali, Ayaan. *The Caged Virgin: An Emancipation Proclamation for Women and Islam.* 1st Free Press ed. New York: Free Press, 2006.

Hirsi Ali, Ayaan. *Infidel.* New York: Free Press, 2007.

Hirsi Ali, Ayaan. 'How to Win the Clash of Civilizations'. *Wall Street Journal,* 18 August 2010.

Hirsi Ali, Ayaan. *Nomad: From Islam to America: A Personal Journey through the Clash of Civilizations.* London: Simon & Schuster, 2010.

Hirsi Ali, Ayaan. *Heretic: Why Islam Needs a Reformation Now.* First edition. New York: Harper, an imprint of HarperCollins Publishers, 2015.

Hofland, Henk. *Opmerkingen over de Chaos.* Amsterdam: Bezige Bij, 1964.

Hofland, Henk. *Tegels Lichten of Ware Verhalen over Autoriteiten in het Land van de Voldongen Feiten.* Contact tijdsdocumenten. Amsterdam: Contact, 1973.

Holman, Theodor. 'Gerard – 49 de Politiek'. *Groene Amsterdammer,* 31 August 1994.

Hooven, Marcel ten. 'Een Machtspartij met Idealen. Een Geschiedenis van het CDA, 1980–2010'. In *De Conjunctuur van de Macht: het Christen Democratisch Appèl 1980–2010,* edited by Gerrit Voerman. Amsterdam: Boom, 2011.

Hooven, Marcel ten. 'Het Conservatieve Offensief'. 9 September 1995.

Hope, Domenique. 'End of History? Not so, Say Critics from Left and Right'. *Sydney Morning Herald,* 13 December 1989.

Houtman, Dick, and Jan Willem Duyvendak. 'Boerka's, Boerkini's En Belastingcenten: Culturele En Politieke Polarisatie in Een Post-Christelijke Samenleving'. In *Polarisatie: Bedreigend En Verrijkend,* edited by Raad voor Maatschappelijke Ontwikkeling, 102–19. Amsterdam: SWP Publishers, 2009.

Huntington, Samuel P. 'Conservatism as an Ideology'. *American Political Science Review* 51, no. 2 (1957): 454–73. https://doi.org/10.2307/1952202.

Huntington, Samuel P. 'No Exit: The Errors of Endism'. *The National Interest,* no. 17 (1989): 3–11.

Huntington, Samuel P. 'The Clash of Civilizations?' *Foreign Affairs* 72, no. 3 (1993): 22–49.

Huntington, Samuel P. *The Clash of Civilizations and the Remaking of World Order.* New York: Simon & Schuster, 1996.

Ignazi, Piero. 'The Silent Counter-Revolution. Hypotheses on the Emergence of Extreme Right-Wing Parties in Europe'. *European Journal of Political Research* 22, no. 1 (1992): 3–34. https://doi.org/10.1111/j.1475-6765.1992.tb00303.x.

Ignazi, Piero. *Extreme Right Parties in Western Europe.* Comparative Politics. Oxford: Oxford University Press, 2003.

Jäger, Anton. 'The Semantic Drift: Images of Populism in Post-War American Historiography and Their Relevance for (European) Political Science'. *Constellations* 24, no. 3 (2017): 310–23. https://doi.org/10.1111/1467-8675.12308.

Jansen, Thijs. 'CDA Moet Conservatieve Verleiding Weerstaan'. *Christen Democratische Verkenningen,* Winter (2004): 5–18.

Janssen, Frans A. *Scheppend Nihilisme: Interviews met Willem Frederik Hermans.* Amsterdam: Loeb & Van der Velden, 1983.

Jong, Alex de. 'The Decline of the Low Countries'. *Jacobin Magazine,* 25 March 2019. https://jacobinmag.com/2019/03/netherlands-forum-voor-democratie-thierry-baudet.

Jong, Sjoerd de. *Een Wereld van Verschil: Wat is er Mis met Cultuurrelativisme?* Amsterdam: De Bezige Bij, 2008.

Jorritsma, Elsje, and Michèle de Waard. 'De SG Is Weer Staatsdienaar, Geen Mooie Zangvogel'. *NRC Handelsblad,* 5 January 2009.

Joustra, Arendo, Tonny van Winssen, Jos de Beus, and Hendrik Jan Schoo. *Dwars en Bewogen: Afscheid van H.J. Schoo (1945–2007)*. Amsterdam: Elsevier/de Volkskrant, 2007.

JOVD. 'Frits Bolkestein over Duitsland, P.J. Oud en de Liberale Doorbraak'. *Driemaster*, 1995.

Kaminski, Matthew. 'Pim's Misfortune – WSJ'. *Wall Street Journal*, 7 May 2002.

Kamp, Elly. *Iedereen Zei, Dat is Pornografie: Willem Frederik Hermans en de Ontvangst van De Tranen der Acacia's*. Amsterdam: Aksant, 2005.

Kellerhuis, Tom. 'Thierry Baudet: "Mijn meningen zijn feiten"'. *HP/De Tijd*, 5 July 2017.

Kennedy, James. 'Building New Babylon: Cultural Change in the Netherlands during the 1960s'. PhD thesis, Iowa University, 1995.

Kennedy, James. 'New Babylon and the Politics of Modernity'. *Sociologische Gids* 44, no. 5/6 (1997): 361–74.

Kennedy, James. *Bezielende Verbanden: Gedachten over Religie, Politiek en Maatschappij in het Moderne Nederland*. Amsterdam: Bakker, 2009.

Kepel, Gilles. *The War for Muslim Minds: Islam and the West*. Cambridge, MA: Belknap Press of Harvard University Press, 2004.

Kepel, Gilles, and Pascale Ghazaleh. *Beyond Terror and Martyrdom: The Future of the Middle East*. Cambridge, MA: Belknap Press of Harvard University Press, 2008.

Keynes, John Maynard. *The General Theory of Employment, Interest and Money*. The Collected Writings of John Maynard Keynes, Vol. 7. London: Macmillan, 1973.

Kieft, Ewoud. *Oorlogsmythen: Willem Frederik Hermans en de Tweede Wereldoorlog*. Amsterdam: De Bezige Bij, 2012.

King, Desmond S. *The New Right: Politics, Markets and Citizenship*. Basingstoke: Macmillan Education, 1987.

Kinneging, Andreas. *Liberalisme: Een Speurtocht naar de Filosofische Grondslagen*. Geschrift Prof. Mr. B.M. Teldersstichting; 65. Den Haag: Prof. Mr. B.M. Teldersstichting, 1988.

Kinneging, Andreas. *Geografie van Goed en Kwaad: Filosofische Essays*. Houten: Spectrum, 2010.

Kist, Reinier. 'Nanninga Kwetst om een Punt te Maken'. *NRC Handelsblad*, 24 October.

Kitschelt, Herbert. *Diversification and Reconfiguration of Party Systems in Postindustrial Democracies*. Bonn: Friedrich Ebert Stiftung, 2004.

Kitschelt, Herbert, and Anthony J. MacGann. *The Radical Right in Western Europe: A Comparative Analysis*. Ann Arbor, MI: The University of Michigan Press, 1995.

Klatch, Rebecca E. *A Generation Divided: The New Left, the New Right, and the 1960s*. Berkeley, CA: University of California Press, 1999.

Klaveren, Kees-Jan van. 'Het onafhankelijkheidssyndroom: een cultuurgeschiedenis van het naoorlogse Nederlandse zorgstelsel'. PhD thesis, University of Amsterdam, 2015. WorldCat.org.

Kleinpaste, Thijs. 'Wie is die Gutmensch? Of misschien beter: wat is de Gutmensch?' *De Groene Amsterdammer*, 16 December 2015.

Kleinpaste, Thijs. 'The New Face of the Dutch Far-Right'. *Foreign Policy*, 28 March 2019. https://foreignpolicy.com/2019/03/28/the-new-face-of-the-dutch-far-right-fvd-thierry-baudet-netherlands-pvv-geert-wilders/.

Knapen, Ben. 'Het Einde van de Geschiedenis Is Nabij'. *NRC Handelsblad*, 12 August 1989.

Koeneman, Lidie, Ruud Koole, Lidie Koeneman, Ida Noomen, and Gerrit Voerman. *Kroniek 1988: Overzicht van Partijpolitieke Gebeurtenissen van het Jaar 1988*. Groningen: Documentatiecentrum Nederlandse Politieke Partijen, 1989.

Kok, Wim. 'Het Bestuurlijke in de Economie: Een Kritiek Op de Nieuwe Zakelijkheid'. In *Lessen Uit Het Verleden: 125 Jaar Vereniging Voor Staathuishoudkunde*, edited by Antonie Knoester, 367–74. Leiden: Stenfert Kroese, 1987.

Koole, Rudolf. 'De Ondergang van de Sociaal-Democratie? De PvdA in Vergelijkend en Historisch Perspectief'. In *Jaarboek Documentatiecentrum Nederlandse Politieke Partijen 1992*, edited by Gerrit Voerman and Rudolf Koole, 73–98. Groningen: Documentatiecentrum Nederlandse Politieke Partijen, 1993.

Kossmann, Ernst. *Politieke Theorie en Geschiedenis: Verspreide Opstellen en Voordrachten Aangeboden Aan de Schrijver bij Zijn Aftreden Als Hoogleraar aan de Rijksuniversiteit Groningen*. Amsterdam: Bert Bakker, 1987.

Kraak, Haro. 'Gutmensch Groeit Langzaam Uit Tot Geuzennaam'. *De Volkskrant*, 21 December 2005.

Kristol, Irving. *Neoconservatism: The Autobiography of an Idea*. New York: Free Press, 1995.

Kristol, Irving. 'The Neoconservative Persuasion'. *The Weekly Standard* 8, no. 47 (2003): 23–5.

Kroes, Rob, Marc Chénetier, and Instituut Amerika. *Neo-Conservatism: Its Emergence in the USA and Europe*. Amsterdam: Free University Press, 1984.

Kumar, Deepa. *Islamophobia and the Politics of Empire*. Chicago, IL: Haymarket Books, 2012.

Lange, Ferdi de. 'Amerikaans En Brits Conservatisme Als Voorland'. In *Ruimte Op Rechts: Conservatieve Onderstroom in de Lage Landen*, edited by Huib Pellikaan and Sebastiaan van der Lubben, 162–79. Utrecht: Spectrum, 2006.

Lange, Sarah de. 'A New Winning Formula? The Programmatic Appeal of the Radical Right'. *Party Politics* 13, no. 4 (2007): 411–35.

Lange, Sarah L. de. 'From Pariah to Power: The Government Participation of Radical Right-Wing Populist Parties in West European Democracies'. PhD thesis, Universiteit van Amsterdam, 2008.

Lans, Jos van der. 'De Kreet Des Volks'. *Vrij Nederland*, 22 June 2002.

Lans, Jos van der, and Antoine Verbij. 'Manifest Voor de Jaren Zeventig'. *Vrij Nederland*, 23 March 2005.

Le Pen, Marine. 'Un Réferendum Pour Sortir de La Crise Migratoire'. *L'Opinion*, 13 January 2016.

Leeuw, Marc de, and Sonja van Wichelen. '"Please, Go Wake Up!" Submission, Hirsi Ali, and the "War on Terror" in the Netherlands'. *Feminist Media Studies* 5, no. 3 (2005): 325–40. https://doi.org/10.1080/14680770500271487.

Lemann, Nicholas. 'The Next World Order: The Hawks' Plan to Reshape the Globe'. *The New Yorker*, 2002, 42–8.

Levitas, Ruth, ed. *The Ideology of the New Right*. Cambridge: Polity Press, 1986.

Lewis, Bernard. 'The Roots of Muslim Rage'. *The Atlantic*, 1990.

Lewis, Bernard. *What Went Wrong? Western Impact and Middle Eastern Response*. Oxford: Oxford University Press, 2002.

Liempt, Ad van. 'Het Raadsel van Reve'. *Andere Tijden*, 16 December 2003.

Ligtenberg, Lucas, and Bob Polak. *Een geschiedenis van Propria Cures, 1890–1990*. Amsterdam: Nijgh en Van Ditmar, 1990.

Lijphart, Arend. *The Politics of Accommodation: Pluralism and Democracy in the Netherlands*. Berkeley, CA: University of California Press, 1968.

Lijphart, Arend. *Verzuiling, pacificatie en kentering in de Nederlandse politiek*. Amsterdam: De Bussy, 1976.

Lijphart, Arend. 'From the Politics of Accommodation to Adversarial Politics in the Netherlands: A Reassessment'. *West European Politics* 12, no. 1 (1989): 139–53. https://doi.org/10.1080/01402388908424727.

Lipset, Seymour Martin, and Earl Raab. *The Politics of Unreason: Right Wing Extremism in America, 1790–1970*. Patterns of American Prejudice Series; 5. New York: Harper & Row, 1970.

List, Gerry van der. 'Hayek en de Nederlandse Politiek'. *De Vrijbrief*, 1993.

Livestro, Joshua. 'Het Conservatieve Moment Is Gekomen'. *NRC Handelsblad*, 3 February 2001.

Lovink, Geert. 'Nihilism and the News'. In *Open! Key Texts 2004, 2012: Art, Culture & the Public Domain*, edited by Jorinde Seijdel, Liesbeth Melis, and Pierre Bouvier, 90–8. Rotterdam: Nai010 Publishers, 2012.

Lovink, Geert. *Zero Comments: Blogging and Critical Internet Culture*. New York: Routledge, 2008.

Lowndes, Joseph E. *From the New Deal to the New Right: Race and the Southern Origins of Modern Conservatism*. New Haven, CT: Yale University Press, 2008.

LPF. *Politiek is Passie: Verkiezingsprogramma Lijst Pim Fortuyn 2003–2007*. Rotterdam: Lijst Pim Fortuyn, 2002.

Lucardie, Paul and Gerrit Voerman. 'Liberaal Patriot of Nationaal Populist? Het Gedachtegoed van Pim Fortuyn'. *Socialisme & Democratie* 59, no. 4 (2002): 32–42.

Lucardie, Paul. 'The Netherlands'. *European Journal of Political Research* 42, no. 7–8 (2003): 1029–36.

Lucardie, Paul. 'The Netherlands: Populism versus Pillarization'. In *Twenty-First Century Populism* edited by Daniele Albertazzi and Duncan McDonnell, 151–65. Basingstoke: Palgrave Macmillan, 2008.

Lucassen, Leo. 'Peeling an Onion: The "Refugee Crisis" from a Historical Perspective'. *Ethnic and Racial Studies* 41, no. 3 (2018): 383–410. https://doi.org/10.1080/01419870 .2017.1355975.

Lucassen, Leo, and Jan Lucassen. *Winnaars en Verliezers: Een Nuchtere Balans van Vijfhonderd Jaar Immigratie*. Amsterdam: Bakker, 2011.

Lucassen, Leo, and Jan Lucassen. 'The Strange Death of Dutch Tolerance: The Timing and Nature of the Pessimist Turn in the Dutch Migration Debate'. *Journal of Modern History* 87, no. 1 (2015): 72–101. https://doi.org/10.1086/681211.

Lyons, Paul. *New Left, New Right, and the Legacy of the Sixties*. Philadelphia, PA: Temple University Press, 1996.

Mahmood, Saba. 'Religion, Feminism and Empire: Islam and the War on Terror'. In *Gendering Religion and Politics: Untangling Modernities*, edited by Hanna Herzog and Ann Braude. New York: Palgrave Macmillan, 2009.

Mair, Peter. 'E. E. Schattschneider's The Semisovereign People'. *Political Studies* 45, no. 5 (1997): 947–54. https://doi.org/10.1111/1467-9248.00122.

Mannheim, Karl. *Ideology and Utopia: An Introduction to the Sociology of Knowledge*. New York: Routledge & Kegan Paul, 1960.

Mannheim, Karl. 'Conservative Thought'. In *From Karl Mannheim*, edited by Kurt Wolff, 132–222. New York: Oxford University Press, 1971.

Marcuse, Herbert. *One Dimensional Man*. London: Sphere Books Ltd., 1968.

McRobbie, Angela. 'Post-feminism and Popular Culture'. *Feminist Media Studies* 4, no. 3 (2004): 255–64. https://doi.org/10.1080/1468077042000309937.

McRobbie, Angela. *Post Feminism and Popular Culture: Bridget Jones and the New Gender Regime*. Duke University Press, 2007.

McRobbie, Angela. *The Aftermath of Feminism: Gender, Culture and Social Change*. London: SAGE, 2009.

Meer, Tom van der. 'Ook Het Verkiezingsprogramma van de PVV Is Niet Links', 5 March 2017. http://stukroodvlees.nl/ook-het-verkiezingsprogramma-van-de-pvv-niet-links/.

Meeus, Tom Jan, and Guus Valk. 'De Buitenlandse Vrienden van Geert Wilders'. *NRC Handelsblad*, 15 May 2010.

Meier, Heinrich, ed. *Carl Schmitt & Leo Strauss: The Hidden Dialogue*. Translated by J. Harvey Lomax. Chicago, IL: University of Chicago Press, 1995.

Meijer, Gerrit. 'Het Neoliberalisme: Neoliberalen Over Economische Orde En Economische Theorie'. PhD thesis, Assen: Koninklijke Van Gorcum, 1988.

Mellink, Bram. 'Tweedracht Maakt Macht. De PvdA, de Doorbraak En de Ontluikende Polarisatiestrategie (1946–1966)'. *BMGN: Low Countries Historical Review* 126, no. 2 (2011): 30–53.

Mellink, Bram. 'Politici Zonder Partij: Sociale Zekerheid En de Geboorte van Het Neo-liberalisme in Nederland (1945–1958)'. *BMGN – Low Countries Historical Review* 132, no. 4 (2017): 25–52.

Mellink, Bram. *Worden Zoals Wij: Onderwijs en de Opkomst van de Geïndividualiseerde Samenleving Sinds 1945*. Amsterdam: Wereldbibliotheek, 2014.

Mepschen, Paul, and Jan Willem Duyvendak. 'European Sexual Nationalisms: The Culturalization of Citizenship and the Sexual Politics of Belonging and Exclusion'. *Perspectives on Europe* 42, no. 1 (2012): 70–6.

Mepschen, Paul, Jan Willem Duyvendak, and Evelien H. Tonkens. 'Sexual Politics, Ori-entalism and Multicultural Citizenship in the Netherlands'. *Sociology* 44, no. 5 (2010): 962–79.

Middendorp, Cees. *Ideology in Dutch Politics: The Democratic System Reconsidered, 1970–1985*. Assen: Van Gorcum, 1991.

Minkenberg, Michael. *Neokonservatismus Und Neue Rechte in Den USA: Neuere Kon-servative Gruppierungen Und Strömungen Im Kontext Sozialen Und Kulturellen Wandels*. Baden-Baden: Nomos, 1990.

Minkenberg, Michael. 'The New Right in Germany. The Transformation of Conserva-tism and the Extreme Right'. *European Journal of Political Research* 22, no. 1 (1992): 55–81.

Mirowski, Philip, and Dieter Plehwe. *The Road from Mont Pèlerin: The Making of the Neoliberal Thought Collective*. Cambridge, MA: Harvard University Press, 2009.

Mourad, Suleiman. 'Riddles of the Book', *New Left Review*, no. 86 (2014): 15–52.

Mudde, Cas. *Populist Radical Right Parties in Europe*. Cambridge: Cambridge University Press, 2007.

Mudde, Cas. 'The Populist Zeitgeist'. *Government and Opposition* 39, no. 4 (2004): 541–63.

Mudde, Cas. 'Wilders Is de Meest Succesvolle Neocon'. *Trouw*, 6 November 2009.

Muis, Jasper, and Tim Immerzeel. 'Causes and Consequences of the Rise of Populist Radical Right Parties and Movements in Europe'. *Current Sociology* 65, no. 6 (2017): 909–30.

Mulisch, Harry. *Bericht aan de Rattenkoning*. Amsterdam: De Bezige Bij, 1966.

Mulisch, Harry. *Het Ironische van de Ironie: Over het Geval G.K. van het Reve*. Manteau marginaal; 6. Brussels: Manteau, 1976.

Nagle, Angela. *Kill All Normies: The Online Culture Wars from Tumblr and 4chan to the Alt-Right and Trump*. Winchester: Zero Books, 2017.

Nash, George H. *The Conservative Intellectual Movement in America since 1945*. 30th anniversary ed. Wilmington, DE: ISI Books, 2014.

Nietzsche, Friedrich. *The Gay Science*. Cambridge: Cambridge University Press, 2001.

Nietzsche, Friedrich. *Beyond Good and Evil: Prelude to a Philosophy of the Future*. Cambridge: Cambridge University Press, 2002.

Norton, Anne. *Leo Strauss and the Politics of American Empire*. New Haven, CT: Yale University Press, 2004.

NRC Handelsblad. 'De Geus: Post Emancipatie Is Overbodig'. *NRC Handelsblad*, 17 November 2003.

NRC Handelsblad. 'GeenStijl: Klacht Tegen Volkskrant'. *NRC Handelsblad*, 22 July 2008.

Obbink, Hans. 'Beleidseconomen Zijn Het Tegenwoordig Veel Te Veel Eens'. *SER Magazine*, 2003.

Offe, Claus. 'New Social Movements: Challenging the Boundaries of Institutional Politics'. *Social Research* 52, no. 4 (1985): 817–68.

Oostveen, Margriet. 'Paniek en Roem'. *NRC*, 12 October 2002. www.nrc.nl/nieuws/2002/10/12/paniek-en-roem-7609656-a874426.

Otterspeer, Willem. *De Mislukkingskunstenaar Deel 1: Willem Frederik Hermans Biografie (1921–1952)*. Amsterdam: De Bezige Bij, 2014.

Oudenampsen, Merijn. 'De Revolte van Nieuwrechts: Neoconservatisme en Postprogressieve Politiek'. *Krisis*, no. 1 (2013): 72–88.

Oudenampsen, Merijn. 'De Dubieuze Psychologie van de Boze Burger'. *De Groene Amsterdammer*, 25 June 2014.

Oudenampsen, Merijn. 'A Dialectic of Freedom: The Dutch Post-War Clash Between Socialism and Neoliberalism'. *Socialism and Democracy* 30, no. 1 (2016): 128–48. https://doi.org/10.1080/08854300.2015.1132648.

Oudenampsen, Merijn. 'Deconstructing Ayaan Hirsi Ali: On Islamism, Neoconservatism, and the Clash of Civilizations'. *Politics, Religion and Ideology* 17, no. 2–3 (2016): 227–48. https://doi.org/10.1080/21567689.2016.1232195.

Oudenampsen, Merijn. 'Opkomst En Voortbestaan van de Derde Weg: Het Raadsel van de Missende Veren'. *B En M: Tijdschrift Voor Beleid, Politiek En Maatschappij* 43, no. 3 (2016): 23–45.

Oudenampsen, Merijn. *Ter Verdediging van Utopia*. Amsterdam: Editie Leesmagazijn, 2016.

Oudenampsen, Merijn. 'In Defence of Utopia'. *Krisis*, no. 1 (2016): 43–59.

Oudenampsen, Merijn. 'The Conservative Embrace of Progressive Values: On the Intellectual Origins of the Swing to the Right in Dutch Politics', PhD thesis, Tilburg University, 2018.

Oudenampsen, Merijn. 'Revolutionairen van deze Tijd'. *De Groene Amsterdammer*, 7 March 2019.

Pam, Max. *Het Bijenspook: Over Dier, Mens en God*. Amsterdam: Prometheus, 2009.

Pauw & Witteman. 'Het Gedachtegoed van Pim Fortuyn'. *Pauw & Witteman*, 6 March 2013.

Peck, Jamie. *Constructions of Neoliberal Reason*. Oxford: Oxford University Press, 2010.

Peeters, Rudolph. 'Dutch Extremist Islamism: Van Gogh's Murderer and His Ideas'. In *Jihadi Terrorism and the Radicalisation Challenge in Europe*, edited by Rik Coolsaet. Aldershot: Ashgate, 2008.

Pellikaan, Huib, and Sebastiaan van der Lubben, eds. *Ruimte op Rechts? Conservatieve Onderstroom in de Lage Landen*. Utrecht: Het Spectrum, 2006.

Pellikaan, Huib, Sarah L. de Lange, and Tom van der Meer. 'Fortuyn's Legacy: Party System Change in the Netherlands'. *Comparative European Politics* 5, no. 3 (2007): 282–302. https://doi.org/10.1057/palgrave.cep.6110097.

Pellikaan, Huib, Sarah L. de Lange, and Tom van der Meer. 'The Centre Does Not Hold: Coalition Politics and Party System Change in the Netherlands, 2002–12'. *Government and Opposition* 53, no. 2 (2018): 231–55.

Pels, Dick. *De Geest van Pim: Het Gedachtegoed van een Politieke Dandy*. Amsterdam: Anthos, 2003.

Pels, Dick. *Een Zwak Voor Nederland: Ideeën voor een Nieuwe Politiek*. Amsterdam: Anthos, 2005.

Pels, Dick. 'Tegen de Verhuftering: Het Nieuwe Nationaal-Individualisme'. *De Groene Amsterdammer*, 4 November 2009.

Pels, Dick. 'Een Paar Apart: Fortuyn En Van Doorn Als Publieke Sociologen'. In *J.A.A. van Doorn En de Nederlandse Sociologie: De Erfenis, Het Debat En de Toekomst*, edited by Jacques Jozef Bernhard Maria van Hoof and Jacobus Adrianus Antonius van Doorn, 87–98. Amsterdam: Pallas Publications, 2010.

Pels, Dick. 'De Hoofdman der Hufters'. *Joop*, 5 October 2011. https://joop.bnnvara.nl/opinies/de-hoofdman-der-hufters.

Pels, Dick. *Het Volk Bestaat Niet: Leiderschap en Populisme in de Mediademocratie*. Amsterdam: De Bezige Bij, 2011.

Phillips-Fein, Kim. *Invisible Hands: The Making of the Conservative Movement from the New Deal to Reagan*. New York: W. W. Norton & Company, 2009.

Piryns, Piet. *Er is Nog Zoveel Ongezegd: Vraaggesprekken met Schrijvers*. Antwerpen Baarn: Houtekiet, 1988.

Polak, Bob. *Het Gezicht van Propria Cures, 1890–2015*. Amsterdam: Stichting Propria Cures, 2015.

Praat, Edwin. *Verrek, het is geen kunstenaar: Gerard Reve en het schrijverschap*. Amsterdam: Amsterdam University Press, 2014.

Prins, Baukje. 'The Nerve to Break Taboos: New Realism in the Dutch Discourse on Multiculturalism'. *JIMI (Journal of International Migration and Integration)/ RIMI (Revue de l'Integration El de La Migration Internationale)* 3, no. 3–4 (2002): 363–79.

Prins, Baukje. *Voorbij de Onschuld: Het Debat Over Integratie in Nederland*. 2nd ed. Amsterdam: Van Gennep, 2004.

Puar, Jasbir K. *Terrorist Assemblages: Homonationalism in Queer Times*. Next Wave. Durham, NC: Duke University Press, 2007.

PVV. 'Een Nieuw-Realistische Visie', 2006. www.pvv.nl/30-visie/publicaties/707-een-nieuw-realistische-visie.html.

PVV. 'Klare Wijn', 2006. www.pvv.nl/index.php/component/content/article/30-publicaties/706-klare-wijn.html.

PVV. 'Plan Voor Een Nieuwe Gouden Eeuw', 2006. www.pvv.nl/30-visie/publicaties/703-een-nieuwe-gouden-eeuw.html.

PVV. 'Een Agenda van Hoop En Optimisme: Een Tijd Om Te Kiezen: PVV 2010–2015'. Den Haag: PVV, 2010.

Quid, Johnny. 'GeenStijl: MANNARCHISME! GeenStijl gaat de man redden', 5 March 2011. www.geenstijl.nl/2477271/mannisme_geenstijl_gaat_de_man/.

Quid, Johnny. 'GL-nerd Dick Pels snapt Huftermanifest niet'. *GeenStijl*, 6 October 2011. www.geenstijl.nl/2725881/glnerd_dick_pels_snapt_hufterm/.

Quid, Johnny. 'GeenStijl: Hoe herken je de moraalneuker op een feestje?', 12 April 2011. www.geenstijl.nl/2516421/hoe_herken_je_de_linkschmensch/.

Quid, Johnny. 'Gefeliciteerd! GeenStijl bestaat 9 jaar!' *GeenStijl*, 10 April 2012. www.geenstijl.nl/2951751/gefeliciteerd_geenstijl_bestaa/.

Quid, Johnny. 'Meest Debiele Kritiek Op GeenStijl Ooit'. *GeenStijl*, 11 August 2013. www.geenstijl.nl/3592341/het_begint_met_tahahaha_hahaha_haha_hahahaha_hahaha/.

Qureshi, Emran, and Michael Anthony Sells. *The New Crusades: Constructing the Muslim Enemy*. Online resource (xii, 416 pages). New York: Columbia University Press, 2003. https://doi.org/10.7312/qure12666.

Quṭb, Sayyid. *Milestones*. Cedar Rapids, IA: Unity Pub. Co., 1981.

Raes, Louis, Jarig van Sinderen, Pieter van Winden, and Guido Biessen. 'Het Maken van Economisch Beleid: De Rol van AEP in de Afgelopen Vijftig Jaar'. *Tijdschrift Voor Politieke Economie* 24, no. 1 (2002): 7–50.

Ranelagh, John. *Thatcher's People: An Insider's Account of the Politics, the Power and the Personalities*. London: Fontana, 1992.

Reagan, Ronald. *Public Papers of the Presidents of the United States: Ronald Reagan, 1982*. New York: Best Books, 1984.

Redactie NRC Handelsblad. 'GeenStijl: Klacht Tegen Volkskrant'. *NRC Handelsblad*, 22 July 2008.

Reekum, Rogier van. 'Out of Character: Debating Dutchness, Narrating Citizenship'. PhD thesis, University of Amsterdam, 2014.

Righart, Hans. *De eindeloze jaren zestig: geschiedenis van een generatieconflict*. Amsterdam: Amsterdam University Press, 2006.

Riley, Denise. *The Words of Selves: Identification, Solidarity, Irony*. Atopia. Stanford, CA: Stanford University Press, 2000.

Robin, Corey. *The Reactionary Mind: Conservatism from Edmund Burke to Sarah Palin*. New York: Oxford University Press, 2011.

Roessel, Aukje van, and Mark Kranenburg. 'Een Partij van Amateurpolitici: Het Intellectueel Gehalte van de VVD'. *NRC Handelsblad*, 12 May 1990.

Rooden, Aukje van. 'Het Gelijk van de Schrijver – Willem Frederik Hermans' Fictieve Discussie Met Jean-Paul Sartre'. *Nederlandse Letterkunde* 17, no. 3 (2012): 159–77. https://doi.org/10.5117/NEDLET2012.3.HET_352.

Rooy, Piet de. *Republiek van rivaliteiten: Nederland sinds 1813*. Amsterdam: Mets & Schilt, 2002.

Rooy, Piet de. *A Tiny Spot on the Earth: The Political Culture of the Netherlands in the Nineteenth and Twentieth Century*. Amsterdam: Amsterdam University Press, 2015. https://doi.org/10.1515/9789048524150.

Rossem, Van. 'Rutger Castricum Is Een HELD'. *GeenStijl*, 1 March 2012. www.geenstijl. nl/2903861/rutger_castricum_is_een_held/.

Roy, Olivier. *Secularism Confronts Islam*. New York: Columbia University Press, 2007.

Roy, Olivier. *The Failure of Political Islam*. Cambridge, MA: Harvard University Press, 1996.

Rubin, Alissa. 'Geert Wilders, Reclusive Provocateur, Rises Before Dutch Vote'. *New York Times*, 27 February 2017.

Rueb, Thomas, and Floor Rusman. 'Zonder Paul Cliteur Was Baudet Bankier Geworden'. *NRC Handelsblad*, 16 October 2017.

Rusman, Floor. 'Over Tien Jaar Zeggen We: In 2014 Kantelde het Debat'. *NRC Handelsblad*, 24 May 2014.

Rusman, Floor. 'Wat Zei Baudet Eigenlijk in zijn Overwinningsspeech?' *NRC Handelsblad*, 21 March 2019.

Rusman, Floor, and Guus Valk. 'Voor Baudet Is Dit Geen Vrijblijvende Denkoefening'. *NRC Handelsblad*, 22 March 2019.

Rutenfrans, Chris. 'Simonis is net zo oppervlakkig als ik vroeger was'. *Trouw*, 3 July 1999. www.trouw.nl/gs-b731c4ae.

Rutte, Mark. 'H.J. Schoo-Lezing: Nederland Bij de Tijd Brengen: Verandering Én Zekerheid'. 2 September 2013.

Rutte, Mark. 'Sterke Mensen, Sterk Land: Over Het Bezielend Verband in de Samenleving'. Presented at the Dreeslezing, Den Haag, 14 October 2013.

Rutten, Frans. *Verval, Herstel en Groei: Lessen voor het Economisch Beleid Gelet op het Leergeld van Twintig Jaar*. Utrecht: LEMMA, 1995.

Rutten, Frans. *Zeven Kabinetten Wijzer: De Nieuwe Zakelijkheid bij het Economische Beleid.* Groningen: Wolters-Noordhoff, 1993.

Said, Edward W. *Orientalism.* London: Penguin, 2003.

Sartre, Jean-Paul. *Being and Nothingness: An Essay on Phenomenological Ontology.* London: Methuen, 1943.

Schattschneider, E.E. *The Semisovereign People: A Realist's View of Democracy in America.* New York: Holt, Rinehart and Winston, 1960.

Scheffer, Paul. 'Het Multiculturele Drama'. *NRC Handelsblad,* 29 January 2000.

Scheffer, Paul. *Het land van aankomst.* Amsterdam: De Bezige Bij, 2007.

Scheffer, Paul. 'The Open Society and Its Immigrants: A Story of Avoidance, Conflict and Accommodation', PhD thesis, Tilburg University, 2010.

Scheffer, Paul. *Immigrant Nations.* Translated by Liz Waters. Cambridge: Polity Press, 2011.

Schendelen, Rinus van. 'Consociational Democracy: The Views of Arend Lijphart and Collected Criticisms'. *The Political Science Reviewer* 15 (1985): 143.

Schinkel, Willem. *Denken in Een Tijd van Sociale Hypochondrie: Aanzet Tot Een Theorie Voorbij de Maatschappij.* Kampen: Klement, 2007.

Schinkel, Willem. *Imagined Societies: A Critique of Immigrant Integration in Western Europe.* Cambridge: Cambridge University Press, 2017.

Schinkel, Willem, and Friso Van Houdt. 'The Double Helix of Cultural Assimilationism and Neo-liberalism: Citizenship in Contemporary Governmentality'. *British Journal of Sociology* 61, no. 4 (2010): 696–715. https://doi.org/10.1111/j.1468-4446.2010.01337.x.

Scholten, Ilja. 'Does Consociationalism Exist? A Critique of the Dutch Experience'. In *Electoral Participation: A Comparative Analysis,* edited by Richard Rose, 329–55. SAGE Studies in Contemporary Political Sociology. London: SAGE, 1980.

Scholten, Ilja. 'Corporatism and the Neo-Liberal Backlash in the Netherlands'. In *Political Stability and Neo-Corporatism: Corporatist Integration and Societal Cleavages in Western Europe,* 120–52. London: SAGE, 1987.

Schoo, Hendrik Jan. *De Verwarde Natie: Dwarse Notities Over Immigratie in Nederland.* Amsterdam: Prometheus, 2000.

Schoo, Hendrik Jan. *Een Bitter Mensbeeld: De Transformatie van een Ontregeld Land.* Amsterdam: Bakker, 2004.

Schoo, Hendrik Jan. 'Het Nieuwe Conservatisme'. *De Volkskrant,* 10 December 2005.

Schoo, Hendrik Jan. *Republiek van Vrije Burgers: Het Onbehagen in de Democratie.* Amsterdam: Bert Bakker, 2008.

Schoo, Hendrik Jan. *Een Ongeregeld Zootje: Over Journalisten en Journalistiek.* Amsterdam: Elsevier, 2009.

Schrover, Marlou, and Willem Schinkel. *The Language of Inclusion and Exclusion in Immigration and Integration.* Ethnic and Racial Studies. London: Routledge, 2014.

Schuyt, Kees. 'Conservatieve Geschiedvervalsing'. *De Volkskrant,* 22 October 2003.

Scott, Joan Wallach. *The Politics of the Veil.* Princeton, NJ: Princeton University Press, 2007.

SCP. *Sociaal en Cultureel Rapport 1998: 25 jaar Sociale Verandering.* Rijswijk: Sociaal en Cultureel Planbureau, 1998.

Sehmer, Alexander. 'Sweden Right-Wingers Plan LGBT March through Stockholm's Muslim-Majority Neighbourhoods'. *Independent,* 25 July 2015.

Seidel, Gill. 'Culture, Nation and "Race" in the British and French New Right'. In *The Ideology of the New Right,* edited by Ruth Levitas, 107–35. Cambridge: Polity Press, 1986.

Serfontijn, Hans. 'Apartheid Enige Oplossing, Mits Menselijk Toegepast'. *Trouw*, 8 March 1983.

Sheehi, Stephen. *Islamophobia: The Ideological Campaign against Muslims*. Atlanta, GA: Clarity Press, 2011.

Sitalsing, Sheila. 'GeenStijlgeneratie bedreigt erop los'. *De Volkskrant*, 18 July 2008.

Sitalsing, Sheila. *Mark: portret van een premier*. Amsterdam: Prometheus, 2016.

Skinner, Quentin. *Visions of Politics/Vol. 1, Regarding Method*. Cambridge: Cambridge University Press, 2002.

Slobodian, Quinn. *Globalists: The End of Empire and the Birth of Neoliberalism*. Harvard University Press, 2018.

Smith, Anna Marie. *New Right Discourse on Race and Sexuality: Britain, 1968–1990*. Cambridge: Cambridge University Press, 1994.

Snel, Bert. 'Zijn Wilders en Fortuyn Vergelijkbaar?' *Civis Mundi Digitaal* 5 (2011).

Sommer, Martin. 'Steeds Harder Lopen'. *De Volkskrant*, 4 September 2008.

Spanje, Joost van. 'Contagious Parties'. *Party Politics* 16, no. 5 (2010): 563–86.

Spruyt, Bart Jan. *Lof van het Conservatisme*. Amsterdam: Balans, 2003.

Spruyt, Bart Jan, and Michiel Visser. 'Conservatief Manifest'. *Trouw*, 18 October 2003. www.trouw.nl/nieuws/conservatief-manifest~b6673e42/.

Spruyt, Bart Jan, and Michiel Visser. *De crisis in Nederland en het conservatieve antwoord*. Den Haag: Edmund Burke Stichting, 2004.

Spruyt, Bart Jan. *De Toekomst van de Stad: Over Geschiedenis en Politiek – Een Boeken-weekessay*. Zoetermeer: Boekencentrum, 2005.

Spruyt, Bart Jan. 'De Zuilen Staan Nog Fier Overeind'. *Historisch Nieuwsblad*, 2005. www.historischnieuwsblad.nl/nl/artikel/6608/de-zuilen-staan-nog-fier-overeind.html.

Spruyt, Bart Jan. 'De Verdediging van het Westen: Leo Strauss, Amerikaans Neoconserv-atisme en de Kansen in Nederland'. In *Ruimte op rechts? Conservatieve onderstroom in de Lage Landen*, edited by Huib Pellikaan and Sebastiaan van der Lubben, 278–98. Utrecht: Het Spectrum, 2006.

Spruyt, Bart Jan. 'In Memoriam H.J. Schoo'. In *Dwars en bewogen: Afscheid van H.J. Schoo (1945–2007)*, edited by Arendo Joustra, Tonny van Winssen, Jos de Beus, and Hendrik Jan Schoo. Amsterdam: Elsevier/de Volkskrant, 2007.

Stacey, Judith. 'The New Conservative Feminism'. *Feminist Studies* 9, no. 3 (1983): 559–83.

Stedman Jones, Daniel. *Masters of the Universe: Hayek, Friedman, and the Birth of Neoliberal Politics*. Princeton, NJ: Princeton University Press, 2014.

Steinfels, Peter. *The Neoconservatives: The Origins of a Movement*. 1st Touchstone ed. New York: Simon and Schuster, 2013.

Sternhell, Zeev. *The Anti-Enlightenment Tradition*. New Haven, CT: Yale University Press, 2010.

Stevers, Theo. *Na Prinsjesdag in De Volkskrant: Kritische Beschouwingen over de Economische en Politieke Zijden van het Begrotingsbeleid der Rijksoverheid*. Leiden: Stenfert Kroese, 1979.

Stokkom, Bas van. *Wat een Hufter! Ergernis, Lichtgeraaktheid en Maatschappelijke Ver-ruwing*. Amsterdam: Boom, 2010.

Stokkom, Bas van. 'Het Klimaat in Nederland Is Wel Degelijk Intoleranter Geworden'. *NRC Handelsblad*, 14 January 2011.

Storey, John. *Cultural Theory and Popular Culture: A Reader*. University of Georgia Press, 2006.

Strauss, Leo. *Natural Right and History*. Charles R. Walgreen Foundation Lectures. Chicago, IL: University of Chicago Press, 1953.

Strauss, Leo. *The City and Man*. Chicago, IL: University of Chicago Press, 1964.

Stuurman, Siep. *Verzuiling, Kapitalisme En Patriarchaat: Aspecten van de Ontwikkeling van de Moderne Staat in Nederland*. Nijmegen: Sun, 1983.

Taggart, Paul A. *Populism*. Buckingham: Open University Press, 2000.

Taguieff, Pierre-André. *Sur la Nouvelle Droite: jalons d'une analyse critique*. Paris: Descartes & Cie, 1994.

Ter Braak, Menno. 'Antisemitisme in Rok'. *De Blaasbalg*, 1939.

Ter Braak, Menno. *De nieuwe elite*. Den Haag: Leopold, 1939.

Thompson, Hunter S., and Ralph Steadman. *Fear and Loathing in Las Vegas: A Savage Journey to the Heart of the American Dream*. London: Paladin, 1972.

Tierolf, Bas, Lisanne Drost, Maaike van. Kapel, and Willem Wagenaar. *Zevende Rapportage Racisme, Antisemitisme en Extreemrechts Geweld in Nederland: Incidenten, Aangiftes, Verdachten en Afhandeling in 2017*. Utrecht: Verwey-Jonker Instituut, 2018.

Tokmetzis, Dimitri, Dennis l'Ami, and Mick van Biezen. 'Thierry Baudet Ontmoette in het Geheim een Amerikaanse Racist van Alt-Right'. *De Correspondent*, 20 December 2017. https://decorrespondent.nl/7738/thierry-baudet-ontmoette-in-het-geheim-een-amerikaanse-racist-van-alt-right/376817386-2d11d76b.

Touwen, Jeroen. 'How Does a Coordinated Market Economy Evolve? Effects of Policy Learning in the Netherlands in the 1980s'. *Labor History* 49, no. 4 (2008): 439–64. https://doi.org/10.1080/00236560802376904.

Tromp, Bart. *Het Falen der Nieuwlichters*. Amsterdam: De Arbeiderspers, 1981.

Tromp, Bart. *Tegen het Vergeten: Degenstoten en Sabelhouwen*. Nieuwegein: Aspekt, 1997.

Tromp, Bart. 'Een Partijloze Democratie, of: Het Einde van de Politieke Partij?' *Socialisme & Democratie*, no. 12 (2001): 544–53.

Tromp, Bart. *Geschriften van een Intellectuele Glazenwasser: De Draagbare Tromp*. Amsterdam: Bert Bakker, 2010.

Trouw. 'Het Is Weer Amsterdam Tegen de Provincie'. *Trouw*, 20 November 2004.

Trouw. 'Hirsi Ali Roept Op Tot een Derde Feministische Golf'. *Trouw*, 10 March 2003.

Trumpbour, John. 'The Clash of Civilizations: Samuel P. Huntington, Bernard Lewis and the Remaking of the Post-Cold War World Order'. In *The New Crusades: Constructing the Muslim Enemy*, edited by Emran Qureshi and Michael Anthony Sells, 88–130. New York: Columbia University Press, 2003. https://doi.org/10.7312/qure12666.

Turpijn, Jouke. *80's Dilemma: Nederland in de Jaren Tachtig*. Amsterdam: Bakker, 2011.

Uitermark, Justus. *Dynamics of Power in Dutch Integration Politics: From Accommodation to Confrontation*. Amsterdam: Amsterdam University Press, 2013. https://doi.org/10.1515/9789048515837.

Uitermark, Justus, Paul Mepschen, and Jan Willem Duyvendak. 'Populism, Sexual Politics, and the Exclusion of Muslims in the Netherlands'. In *European States and Their Muslim Citizens: The Impact of Institutions on Perceptions and Boundaries*, edited by John R. Bowen, Christophe Bertossi, Jan Willem Duyvendak, and Mona Lena Krook, 88–130. New York: Cambridge University Press, 2013. https://doi.org/10.1017/CBO9781139839174

Vaïsse, Justin. *Neoconservatism: The Biography of a Movement*. Cambridge, MA: Belknap Press of Harvard University Press, 2010.

Valk, Guus. 'Het Conservatieve Moment is Voorbij'. *NRC Handelsblad*, 26 August 2006.

Van Houdt, Friso, and Willem Schinkel. 'A Genealogy of Neoliberal Communitarianism'. *Theoretical Criminology* 17, no. 4 (2013): 493–516.

Veer, Peter van der. 'Pim Fortuyn, Theo van Gogh, and the Politics of Tolerance in the Netherlands'. *Public Culture* 18, no. 1 (2006): 111–24. https://doi.org/10.1215/0899 2363-18-1-111.

Viguerie, Richard A. *The New Right: We're Ready to Lead*. Falls Church, VA: Viguerie Co., 1981.

Vink, Jaffe. 'De Neoconservatieve Revolutie'. *Trouw*, 12 February 2006. www.trouw.nl/ nieuws/vink-de-neoconservatieve-revolutie~bc29ff0f/.

Vink, Jaffe, and Chris Rutenfrans. *De Terugkeer van de Geschiedenis: Letter & Geest*. Amsterdam: Trouw; Augustus, 2005.

Visser, Jelle, and Anton Hemerijck. *'A Dutch Miracle': Job Growth, Welfare Reform and Corporatism in the Netherlands*. Changing Welfare States. Amsterdam: Amsterdam University Press, 1997.

Voerman, Gerrit, ed. *De Conjunctuur van de Macht: Het Christen Democratisch Appèl 1980–2010*. Amsterdam: Boom, 2011.

Volkspartij voor Vrijheid en, Democratie. *Discussienota Liberaal Bestek '90: 'Een Kansrijke Toekomstverantwoorde Vrijheid'*. Den Haag: VVD, 1988.

Vossen, Koen. 'Classifying Wilders: The Ideological Development of Geert Wilders and His Party for Freedom'. *Politics* 31, no. 3 (2011): 179–89. https://doi.org/10.1111/ j.1467-9256.2011.01417.

Vossen, Koen. *Rondom Wilders: portret van de PVV*. Amsterdam: Boom, 2013.

Vossen, Koen. *The Power of Populism: Geert Wilders and the Party for Freedom in the Netherlands*. London: Routledge, 2017.

Vries, Joost de. 'Reaguurders in de digitale onderbuik'. *De Groene Amsterdammer*, 12 December 2008.

Vries, Joost de. 'Meet Thierry Baudet, the Suave New Face of Dutch Rightwing Populism'. *Guardian*, 3 April 2019, sec. Opinion. www.theguardian.com/commentisfree/ 2019/apr/03/thierry-baudet-dutch-rightwing-populism.

Vuijsje, Herman. *Correct: Weldenkend Nederland sinds de Jaren Zestig*. Amsterdam: Contact, 1997.

Vuijsje, Herman. *The Politically Correct Netherlands Since the 1960s*. Translated by Mark T. Hooker. Westport, CT: Greenwood Press, 2000.

Walpen, Bernhard Josef Antonio. 'Der Plan, Das Planen Zu Beenden: Eine Hegemo- nietheoretische Studie Zur Mont Pèlerin Society'. PhD thesis, University of Amsterdam, 2004.

Wansink, Hans. *De Conservatieve Golf*. Amsterdam: Prometheus, 1996.

Wansink, Hans, and Frank Poorthuis. 'De islam is een achterlijke cultuur'. *De Volkskrant*, 9 February 2002.

Weber, Max. *From Max Weber: Essays in Sociology*. Translated by Hans H. Gerth. London: International Library of Sociology and Social Reconstruction, 1970.

Weezel, Max van, and Leonard Ornstein. *Frits Bolkestein: Portret van een Liberale Vrijbuiter*. Amsterdam: Prometheus, 1999.

Weezel, Max van. 'De Inkapselingsstrategie van Het CDA'. *Vrij Nederland*, 25 April 2012.

Weijers, Ido. *Terug naar het Behouden Huis: Romanschrijvers en Wetenschappers in de Jaren Vijftig*. Amsterdam: SUA, 1991.

Wekker, Gloria, and Rosi Braidotti. *Praten in het donker: multiculturalisme en anti- racisme in feministisch perspectief*. Kampen: Kok Agora, 1996.

Wekker, Gloria. *White Innocence: Paradoxes of Colonialism and Race*. Durham, NC: Duke University Press, 2016.

Wiktorowicz, Quintan, and John Kaltner. 'Killing in the Name of Islam: Al-Qaeda's Justification for September 11'. *Middle East Policy* 10, no. 2 (2003): 76–92.

Wilders, Geert. 'Stop de vakbondsmacht', *NRC*, 15 February 2001.

Wilders, Geert, and Ayaan Hirsi Ali. 'Het Is Tijd Voor Een Liberale Jihad'. *NRC Handelsblad*, 12 April 2003.

Wilders, Geert, and Wilders Groep. *Kies voor vrijheid: een eerlijk antwoord*. [S.l.]: Groep Wilders, 2005.

Wilders, Geert. *Marked for Death: Islam's War against the West and Me*. Washington, DC: Regnery, 2012.

Williams, Raymond. *Marxism and Literature*. Oxford: Oxford University Press, 1977.

Williams, Raymond, and Ederyn Williams. *Television: Technology and Cultural Form*. London: Routledge, 2003.

Winter, Leon de. *De Vijand: Een Opstel*. Amsterdam: De Bezige Bij, 2004.

Witteveen, Willem. 'Edmund Burke, Profeet van de Vooruitstrevendheid'. *Socialisme en Democratie* 62, no. 1 (2005): 48–56.

Woods, Roger. *Germany's New Right as Culture and Politics*. Basingstoke: Palgrave Macmillan, 2007.

Wynia, Syp. 'Meebuigen met de Moslims: Hoe de Islam Nederland Verandert'. *Elsevier Weekblad*, 14 April 2017. www.elsevierweekblad.nl/opinie/opinie/2017/04/meebuigen-met-de-moslims-hoe-de-islam-nederland-verandert-490086/.

Wynia, Syp, and Sytze van der Zee. 'Lubbers: "Geen Zin in Nog Een Sanering"'. *Het Parool*, 10 June 1989.

Yaghi, Adam. 'Popular Testimonial Literature by American Cultural Conservatives of Arab or Muslim Descent: Narrating the Self, Translating (an)Other'. *Middle East Critique* 25, no. 1 (2016): 83–98. https://doi.org/10.1080/19436149.2015.1107996.

Zahn, Ernest. *Regenten, rebellen en reformatoren: een visie op Nederland en de Nederlanders*. Translated by Dik Linthout. Amsterdam: Contact, 1989.

Zenk, Thomas. 'New Atheism'. In *The Oxford Handbook of Atheism*, edited by Stephen Bullivant and Michael Ruse, 245–62, Oxford: Oxford University Press, 2013.

Zuidhof, Petrus Willem. 'Imagining Markets: The Discursive Politics of Neoliberalism'. PhD thesis, Erasmus Universiteit Rotterdam, 2012.

Zúquete, José Pedro. *The Identitarians: The Movement against Globalism and Islam in Europe*. Notre Dame, IN: University of Notre Dame Press, 2018.

Zwart, Tom de. 'VVD-Partijraad Verwijst Politiek Moralisme naar de Vestmaalt'. *De Volkskrant*, 24 June 1996.

Index

Printed in the United States
By Bookmasters

Printed in the United States
By Bookmasters